BLACK HAMMER

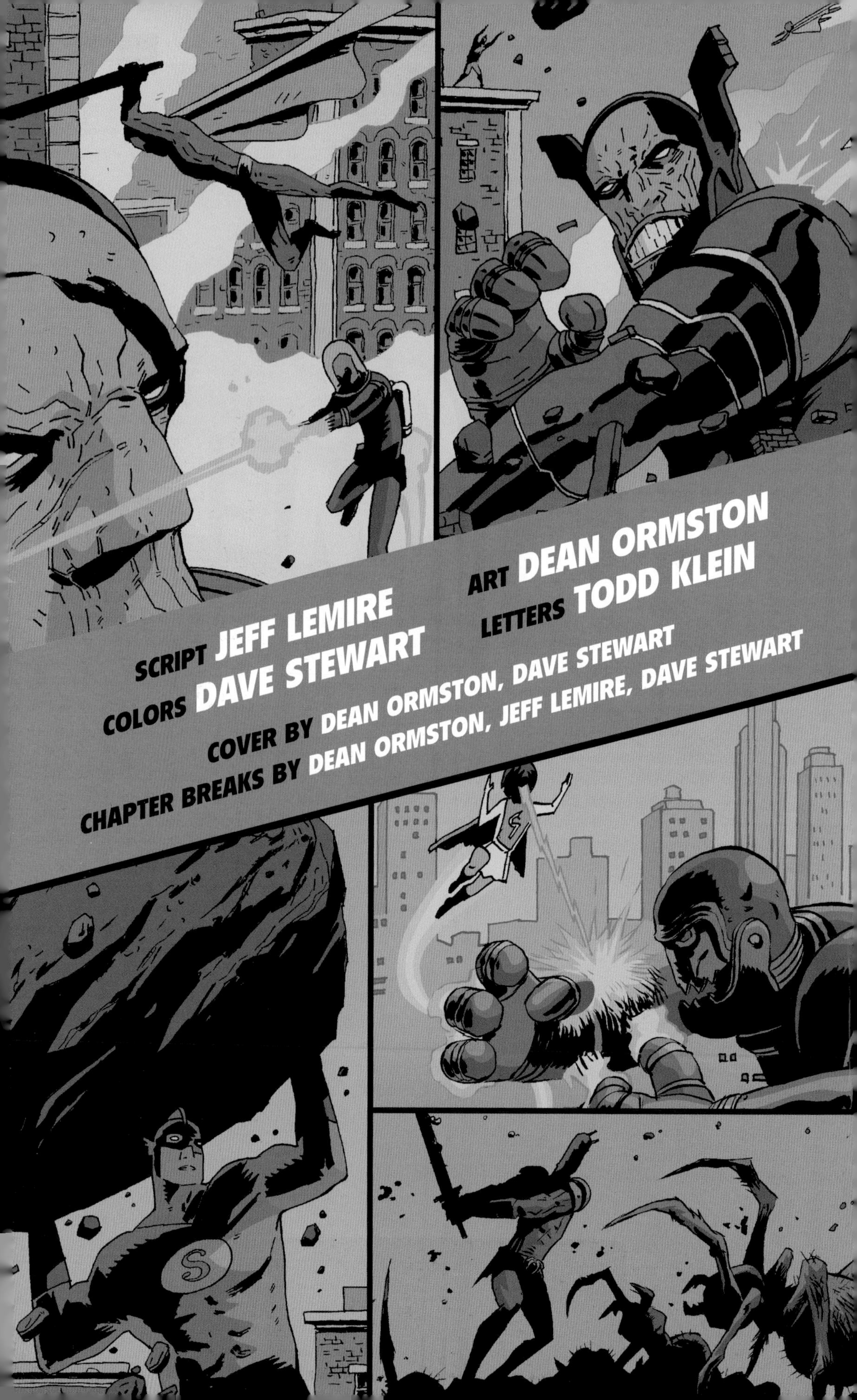

SCRIPT **JEFF LEMIRE** ART **DEAN ORMSTON**
COLORS **DAVE STEWART** LETTERS **TODD KLEIN**
COVER BY DEAN ORMSTON, DAVE STEWART
CHAPTER BREAKS BY DEAN ORMSTON, JEFF LEMIRE, DAVE STEWART

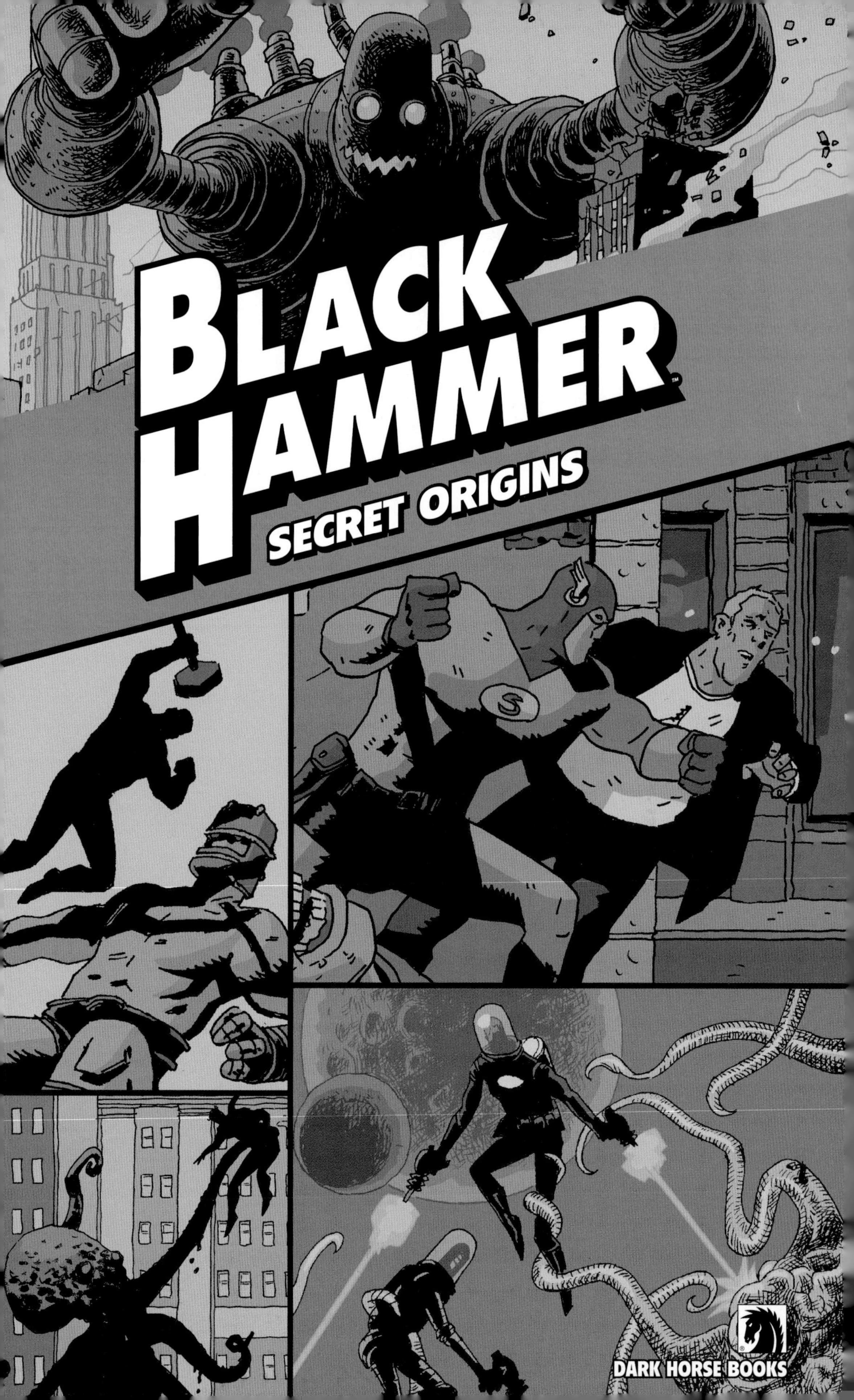
BLACK HAMMER™
SECRET ORIGINS
DARK HORSE BOOKS

PRESIDENT AND PUBLISHER
MIKE RICHARDSON

COLLECTION EDITOR
DANIEL CHABON

SERIES EDITORS
BRENDAN WRIGHT
DANIEL CHABON

ASSISTANT EDITORS
IAN TUCKER
CARDNER CLARK

DESIGNER
RICK DeLUCCO

DIGITAL ART TECHNICIAN
CHRISTINA McKENZIE

SPECIAL THANKS TO DIANA SCHUTZ

BLACK HAMMER VOLUME 1: SECRET ORIGINS

This volume collects issues #1–#6 of the Dark Horse Comics series *Black Hammer*.

Library of Congress Cataloging-in-Publication Data

Names: Lemire, Jeff, author, artist. | Ormston, Dean, artist. | Stewart,
  Dave, colourist. | Klein, Todd, letterer.
Title: Black Hammer. Volume 1, Secret origins / script by Jeff Lemire ; art
  by Dean Ormston ; colors by Dave Stewart ; letters by Todd Klein ; cover
  by Dean Ormston with Dave Stewart ; chapter breaks by Dean Ormston, Jeff
  Lemire, and Dave Stewart.
Other titles: Secret origins
Description: First edition. | Milwaukie, OR : Dark Horse Books, 2017. | "This
  volume collects issues #1–#6 of the Dark Horse Comics series Black
  Hammer"--Title page verso.
Identifiers: LCCN 2016045234 | ISBN 9781616557867 (paperback)
Subjects: LCSH: Comic books, strips, etc. | BISAC: COMICS & GRAPHIC NOVELS /
  Superheroes.
Classification: LCC PN6728.B51926 L46 2017 | DDC 741.5/973--dc23
LC record available at https://lccn.loc.gov/2016045234

Published by
Dark Horse Books
A division of Dark Horse Comics, Inc.
10956 SE Main Street
Milwaukie, OR 97222

DarkHorse.com

To find a comics shop in your area, call the Comic Shop Locator Service toll-free at 1-888-266-4226.
International Licensing: (503) 905-2377

First edition: March 2017
ISBN 978-1-61655-786-7

10 9 8 7 6 5 4 3 2 1
Printed in China

NEIL HANKERSON Executive Vice President TOM WEDDLE Chief Financial Officer RANDY STRADLEY Vice President of Publishing MATT PARKINSON Vice President of Marketing DAVID SCROGGY Vice President of Product Development DALE LAFOUNTAIN Vice President of Information Technology CARA NIECE Vice President of Production and Scheduling NICK McWHORTER Vice President of Media Licensing MARK BERNARDI Vice President of Digital and Book Trade Sales KEN LIZZI General Counsel DAVE MARSHALL Editor in Chief DAVEY ESTRADA Editorial Director SCOTT ALLIE Executive Senior Editor CHRIS WARNER Senior Books Editor CARY GRAZZINI Director of Specialty Projects LIA RIBACCHI Art Director VANESSA TODD Director of Print Purchasing MATT DRYER Director of Digital Art and Prepress SARAH ROBERTSON Director of Product Sales MICHAEL GOMBOS Director of International Publishing and Licensing

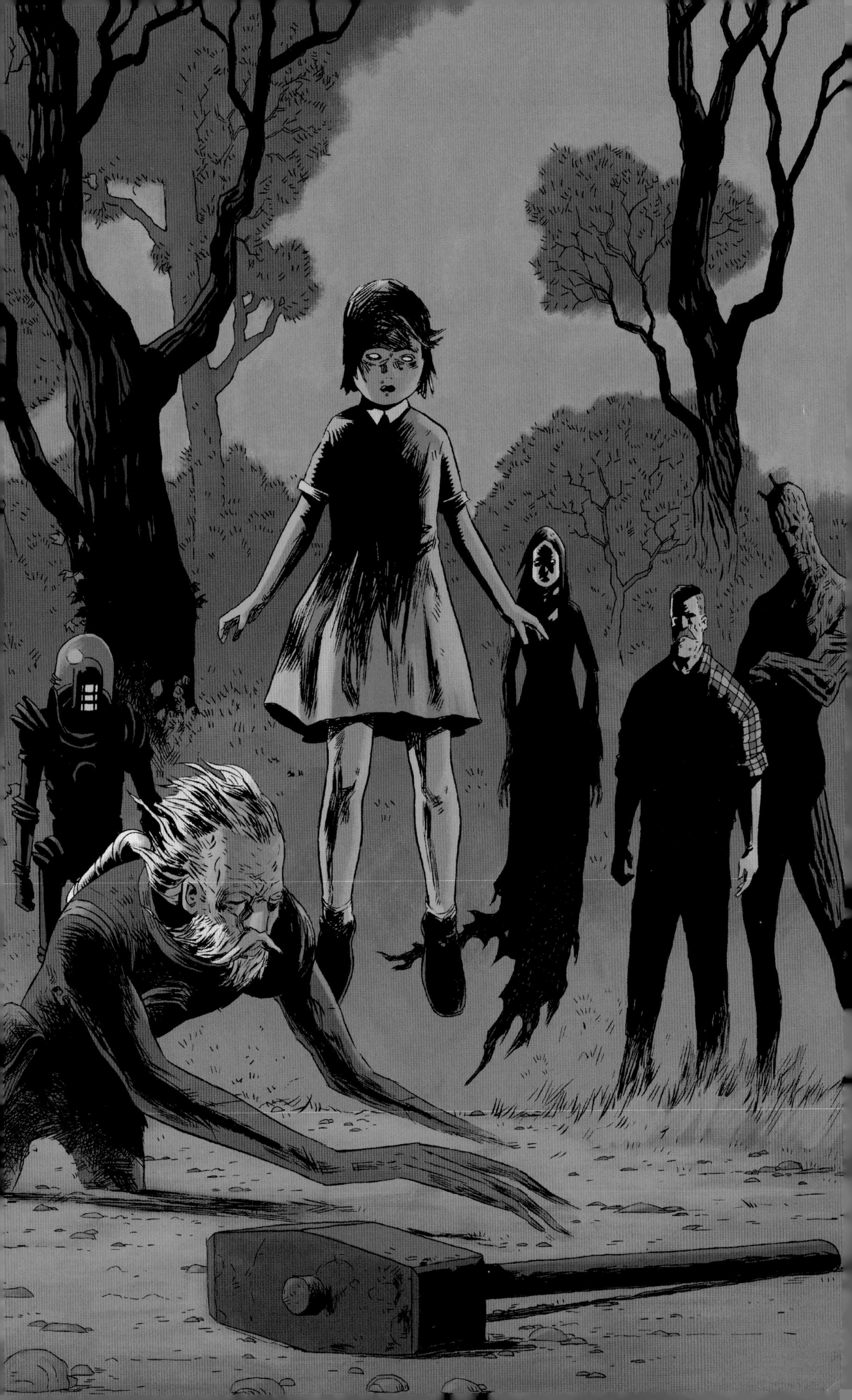

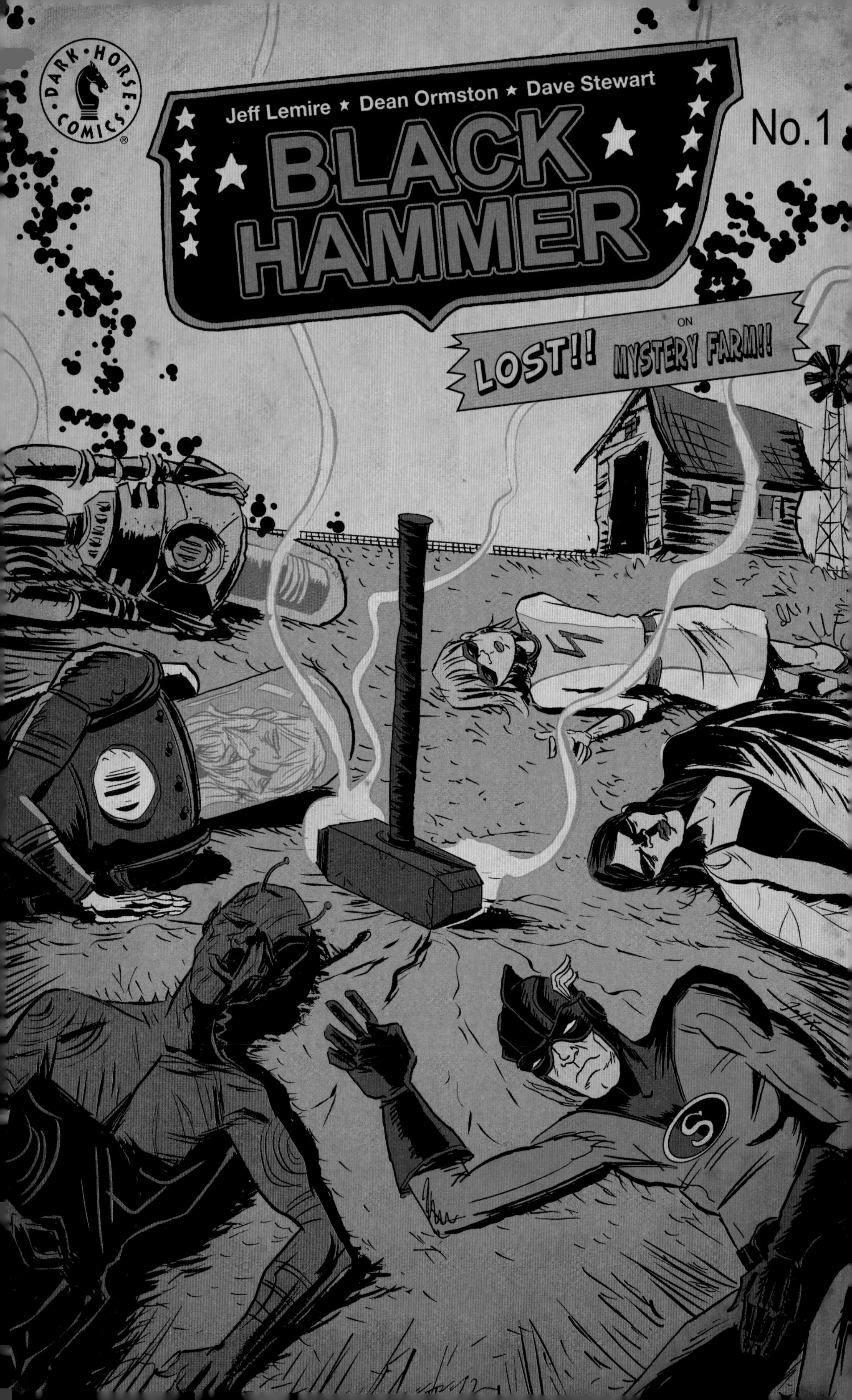
DARK HORSE COMICS
Jeff Lemire ★ Dean Ormston ★ Dave Stewart
No.1
BLACK HAMMER
LOST!! ON MYSTERY FARM!!

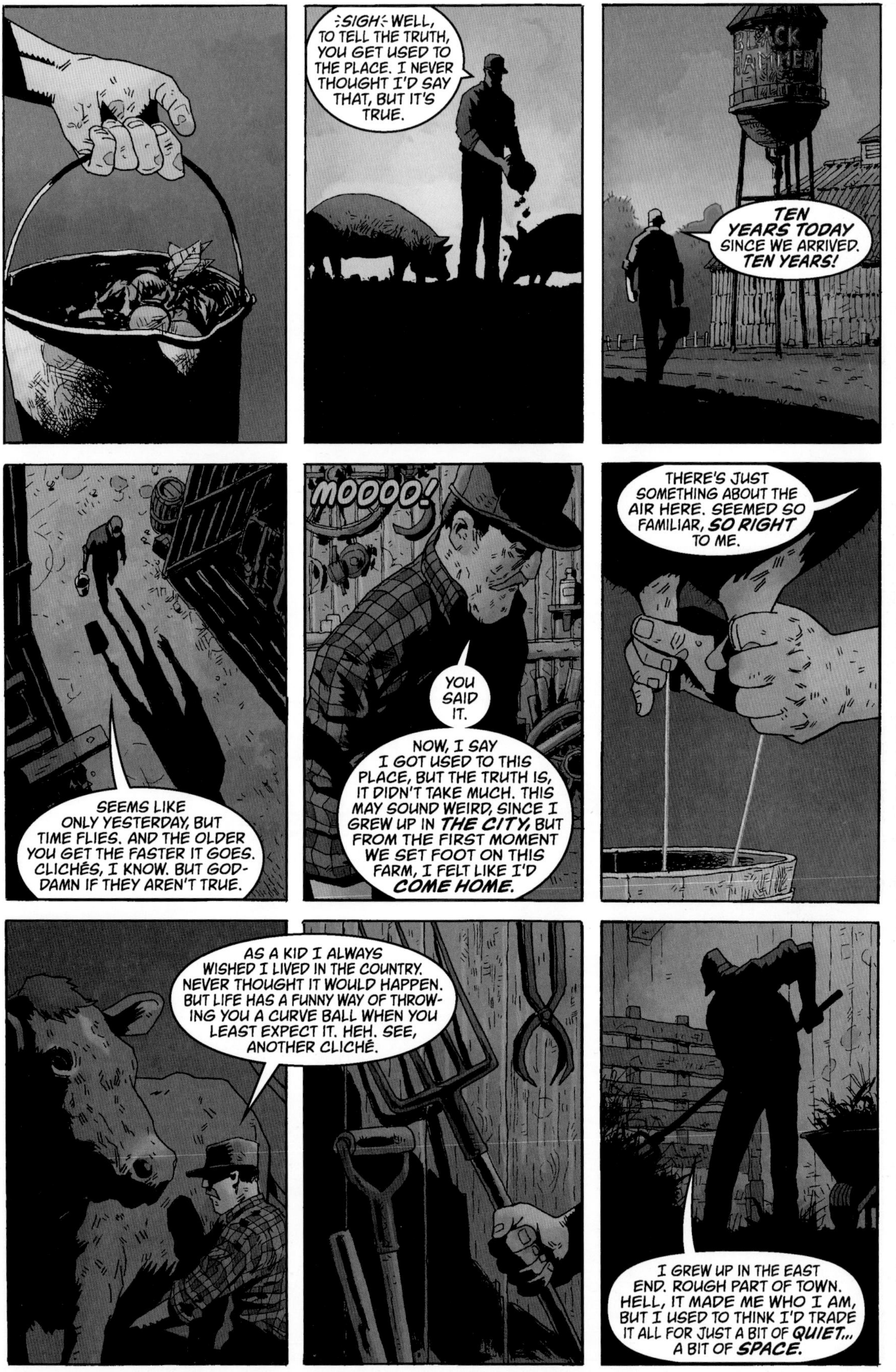

-SIGH- WELL, TO TELL THE TRUTH, YOU GET USED TO THE PLACE. I NEVER THOUGHT I'D SAY THAT, BUT IT'S TRUE.
BLACK HAMMER
TEN YEARS TODAY SINCE WE ARRIVED. TEN YEARS!
SEEMS LIKE ONLY YESTERDAY, BUT TIME FLIES. AND THE OLDER YOU GET THE FASTER IT GOES. CLICHÉS, I KNOW. BUT GOD-DAMN IF THEY AREN'T TRUE.
MOOOO!
YOU SAID IT.
NOW, I SAY I GOT USED TO THIS PLACE, BUT THE TRUTH IS, IT DIDN'T TAKE MUCH. THIS MAY SOUND WEIRD, SINCE I GREW UP IN THE CITY, BUT FROM THE FIRST MOMENT WE SET FOOT ON THIS FARM, I FELT LIKE I'D COME HOME.
THERE'S JUST SOMETHING ABOUT THE AIR HERE. SEEMED SO FAMILIAR, SO RIGHT TO ME.
AS A KID I ALWAYS WISHED I LIVED IN THE COUNTRY. NEVER THOUGHT IT WOULD HAPPEN. BUT LIFE HAS A FUNNY WAY OF THROWING YOU A CURVE BALL WHEN YOU LEAST EXPECT IT. HEH. SEE, ANOTHER CLICHÉ.
I GREW UP IN THE EAST END. ROUGH PART OF TOWN. HELL, IT MADE ME WHO I AM, BUT I USED TO THINK I'D TRADE IT ALL FOR JUST A BIT OF QUIET... A BIT OF SPACE.

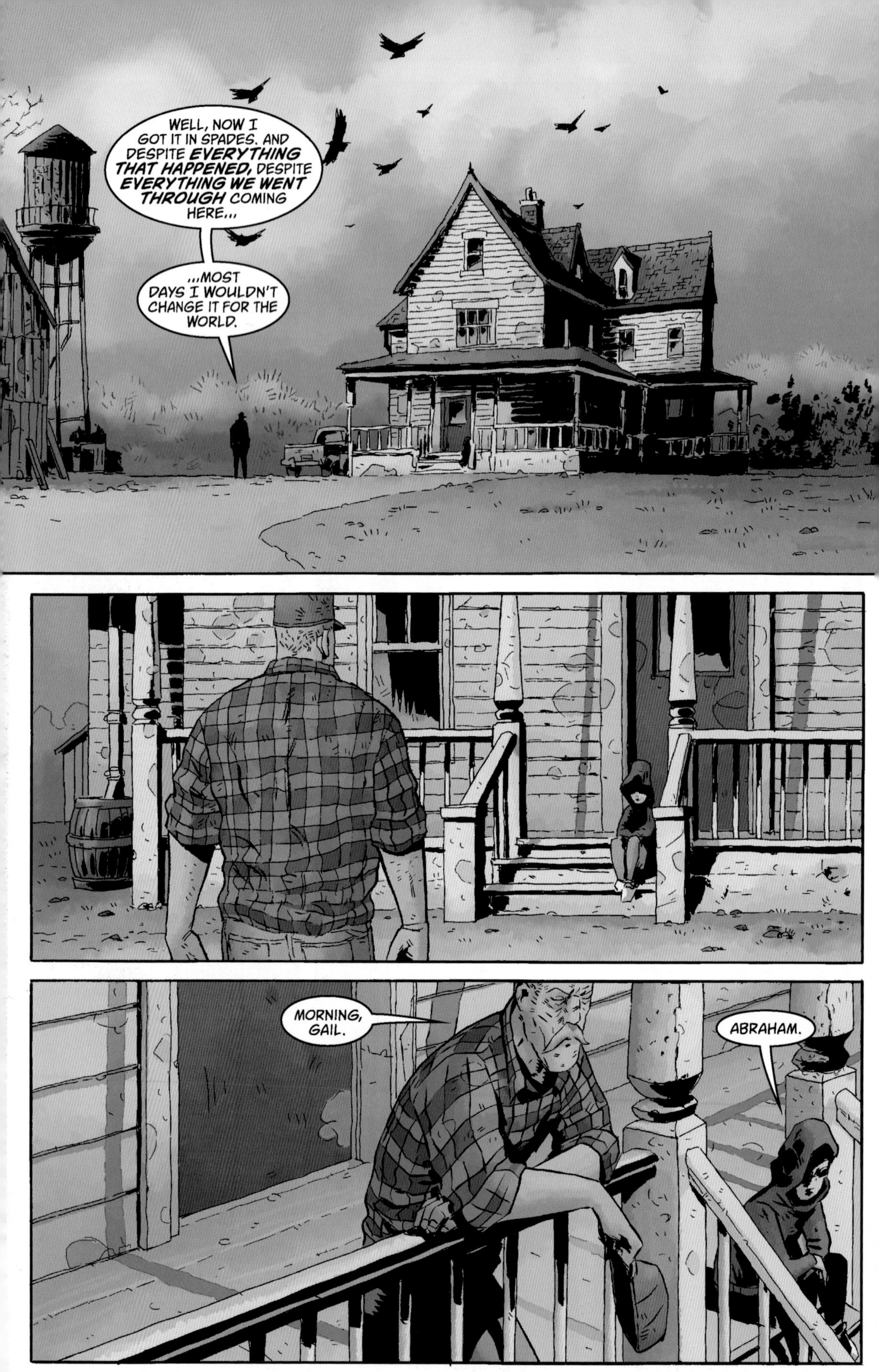
WELL, NOW I GOT IT IN SPADES. AND DESPITE **EVERYTHING THAT HAPPENED,** DESPITE **EVERYTHING WE WENT THROUGH** COMING HERE...
...MOST DAYS I WOULDN'T CHANGE IT FOR THE WORLD.
MORNING, GAIL.
ABRAHAM.

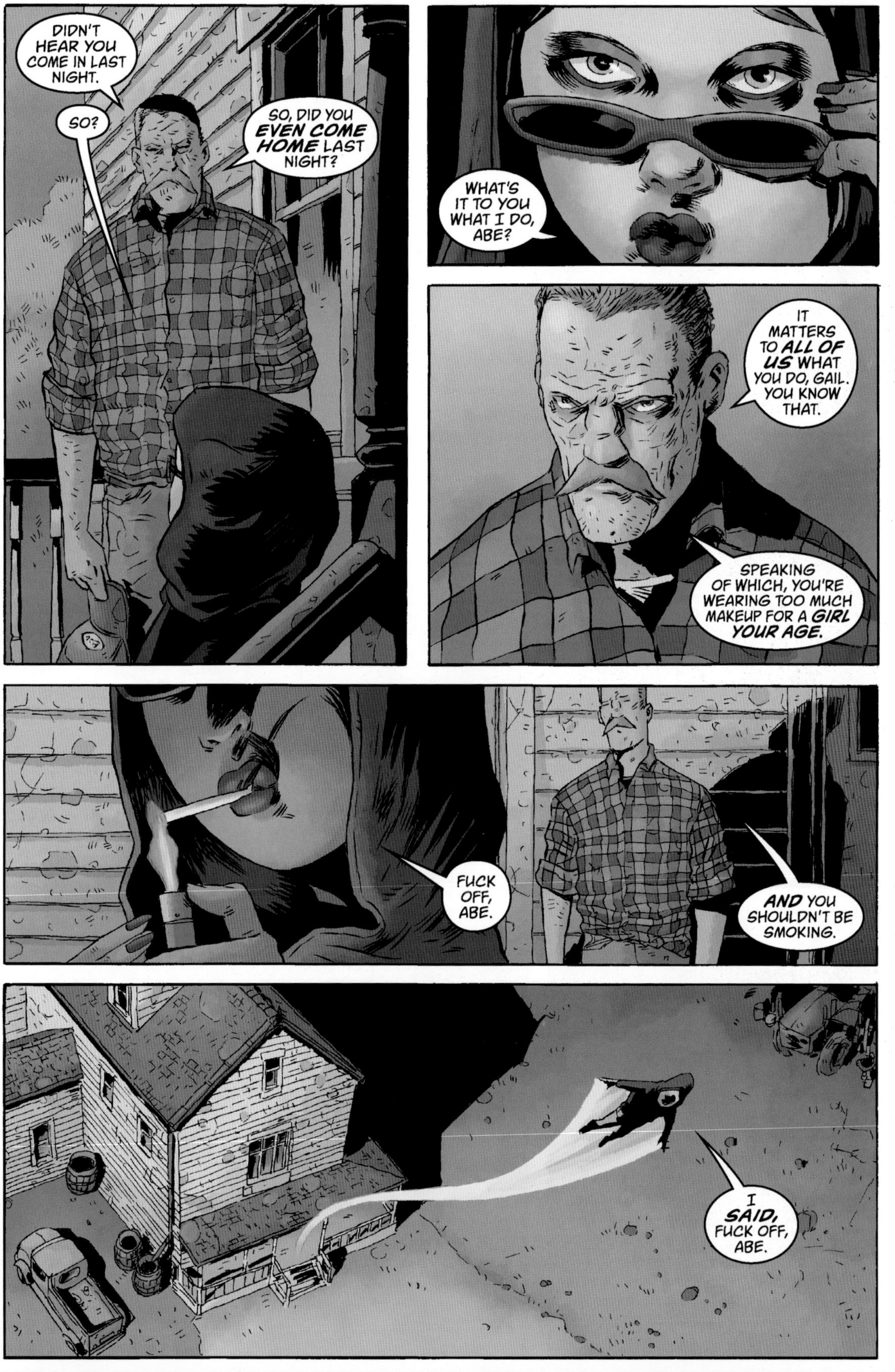
DIDN'T HEAR YOU COME IN LAST NIGHT.
SO?
SO, DID YOU *EVEN COME HOME* LAST NIGHT?
WHAT'S IT TO YOU WHAT I DO, ABE?
IT MATTERS TO *ALL OF US* WHAT YOU DO, GAIL. YOU KNOW THAT.
SPEAKING OF WHICH, YOU'RE WEARING TOO MUCH MAKEUP FOR A *GIRL YOUR AGE*.
FUCK OFF, ABE.
AND YOU SHOULDN'T BE SMOKING.
I *SAID,* FUCK OFF, ABE.

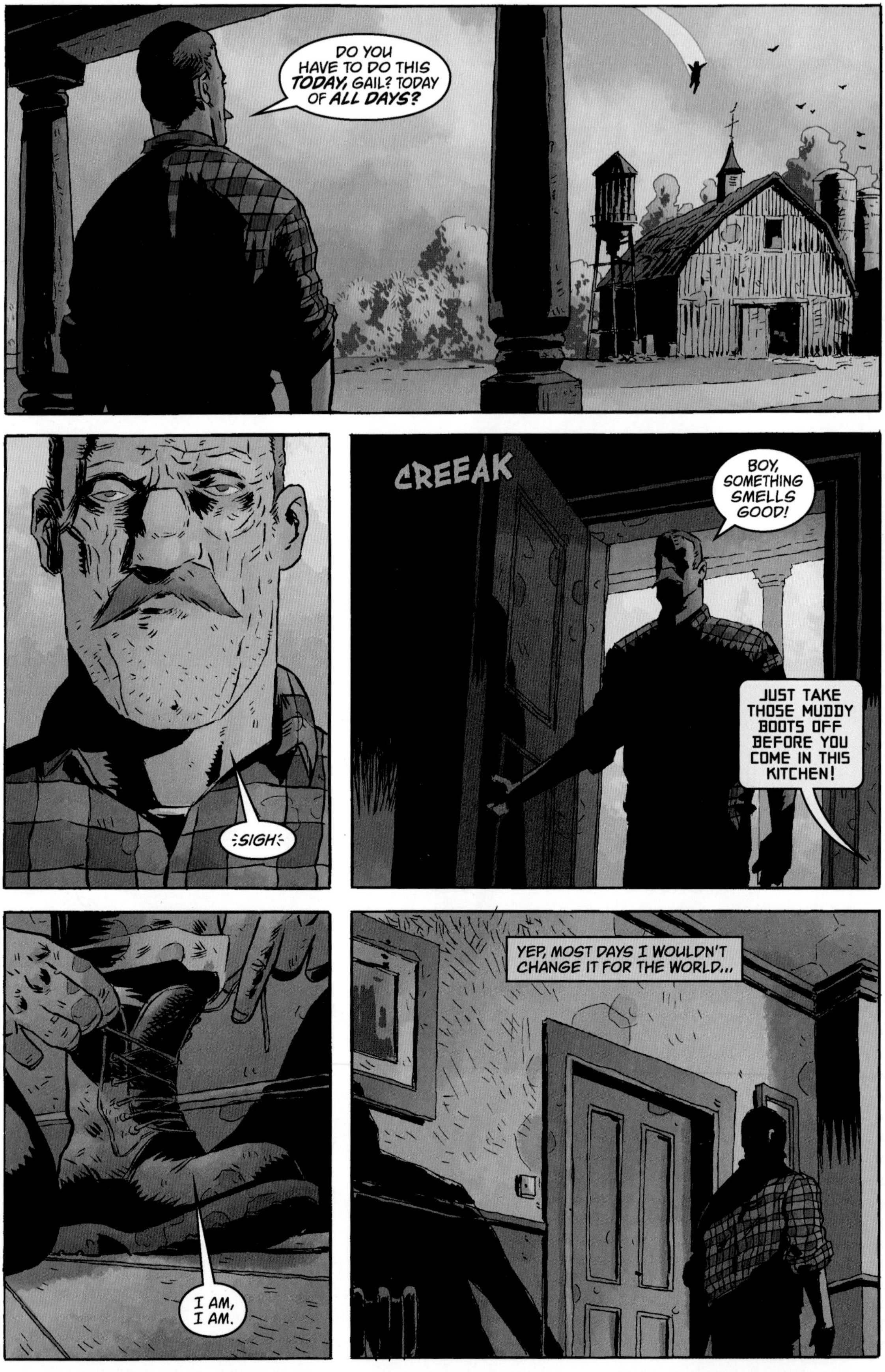
DO YOU HAVE TO DO THIS TODAY, GAIL? TODAY OF ALL DAYS?
SIGH
CREEAK
BOY, SOMETHING SMELLS GOOD!
JUST TAKE THOSE MUDDY BOOTS OFF BEFORE YOU COME IN THIS KITCHEN!
I AM, I AM.
YEP, MOST DAYS I WOULDN'T CHANGE IT FOR THE WORLD...

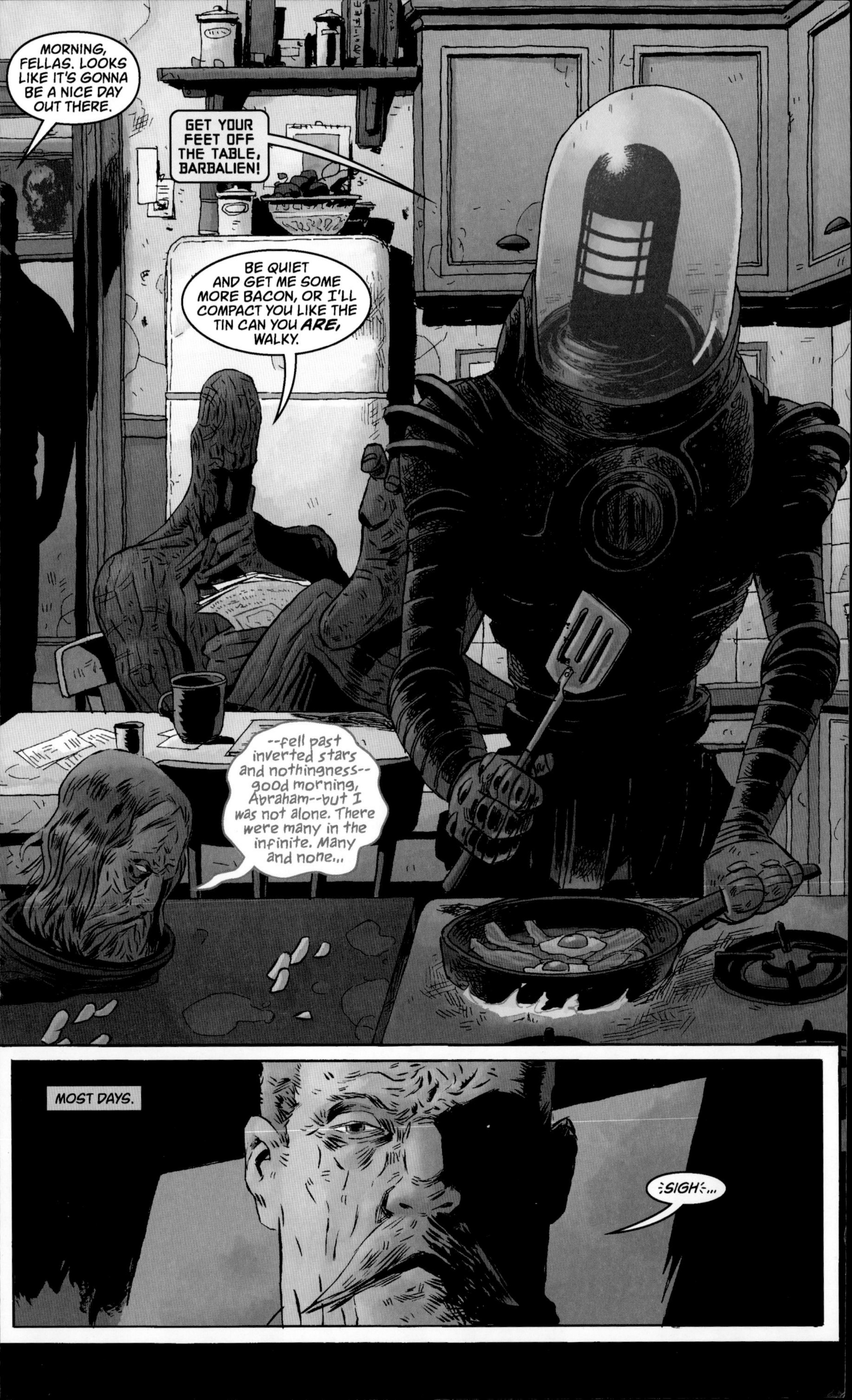
MORNING, FELLAS. LOOKS LIKE IT'S GONNA BE A NICE DAY OUT THERE.
GET YOUR FEET OFF THE TABLE, BARBALIEN!
BE QUIET AND GET ME SOME MORE BACON, OR I'LL COMPACT YOU LIKE THE TIN CAN YOU *ARE,* WALKY.
--fell past inverted stars and nothingness--good morning, Abraham--but I was not alone. There were many in the infinite. Many and none...
MOST DAYS.
SIGH...

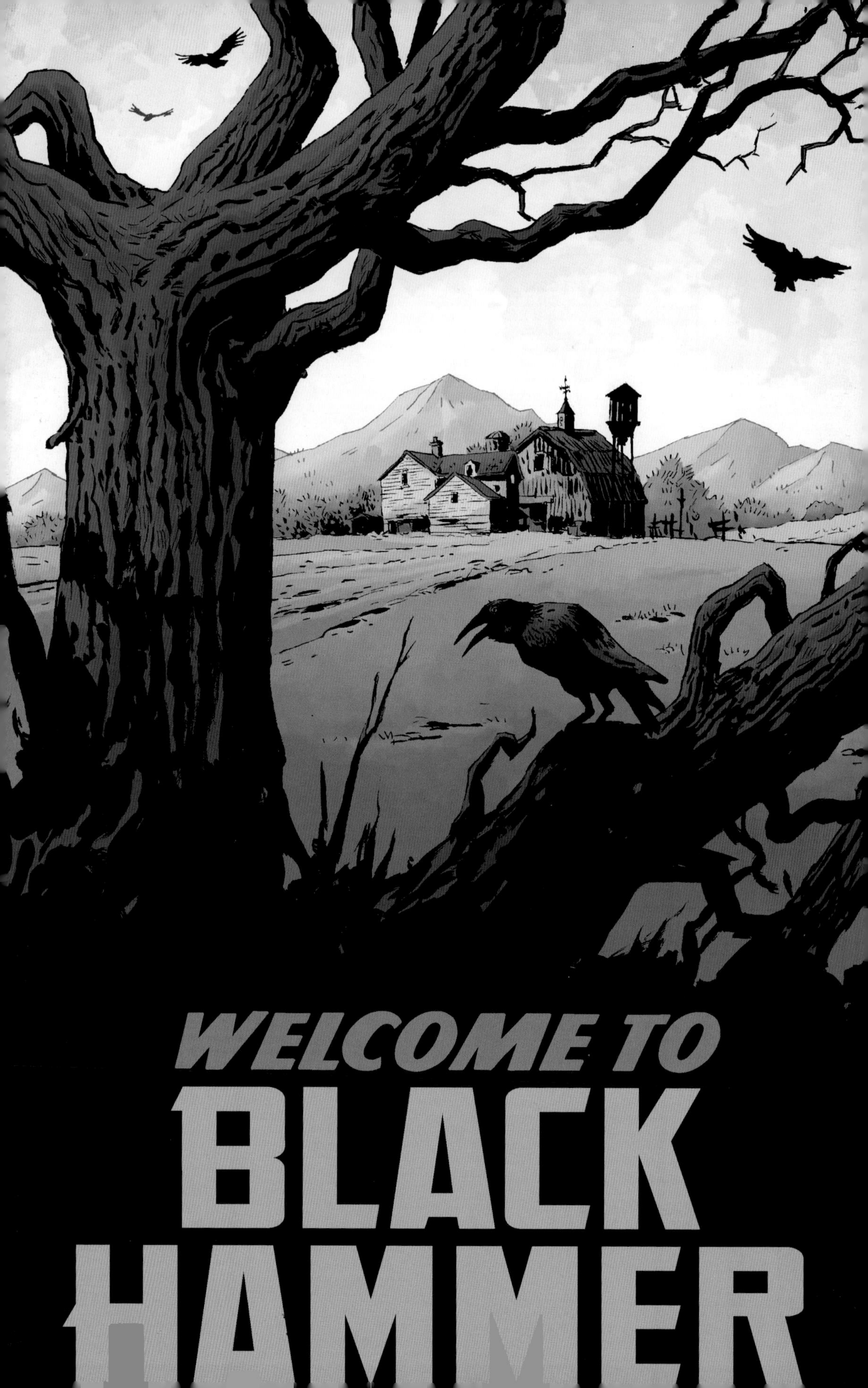
WELCOME TO
BLACK
HAMMER

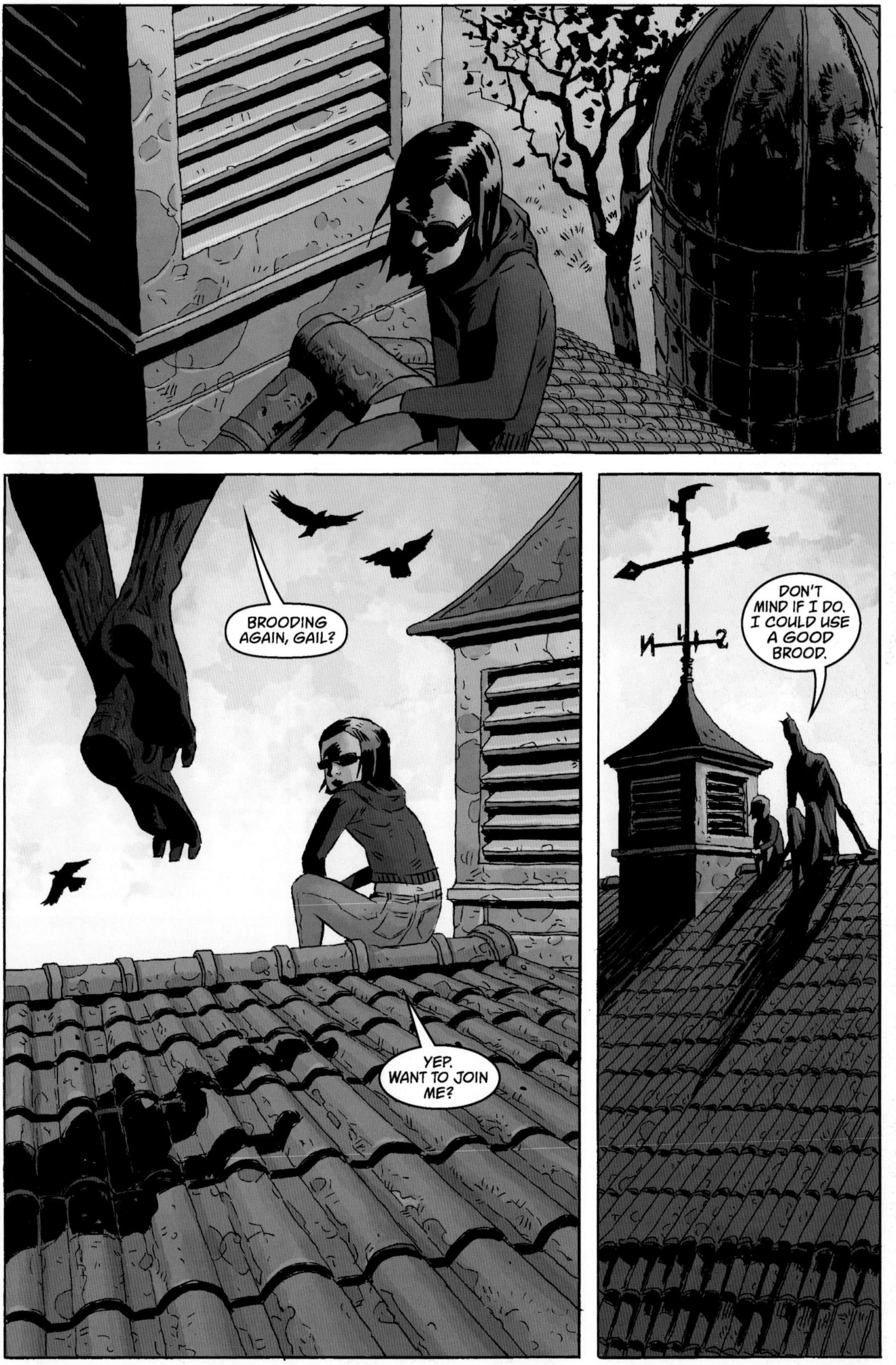
BROODING AGAIN, GAIL?
YEP. WANT TO JOIN ME?
DON'T MIND IF I DO. I COULD USE A GOOD BROOD.

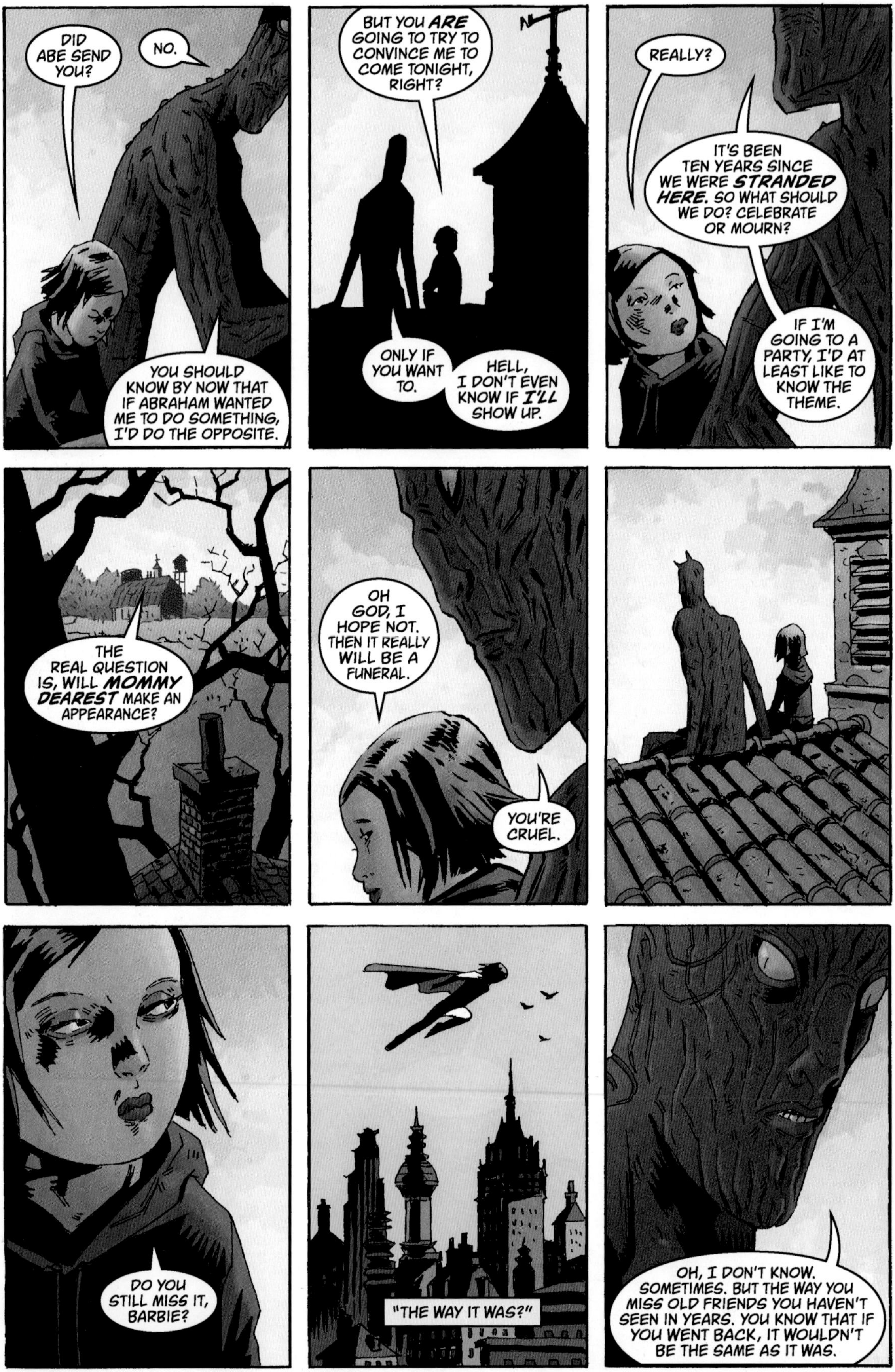
DID ABE SEND YOU?
NO.
YOU SHOULD KNOW BY NOW THAT IF ABRAHAM WANTED ME TO DO SOMETHING, I'D DO THE OPPOSITE.
BUT YOU ARE GOING TO TRY TO CONVINCE ME TO COME TONIGHT, RIGHT?
ONLY IF YOU WANT TO.
HELL, I DON'T EVEN KNOW IF I'LL SHOW UP.
REALLY?
IT'S BEEN TEN YEARS SINCE WE WERE STRANDED HERE. SO WHAT SHOULD WE DO? CELEBRATE OR MOURN?
IF I'M GOING TO A PARTY, I'D AT LEAST LIKE TO KNOW THE THEME.
THE REAL QUESTION IS, WILL MOMMY DEAREST MAKE AN APPEARANCE?
OH GOD, I HOPE NOT. THEN IT REALLY WILL BE A FUNERAL.
YOU'RE CRUEL.
DO YOU STILL MISS IT, BARBIE?
"THE WAY IT WAS?"
OH, I DON'T KNOW. SOMETIMES. BUT THE WAY YOU MISS OLD FRIENDS YOU HAVEN'T SEEN IN YEARS. YOU KNOW THAT IF YOU WENT BACK, IT WOULDN'T BE THE SAME AS IT WAS.

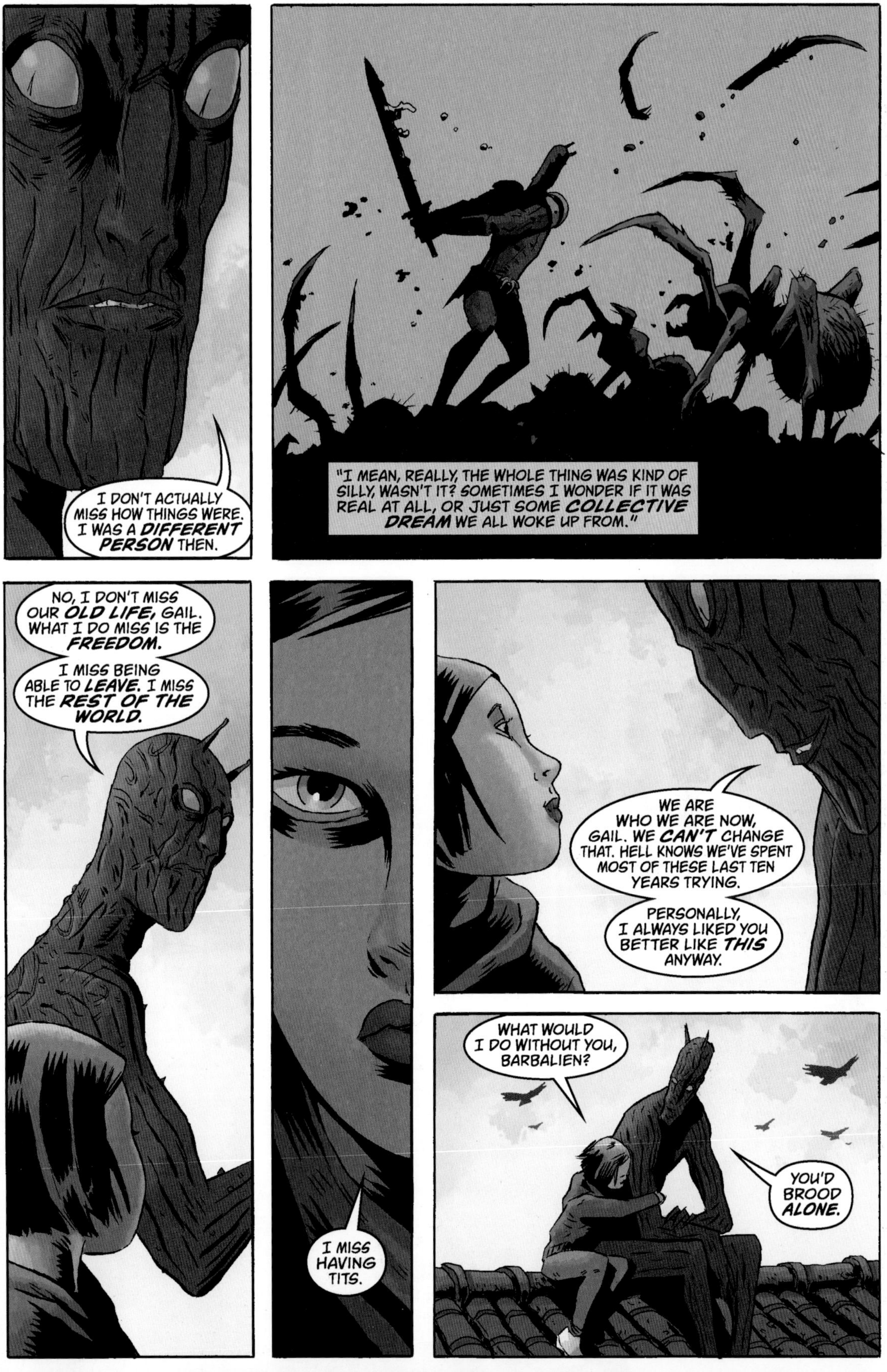
I DON'T ACTUALLY MISS HOW THINGS WERE. I WAS A DIFFERENT PERSON THEN.
"I MEAN, REALLY, THE WHOLE THING WAS KIND OF SILLY, WASN'T IT? SOMETIMES I WONDER IF IT WAS REAL AT ALL, OR JUST SOME COLLECTIVE DREAM WE ALL WOKE UP FROM."
NO, I DON'T MISS OUR OLD LIFE, GAIL. WHAT I DO MISS IS THE FREEDOM.
I MISS BEING ABLE TO LEAVE. I MISS THE REST OF THE WORLD.
I MISS HAVING TITS.
WE ARE WHO WE ARE NOW, GAIL. WE CAN'T CHANGE THAT. HELL KNOWS WE'VE SPENT MOST OF THESE LAST TEN YEARS TRYING.
PERSONALLY, I ALWAYS LIKED YOU BETTER LIKE THIS ANYWAY.
WHAT WOULD I DO WITHOUT YOU, BARBALIEN?
YOU'D BROOD ALONE.

AH, COLONEL WEIRD. I WASN'T SURE WE WOULD SEE YOU AGAIN TODAY.

KZT

Of course you'll see me, Talky-Walky. I'm right here.

THAT'S NOT WHAT I--

IT'S JUST, YOU'VE BEEN SPENDING MORE AND MORE TIME *AWAY*, THESE PAST WEEKS.

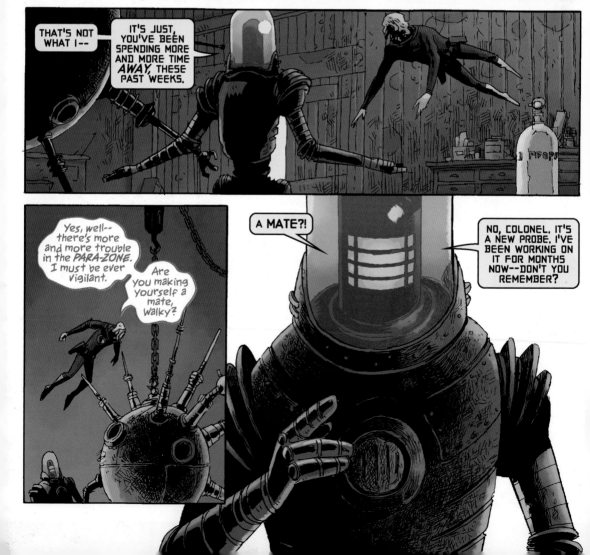

Yes, well-- there's more and more trouble in the *PARA-ZONE*. I must be ever vigilant.

Are you making yourself a mate, Walky?

A MATE?!

NO, COLONEL. IT'S A NEW PROBE. I'VE BEEN WORKING ON IT FOR MONTHS NOW--DON'T YOU REMEMBER?

A probe? Oh...yes. Of course.

I INTEND TO LAUNCH IT PAST THE PERIMETER OF THE TOWN SOON. JUST A FEW MORE ADJUSTMENTS TO THE THRUSTERS AND IT WILL BE READY.

I HAVE A GOOD FEELING ABOUT THIS ONE, COLONEL. I THINK IT MIGHT FINALLY BE THE ONE TO *MAKE CONTACT.*

You never give up, do you, Walky?

"You were always such a loyal and diligent friend."

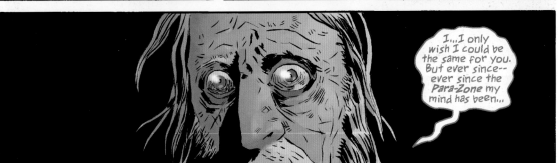

I...I only wish I could be the same for you. But ever since-- ever since the *Para-Zone* my mind has been...

Well, I haven't been myself, have I?

NONSENSE, COLONEL. YOU'LL ALWAYS BE MY COMMANDING OFFICER.

I...

Ah! What's this, then? Are you building yourself a *MATE,* Walky?

NO, I TOLD YOU, IT'S--

Must be ever vigilant, Talky-Walky. The Para-Zone needs me... inverted stars and hordes of Nothing Beasts. Can't let them out...

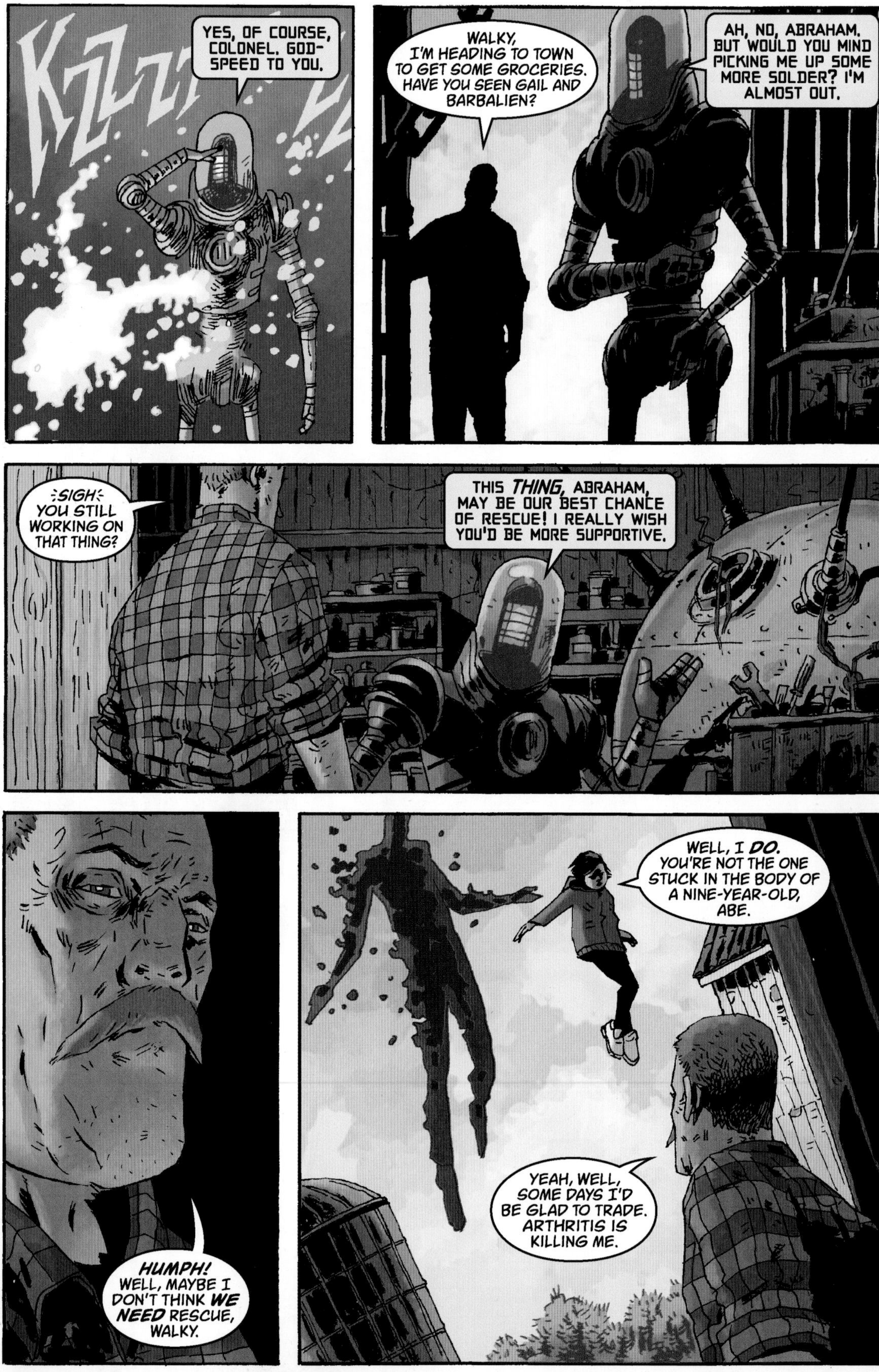
KZZZT
YES, OF COURSE, COLONEL. GOD-SPEED TO YOU.
WALKY, I'M HEADING TO TOWN TO GET SOME GROCERIES. HAVE YOU SEEN GAIL AND BARBALIEN?
AH, NO, ABRAHAM. BUT WOULD YOU MIND PICKING ME UP SOME MORE SOLDER? I'M ALMOST OUT.
SIGH YOU STILL WORKING ON THAT THING?
THIS THING, ABRAHAM, MAY BE OUR BEST CHANCE OF RESCUE! I REALLY WISH YOU'D BE MORE SUPPORTIVE.
HUMPH! WELL, MAYBE I DON'T THINK WE NEED RESCUE, WALKY.
WELL, I DO. YOU'RE NOT THE ONE STUCK IN THE BODY OF A NINE-YEAR-OLD, ABE.
YEAH, WELL, SOME DAYS I'D BE GLAD TO TRADE. ARTHRITIS IS KILLING ME.

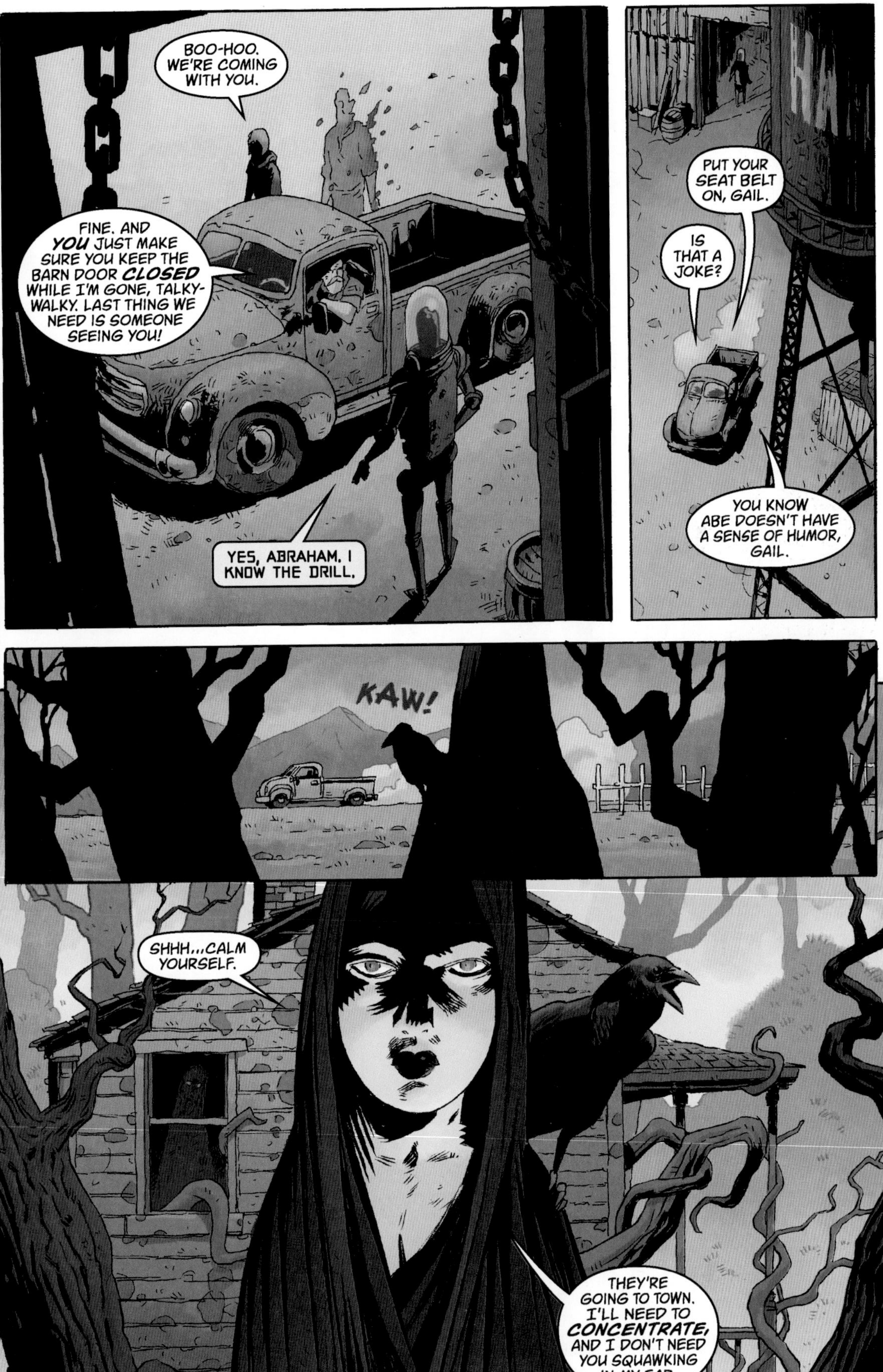
BOO-HOO. WE'RE COMING WITH YOU.
FINE. AND YOU JUST MAKE SURE YOU KEEP THE BARN DOOR CLOSED WHILE I'M GONE, TALKY-WALKY. LAST THING WE NEED IS SOMEONE SEEING YOU!
YES, ABRAHAM. I KNOW THE DRILL.
PUT YOUR SEAT BELT ON, GAIL.
IS THAT A JOKE?
YOU KNOW ABE DOESN'T HAVE A SENSE OF HUMOR, GAIL.
KAW!
SHHH...CALM YOURSELF.
THEY'RE GOING TO TOWN. I'LL NEED TO CONCENTRATE, AND I DON'T NEED YOU SQUAWKING IN MY EAR.

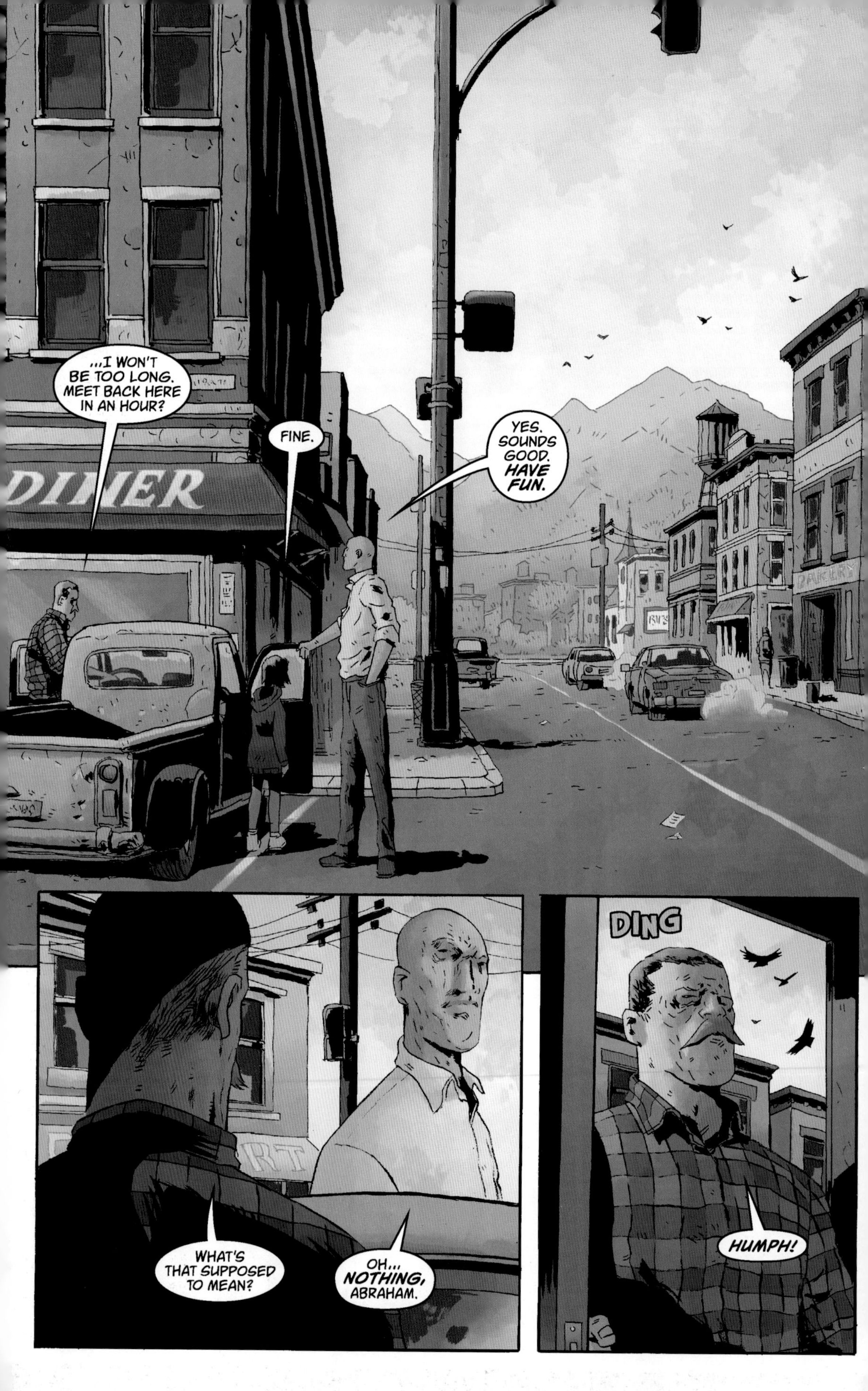
...I WON'T BE TOO LONG. MEET BACK HERE IN AN HOUR?
FINE.
YES. SOUNDS GOOD. HAVE FUN.
DINER
WHAT'S THAT SUPPOSED TO MEAN?
OH... NOTHING, ABRAHAM.
DING
HUMPH!

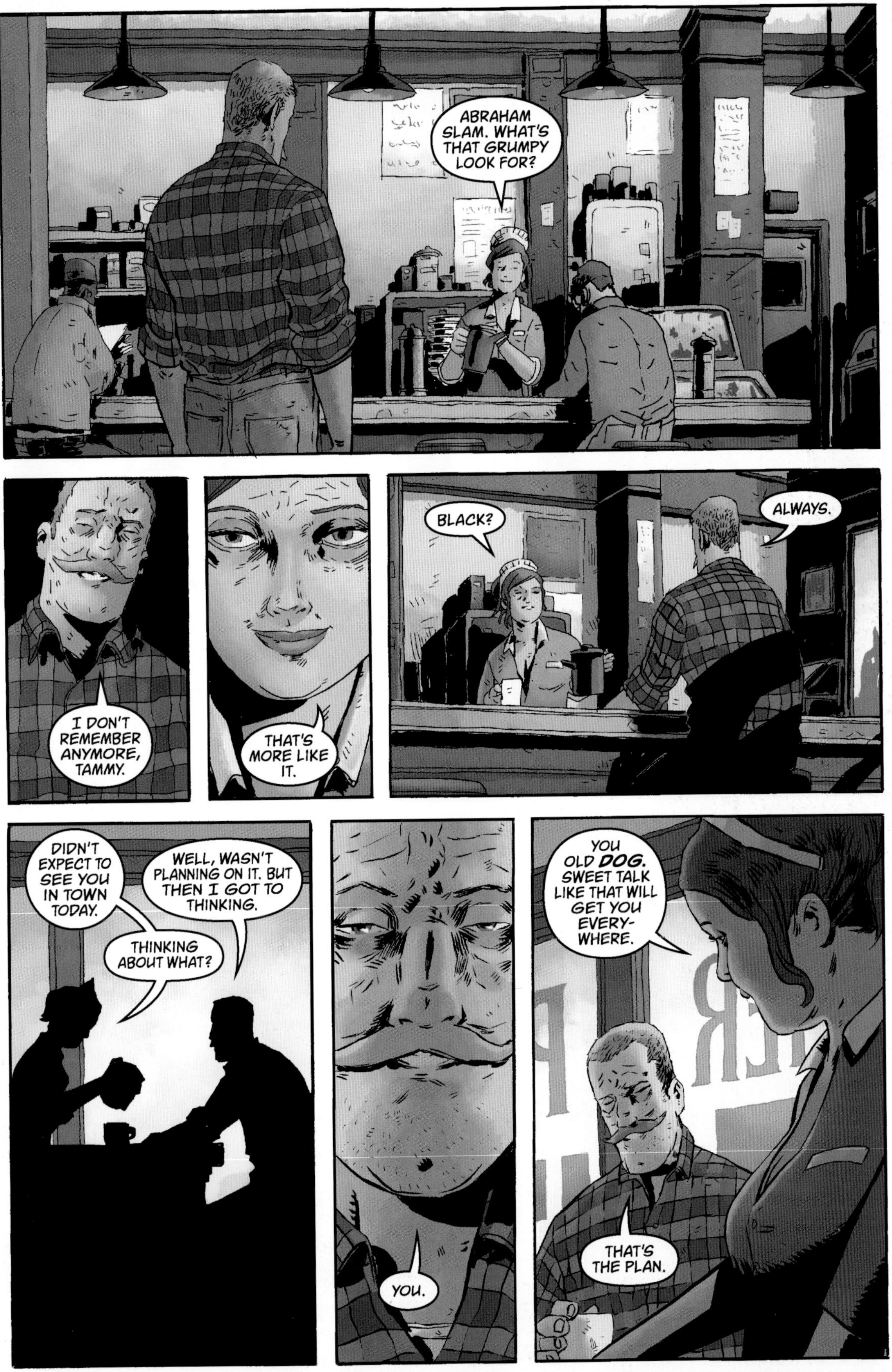
ABRAHAM SLAM. WHAT'S THAT GRUMPY LOOK FOR?
I DON'T REMEMBER ANYMORE, TAMMY.
THAT'S MORE LIKE IT.
BLACK?
ALWAYS.
DIDN'T EXPECT TO SEE YOU IN TOWN TODAY.
WELL, WASN'T PLANNING ON IT. BUT THEN I GOT TO THINKING.
THINKING ABOUT WHAT?
YOU.
YOU OLD DOG. SWEET TALK LIKE THAT WILL GET YOU EVERY-WHERE.
THAT'S THE PLAN.

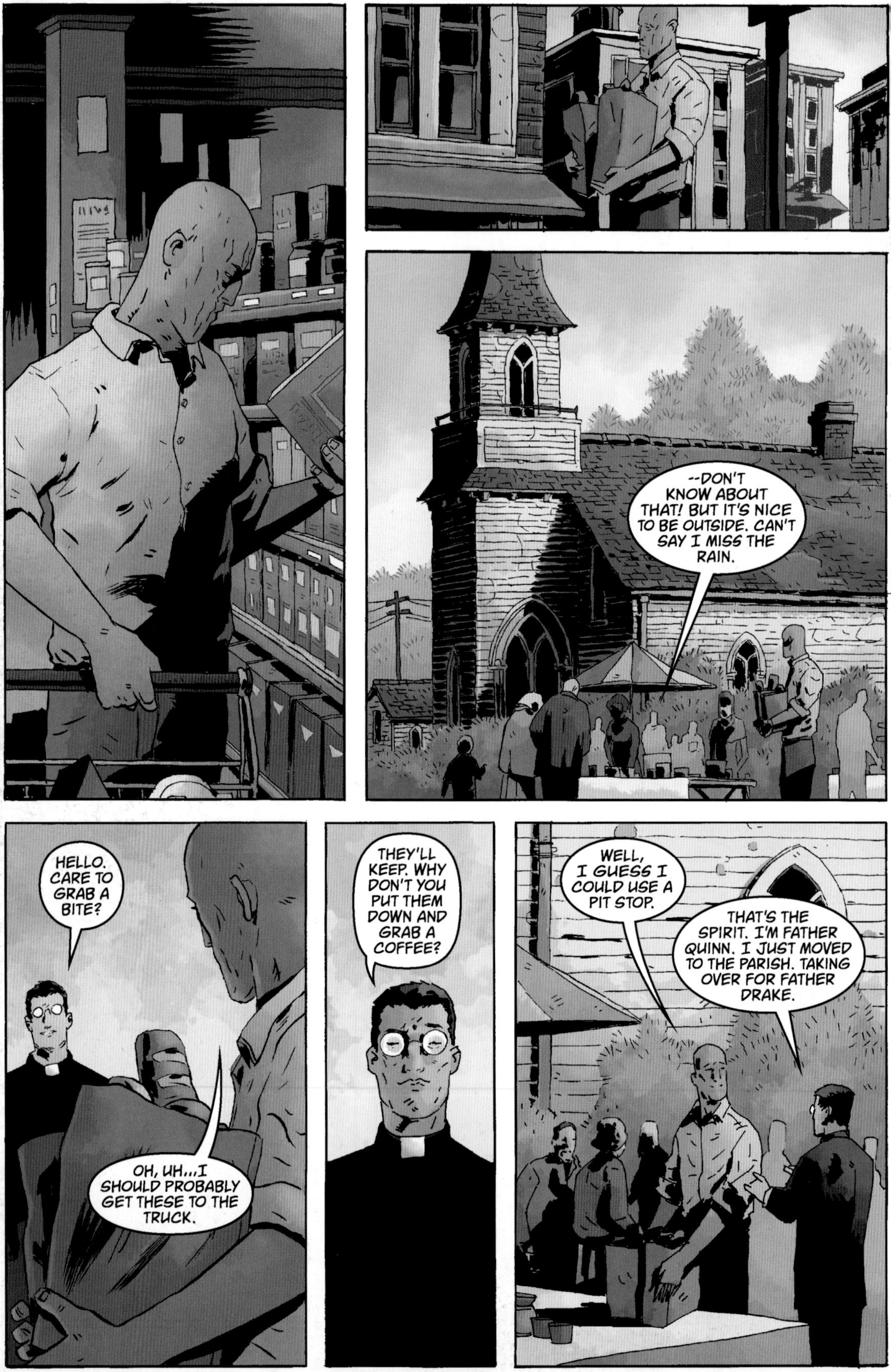
--DON'T KNOW ABOUT THAT! BUT IT'S NICE TO BE OUTSIDE. CAN'T SAY I MISS THE RAIN.
HELLO. CARE TO GRAB A BITE?
OH, UH...I SHOULD PROBABLY GET THESE TO THE TRUCK.
THEY'LL KEEP. WHY DON'T YOU PUT THEM DOWN AND GRAB A COFFEE?
WELL, I GUESS I COULD USE A PIT STOP.
THAT'S THE SPIRIT. I'M FATHER QUINN. I JUST MOVED TO THE PARISH. TAKING OVER FOR FATHER DRAKE.

OH, UH... MARK MARKZ. I, UH--I DIDN'T KNOW FATHER DRAKE VERY WELL, I'M AFRAID.

AH, NOT A CHURCHGOING MAN, THEN?

UH...NOT AS MUCH THESE DAYS. I'VE LAPSED.

WELL, YOU'LL HAVE TO PUT THE COFFEE BACK THEN, I'M AFRAID.

...

I'M JOKING.

AH, OKAY. GOOD.

SO...I GUESS I SHOULD MAKE MY SALES PITCH.

THE BOSS IS ALWAYS WATCHING, RIGHT?

HA, YES. BUT IT WOULD BE GREAT TO SEE YOU OUT AT MASS. NO PRESSURE, BUT MAYBE IT'S TIME YOU GAVE IT ANOTHER SHOT?

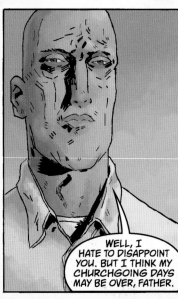

WELL, I HATE TO DISAPPOINT YOU. BUT I THINK MY CHURCHGOING DAYS MAY BE OVER, FATHER.

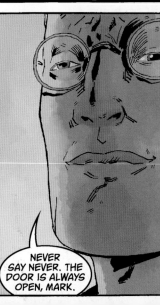

NEVER SAY NEVER. THE DOOR IS ALWAYS OPEN, MARK.

MARK MARKZ. WHAT IS THAT? EASTERN EUROPEAN?

UH...IT'S SWEDISH.

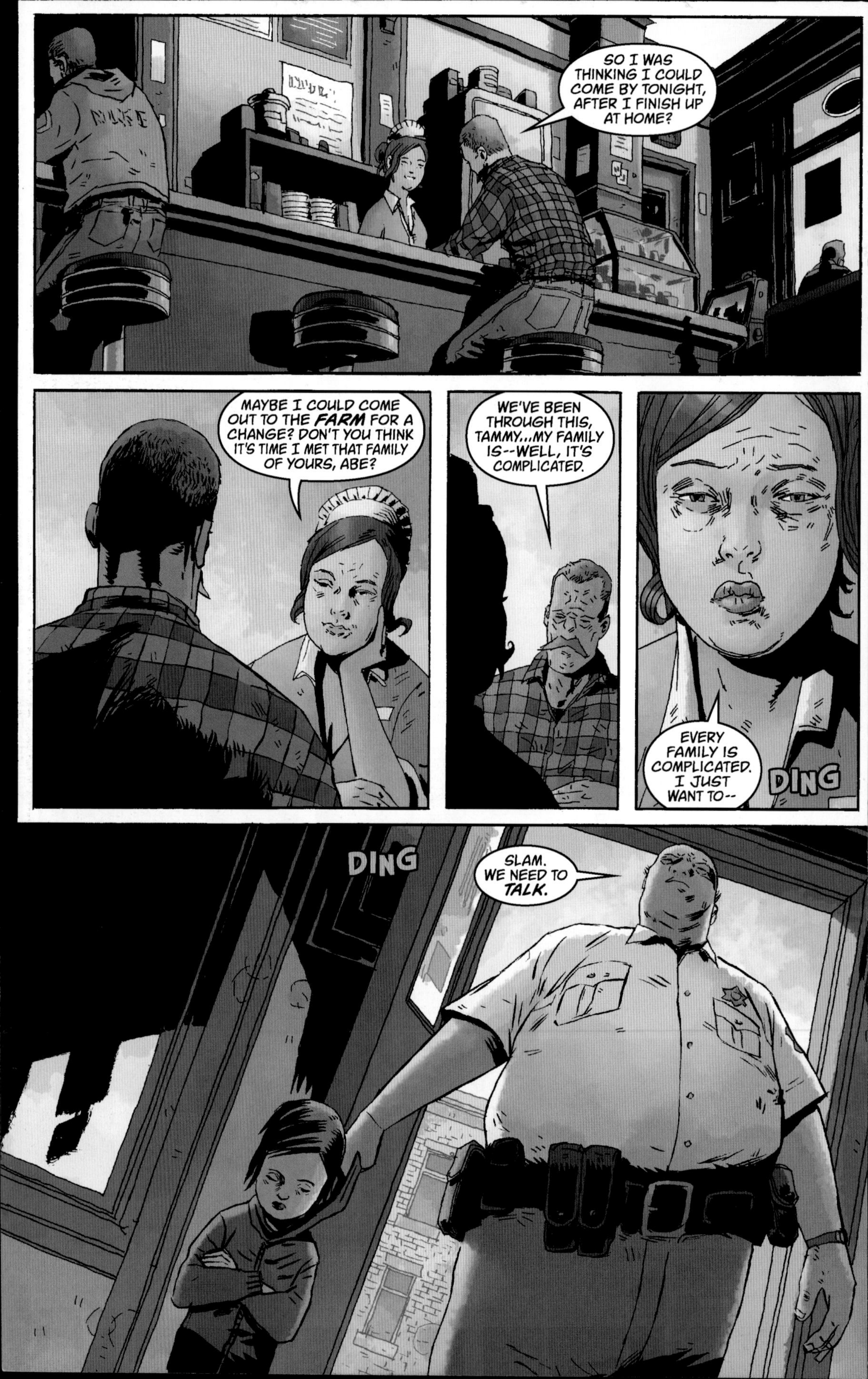
SO I WAS THINKING I COULD COME BY TONIGHT, AFTER I FINISH UP AT HOME?
MAYBE I COULD COME OUT TO THE FARM FOR A CHANGE? DON'T YOU THINK IT'S TIME I MET THAT FAMILY OF YOURS, ABE?
WE'VE BEEN THROUGH THIS, TAMMY... MY FAMILY IS--WELL, IT'S COMPLICATED.
EVERY FAMILY IS COMPLICATED. I JUST WANT TO--
DING
DING
SLAM. WE NEED TO TALK.

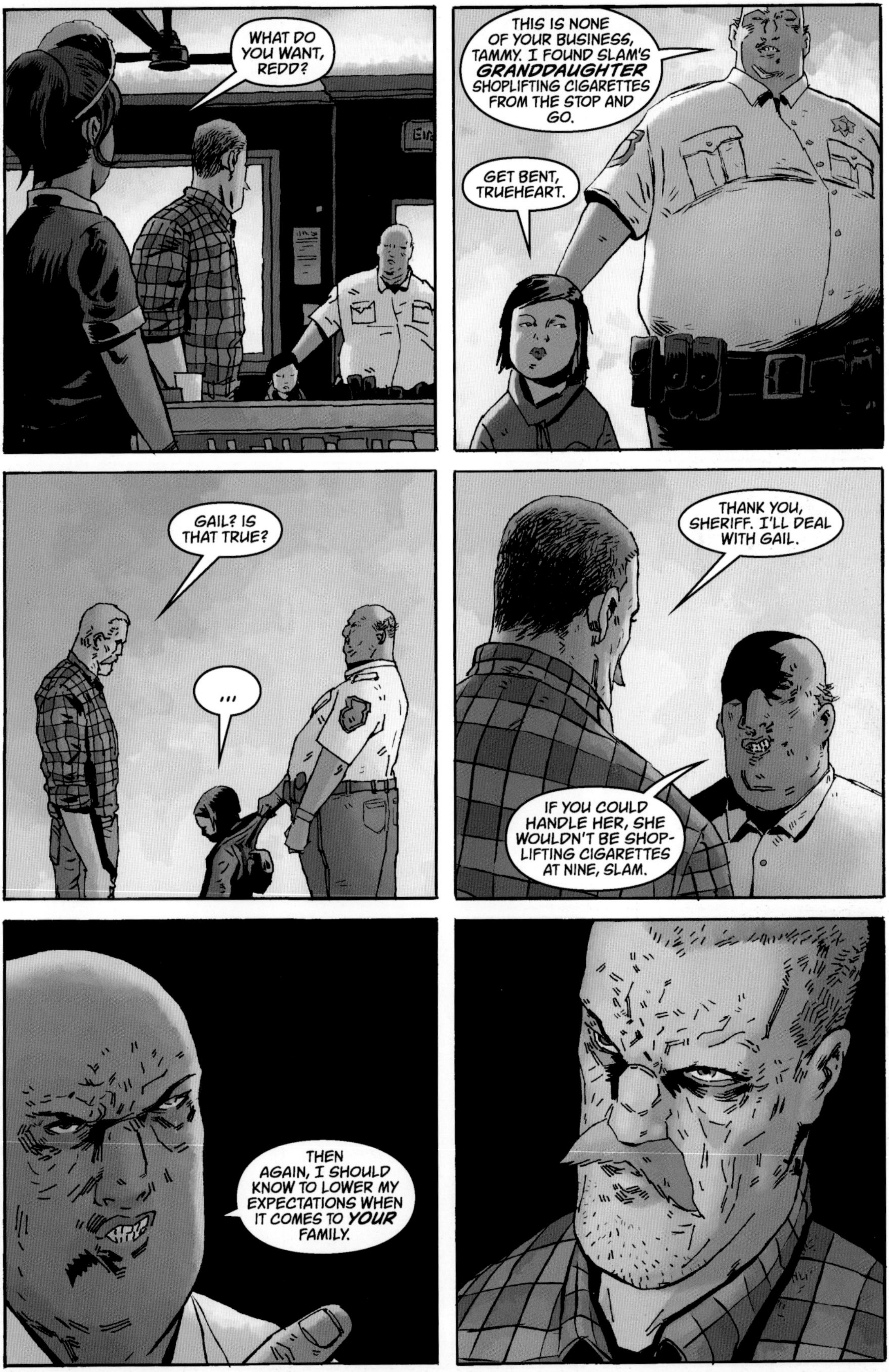
WHAT DO YOU WANT, REDD?
THIS IS NONE OF YOUR BUSINESS, TAMMY. I FOUND SLAM'S **GRANDDAUGHTER** SHOPLIFTING CIGARETTES FROM THE STOP AND GO.
GET BENT, TRUEHEART.
GAIL? IS THAT TRUE?
...
THANK YOU, SHERIFF. I'LL DEAL WITH GAIL.
IF YOU COULD HANDLE HER, SHE WOULDN'T BE SHOP-LIFTING CIGARETTES AT NINE, SLAM.
THEN AGAIN, I SHOULD KNOW TO LOWER MY EXPECTATIONS WHEN IT COMES TO ***YOUR*** FAMILY.

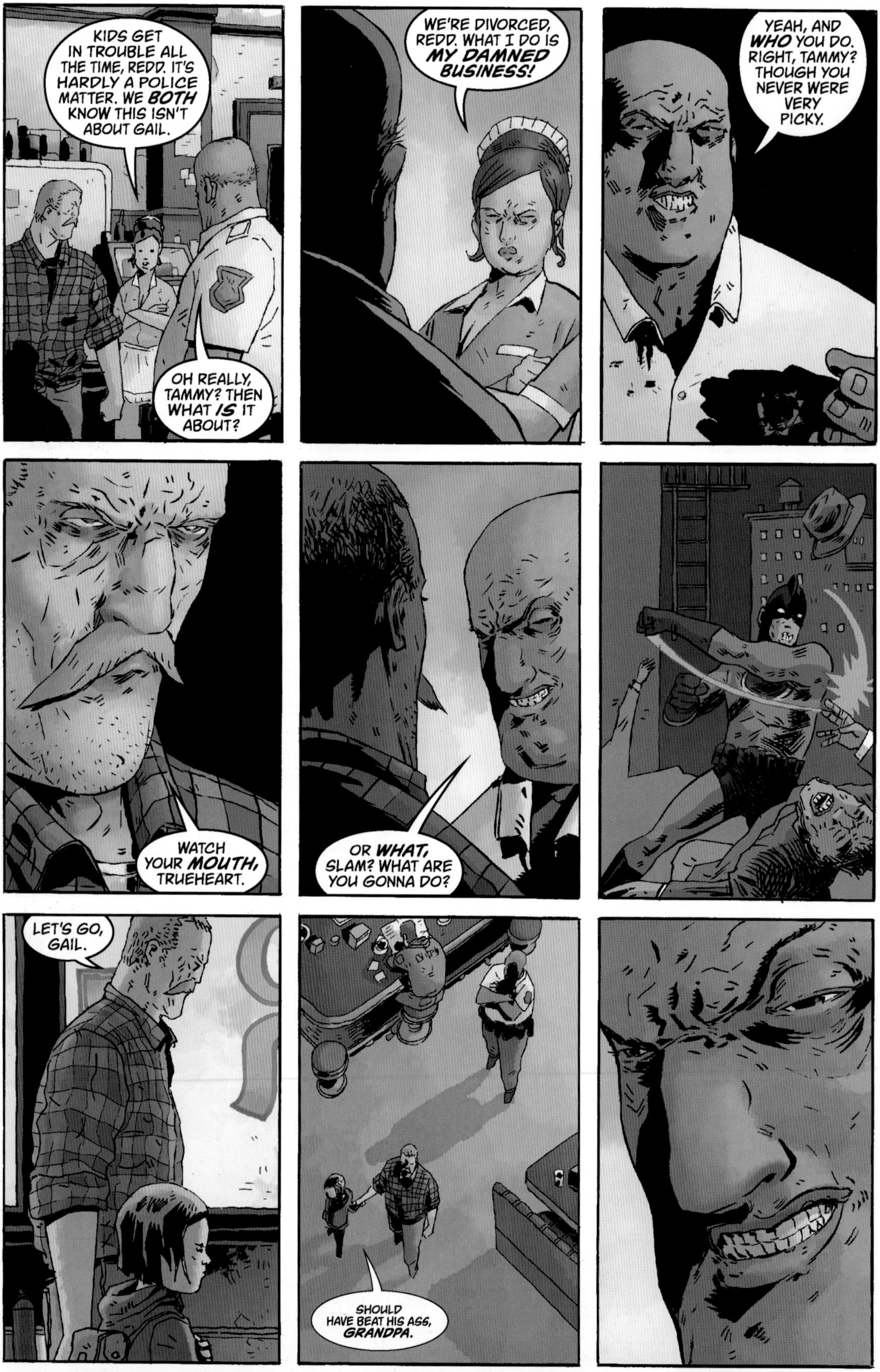
KIDS GET IN TROUBLE ALL THE TIME, REDD. IT'S HARDLY A POLICE MATTER. WE BOTH KNOW THIS ISN'T ABOUT GAIL.
OH REALLY, TAMMY? THEN WHAT IS IT ABOUT?
WE'RE DIVORCED, REDD. WHAT I DO IS MY DAMNED BUSINESS!
YEAH, AND WHO YOU DO. RIGHT, TAMMY? THOUGH YOU NEVER WERE VERY PICKY.
WATCH YOUR MOUTH, TRUEHEART.
OR WHAT, SLAM? WHAT ARE YOU GONNA DO?
LET'S GO, GAIL.
SHOULD HAVE BEAT HIS ASS, GRANDPA.

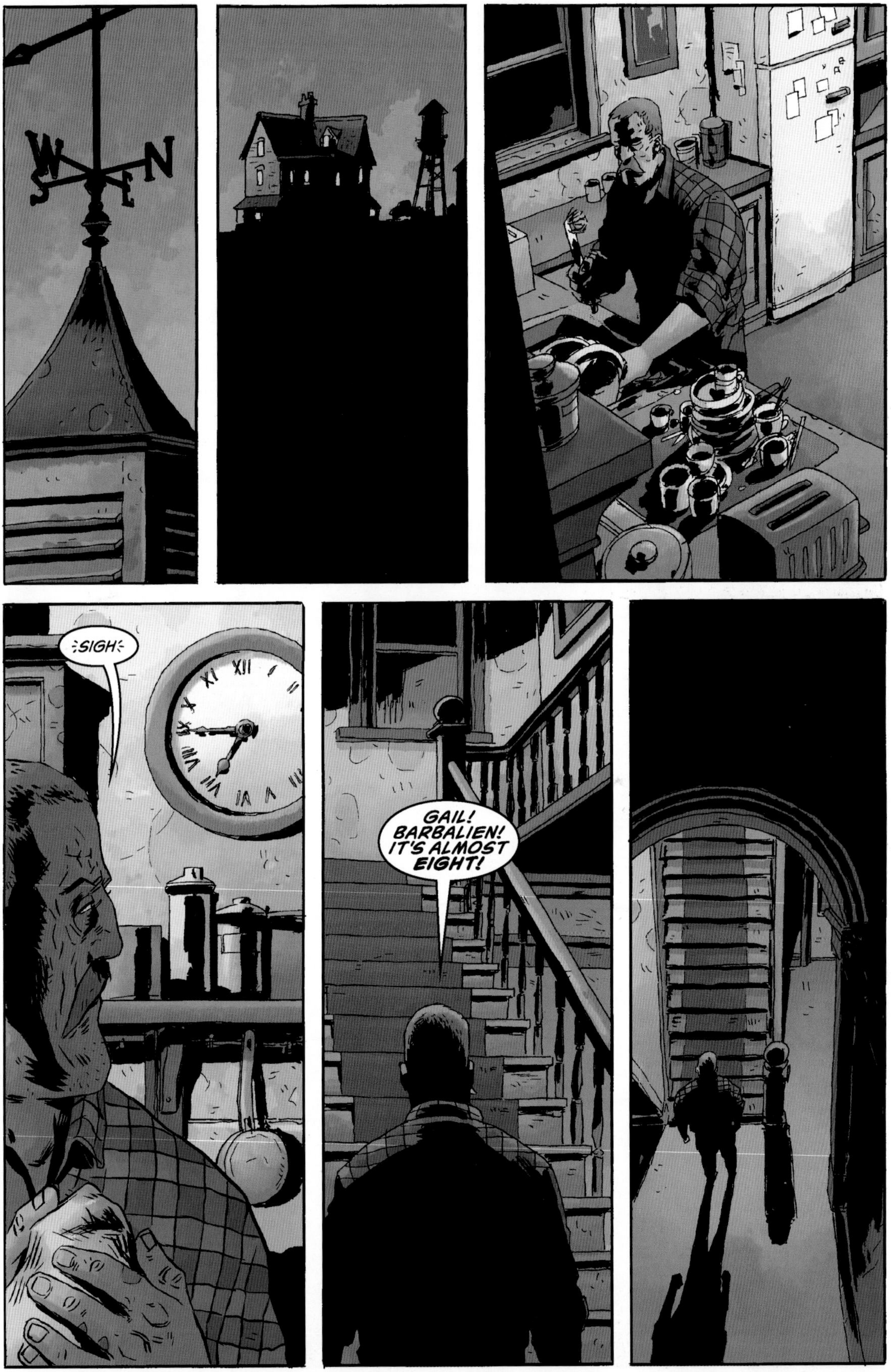
SIGH
GAIL! BARBALIEN! IT'S ALMOST EIGHT!

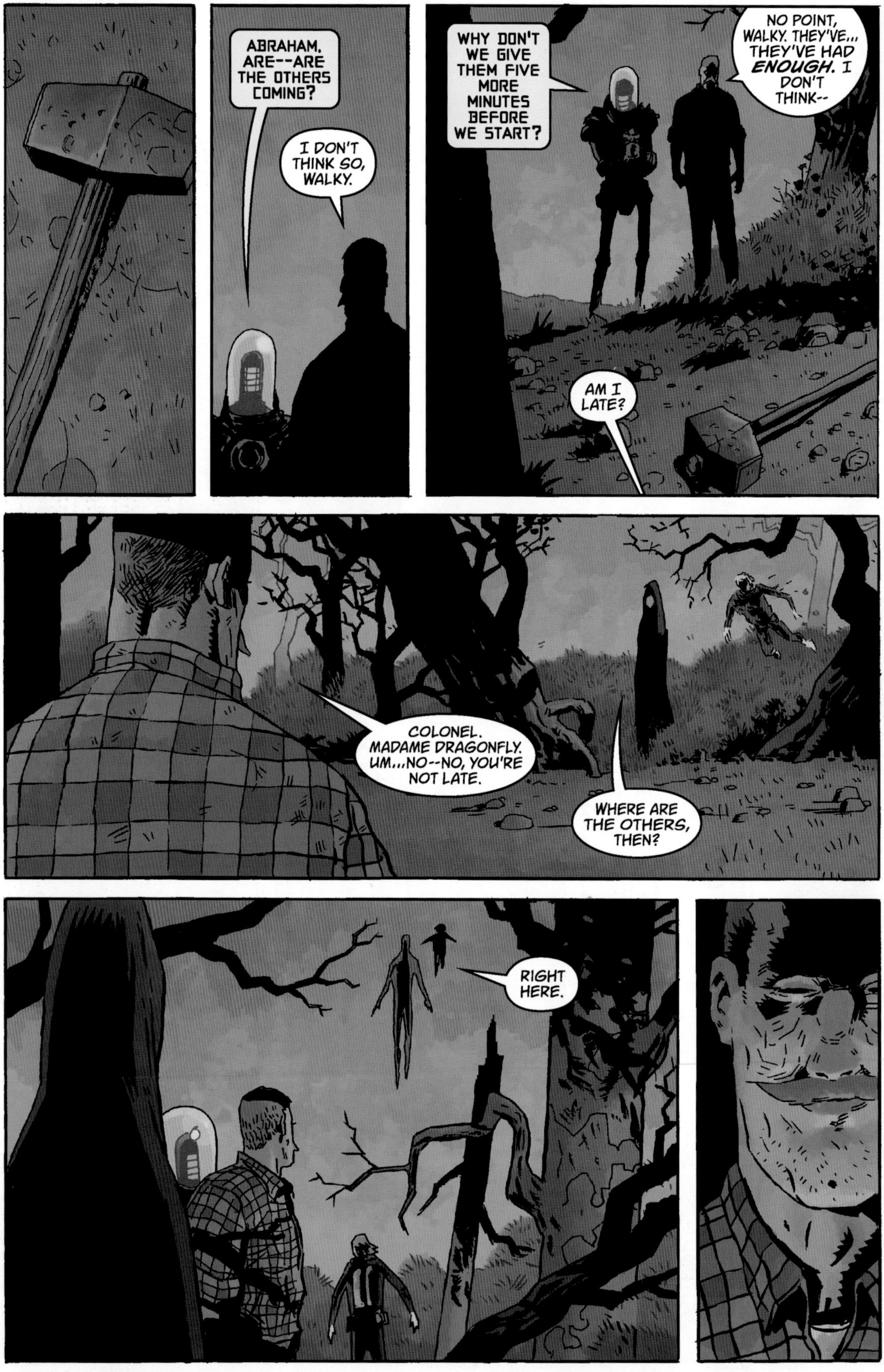
ABRAHAM. ARE--ARE THE OTHERS COMING?
I DON'T THINK SO, WALKY.
WHY DON'T WE GIVE THEM FIVE MORE MINUTES BEFORE WE START?
NO POINT, WALKY. THEY'VE... THEY'VE HAD **ENOUGH**. I DON'T THINK--
AM I LATE?
COLONEL. MADAME DRAGONFLY. UM...NO--NO, YOU'RE NOT LATE.
WHERE ARE THE OTHERS, THEN?
RIGHT HERE.

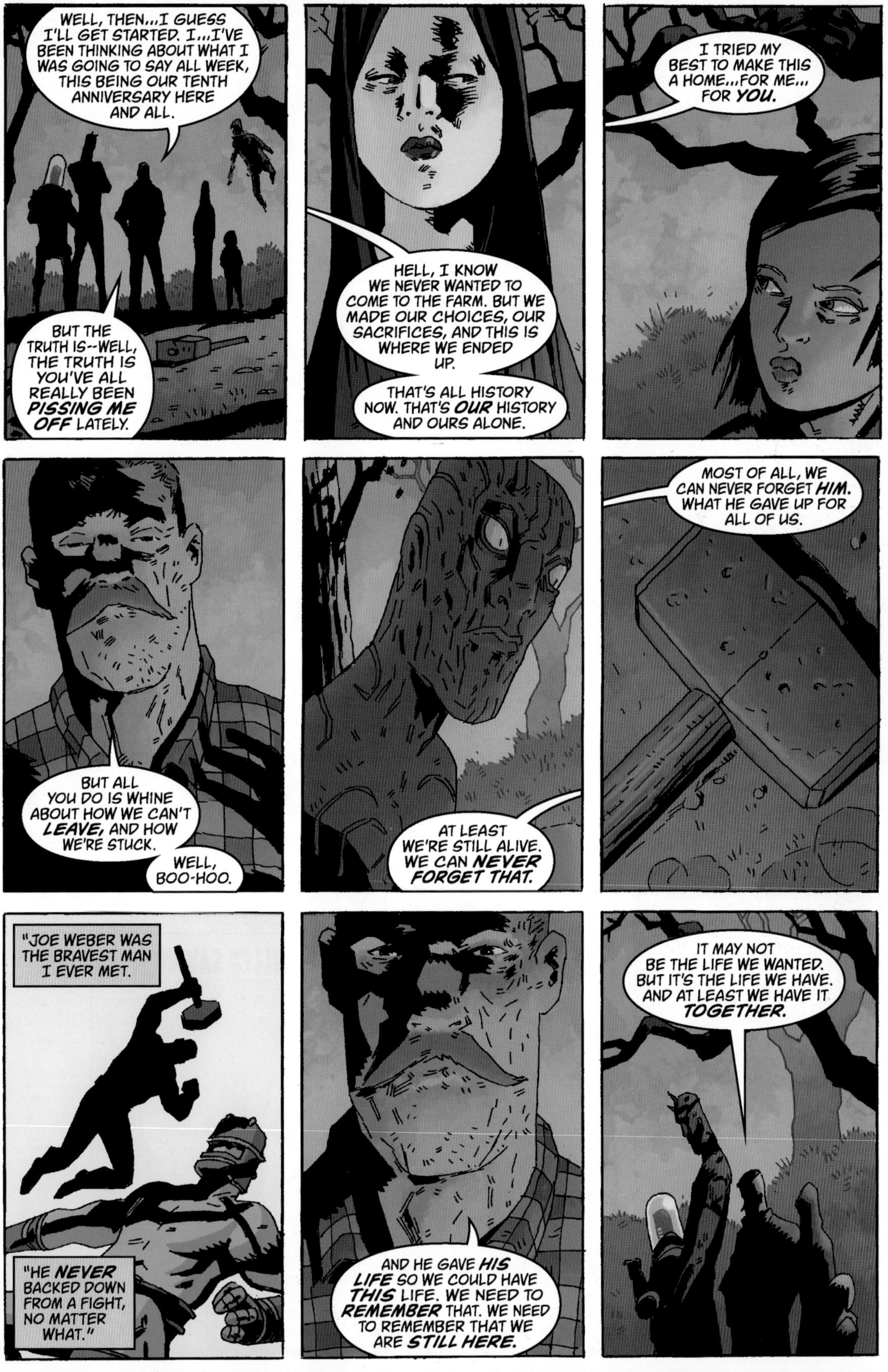
WELL, THEN...I GUESS I'LL GET STARTED. I...I'VE BEEN THINKING ABOUT WHAT I WAS GOING TO SAY ALL WEEK, THIS BEING OUR TENTH ANNIVERSARY HERE AND ALL.
BUT THE TRUTH IS--WELL, THE TRUTH IS YOU'VE ALL REALLY BEEN PISSING ME OFF LATELY.
HELL, I KNOW WE NEVER WANTED TO COME TO THE FARM. BUT WE MADE OUR CHOICES, OUR SACRIFICES, AND THIS IS WHERE WE ENDED UP.
THAT'S ALL HISTORY NOW. THAT'S OUR HISTORY AND OURS ALONE.
I TRIED MY BEST TO MAKE THIS A HOME...FOR ME... FOR YOU.
BUT ALL YOU DO IS WHINE ABOUT HOW WE CAN'T LEAVE, AND HOW WE'RE STUCK.
WELL, BOO-HOO.
AT LEAST WE'RE STILL ALIVE. WE CAN NEVER FORGET THAT.
MOST OF ALL, WE CAN NEVER FORGET HIM. WHAT HE GAVE UP FOR ALL OF US.
"JOE WEBER WAS THE BRAVEST MAN I EVER MET.
"HE NEVER BACKED DOWN FROM A FIGHT, NO MATTER WHAT."
AND HE GAVE HIS LIFE SO WE COULD HAVE THIS LIFE. WE NEED TO REMEMBER THAT. WE NEED TO REMEMBER THAT WE ARE STILL HERE.
IT MAY NOT BE THE LIFE WE WANTED. BUT IT'S THE LIFE WE HAVE. AND AT LEAST WE HAVE IT TOGETHER.

Ten years.

Ten years ago today since they saved *Spiral City* and disappeared.

To most, they don't seem real anymore. Like urban legends... ghost stories.

But they *were real.* I know, because *I was there.* I was only thirteen, but I remember the terror...the fear.

It's still there, in the air. It infected the city and never left us.

GLOBAL PLANET

SPIRAL CITY'S GREATEST NEWSPAPER   ESTABLISHED 1902

HEROES KILLED SAVING SPIRAL CITY

Anti-God Destroyed

BLACK OF HAMMER

GOLDEN SMALL LOCK

They stopped him. They defeated the Anti-God and saved us all.

In the aftermath, their bodies were never found. They were presumed to have been obliterated in the final battle.

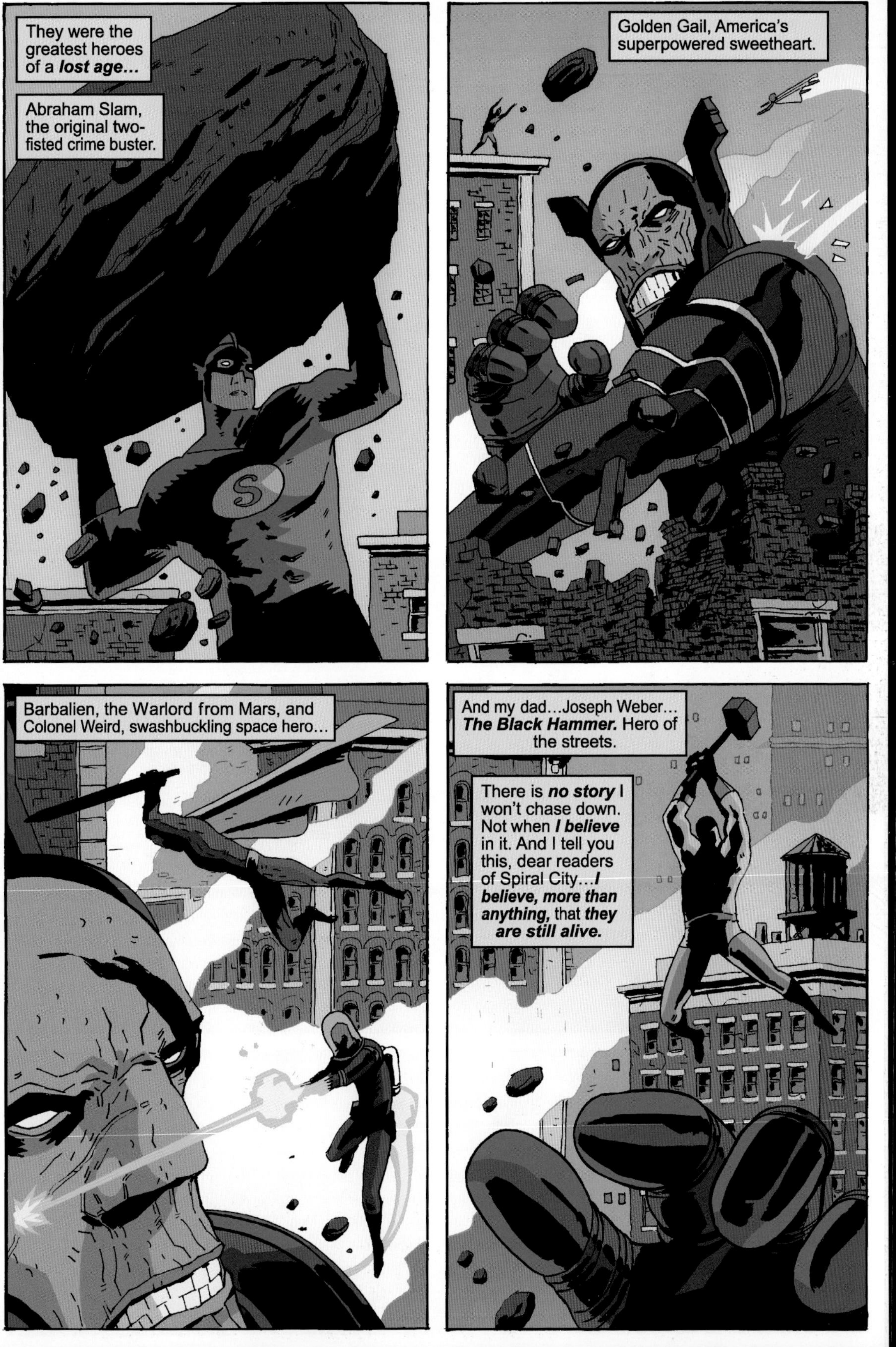
They were the greatest heroes of a *lost age...*
Abraham Slam, the original two-fisted crime buster.
Golden Gail, America's superpowered sweetheart.
Barbalien, the Warlord from Mars, and Colonel Weird, swashbuckling space hero...
And my dad...Joseph Weber... ***The Black Hammer.*** Hero of the streets.
There is ***no story*** I won't chase down. Not when ***I believe*** in it. And I tell you this, dear readers of Spiral City...***I believe, more than anything,*** that ***they are still alive.***

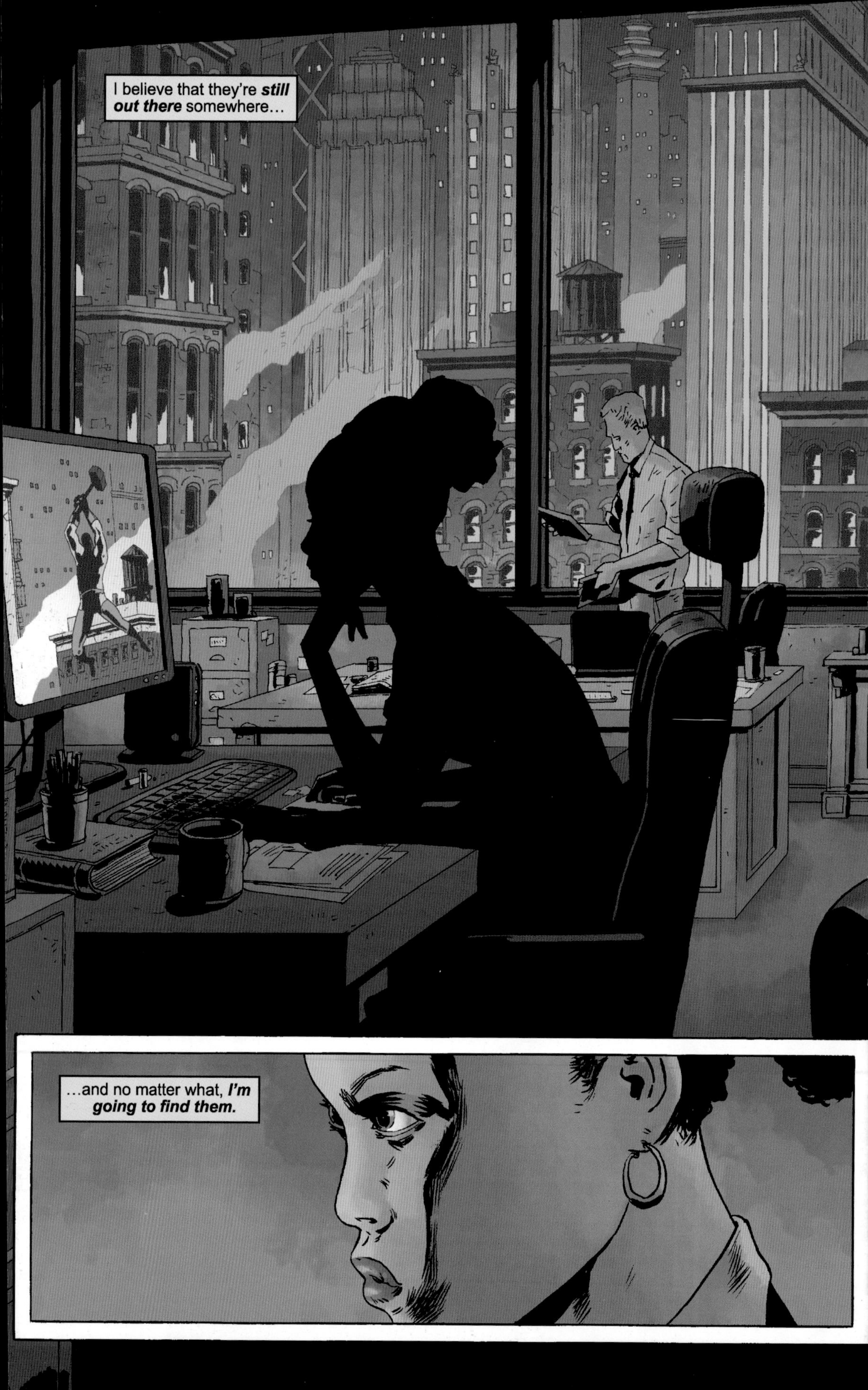
I believe that they're ***still out there*** somewhere…
…and no matter what, ***I'm going to find them.***

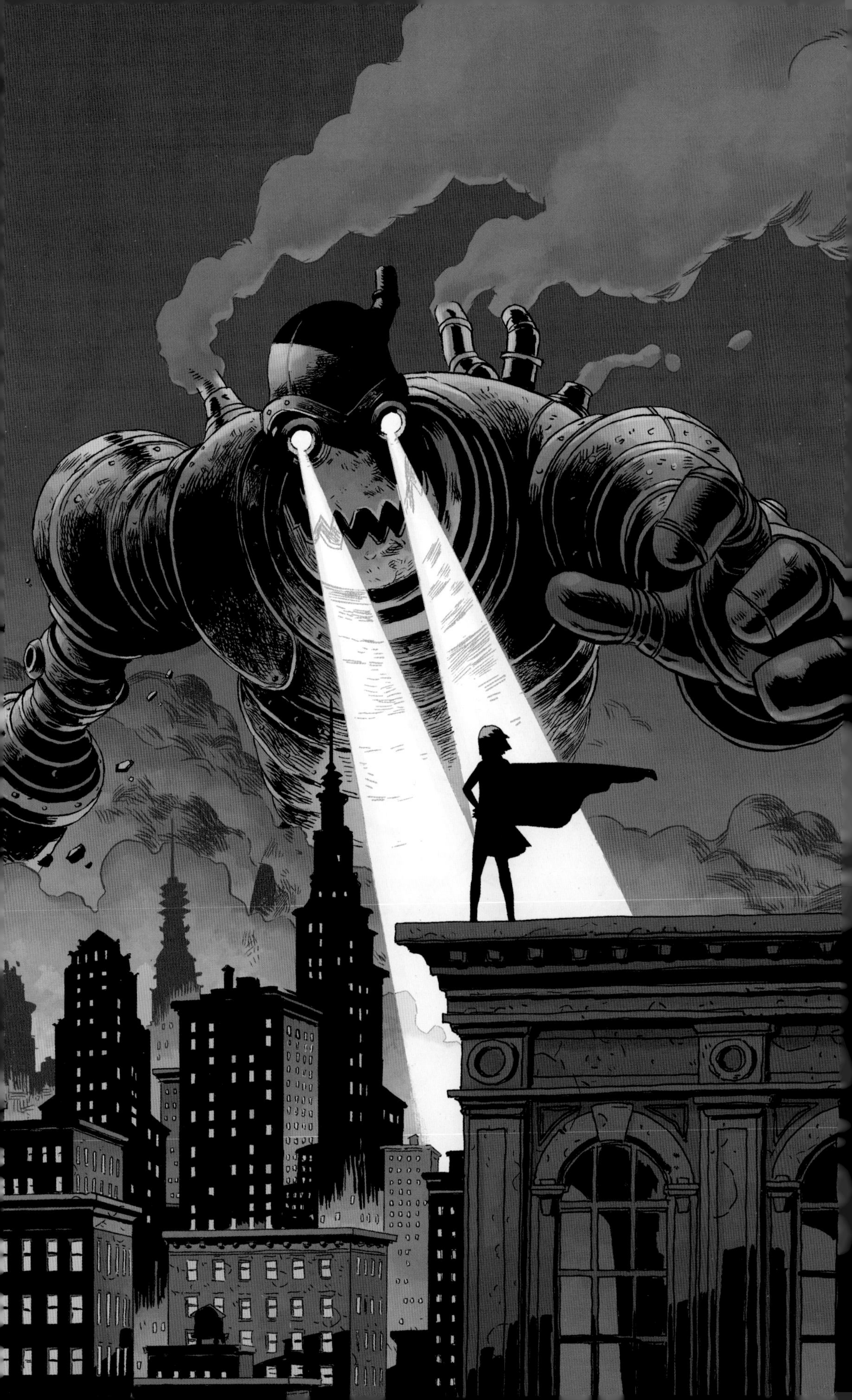

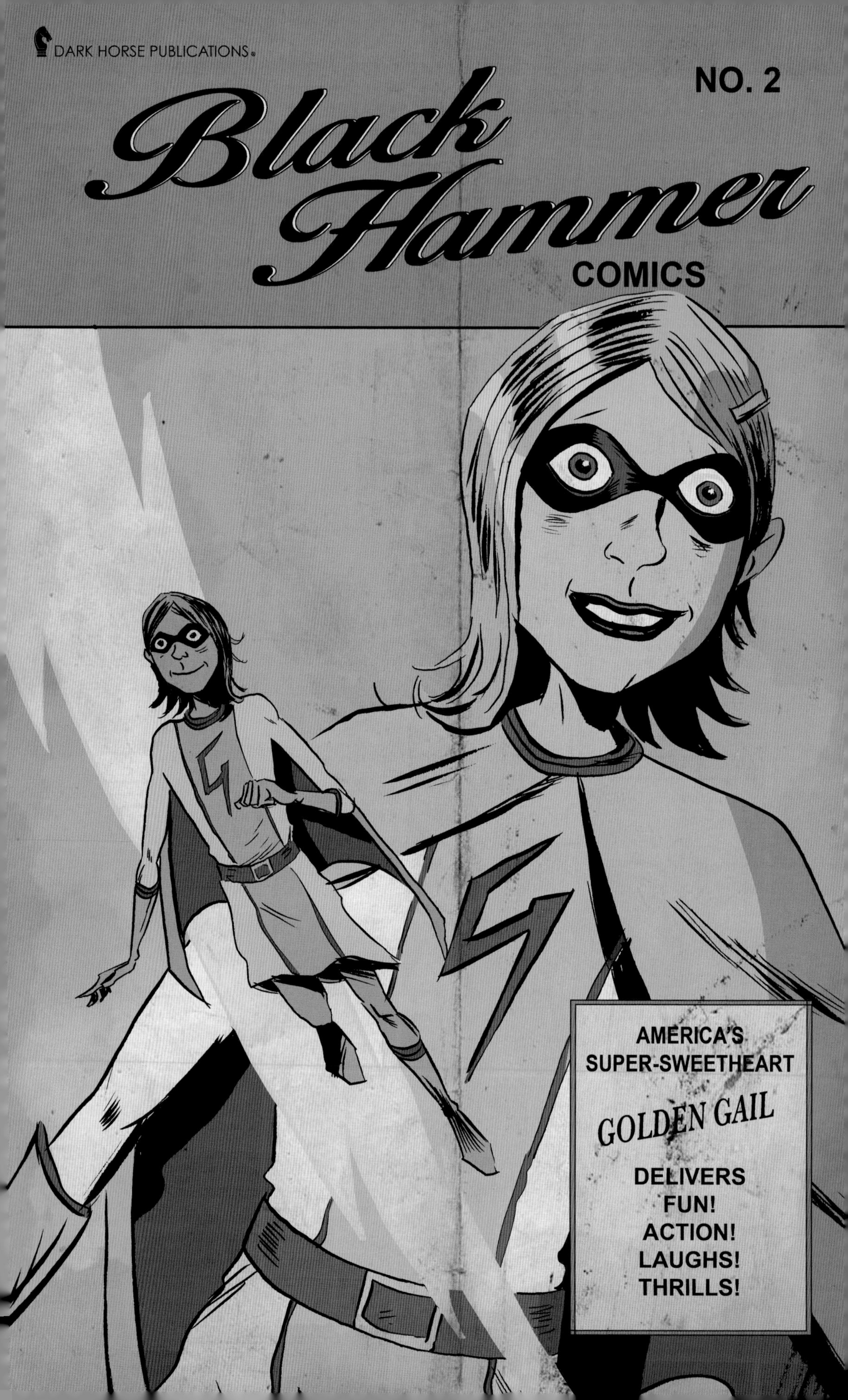
DARK HORSE PUBLICATIONS
NO. 2
Black Hammer
COMICS
AMERICA'S SUPER-SWEETHEART
GOLDEN GAIL
DELIVERS FUN! ACTION! LAUGHS! THRILLS!

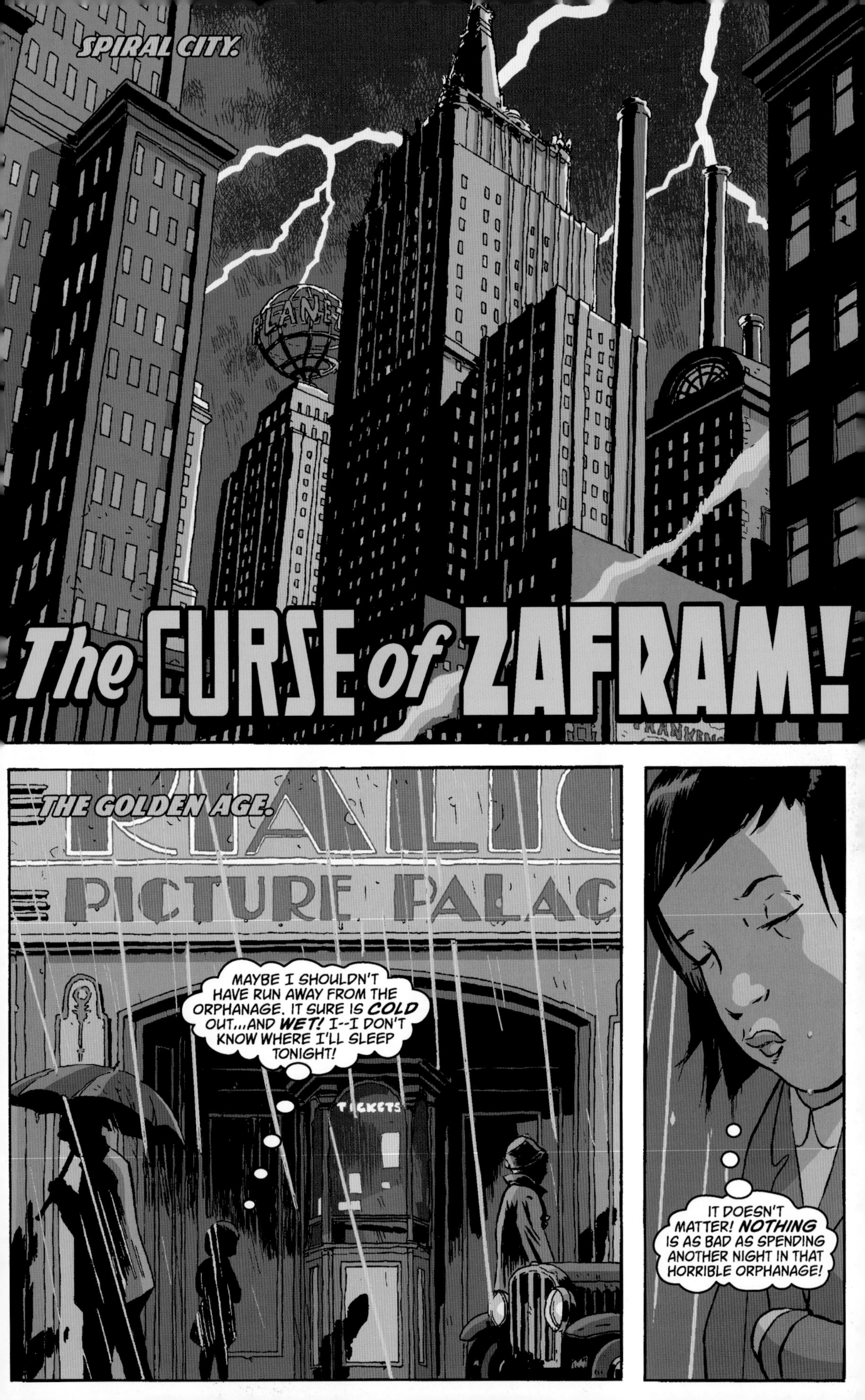
SPIRAL CITY.
PLANET
The CURSE of ZAFRAM!
THE GOLDEN AGE.
PICTURE PALAC
MAYBE I SHOULDN'T HAVE RUN AWAY FROM THE ORPHANAGE. IT SURE IS COLD OUT...AND WET! I--I DON'T KNOW WHERE I'LL SLEEP TONIGHT!
TICKETS
IT DOESN'T MATTER! NOTHING IS AS BAD AS SPENDING ANOTHER NIGHT IN THAT HORRIBLE ORPHANAGE!

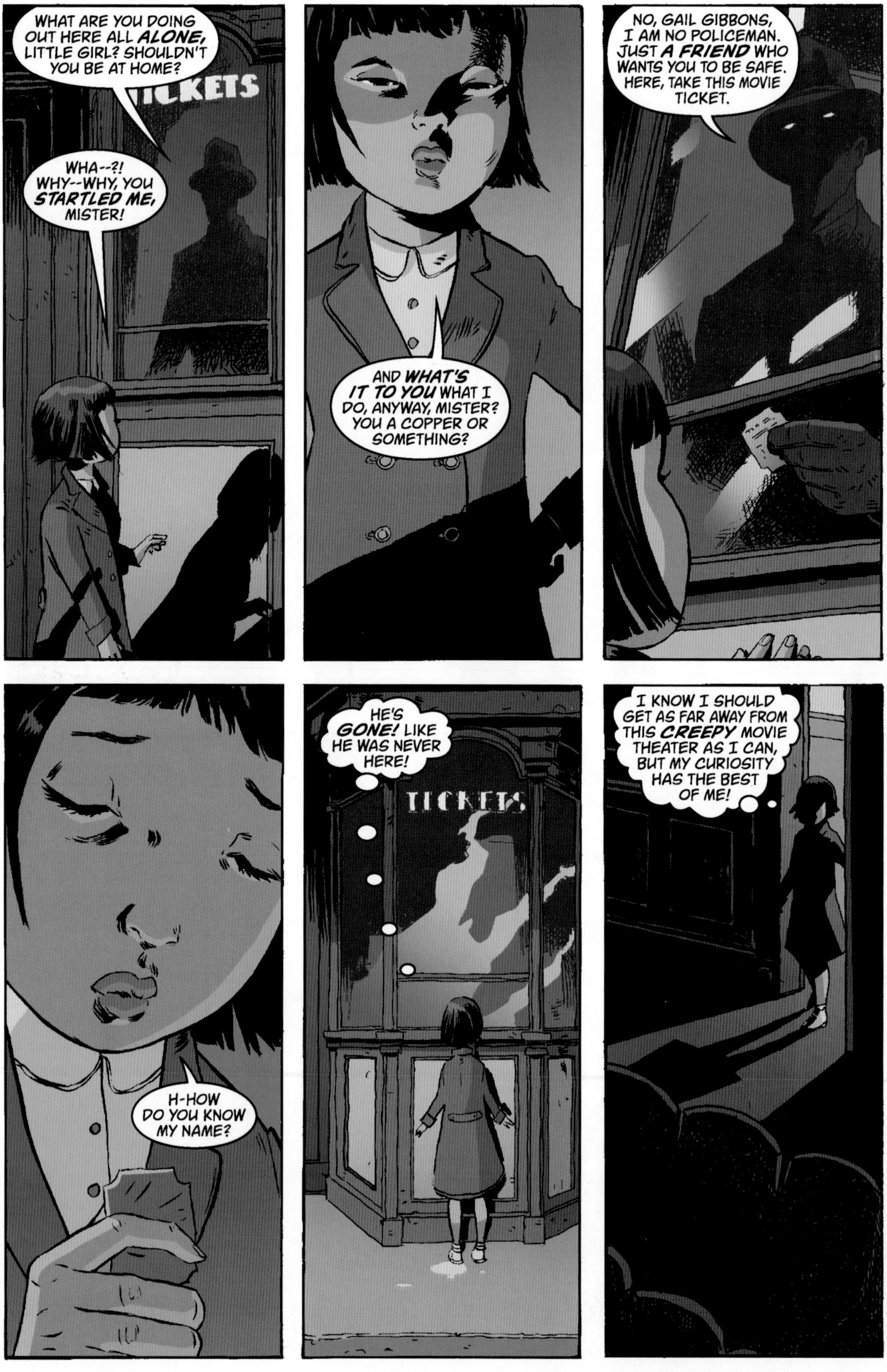

WHAT ARE YOU DOING OUT HERE ALL ALONE, LITTLE GIRL? SHOULDN'T YOU BE AT HOME?
TICKETS
WHA--?! WHY--WHY, YOU STARTLED ME, MISTER!
AND WHAT'S IT TO YOU WHAT I DO, ANYWAY, MISTER? YOU A COPPER OR SOMETHING?
NO, GAIL GIBBONS, I AM NO POLICEMAN. JUST A FRIEND WHO WANTS YOU TO BE SAFE. HERE, TAKE THIS MOVIE TICKET.
H-HOW DO YOU KNOW MY NAME?
HE'S GONE! LIKE HE WAS NEVER HERE!
TICKETS
I KNOW I SHOULD GET AS FAR AWAY FROM THIS CREEPY MOVIE THEATER AS I CAN, BUT MY CURIOSITY HAS THE BEST OF ME!

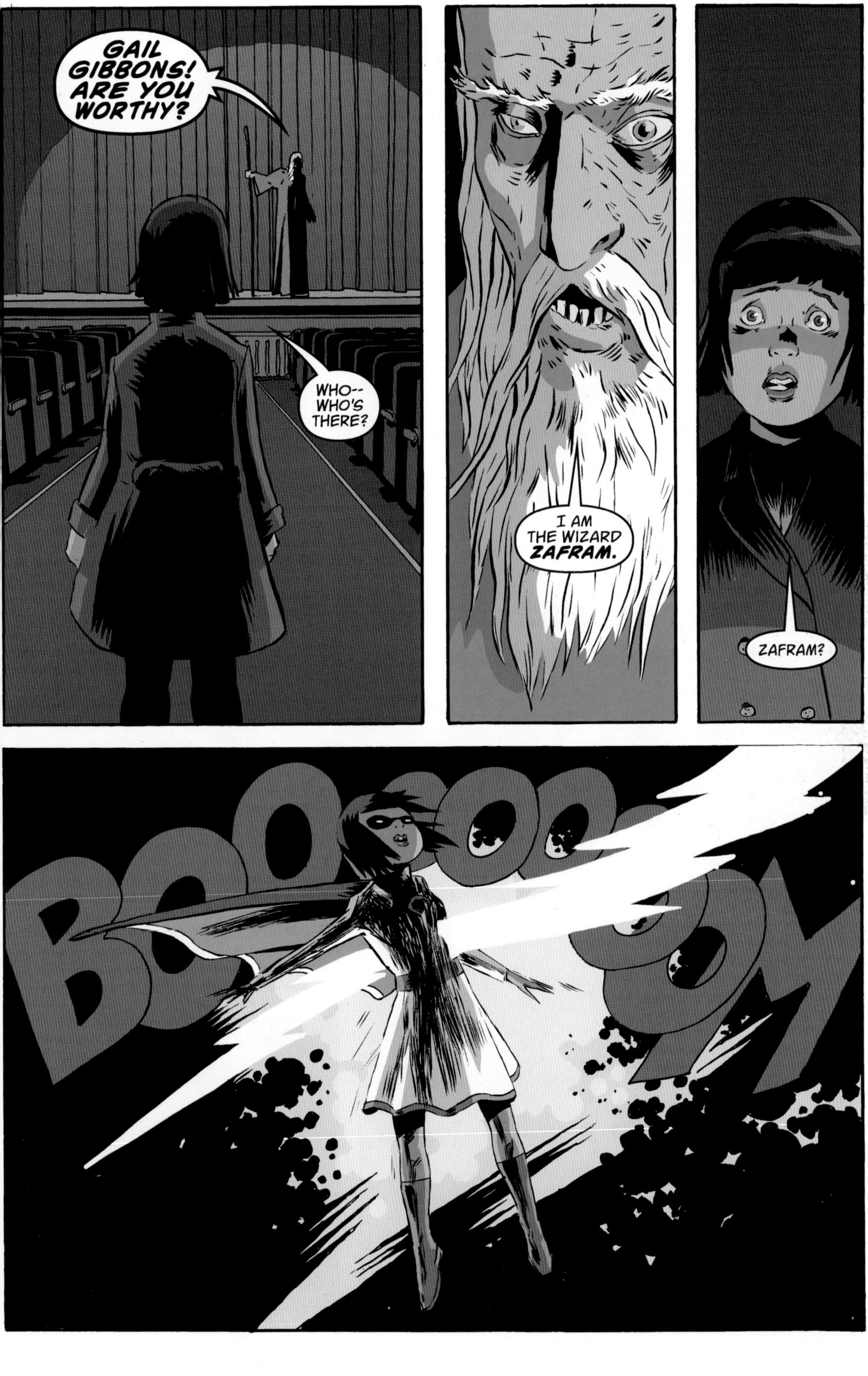
GAIL GIBBONS! ARE YOU WORTHY?
WHO-- WHO'S THERE?
I AM THE WIZARD ZAFRAM.
ZAFRAM?
BOOOOOOOOOOOM

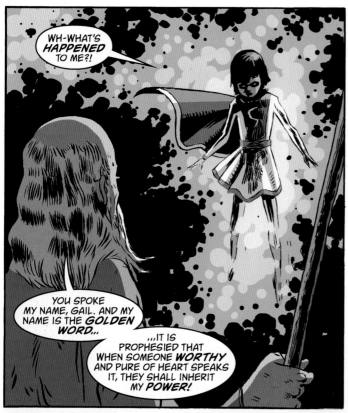

WH-WHAT'S *HAPPENED* TO ME?!

YOU SPOKE MY NAME, GAIL. AND MY NAME IS THE *GOLDEN WORD*...

...IT IS PROPHESIED THAT WHEN SOMEONE *WORTHY* AND PURE OF HEART SPEAKS IT, THEY SHALL INHERIT MY *POWER!*

THIS IS INCREDIBLE! I--I CAN *FLY*, AND I FEEL SO *STRONG!*

YES! YOU SEE, I HAVE BEEN IMPRISONED HERE IN THIS WORLD BETWEEN WORLDS FOR *EONS*. AND NOW, WITH MY POWER SAFE INSIDE OF *YOU*...

...I CAN BE *FREE* AT LAST!

HOLD ON! I'LL...I'LL GET *HELP!*

NO! I NEED NO HELP. AND I WILL *ALWAYS* BE WITH YOU, GAIL...IN YOUR HEART. YOU ONLY NEED TO SAY MY NAME.

SAY IT, GAIL...SAY IT AGAIN. SAY MY *NAME.*

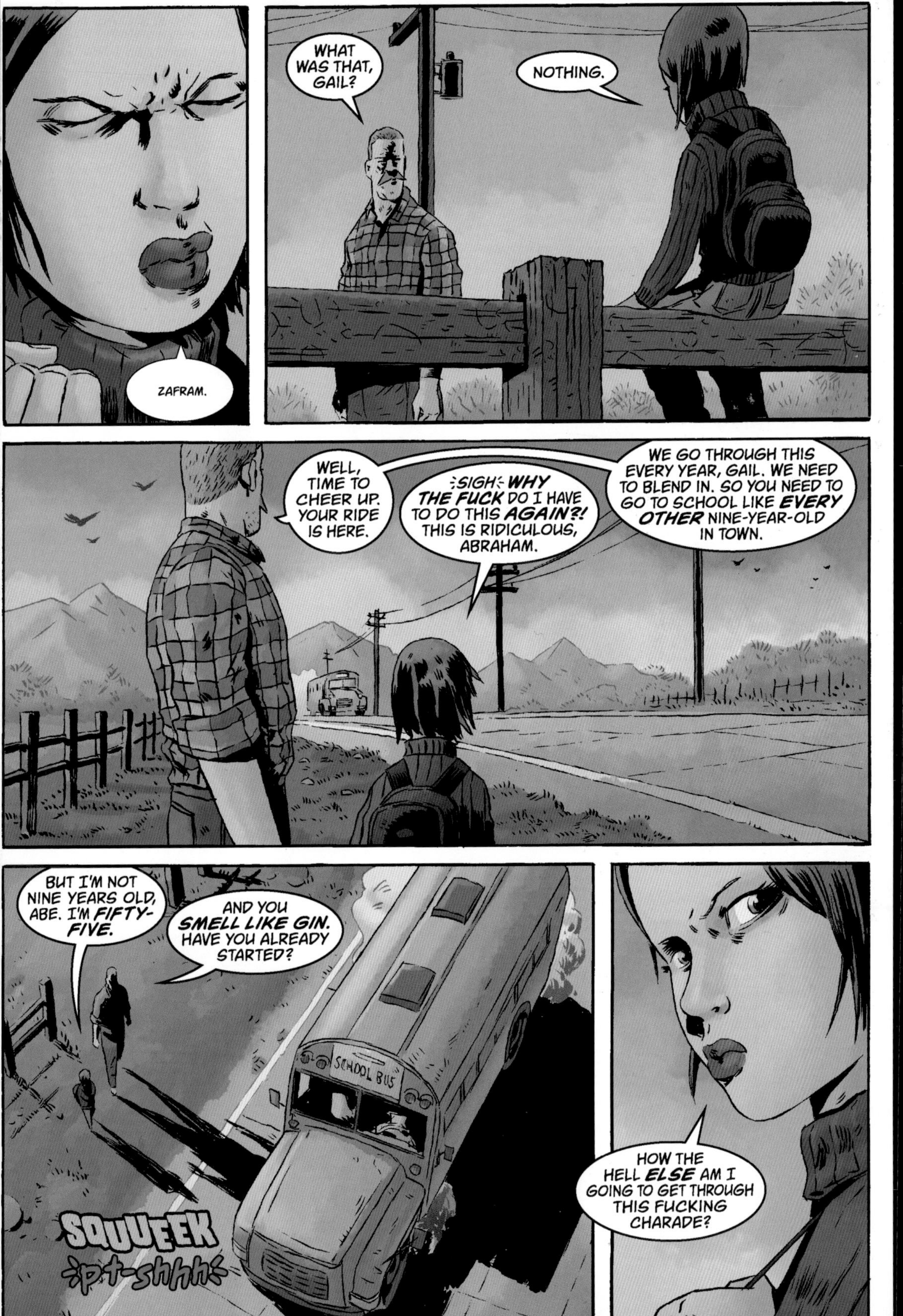
ZAFRAM.
WHAT WAS THAT, GAIL?
NOTHING.
WELL, TIME TO CHEER UP. YOUR RIDE IS HERE.
SIGH WHY THE FUCK DO I HAVE TO DO THIS AGAIN?! THIS IS RIDICULOUS, ABRAHAM.
WE GO THROUGH THIS EVERY YEAR, GAIL. WE NEED TO BLEND IN. SO YOU NEED TO GO TO SCHOOL LIKE EVERY OTHER NINE-YEAR-OLD IN TOWN.
BUT I'M NOT NINE YEARS OLD, ABE. I'M FIFTY-FIVE.
AND YOU SMELL LIKE GIN. HAVE YOU ALREADY STARTED?
SCHOOL BUS
SQUUEEK
pt-shhh
HOW THE HELL ELSE AM I GOING TO GET THROUGH THIS FUCKING CHARADE?

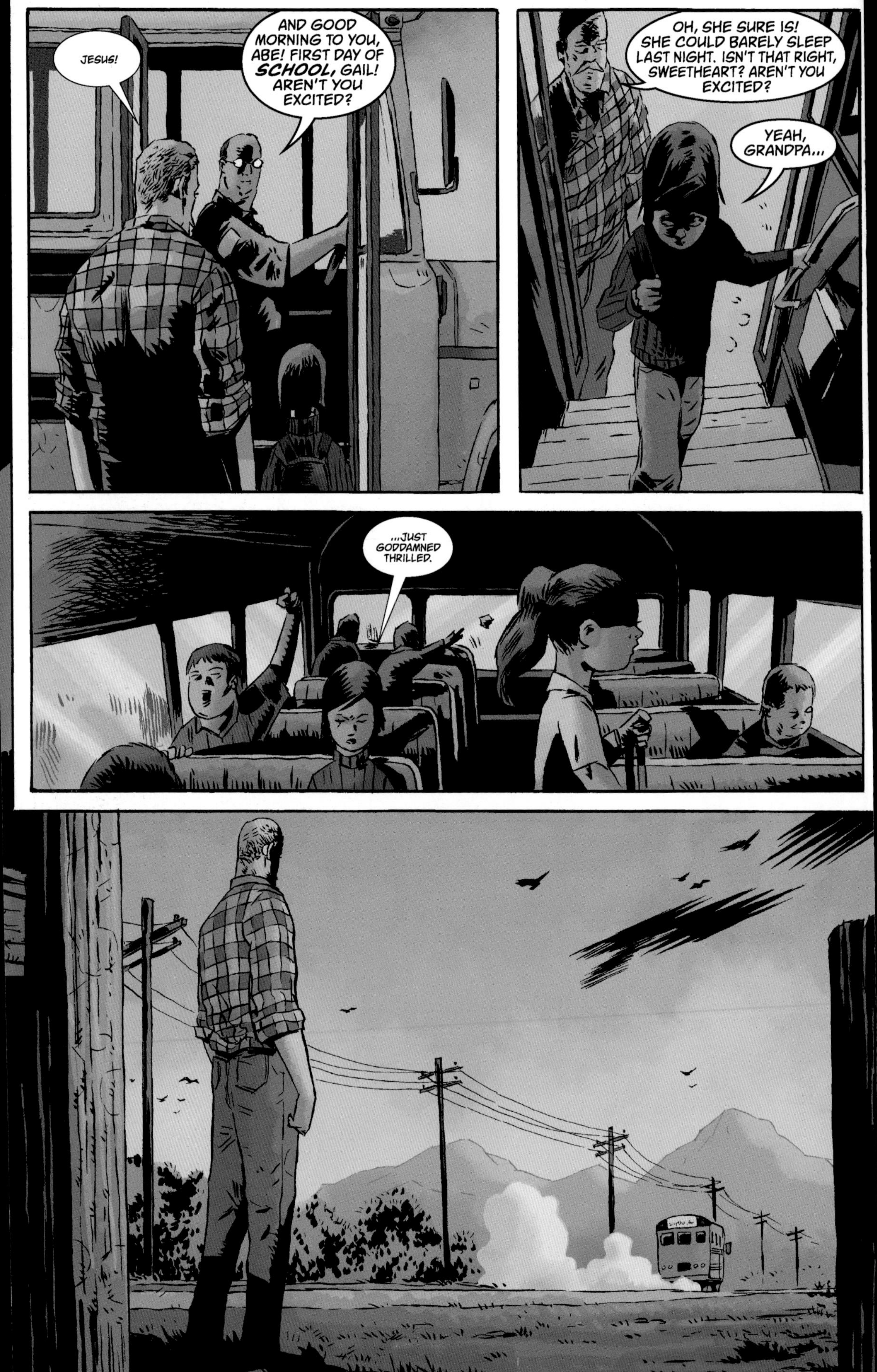
JESUS!
AND GOOD MORNING TO YOU, ABE! FIRST DAY OF SCHOOL, GAIL! AREN'T YOU EXCITED?
OH, SHE SURE IS! SHE COULD BARELY SLEEP LAST NIGHT. ISN'T THAT RIGHT, SWEETHEART? AREN'T YOU EXCITED?
YEAH, GRANDPA...
...JUST GODDAMNED THRILLED.

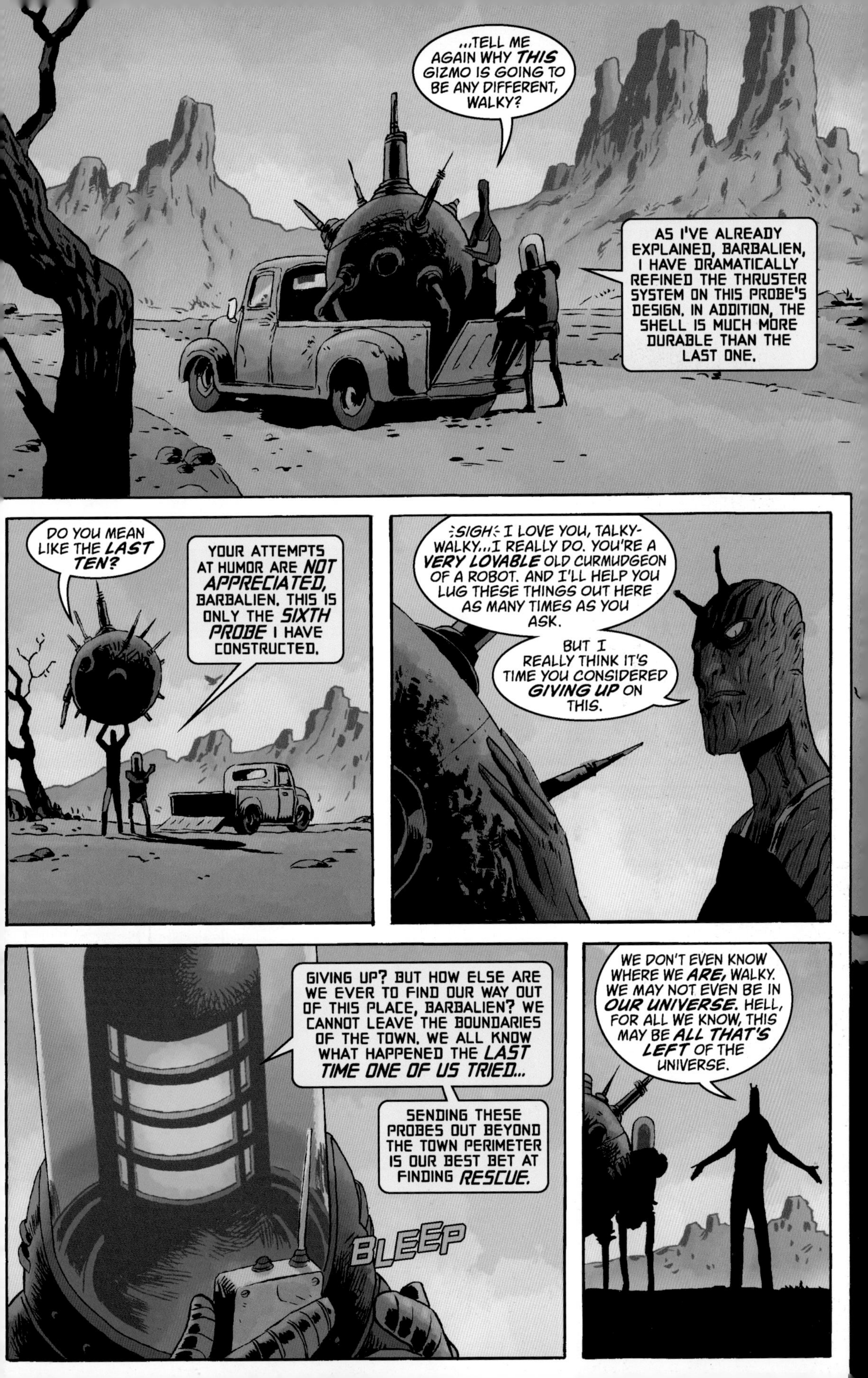
...TELL ME AGAIN WHY THIS GIZMO IS GOING TO BE ANY DIFFERENT, WALKY?
AS I'VE ALREADY EXPLAINED, BARBALIEN, I HAVE DRAMATICALLY REFINED THE THRUSTER SYSTEM ON THIS PROBE'S DESIGN. IN ADDITION, THE SHELL IS MUCH MORE DURABLE THAN THE LAST ONE.
DO YOU MEAN LIKE THE LAST TEN?
YOUR ATTEMPTS AT HUMOR ARE NOT APPRECIATED, BARBALIEN. THIS IS ONLY THE SIXTH PROBE I HAVE CONSTRUCTED.
:SIGH: I LOVE YOU, TALKY-WALKY...I REALLY DO. YOU'RE A VERY LOVABLE OLD CURMUDGEON OF A ROBOT. AND I'LL HELP YOU LUG THESE THINGS OUT HERE AS MANY TIMES AS YOU ASK.
BUT I REALLY THINK IT'S TIME YOU CONSIDERED GIVING UP ON THIS.
GIVING UP? BUT HOW ELSE ARE WE EVER TO FIND OUR WAY OUT OF THIS PLACE, BARBALIEN? WE CANNOT LEAVE THE BOUNDARIES OF THE TOWN. WE ALL KNOW WHAT HAPPENED THE LAST TIME ONE OF US TRIED...
SENDING THESE PROBES OUT BEYOND THE TOWN PERIMETER IS OUR BEST BET AT FINDING RESCUE.
BLEEP
WE DON'T EVEN KNOW WHERE WE ARE, WALKY. WE MAY NOT EVEN BE IN OUR UNIVERSE. HELL, FOR ALL WE KNOW, THIS MAY BE ALL THAT'S LEFT OF THE UNIVERSE.

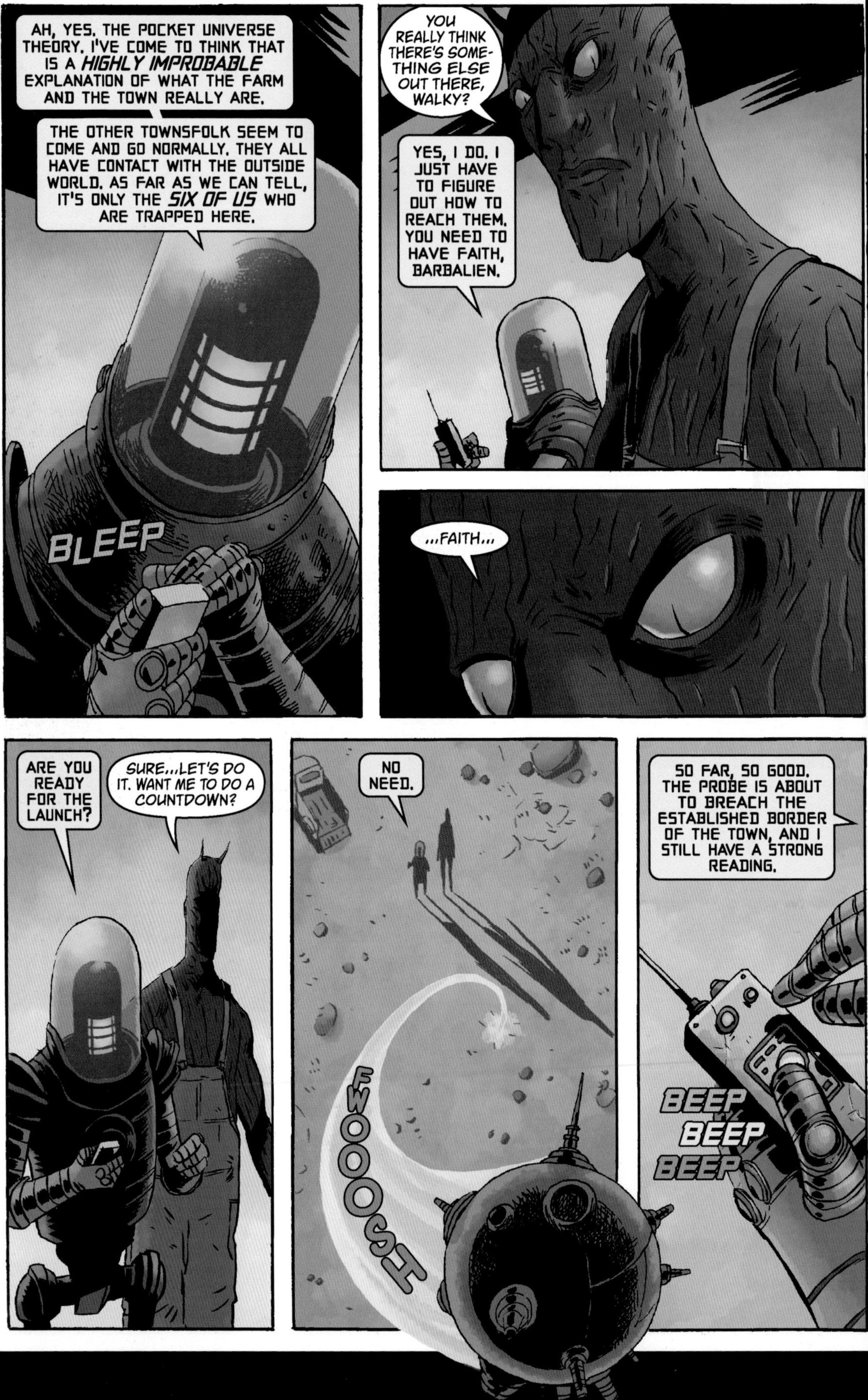

AH, YES. THE POCKET UNIVERSE THEORY. I'VE COME TO THINK THAT IS A *HIGHLY IMPROBABLE* EXPLANATION OF WHAT THE FARM AND THE TOWN REALLY ARE.
THE OTHER TOWNSFOLK SEEM TO COME AND GO NORMALLY. THEY ALL HAVE CONTACT WITH THE OUTSIDE WORLD. AS FAR AS WE CAN TELL, IT'S ONLY THE *SIX OF US* WHO ARE TRAPPED HERE.
BLEEP
YOU REALLY THINK THERE'S SOMETHING ELSE OUT THERE, WALKY?
YES, I DO. I JUST HAVE TO FIGURE OUT HOW TO REACH THEM. YOU NEED TO HAVE FAITH, BARBALIEN.
...FAITH...
ARE YOU READY FOR THE LAUNCH?
SURE...LET'S DO IT. WANT ME TO DO A COUNTDOWN?
NO NEED.
FWOOOSH
SO FAR, SO GOOD. THE PROBE IS ABOUT TO BREACH THE ESTABLISHED BORDER OF THE TOWN, AND I STILL HAVE A STRONG READING.
BEEP
BEEP
BEEP

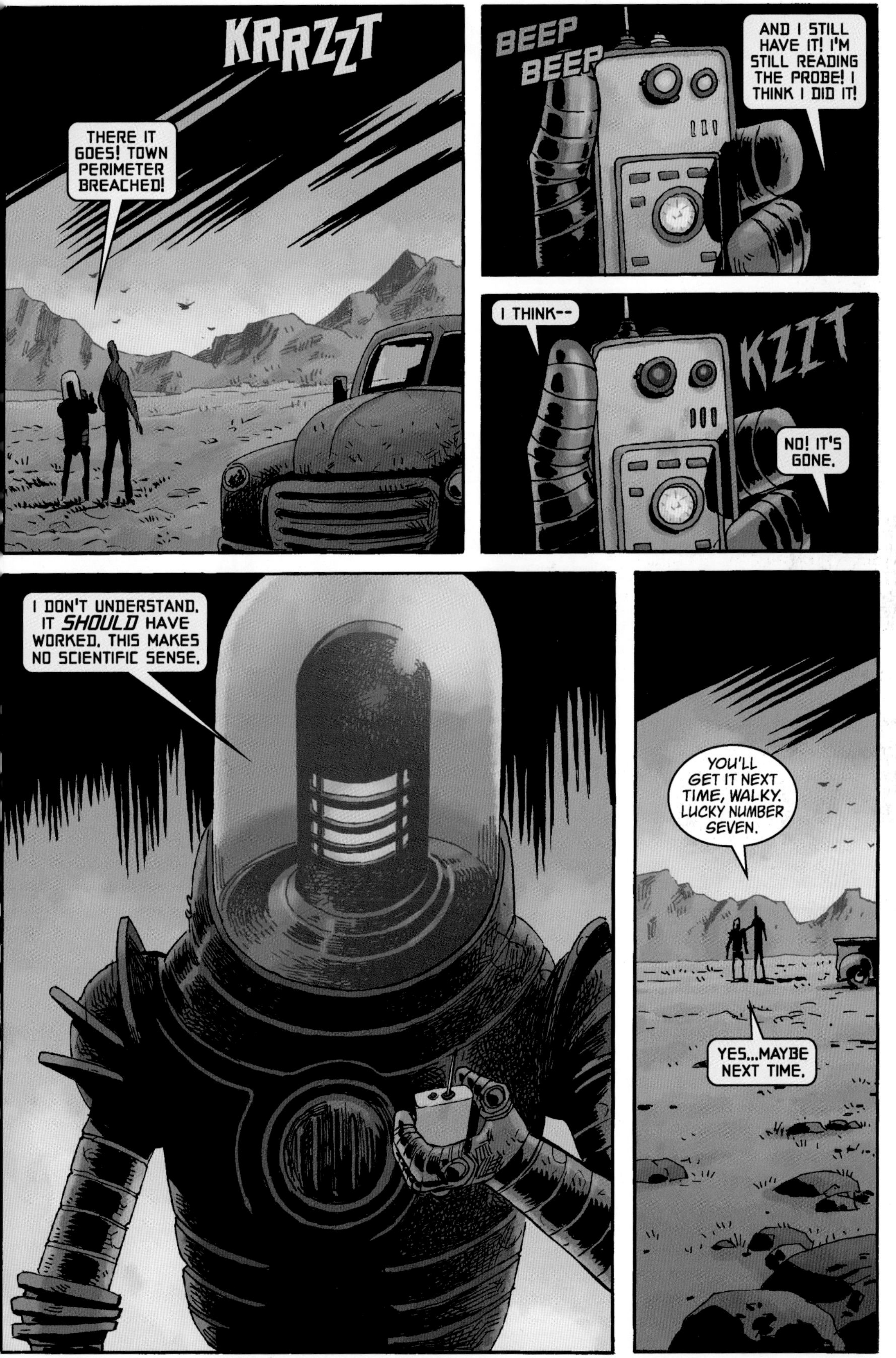
KRRZZT
THERE IT GOES! TOWN PERIMETER BREACHED!
BEEP BEEP
AND I STILL HAVE IT! I'M STILL READING THE PROBE! I THINK I DID IT!
I THINK--
KZZZT
NO! IT'S GONE.
I DON'T UNDERSTAND. IT *SHOULD* HAVE WORKED. THIS MAKES NO SCIENTIFIC SENSE.
YOU'LL GET IT NEXT TIME, WALKY. LUCKY NUMBER SEVEN.
YES...MAYBE NEXT TIME.

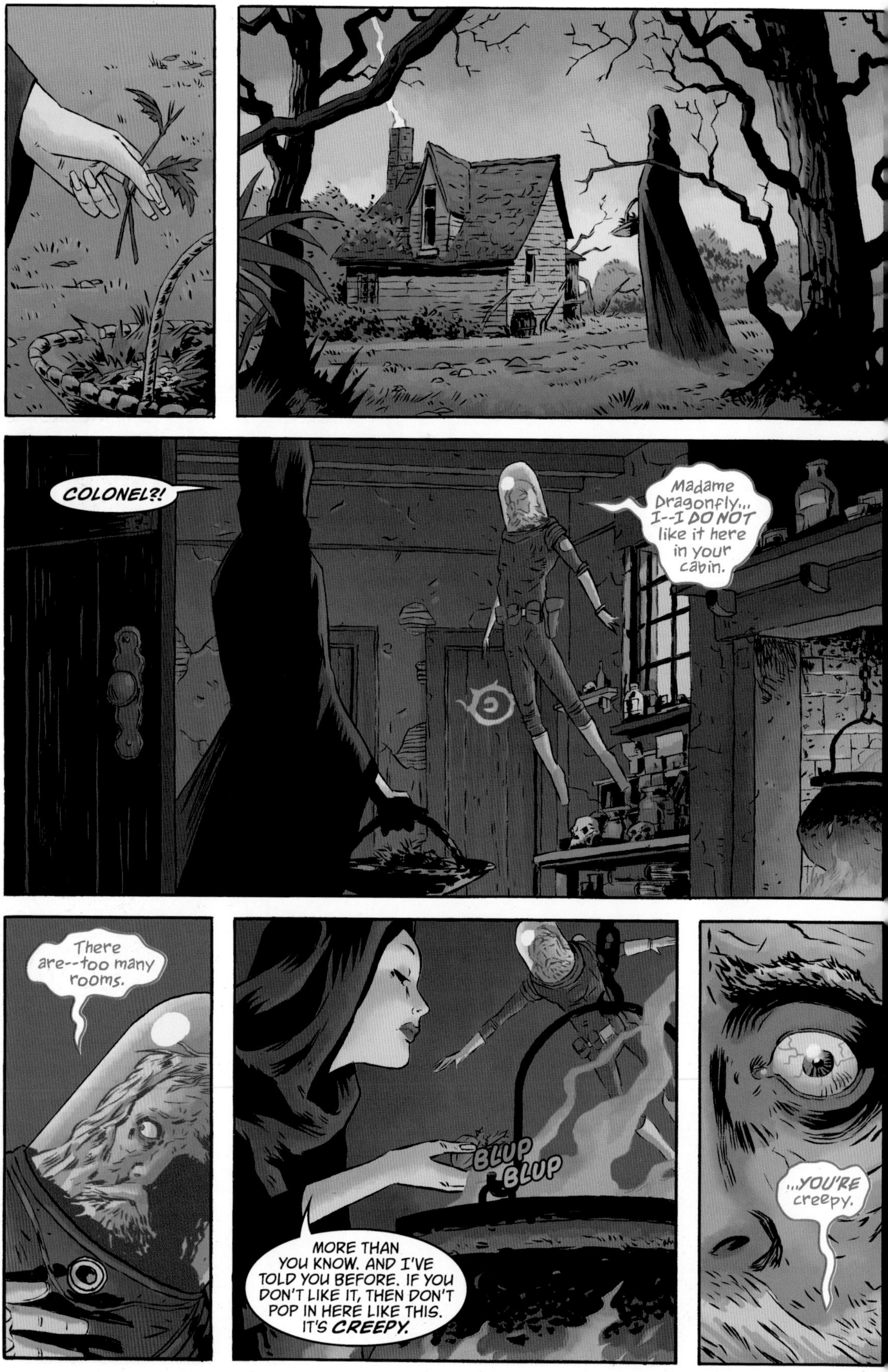
COLONEL?!
Madame Dragonfly... I--I DO NOT like it here in your cabin.
There are--too many rooms.
BLUP BLUP
MORE THAN YOU KNOW. AND I'VE TOLD YOU BEFORE. IF YOU DON'T LIKE IT, THEN DON'T POP IN HERE LIKE THIS. IT'S CREEPY.
...YOU'RE creepy.

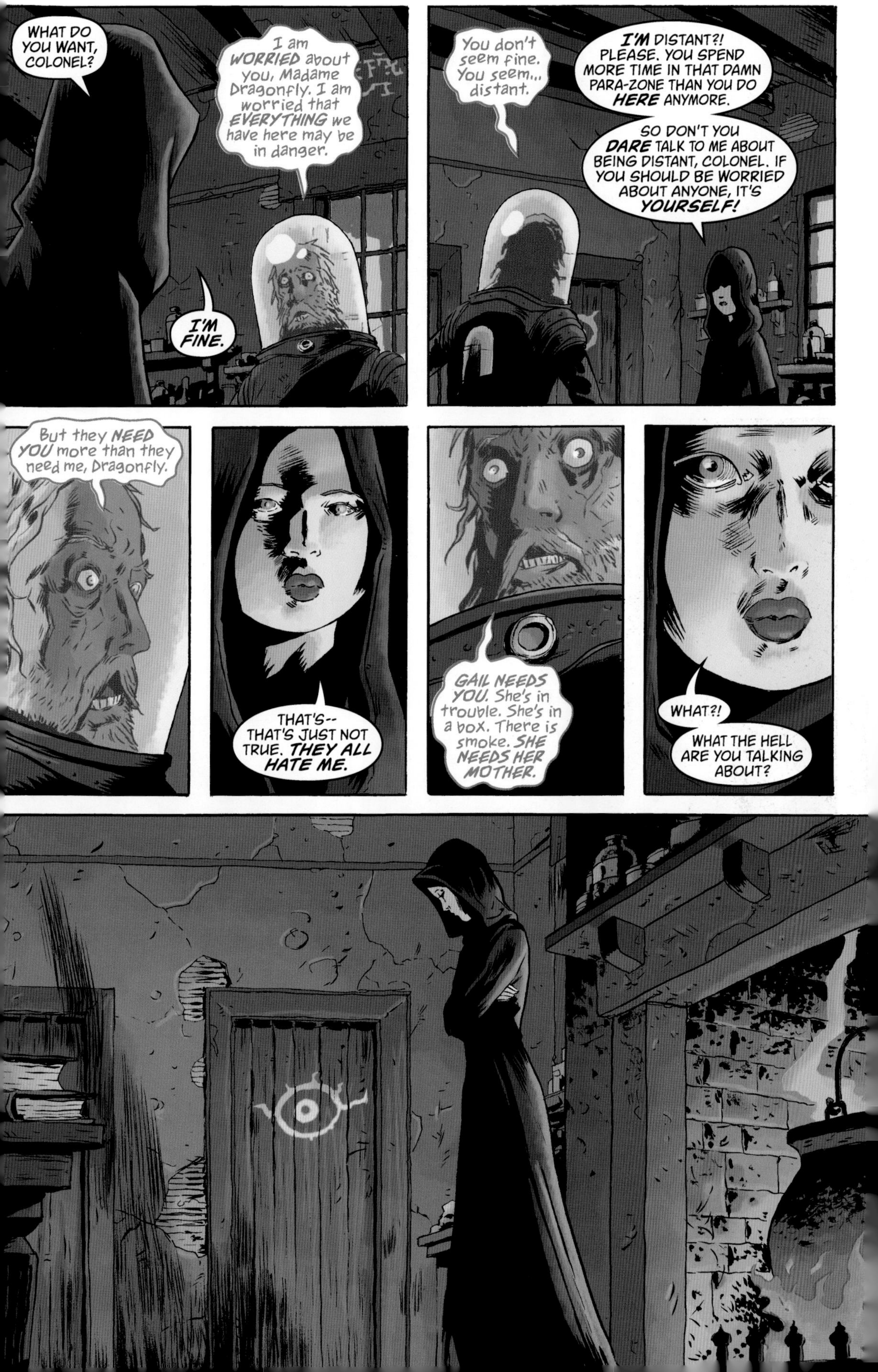
WHAT DO YOU WANT, COLONEL?
I am WORRIED about you, Madame Dragonfly. I am worried that EVERYTHING we have here may be in danger.
I'M FINE.
You don't seem fine. You seem... distant.
I'M DISTANT?! PLEASE. YOU SPEND MORE TIME IN THAT DAMN PARA-ZONE THAN YOU DO HERE ANYMORE.
SO DON'T YOU DARE TALK TO ME ABOUT BEING DISTANT, COLONEL. IF YOU SHOULD BE WORRIED ABOUT ANYONE, IT'S YOURSELF!
But they NEED YOU more than they need me, Dragonfly.
THAT'S-- THAT'S JUST NOT TRUE. THEY ALL HATE ME.
GAIL NEEDS YOU. She's in trouble. She's in a box. There is smoke. SHE NEEDS HER MOTHER.
WHAT?!
WHAT THE HELL ARE YOU TALKING ABOUT?

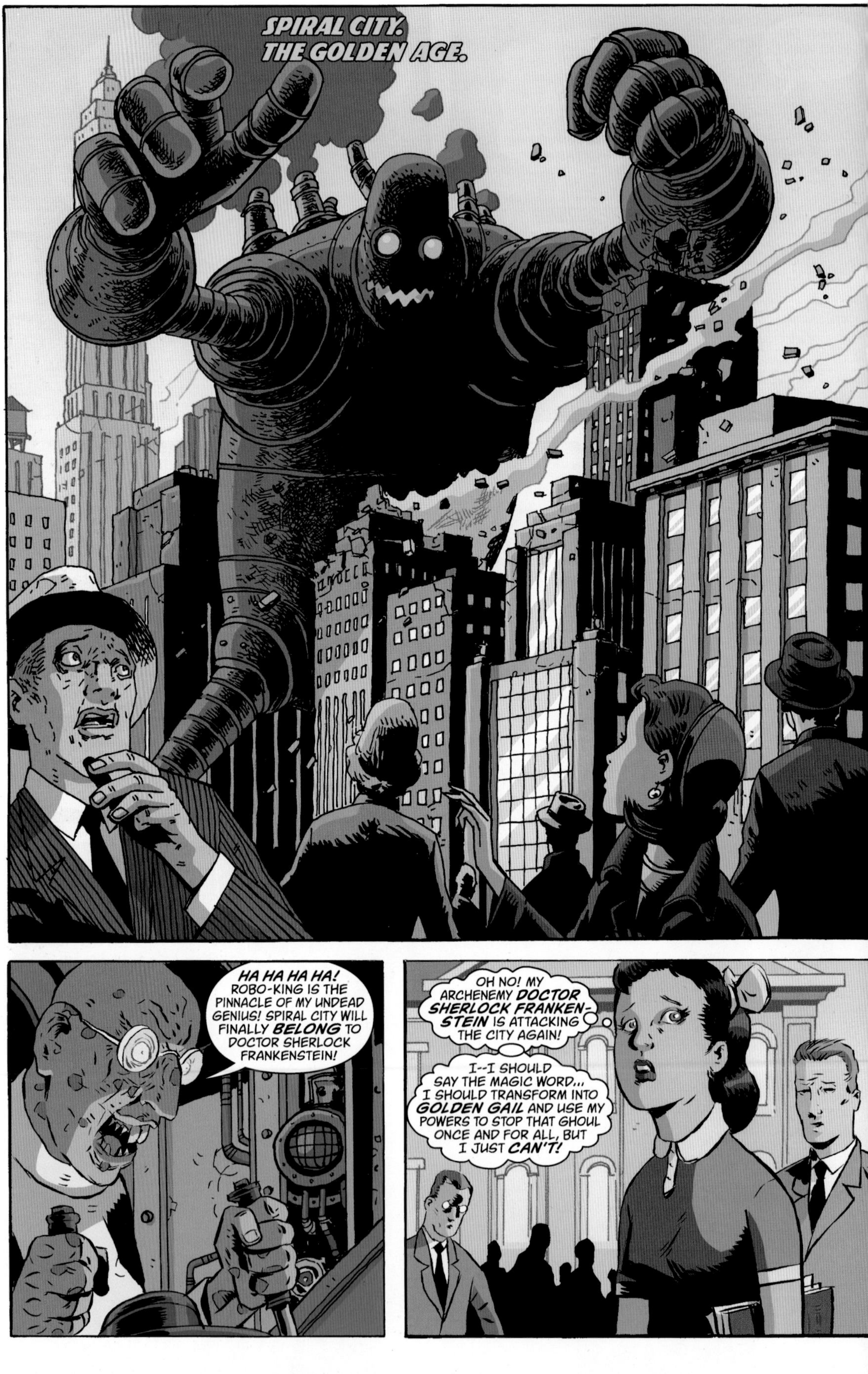
SPIRAL CITY.
THE GOLDEN AGE.
HA HA HA HA! ROBO-KING IS THE PINNACLE OF MY UNDEAD GENIUS! SPIRAL CITY WILL FINALLY BELONG TO DOCTOR SHERLOCK FRANKENSTEIN!
OH NO! MY ARCHENEMY DOCTOR SHERLOCK FRANKEN-STEIN IS ATTACKING THE CITY AGAIN!
I--I SHOULD SAY THE MAGIC WORD... I SHOULD TRANSFORM INTO GOLDEN GAIL AND USE MY POWERS TO STOP THAT GHOUL ONCE AND FOR ALL, BUT I JUST CAN'T!

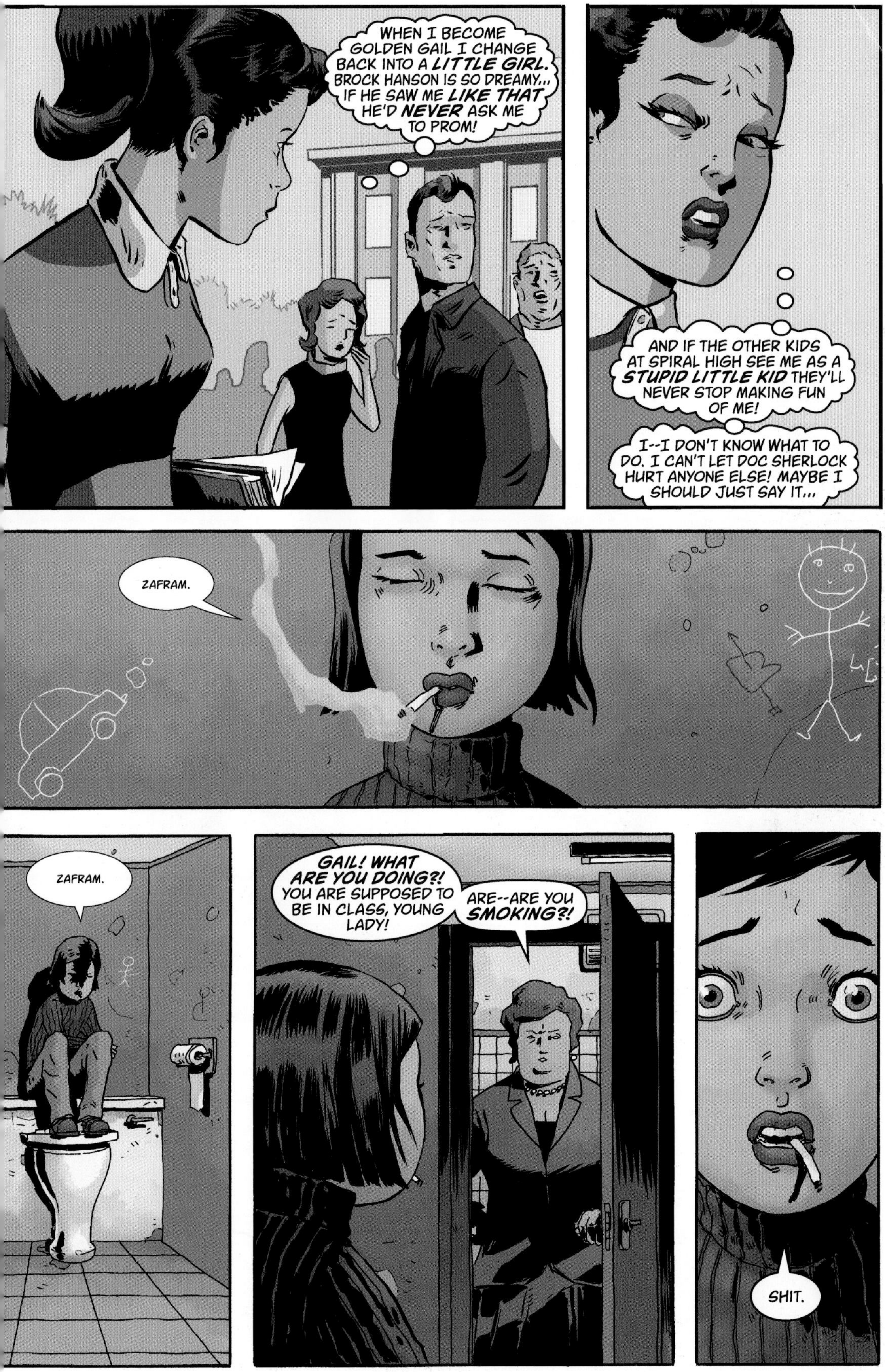
WHEN I BECOME GOLDEN GAIL I CHANGE BACK INTO A LITTLE GIRL. BROCK HANSON IS SO DREAMY... IF HE SAW ME LIKE THAT HE'D NEVER ASK ME TO PROM!
AND IF THE OTHER KIDS AT SPIRAL HIGH SEE ME AS A STUPID LITTLE KID THEY'LL NEVER STOP MAKING FUN OF ME!
I--I DON'T KNOW WHAT TO DO. I CAN'T LET DOC SHERLOCK HURT ANYONE ELSE! MAYBE I SHOULD JUST SAY IT...
ZAFRAM.
ZAFRAM.
GAIL! WHAT ARE YOU DOING?! YOU ARE SUPPOSED TO BE IN CLASS, YOUNG LADY!
ARE--ARE YOU SMOKING?!
SHIT.

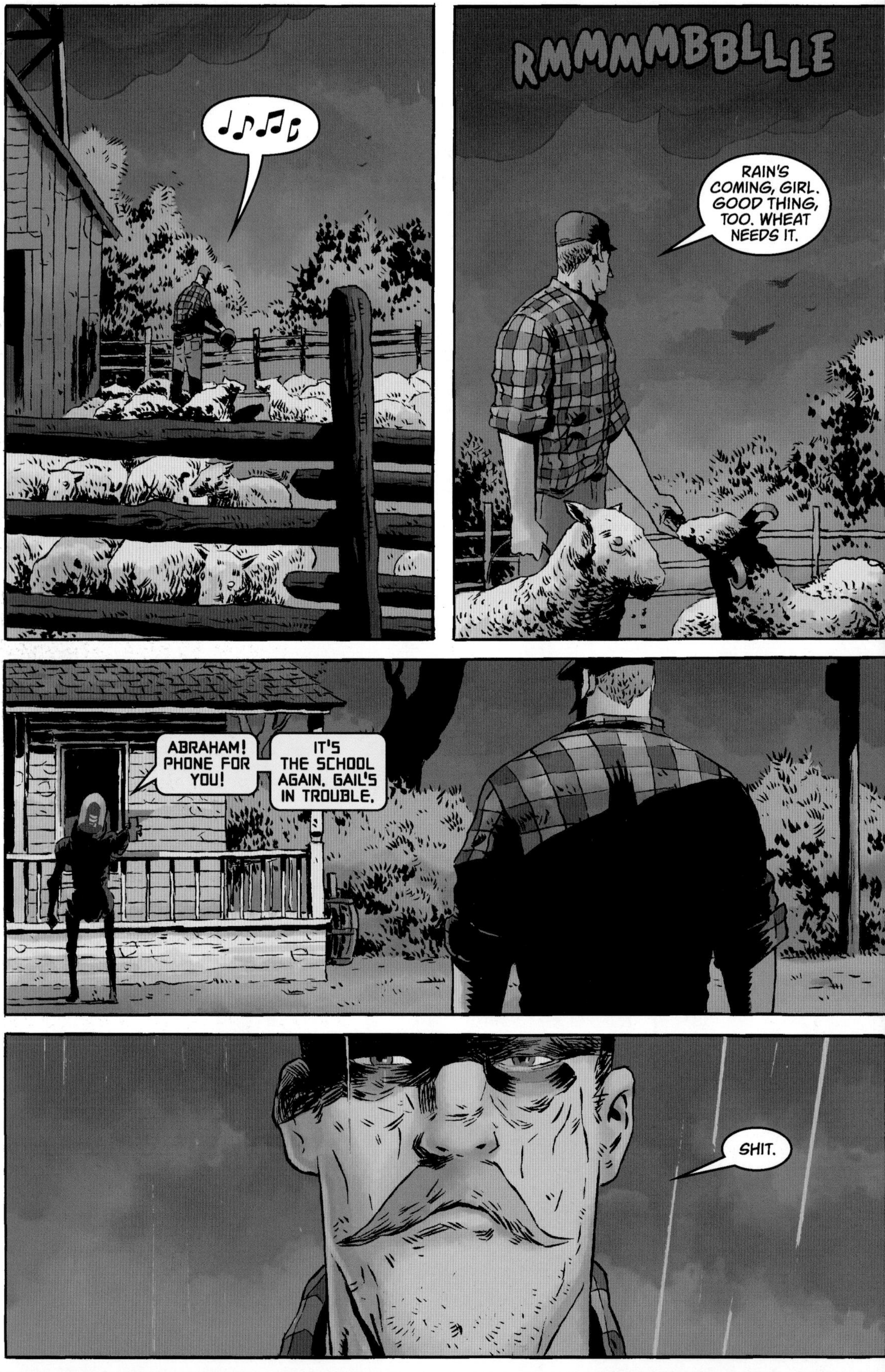
♩♪♫♬
RMMMMBBLLLE
RAIN'S COMING, GIRL. GOOD THING, TOO. WHEAT NEEDS IT.
ABRAHAM! PHONE FOR YOU!
IT'S THE SCHOOL AGAIN. GAIL'S IN TROUBLE.
SHIT.

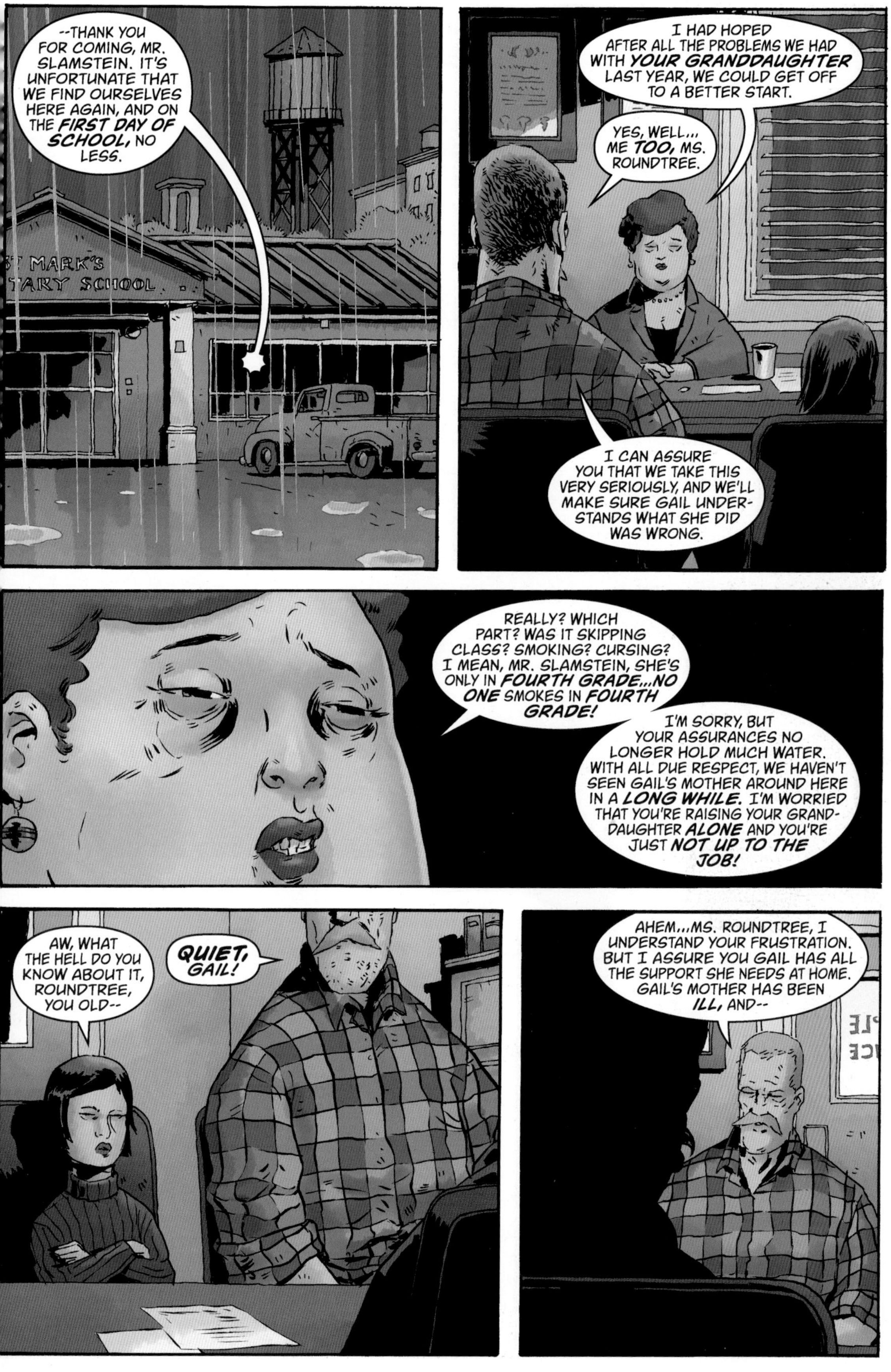
ST MARK'S
TARY SCHOOL
--THANK YOU FOR COMING, MR. SLAMSTEIN. IT'S UNFORTUNATE THAT WE FIND OURSELVES HERE AGAIN, AND ON THE FIRST DAY OF SCHOOL, NO LESS.
I HAD HOPED AFTER ALL THE PROBLEMS WE HAD WITH YOUR GRANDDAUGHTER LAST YEAR, WE COULD GET OFF TO A BETTER START.
YES, WELL... ME TOO, MS. ROUNDTREE.
I CAN ASSURE YOU THAT WE TAKE THIS VERY SERIOUSLY, AND WE'LL MAKE SURE GAIL UNDERSTANDS WHAT SHE DID WAS WRONG.
REALLY? WHICH PART? WAS IT SKIPPING CLASS? SMOKING? CURSING? I MEAN, MR. SLAMSTEIN, SHE'S ONLY IN FOURTH GRADE...NO ONE SMOKES IN FOURTH GRADE!
I'M SORRY, BUT YOUR ASSURANCES NO LONGER HOLD MUCH WATER. WITH ALL DUE RESPECT, WE HAVEN'T SEEN GAIL'S MOTHER AROUND HERE IN A LONG WHILE. I'M WORRIED THAT YOU'RE RAISING YOUR GRANDDAUGHTER ALONE AND YOU'RE JUST NOT UP TO THE JOB!
AW, WHAT THE HELL DO YOU KNOW ABOUT IT, ROUNDTREE, YOU OLD--
QUIET, GAIL!
AHEM...MS. ROUNDTREE, I UNDERSTAND YOUR FRUSTRATION. BUT I ASSURE YOU GAIL HAS ALL THE SUPPORT SHE NEEDS AT HOME. GAIL'S MOTHER HAS BEEN ILL, AND--

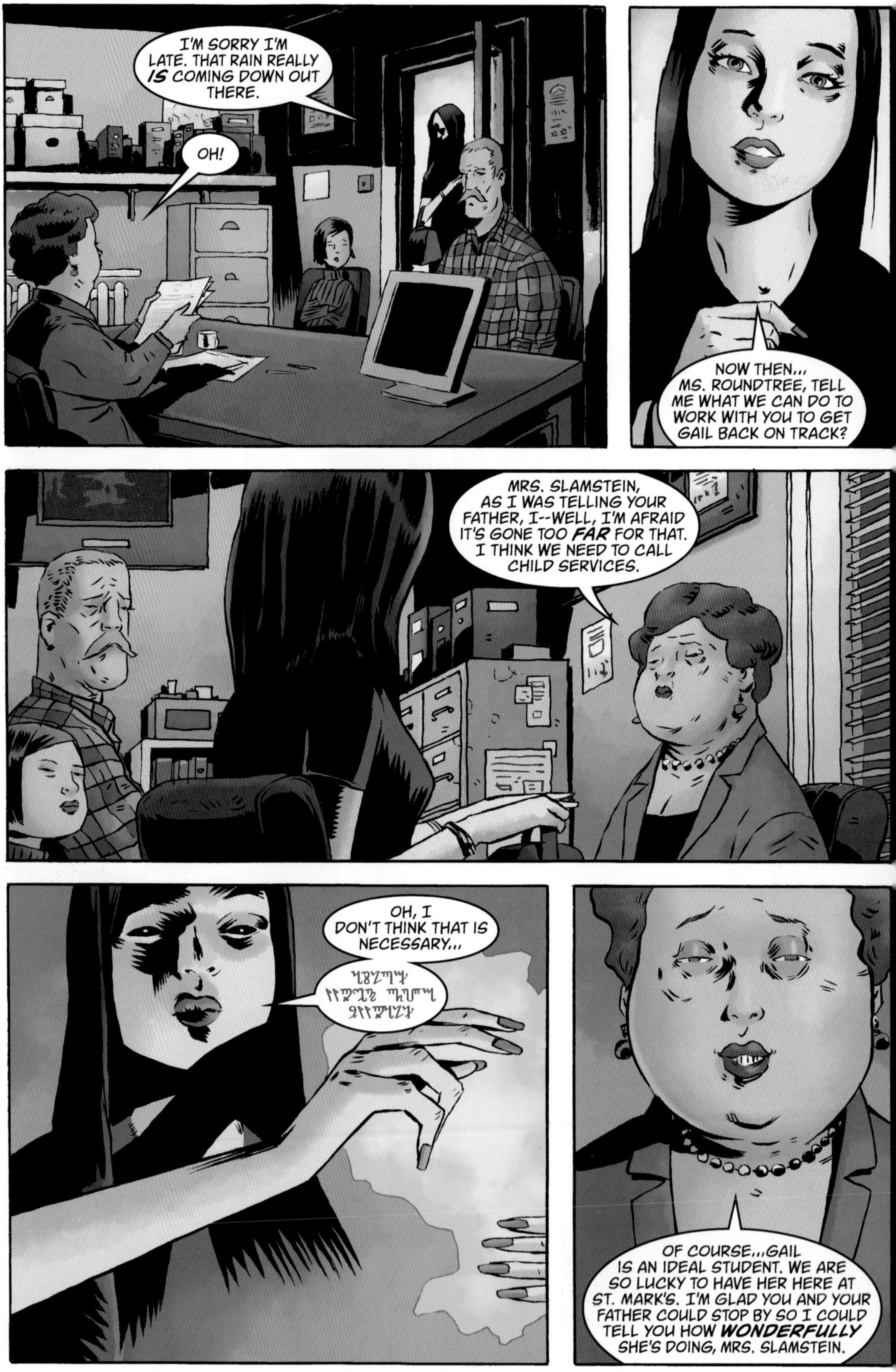
I'M SORRY I'M LATE. THAT RAIN REALLY IS COMING DOWN OUT THERE.
OH!
NOW THEN... MS. ROUNDTREE, TELL ME WHAT WE CAN DO TO WORK WITH YOU TO GET GAIL BACK ON TRACK?
MRS. SLAMSTEIN, AS I WAS TELLING YOUR FATHER, I--WELL, I'M AFRAID IT'S GONE TOO FAR FOR THAT. I THINK WE NEED TO CALL CHILD SERVICES.
OH, I DON'T THINK THAT IS NECESSARY...
OF COURSE...GAIL IS AN IDEAL STUDENT. WE ARE SO LUCKY TO HAVE HER HERE AT ST. MARK'S. I'M GLAD YOU AND YOUR FATHER COULD STOP BY SO I COULD TELL YOU HOW WONDERFULLY SHE'S DOING, MRS. SLAMSTEIN.

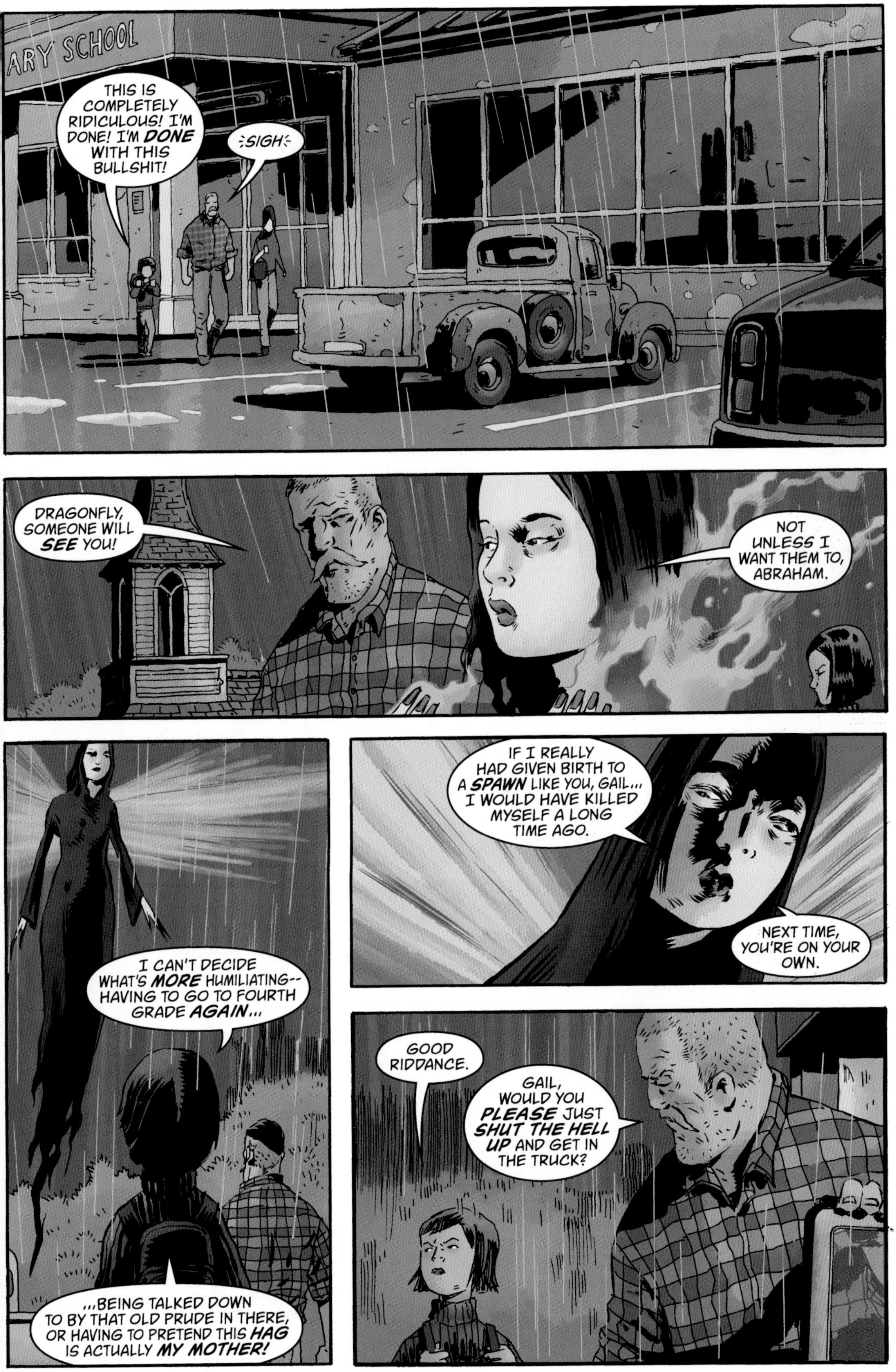
ARY SCHOOL
THIS IS COMPLETELY RIDICULOUS! I'M DONE! I'M DONE WITH THIS BULLSHIT!
SIGH
DRAGONFLY, SOMEONE WILL SEE YOU!
NOT UNLESS I WANT THEM TO, ABRAHAM.
IF I REALLY HAD GIVEN BIRTH TO A SPAWN LIKE YOU, GAIL... I WOULD HAVE KILLED MYSELF A LONG TIME AGO.
NEXT TIME, YOU'RE ON YOUR OWN.
I CAN'T DECIDE WHAT'S MORE HUMILIATING-- HAVING TO GO TO FOURTH GRADE AGAIN...
...BEING TALKED DOWN TO BY THAT OLD PRUDE IN THERE, OR HAVING TO PRETEND THIS HAG IS ACTUALLY MY MOTHER!
GOOD RIDDANCE.
GAIL, WOULD YOU PLEASE JUST SHUT THE HELL UP AND GET IN THE TRUCK?

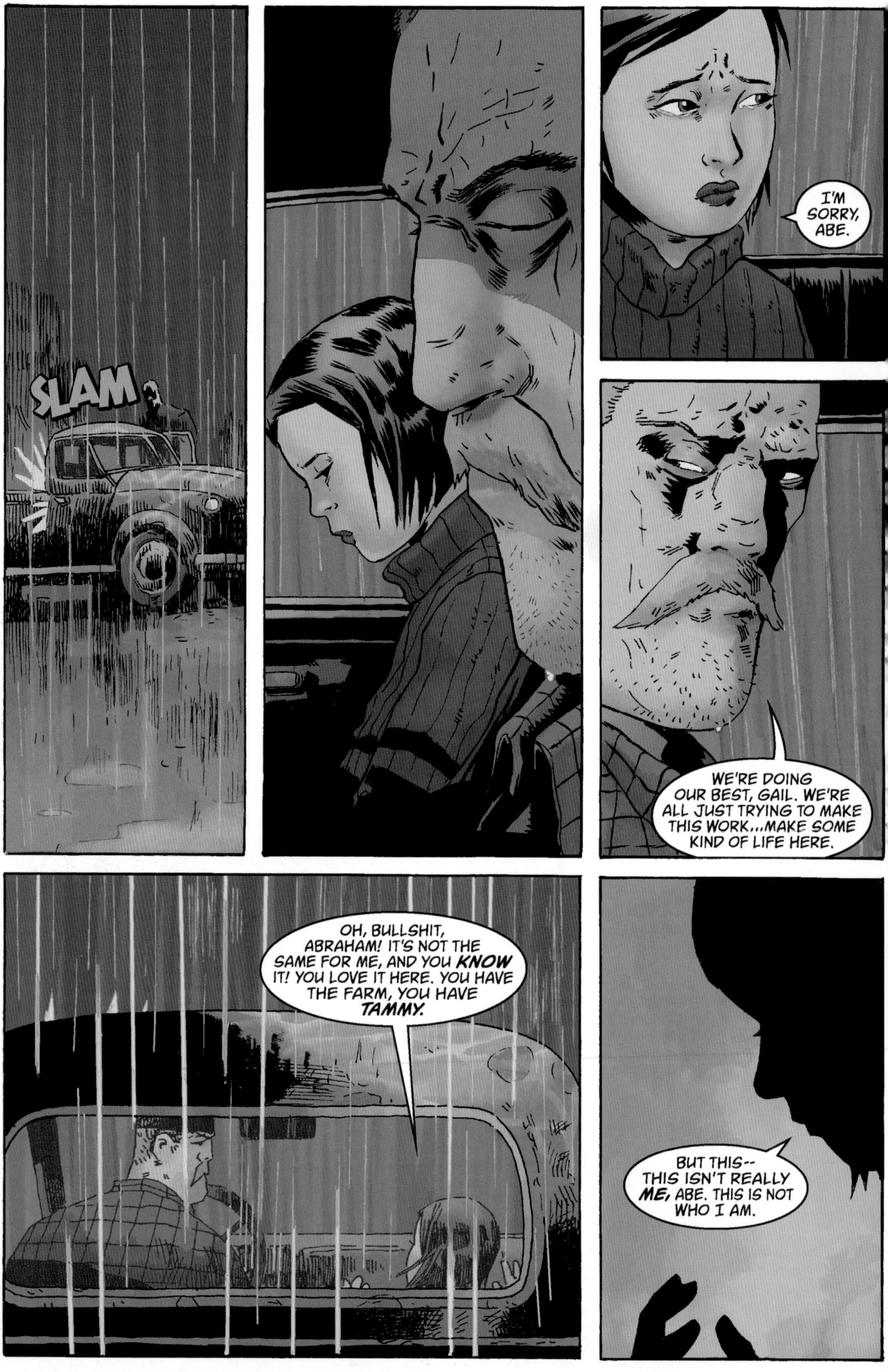
SLAM
I'M SORRY, ABE.
WE'RE DOING OUR BEST, GAIL. WE'RE ALL JUST TRYING TO MAKE THIS WORK...MAKE SOME KIND OF LIFE HERE.
OH, BULLSHIT, ABRAHAM! IT'S NOT THE SAME FOR ME, AND YOU KNOW IT! YOU LOVE IT HERE. YOU HAVE THE FARM, YOU HAVE TAMMY.
BUT THIS-- THIS ISN'T REALLY ME, ABE. THIS IS NOT WHO I AM.

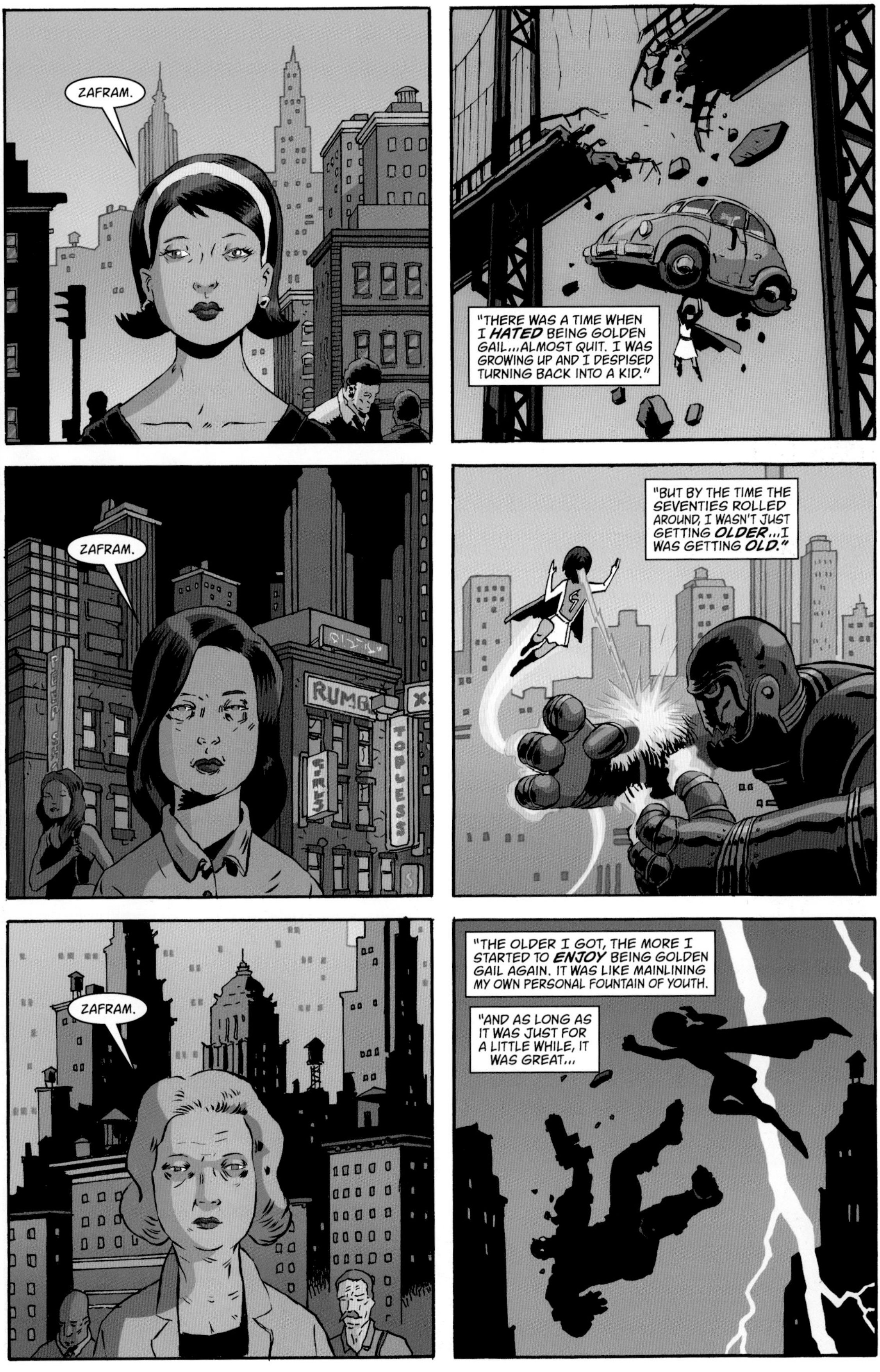
ZAFRAM.
"THERE WAS A TIME WHEN I HATED BEING GOLDEN GAIL...ALMOST QUIT. I WAS GROWING UP AND I DESPISED TURNING BACK INTO A KID."
ZAFRAM.
"BUT BY THE TIME THE SEVENTIES ROLLED AROUND, I WASN'T JUST GETTING OLDER...I WAS GETTING OLD."
RUMB
TOPLESS
GIRLS
ZAFRAM.
"THE OLDER I GOT, THE MORE I STARTED TO ENJOY BEING GOLDEN GAIL AGAIN. IT WAS LIKE MAINLINING MY OWN PERSONAL FOUNTAIN OF YOUTH.
"AND AS LONG AS IT WAS JUST FOR A LITTLE WHILE, IT WAS GREAT...

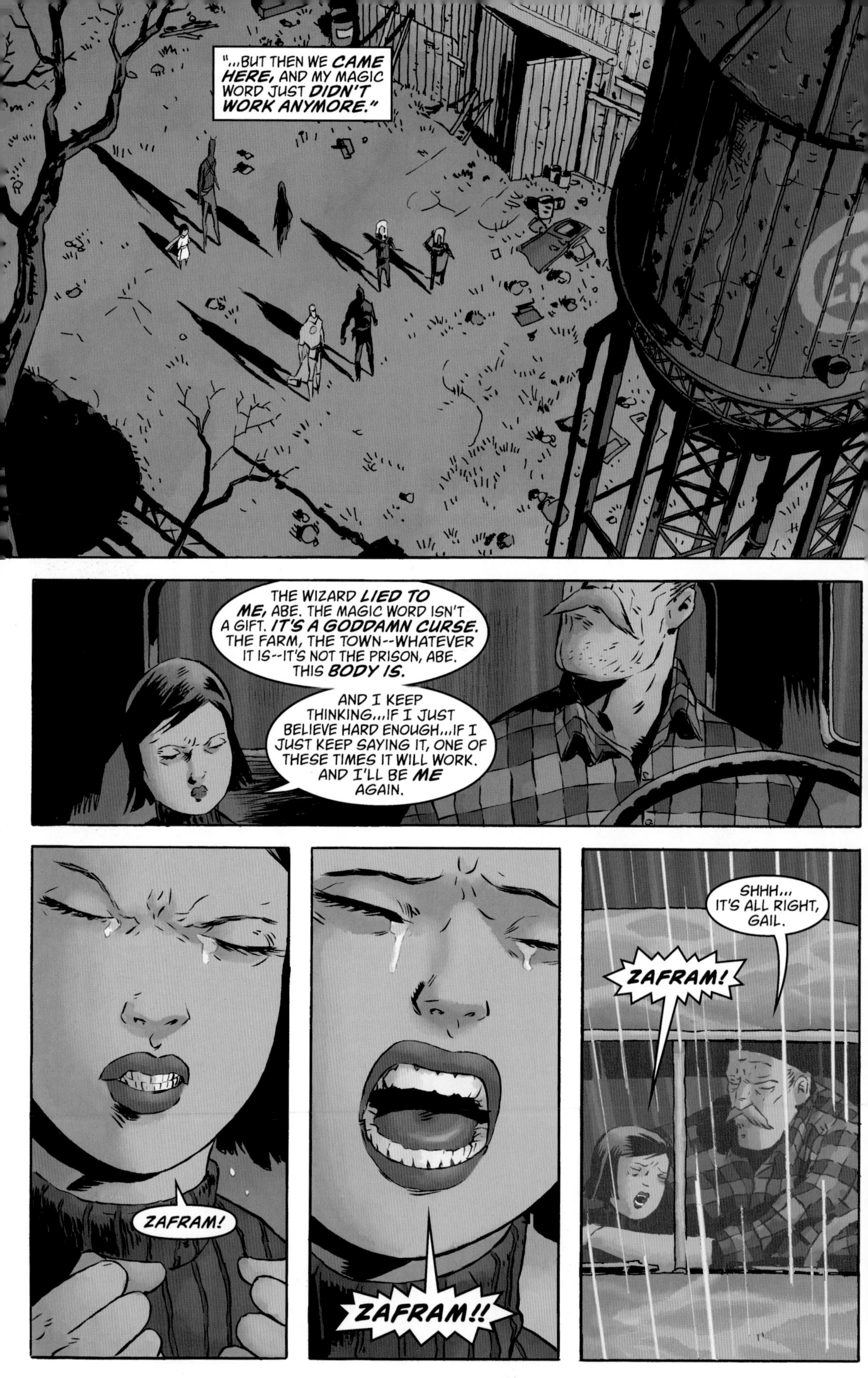
"...BUT THEN WE CAME HERE, AND MY MAGIC WORD JUST DIDN'T WORK ANYMORE."
THE WIZARD LIED TO ME, ABE. THE MAGIC WORD ISN'T A GIFT. IT'S A GODDAMN CURSE. THE FARM, THE TOWN--WHATEVER IT IS--IT'S NOT THE PRISON, ABE. THIS BODY IS.
AND I KEEP THINKING...IF I JUST BELIEVE HARD ENOUGH...IF I JUST KEEP SAYING IT, ONE OF THESE TIMES IT WILL WORK. AND I'LL BE ME AGAIN.
ZAFRAM!
ZAFRAM!!
SHHH... IT'S ALL RIGHT, GAIL.
ZAFRAM!

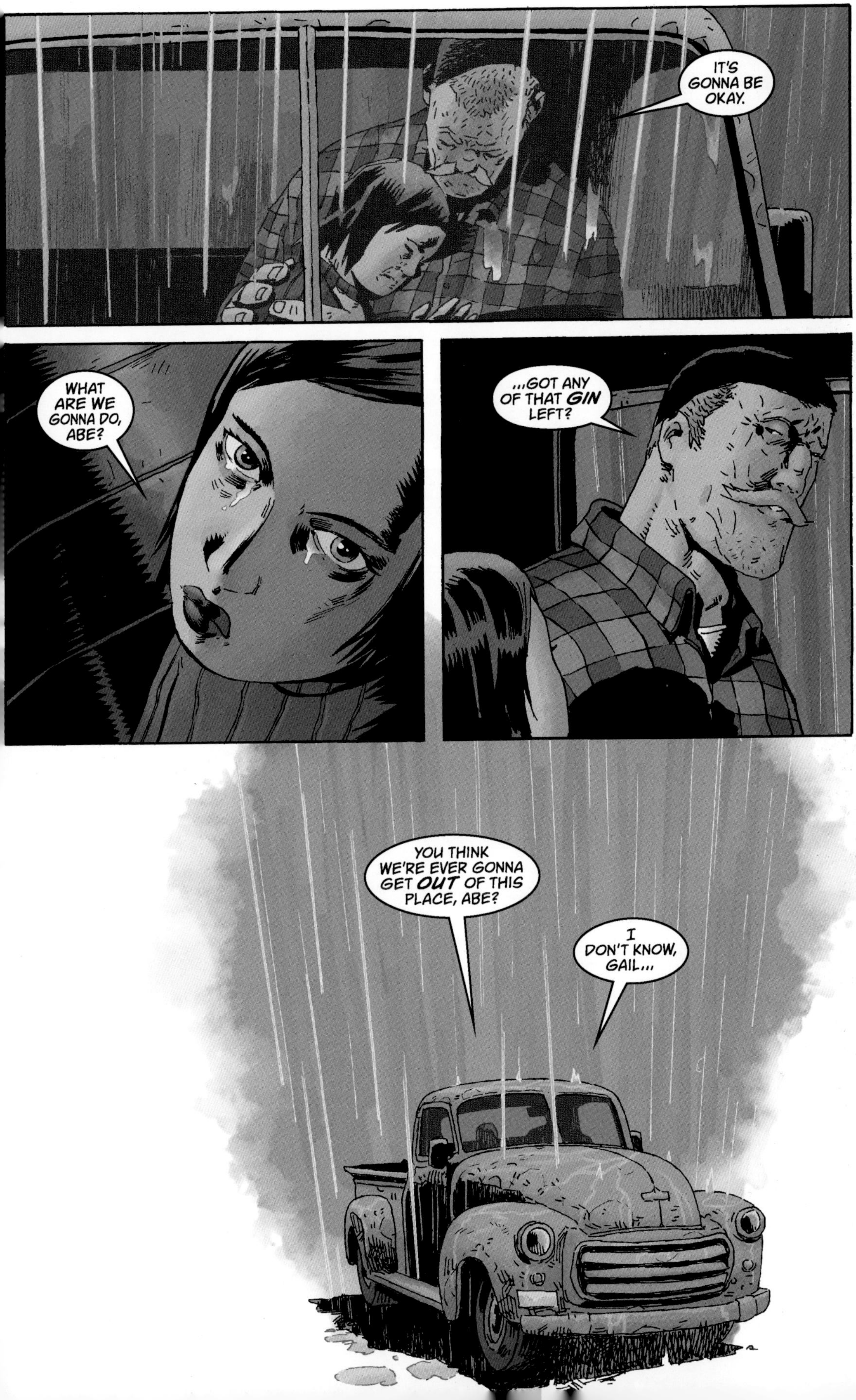
IT'S GONNA BE OKAY.
WHAT ARE WE GONNA DO, ABE?
...GOT ANY OF THAT GIN LEFT?
YOU THINK WE'RE EVER GONNA GET OUT OF THIS PLACE, ABE?
I DON'T KNOW, GAIL...

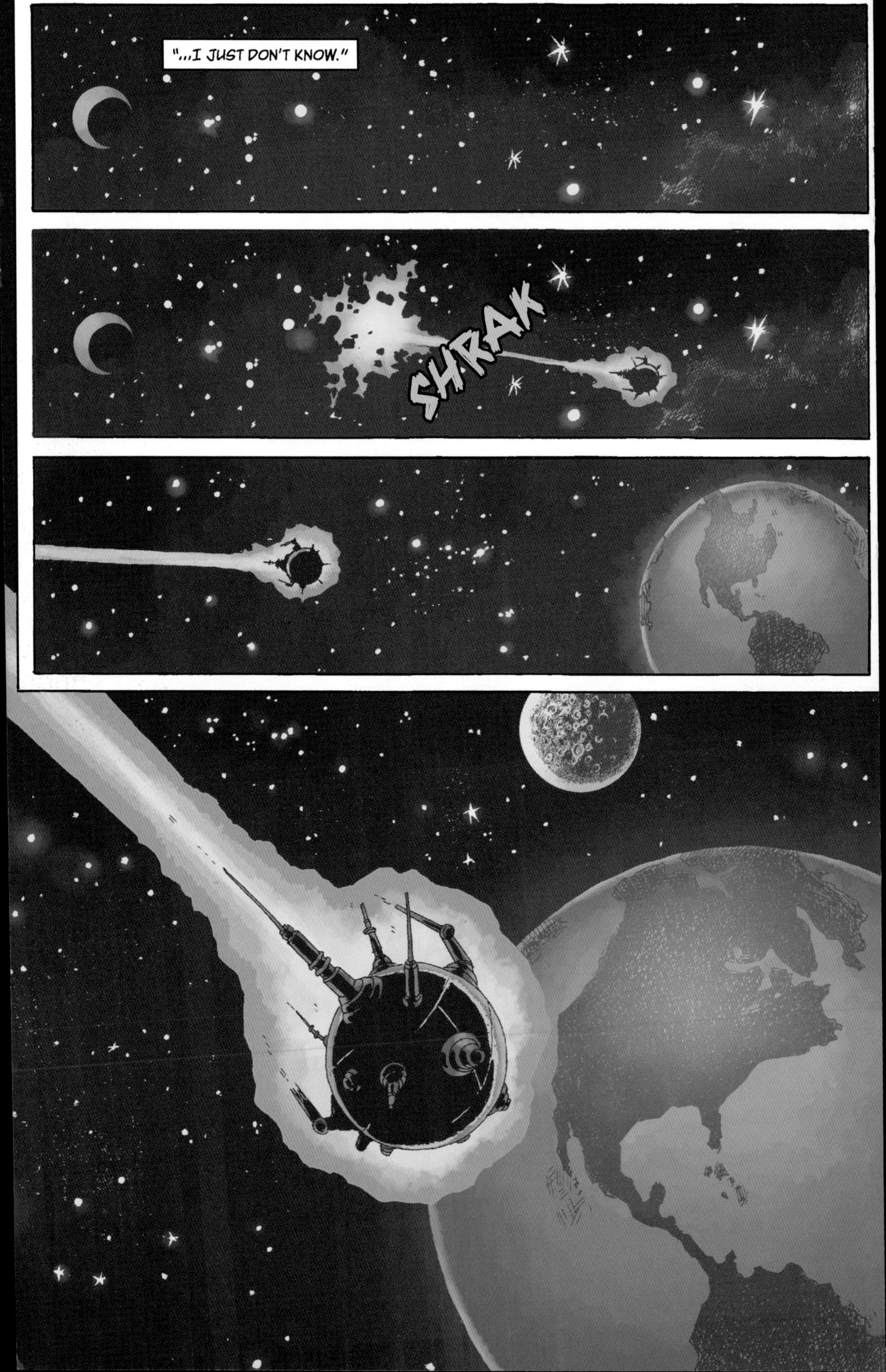
"...I JUST DON'T KNOW."
SHRAK

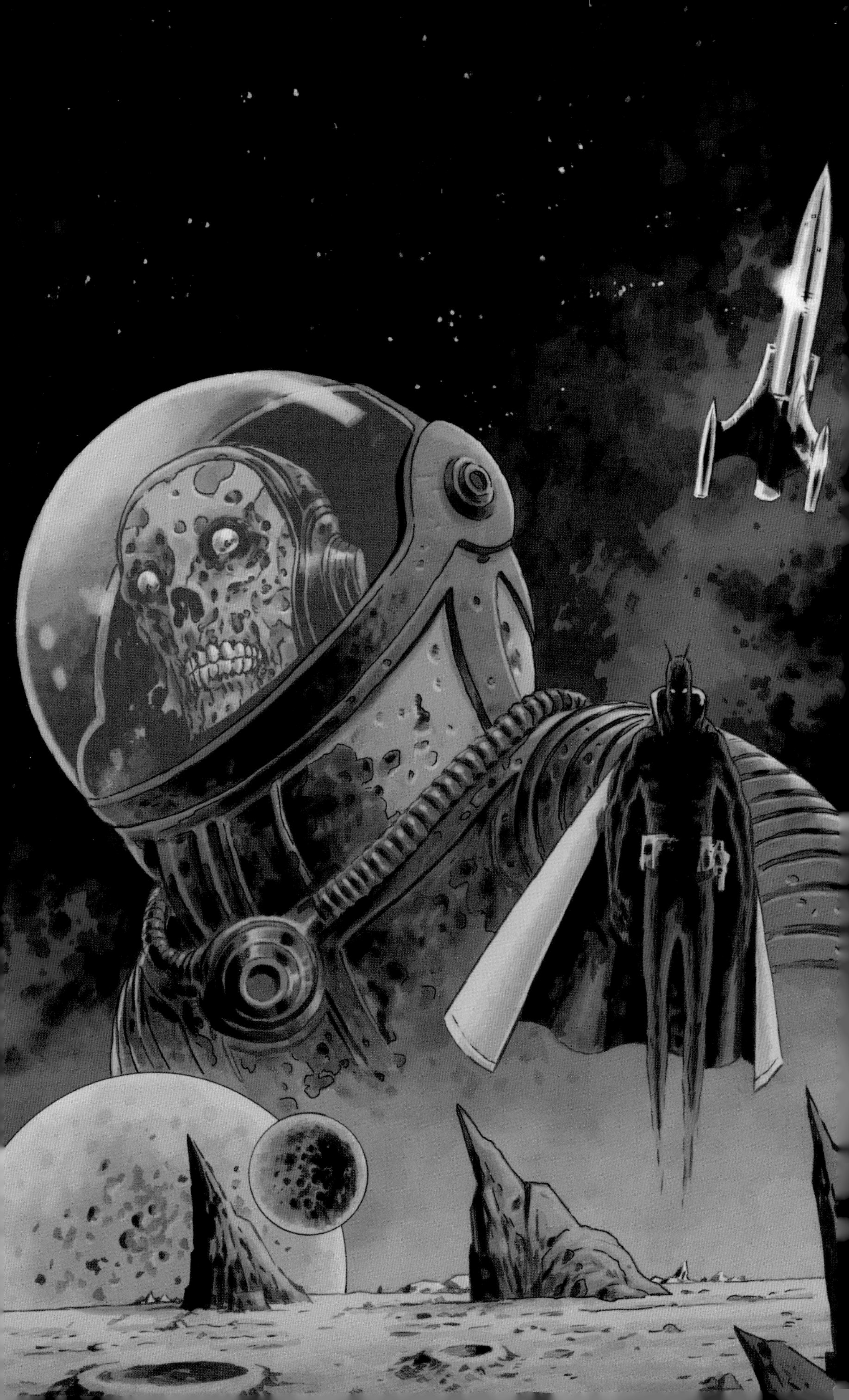

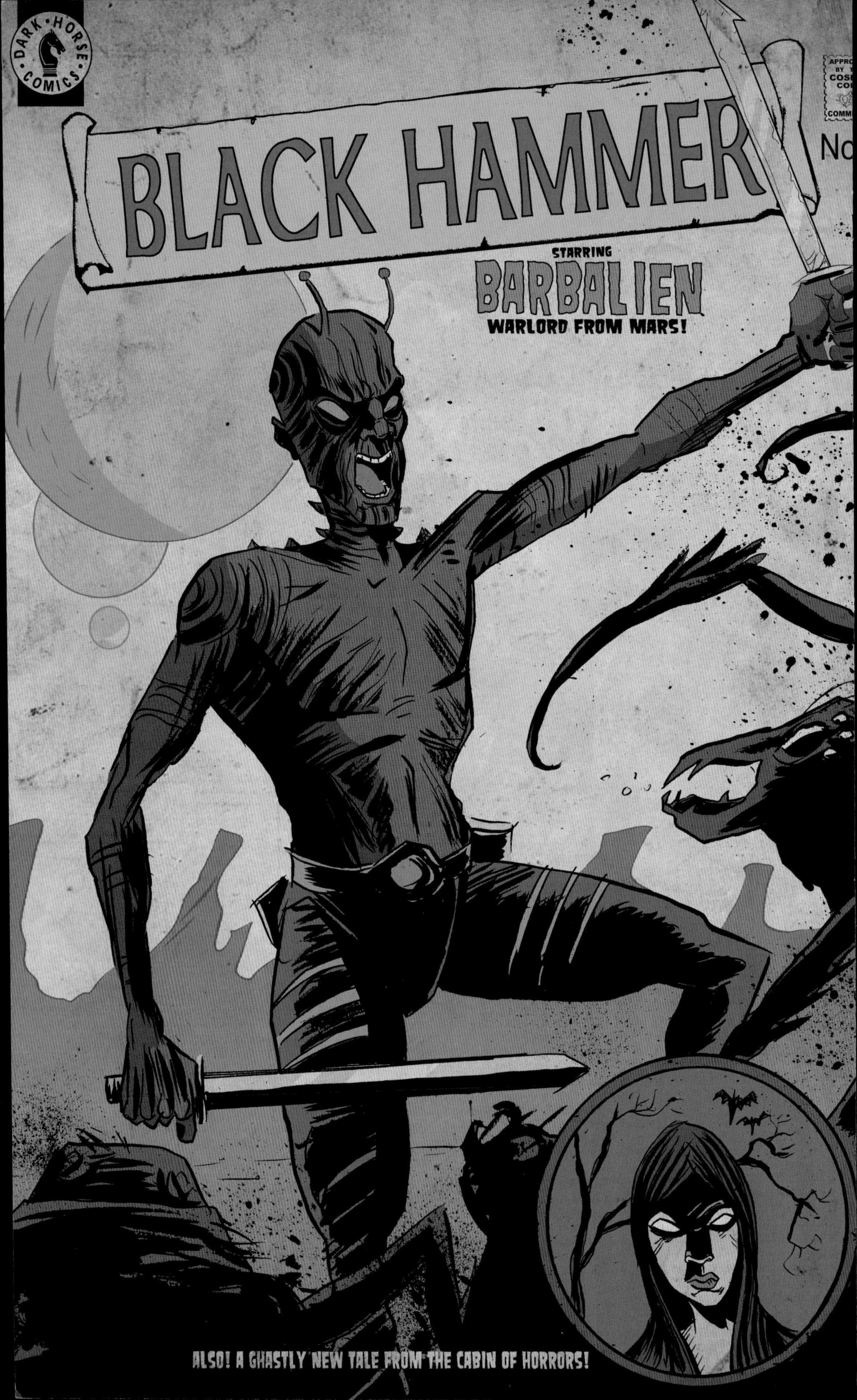
DARK HORSE COMICS
BLACK HAMMER
STARRING
BARBALIEN
WARLORD FROM MARS!
ALSO! A GHASTLY NEW TALE FROM THE CABIN OF HORRORS!

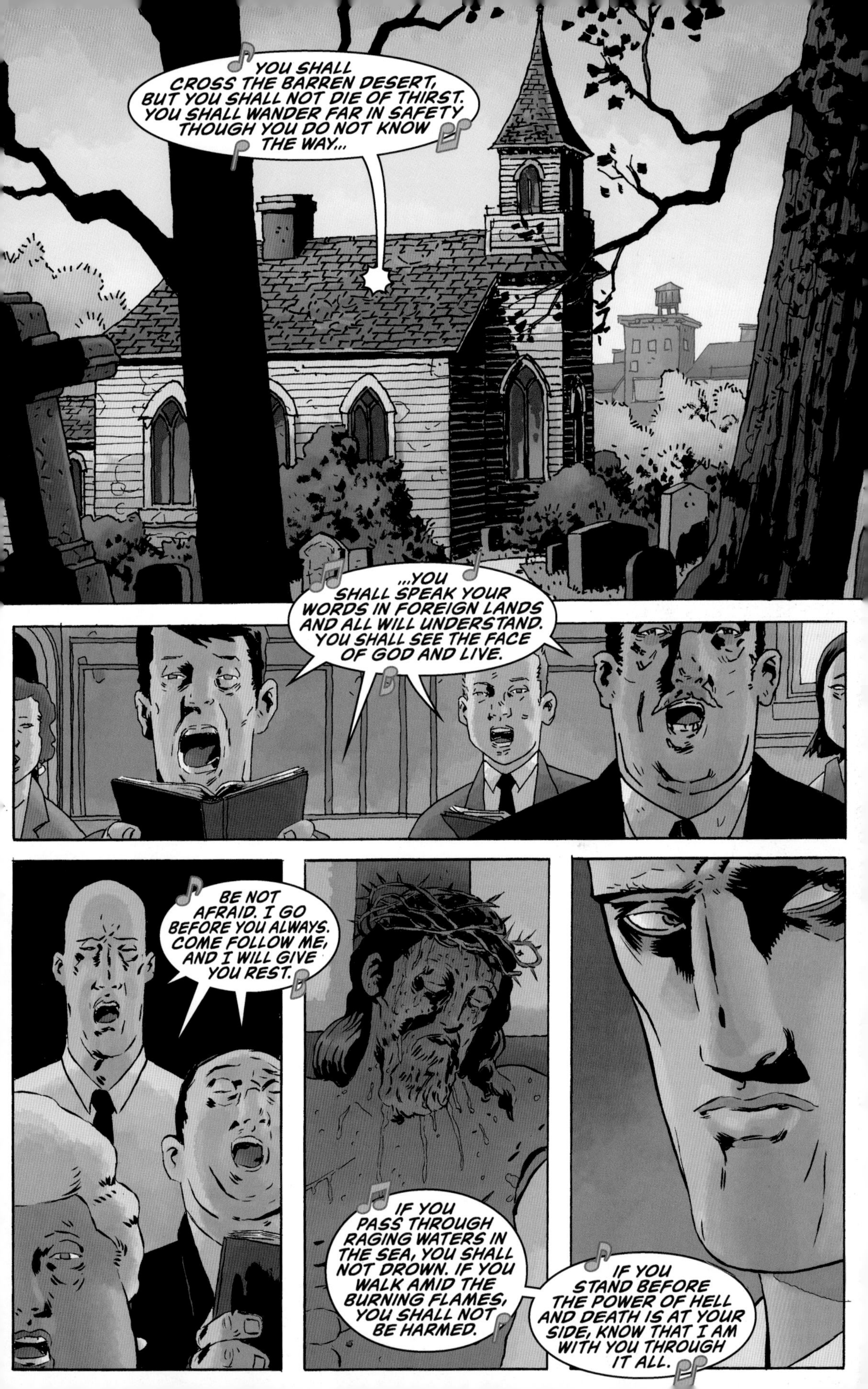
YOU SHALL CROSS THE BARREN DESERT, BUT YOU SHALL NOT DIE OF THIRST. YOU SHALL WANDER FAR IN SAFETY THOUGH YOU DO NOT KNOW THE WAY...
...YOU SHALL SPEAK YOUR WORDS IN FOREIGN LANDS AND ALL WILL UNDERSTAND. YOU SHALL SEE THE FACE OF GOD AND LIVE.
BE NOT AFRAID. I GO BEFORE YOU ALWAYS. COME FOLLOW ME, AND I WILL GIVE YOU REST.
IF YOU PASS THROUGH RAGING WATERS IN THE SEA, YOU SHALL NOT DROWN. IF YOU WALK AMID THE BURNING FLAMES, YOU SHALL NOT BE HARMED.
IF YOU STAND BEFORE THE POWER OF HELL AND DEATH IS AT YOUR SIDE, KNOW THAT I AM WITH YOU THROUGH IT ALL.

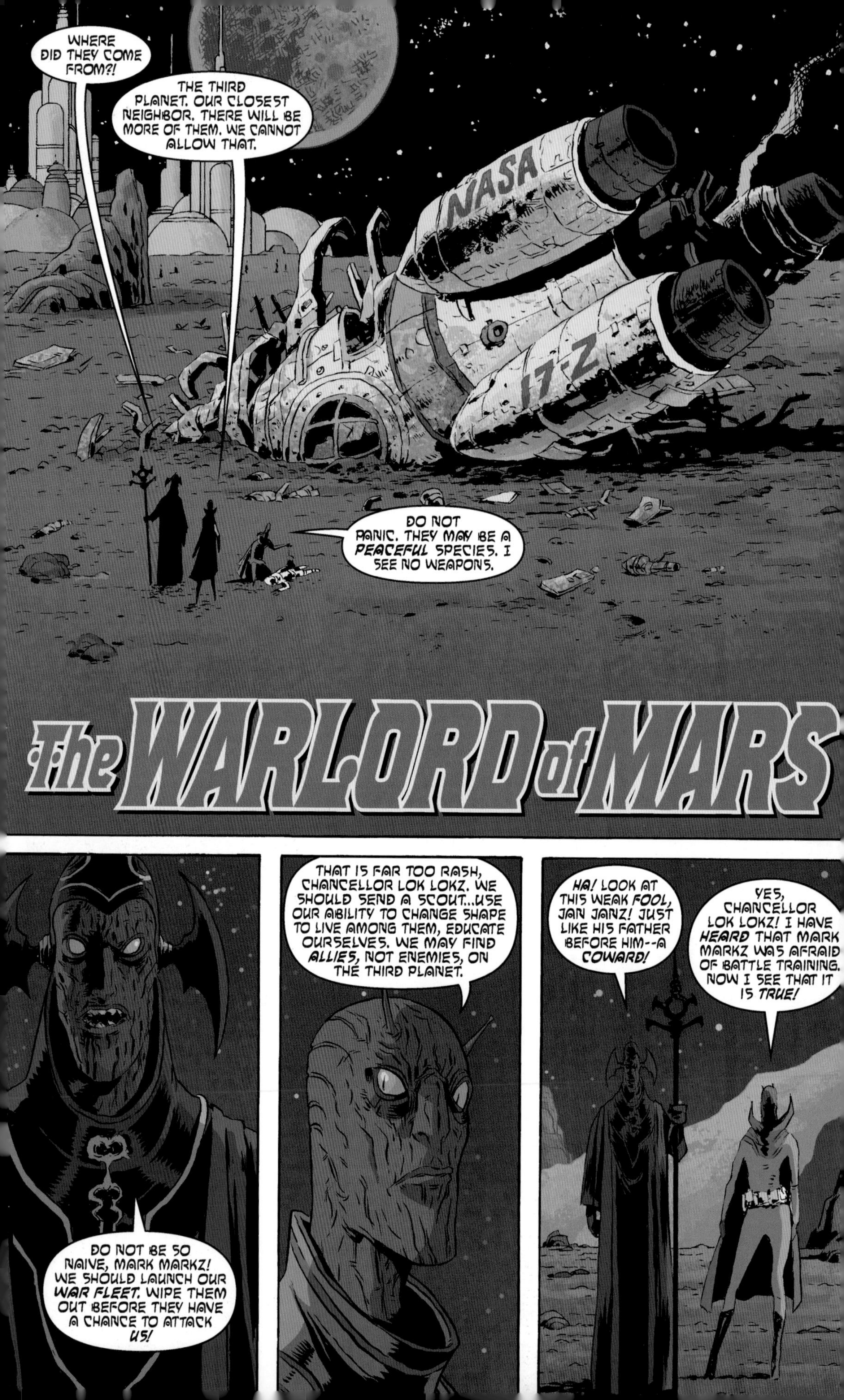

WHERE DID THEY COME FROM?!
THE THIRD PLANET. OUR CLOSEST NEIGHBOR. THERE WILL BE MORE OF THEM. WE CANNOT ALLOW THAT.
NASA
17-Z
DO NOT PANIC. THEY MAY BE A *PEACEFUL* SPECIES. I SEE NO WEAPONS.
The WARLORD of MARS
DO NOT BE SO NAIVE, MARK MARKZ! WE SHOULD LAUNCH OUR *WAR FLEET*. WIPE THEM OUT BEFORE THEY HAVE A CHANCE TO ATTACK *US!*
THAT IS FAR TOO RASH, CHANCELLOR LOK LOKZ. WE SHOULD SEND A SCOUT...USE OUR ABILITY TO CHANGE SHAPE TO LIVE AMONG THEM, EDUCATE OURSELVES. WE MAY FIND *ALLIES*, NOT ENEMIES, ON THE THIRD PLANET.
HA! LOOK AT THIS WEAK *FOOL*, JAN JANZ! JUST LIKE HIS FATHER BEFORE HIM--A *COWARD!*
YES, CHANCELLOR LOK LOKZ! I HAVE *HEARD* THAT MARK MARKZ WAS AFRAID OF BATTLE TRAINING. NOW I SEE THAT IT IS *TRUE!*

MY FATHER DIED UNITING THE RED TRIBES OF MARS. HE DID IT WITH HIS WORDS, NOT HIS SWORD. THAT DID NOT MAKE HIM A COWARD.

YOU REALLY THINK WE SHOULD INVESTIGATE THE HOME OF THESE INVADERS, MARKZ?

THESE ARE *NOT THE ONLY RUMORS* I HAVE HEARD ABOUT YOU, MARKZ...

AND I TRY TO LIVE MY LIFE BY THE SAME PRINCIPLE. AS FOR THESE *OTHER RUMORS*, CHANCELLOR LOK LOKZ, I WILL NOT DIGNIFY THEM WITH A RESPONSE.

¡UNGH!¿

KRAK

SPLORT

THEN I VOLUNTEER *YOU*, OUR *GREAT DIPLOMAT*, FOR THE MISSION.

ME?! B-BUT CHANCELLOR--I HAVE NO TRAINING IN SPACE FLIGHT OR ESPIONAGE!

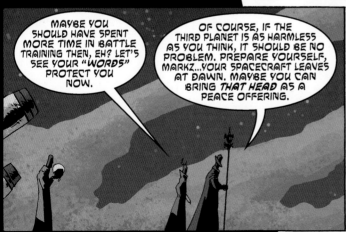

MAYBE YOU SHOULD HAVE SPENT MORE TIME IN BATTLE TRAINING THEN, EH? LET'S SEE YOUR *"WORDS"* PROTECT YOU NOW.

OF COURSE, IF THE THIRD PLANET IS AS HARMLESS AS YOU THINK, IT SHOULD BE NO PROBLEM. PREPARE YOURSELF, MARKZ...YOUR SPACECRAFT LEAVES AT DAWN. MAYBE YOU CAN BRING *THAT HEAD* AS A PEACE OFFERING.

♪ BLESSED ARE YOUR POOR, FOR THE KINGDOM SHALL BE THEIRS. BLESSED ARE YOU THAT WEEP AND MOURN, FOR ONE DAY YOU SHALL LAUGH-- ♪

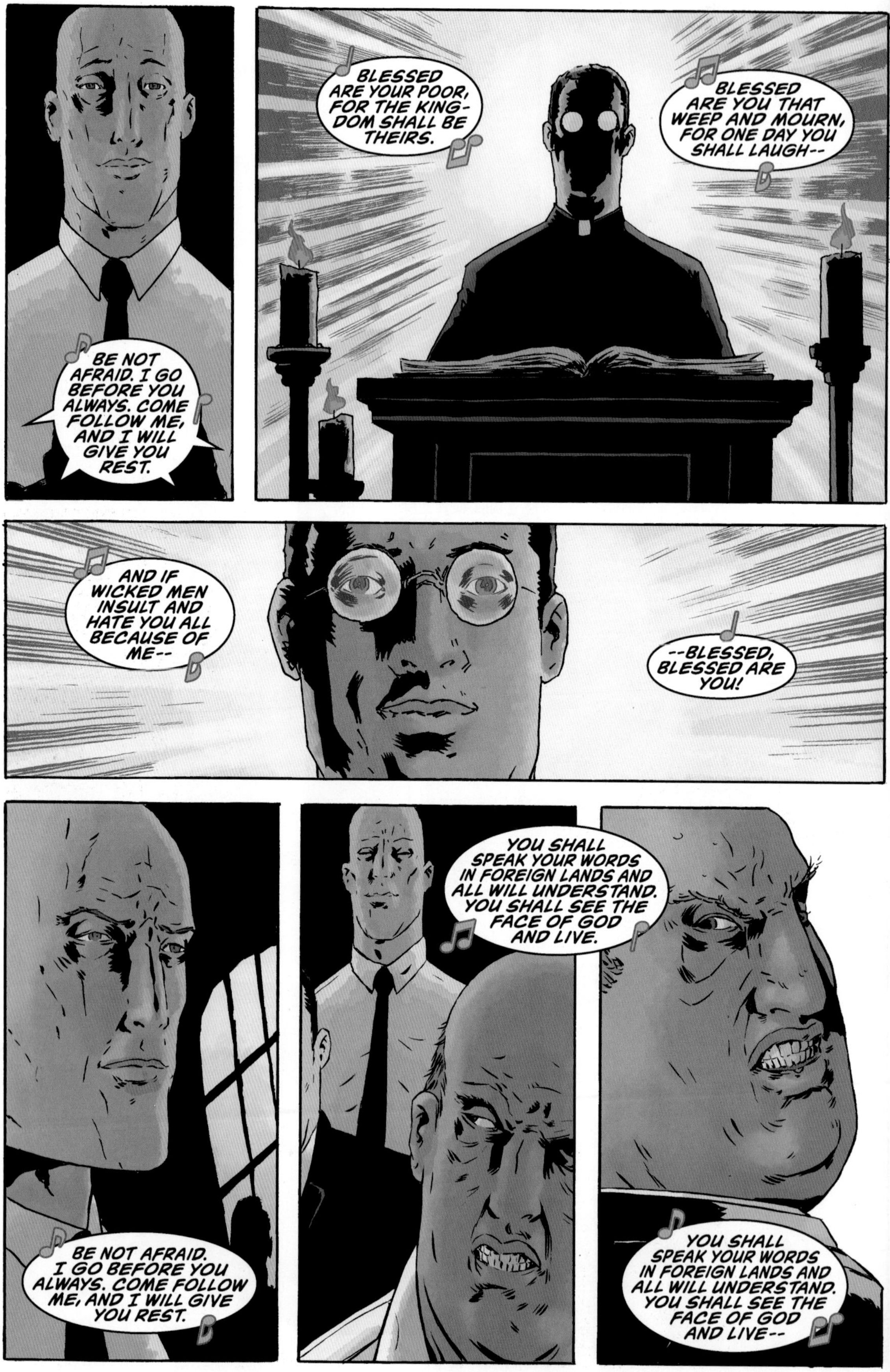
BE NOT AFRAID. I GO BEFORE YOU ALWAYS. COME FOLLOW ME, AND I WILL GIVE YOU REST.
BLESSED ARE YOUR POOR, FOR THE KING-DOM SHALL BE THEIRS.
BLESSED ARE YOU THAT WEEP AND MOURN, FOR ONE DAY YOU SHALL LAUGH--
AND IF WICKED MEN INSULT AND HATE YOU ALL BECAUSE OF ME--
--BLESSED, BLESSED ARE YOU!
BE NOT AFRAID. I GO BEFORE YOU ALWAYS. COME FOLLOW ME, AND I WILL GIVE YOU REST.
YOU SHALL SPEAK YOUR WORDS IN FOREIGN LANDS AND ALL WILL UNDERSTAND. YOU SHALL SEE THE FACE OF GOD AND LIVE.
YOU SHALL SPEAK YOUR WORDS IN FOREIGN LANDS AND ALL WILL UNDERSTAND. YOU SHALL SEE THE FACE OF GOD AND LIVE--

WELL, ABE, I DIDN'T EXPECT *THAT* WHEN YOU SAID YOU WERE GOING TO STOP BY THE DINER LAST NIGHT.

OUR FIRST SLEEPOVER. HOW'D I DO?

NOT BAD FOR AN OLD MAN.

SO, AM I GOING TO GET TO SLEEP OVER AT *YOUR* HOUSE NEXT?

...

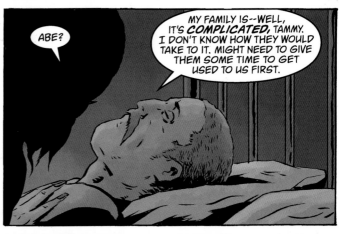

ABE?

MY FAMILY IS--WELL, IT'S *COMPLICATED*, TAMMY. I DON'T KNOW HOW THEY WOULD TAKE TO IT. MIGHT NEED TO GIVE THEM SOME TIME TO GET USED TO US FIRST.

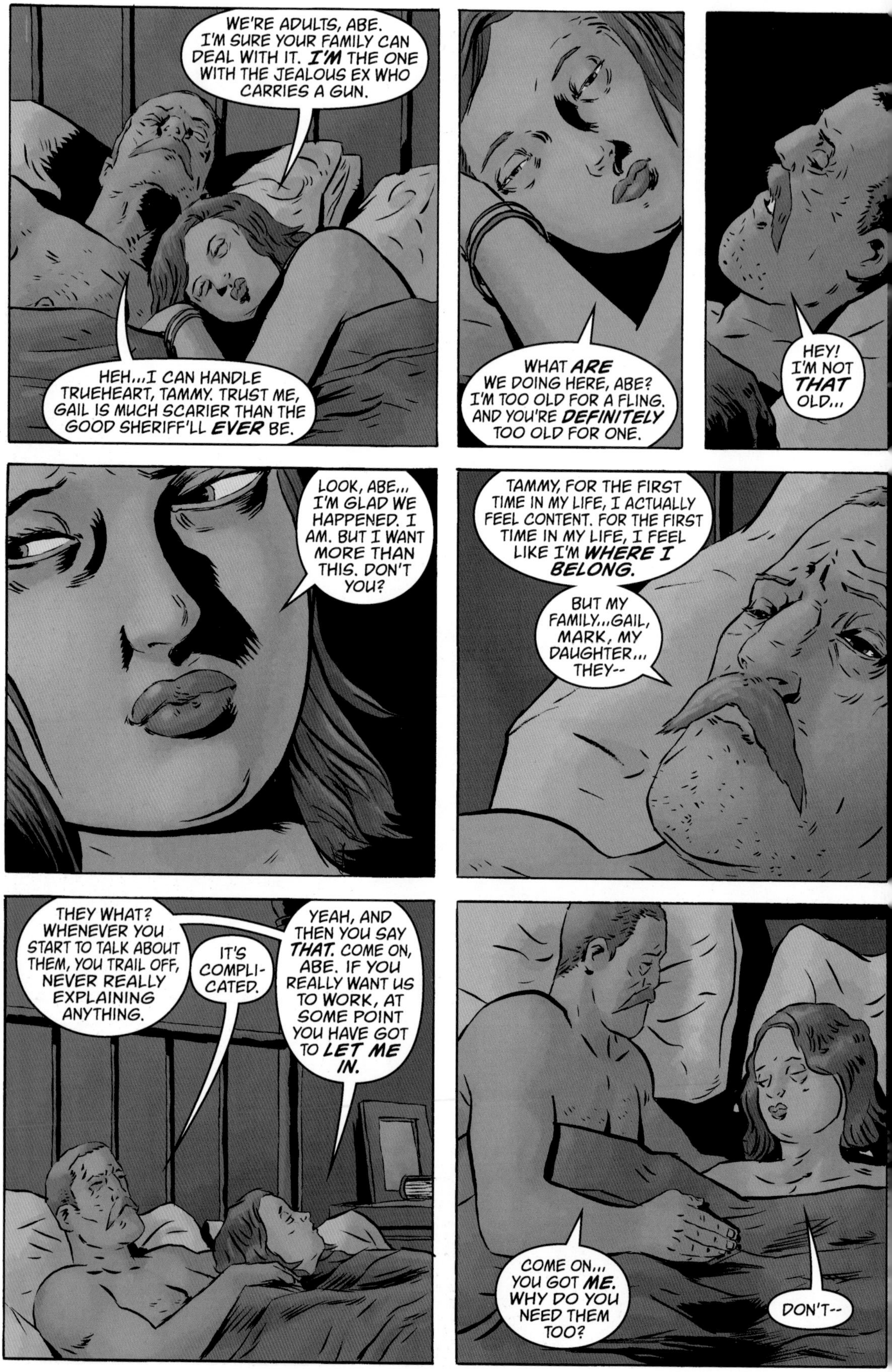
WE'RE ADULTS, ABE. I'M SURE YOUR FAMILY CAN DEAL WITH IT. I'M THE ONE WITH THE JEALOUS EX WHO CARRIES A GUN.
HEH...I CAN HANDLE TRUEHEART, TAMMY. TRUST ME, GAIL IS MUCH SCARIER THAN THE GOOD SHERIFF'LL EVER BE.
WHAT ARE WE DOING HERE, ABE? I'M TOO OLD FOR A FLING. AND YOU'RE DEFINITELY TOO OLD FOR ONE.
HEY! I'M NOT THAT OLD...
LOOK, ABE... I'M GLAD WE HAPPENED. I AM. BUT I WANT MORE THAN THIS. DON'T YOU?
TAMMY, FOR THE FIRST TIME IN MY LIFE, I ACTUALLY FEEL CONTENT. FOR THE FIRST TIME IN MY LIFE, I FEEL LIKE I'M WHERE I BELONG.
BUT MY FAMILY...GAIL, MARK, MY DAUGHTER... THEY--
THEY WHAT? WHENEVER YOU START TO TALK ABOUT THEM, YOU TRAIL OFF, NEVER REALLY EXPLAINING ANYTHING.
IT'S COMPLI-CATED.
YEAH, AND THEN YOU SAY THAT. COME ON, ABE. IF YOU REALLY WANT US TO WORK, AT SOME POINT YOU HAVE GOT TO LET ME IN.
COME ON... YOU GOT ME. WHY DO YOU NEED THEM TOO?
DON'T--

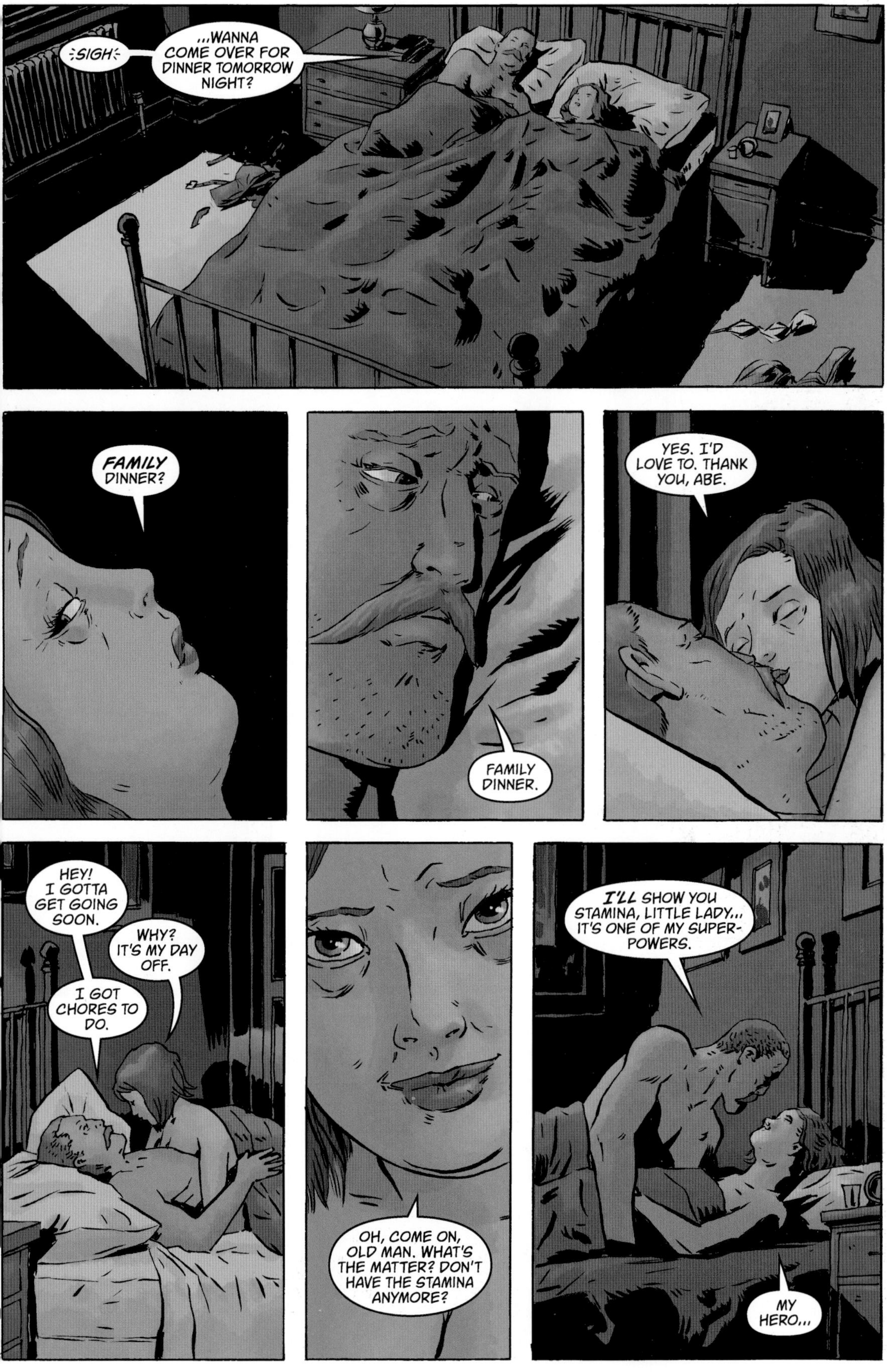

SIGH
...WANNA COME OVER FOR DINNER TOMORROW NIGHT?
FAMILY DINNER?
FAMILY DINNER.
YES. I'D LOVE TO. THANK YOU, ABE.
HEY! I GOTTA GET GOING SOON.
WHY? IT'S MY DAY OFF.
I GOT CHORES TO DO.
OH, COME ON, OLD MAN. WHAT'S THE MATTER? DON'T HAVE THE STAMINA ANYMORE?
I'LL SHOW YOU STAMINA, LITTLE LADY... IT'S ONE OF MY SUPER-POWERS.
MY HERO...

DIDN'T THINK I'D EVER SEE ONE A YOU HERE.

ONE OF *US*, SHERIFF?

DIDN'T THINK YOU OR *YOUR FAMILY* WERE THE CHURCH-GOING TYPE.

YOU DON'T KNOW A THING ABOUT MY FAMILY, TRUE-HEART.

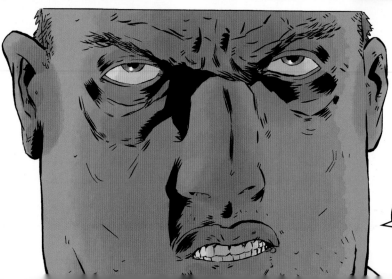

NO...NO ONE SEEMS TO KNOW MUCH OF *ANYTHING* ABOUT YOU. ALMOST LIKE YOU WANT TO KEEP IT THAT WAY.

MY EXPERIENCE, PEOPLE USUALLY ONLY DO THAT WHEN THEY HAVE *SOMETHING TO HIDE*.

UH-HUH. WELL, I KNOW HOW WORLDLY AND EXPERIENCED YOU ARE, SHERIFF. HAVE YOU EVER EVEN LEFT THIS TOWN?

JUST BECAUSE WE LIKE OUR PRIVACY DOESN'T MEAN WE'RE THE ENEMY.

NO...BUT MAYBE YOU'RE HERE BECAUSE YOU'VE DEVELOPED A GUILTY CONSCIENCE ABOUT SOMETHING? OR *SOMEONE?*

AFTERNOON. SEND MY BEST WISHES TO ABE, WILL YOU?

ALWAYS A PLEASURE, SHERIFF.

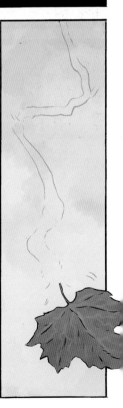

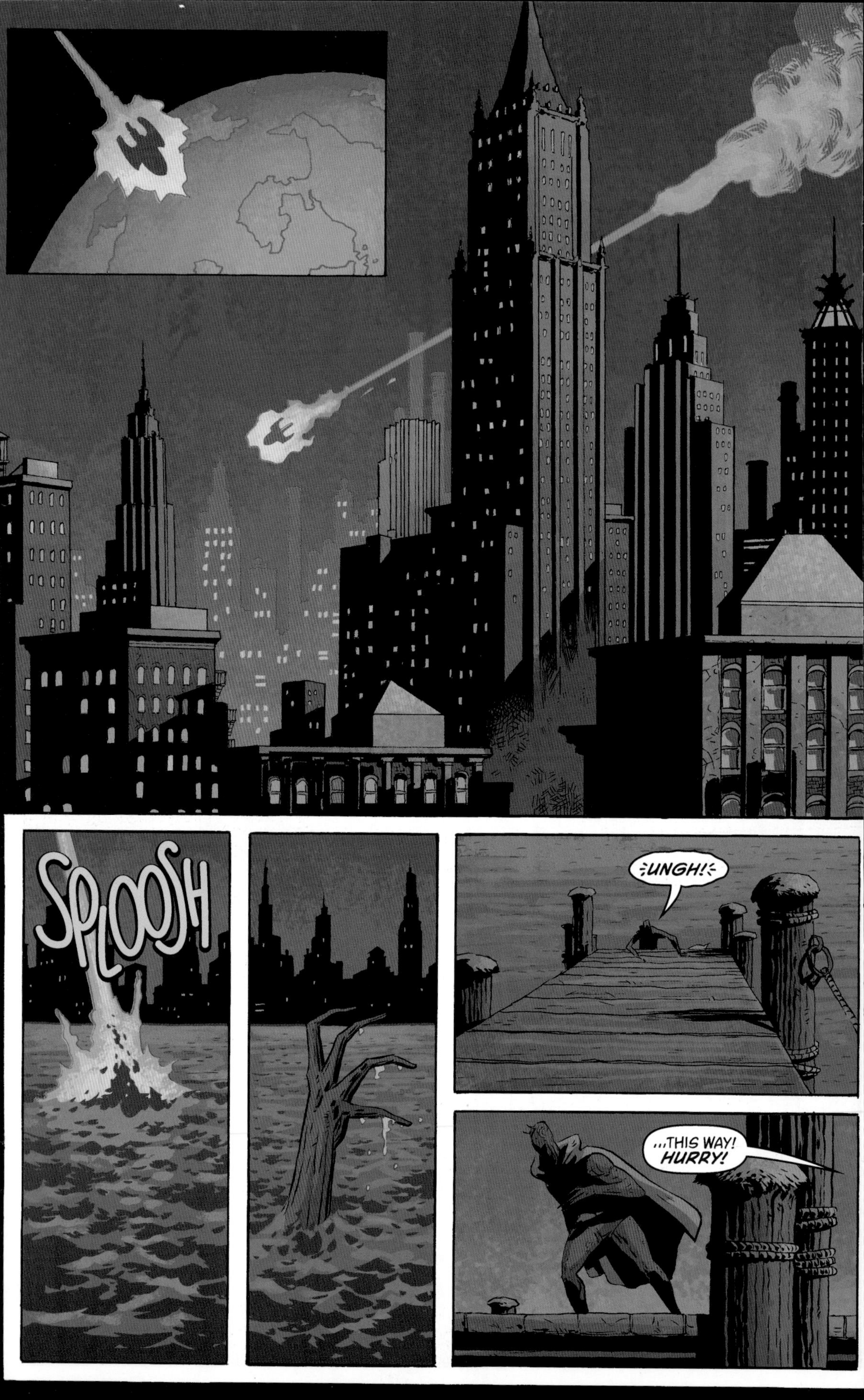
SPLOOSH
UNGH!
...THIS WAY! HURRY!

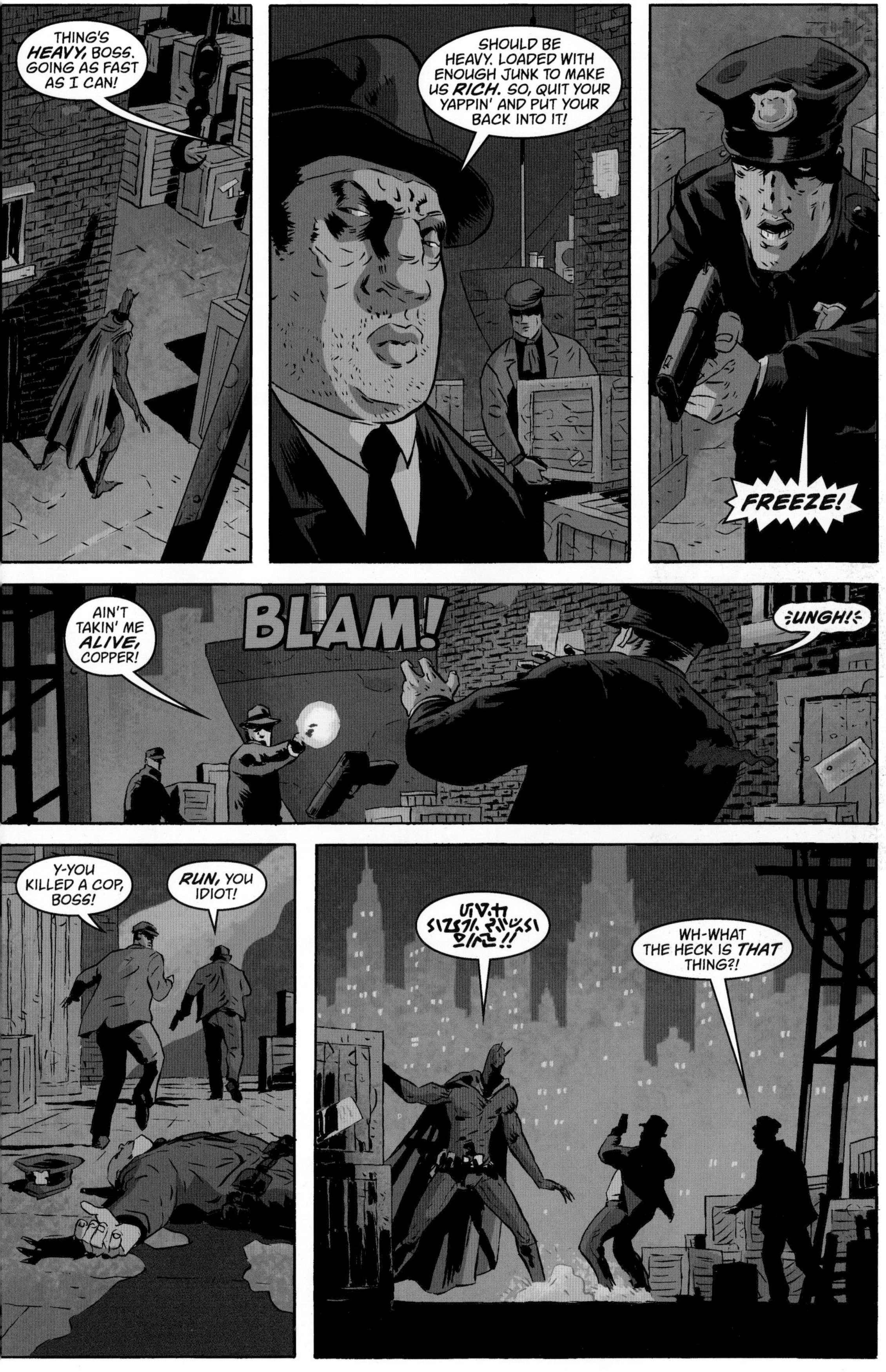
THING'S HEAVY, BOSS. GOING AS FAST AS I CAN!
SHOULD BE HEAVY. LOADED WITH ENOUGH JUNK TO MAKE US RICH. SO, QUIT YOUR YAPPIN' AND PUT YOUR BACK INTO IT!
FREEZE!
AIN'T TAKIN' ME ALIVE, COPPER!
BLAM!
UNGH!
Y-YOU KILLED A COP, BOSS!
RUN, YOU IDIOT!
WH-WHAT THE HECK IS THAT THING?!

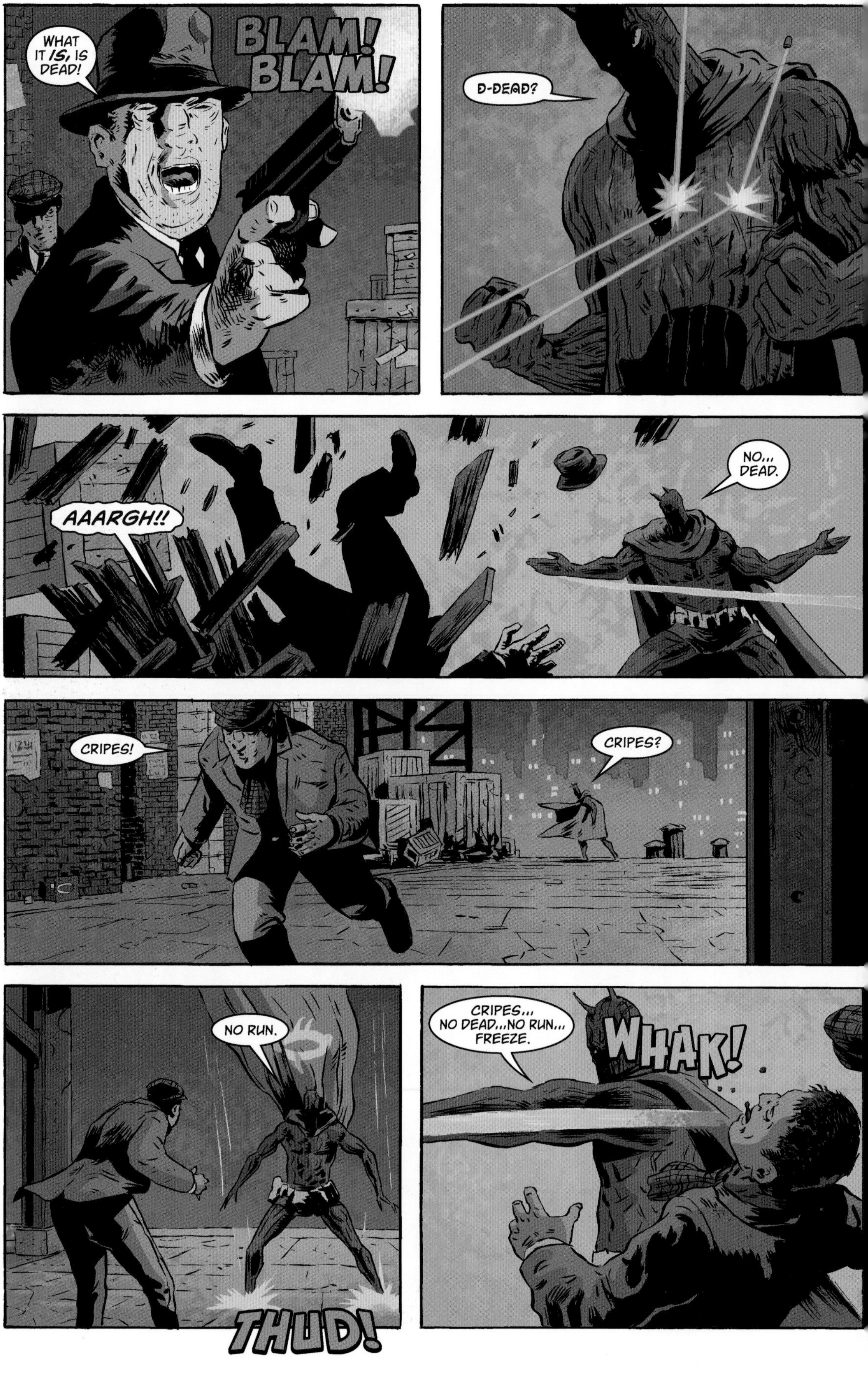
WHAT IT IS, IS DEAD!
BLAM! BLAM!
D-DEAD?
AAARGH!!
NO... DEAD.
CRIPES!
CRIPES?
NO RUN.
THUD!
CRIPES... NO DEAD...NO RUN... FREEZE.
WHAK!

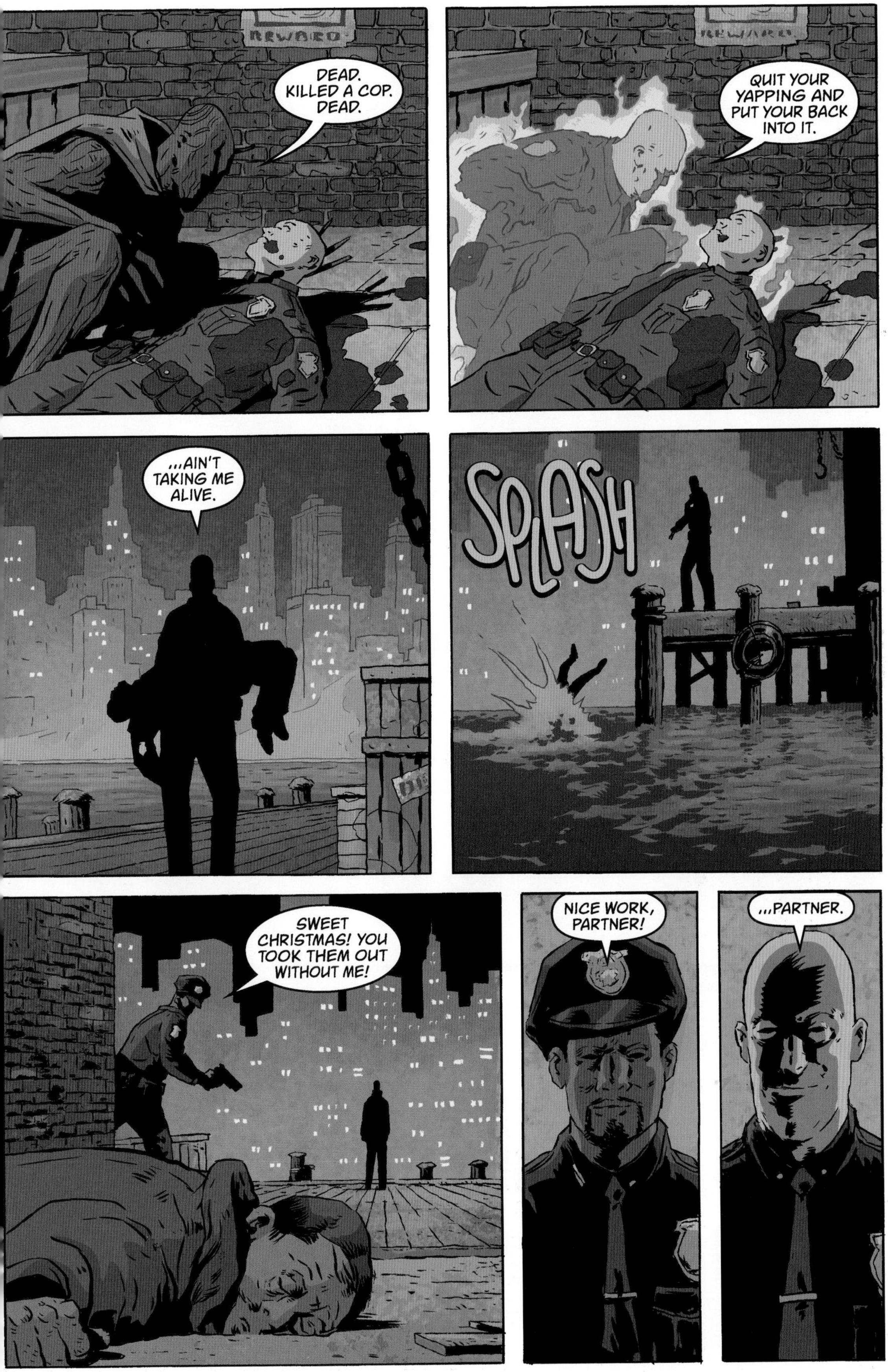
DEAD. KILLED A COP. DEAD.
QUIT YOUR YAPPING AND PUT YOUR BACK INTO IT.
...AIN'T TAKING ME ALIVE.
SPLASH
SWEET CHRISTMAS! YOU TOOK THEM OUT WITHOUT ME!
NICE WORK, PARTNER!
...PARTNER.

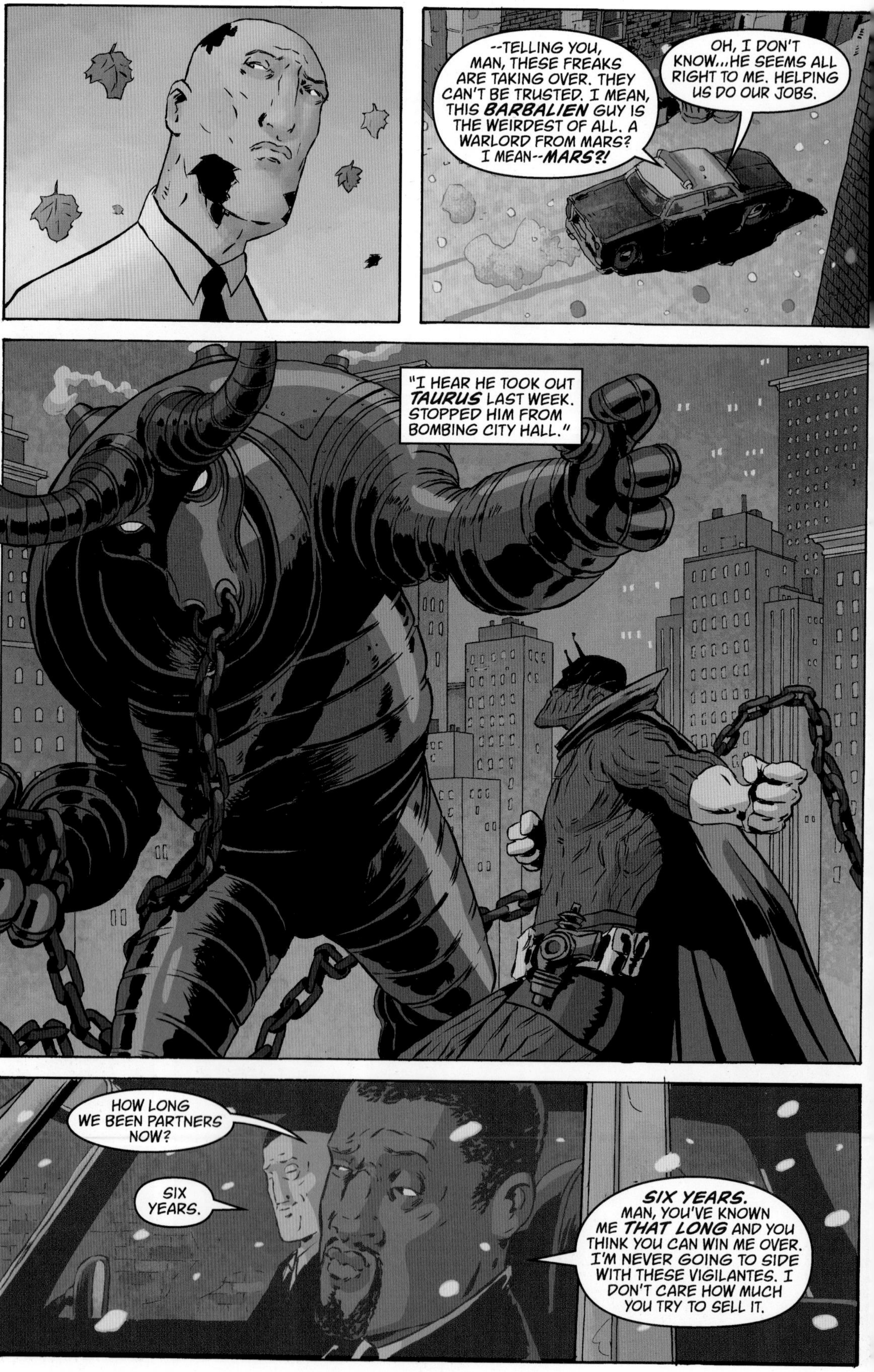

--TELLING YOU, MAN, THESE FREAKS ARE TAKING OVER. THEY CAN'T BE TRUSTED. I MEAN, THIS BARBALIEN GUY IS THE WEIRDEST OF ALL. A WARLORD FROM MARS? I MEAN--MARS?!
OH, I DON'T KNOW...HE SEEMS ALL RIGHT TO ME. HELPING US DO OUR JOBS.
"I HEAR HE TOOK OUT TAURUS LAST WEEK. STOPPED HIM FROM BOMBING CITY HALL."
HOW LONG WE BEEN PARTNERS NOW?
SIX YEARS.
SIX YEARS. MAN, YOU'VE KNOWN ME THAT LONG AND YOU THINK YOU CAN WIN ME OVER. I'M NEVER GOING TO SIDE WITH THESE VIGILANTES. I DON'T CARE HOW MUCH YOU TRY TO SELL IT.

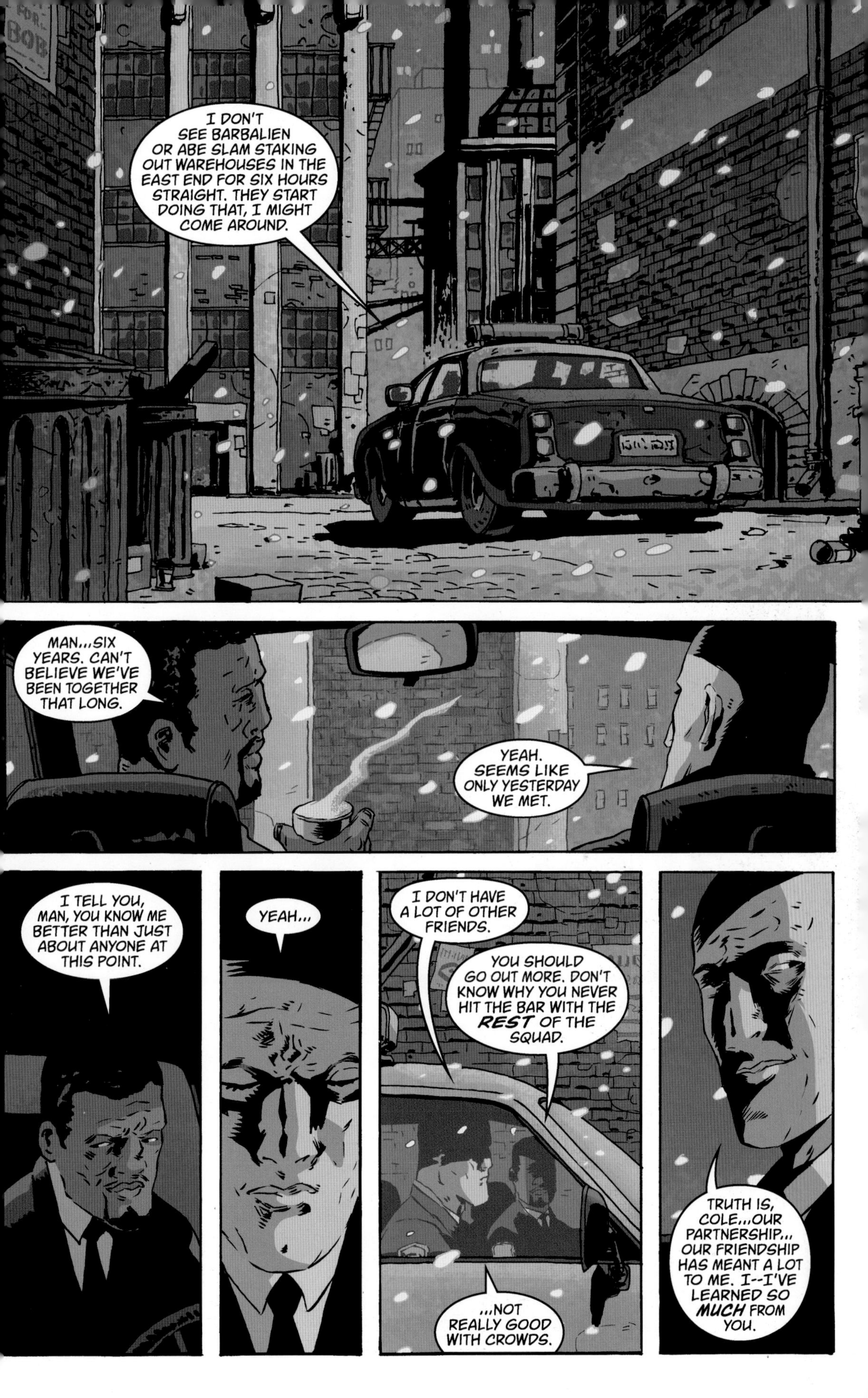
I DON'T SEE BARBALIEN OR ABE SLAM STAKING OUT WAREHOUSES IN THE EAST END FOR SIX HOURS STRAIGHT. THEY START DOING THAT, I MIGHT COME AROUND.
MAN...SIX YEARS. CAN'T BELIEVE WE'VE BEEN TOGETHER THAT LONG.
YEAH. SEEMS LIKE ONLY YESTERDAY WE MET.
I TELL YOU, MAN, YOU KNOW ME BETTER THAN JUST ABOUT ANYONE AT THIS POINT.
YEAH...
I DON'T HAVE A LOT OF OTHER FRIENDS.
YOU SHOULD GO OUT MORE. DON'T KNOW WHY YOU NEVER HIT THE BAR WITH THE REST OF THE SQUAD.
...NOT REALLY GOOD WITH CROWDS.
TRUTH IS, COLE...OUR PARTNERSHIP... OUR FRIENDSHIP HAS MEANT A LOT TO ME. I--I'VE LEARNED SO MUCH FROM YOU.

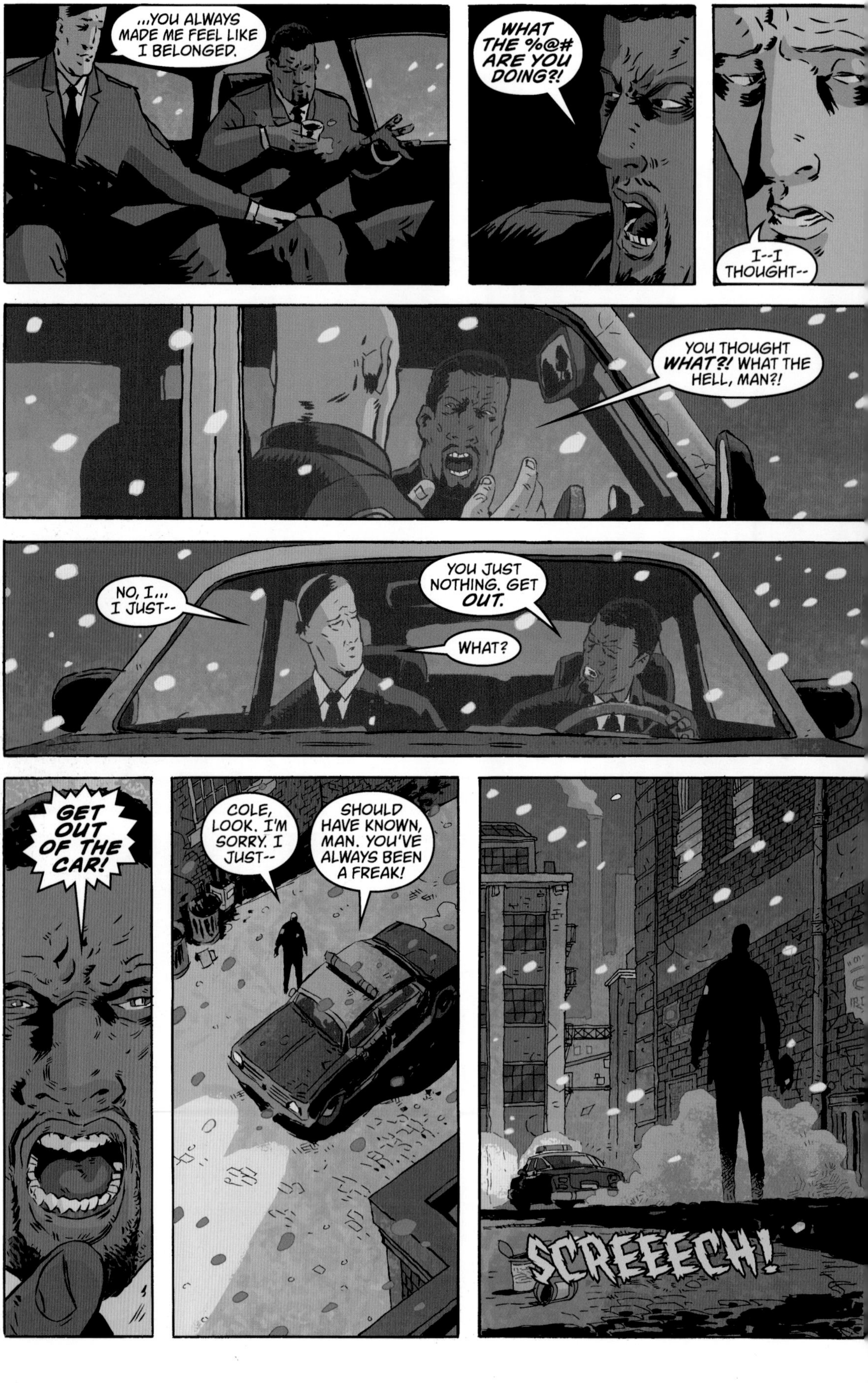
...YOU ALWAYS MADE ME FEEL LIKE I BELONGED.
WHAT THE %@# ARE YOU DOING?!
I--I THOUGHT--
YOU THOUGHT WHAT?! WHAT THE HELL, MAN?!
NO, I... I JUST--
YOU JUST NOTHING. GET OUT.
WHAT?
GET OUT OF THE CAR!
COLE, LOOK. I'M SORRY. I JUST--
SHOULD HAVE KNOWN, MAN. YOU'VE ALWAYS BEEN A FREAK!
SCREEECH!

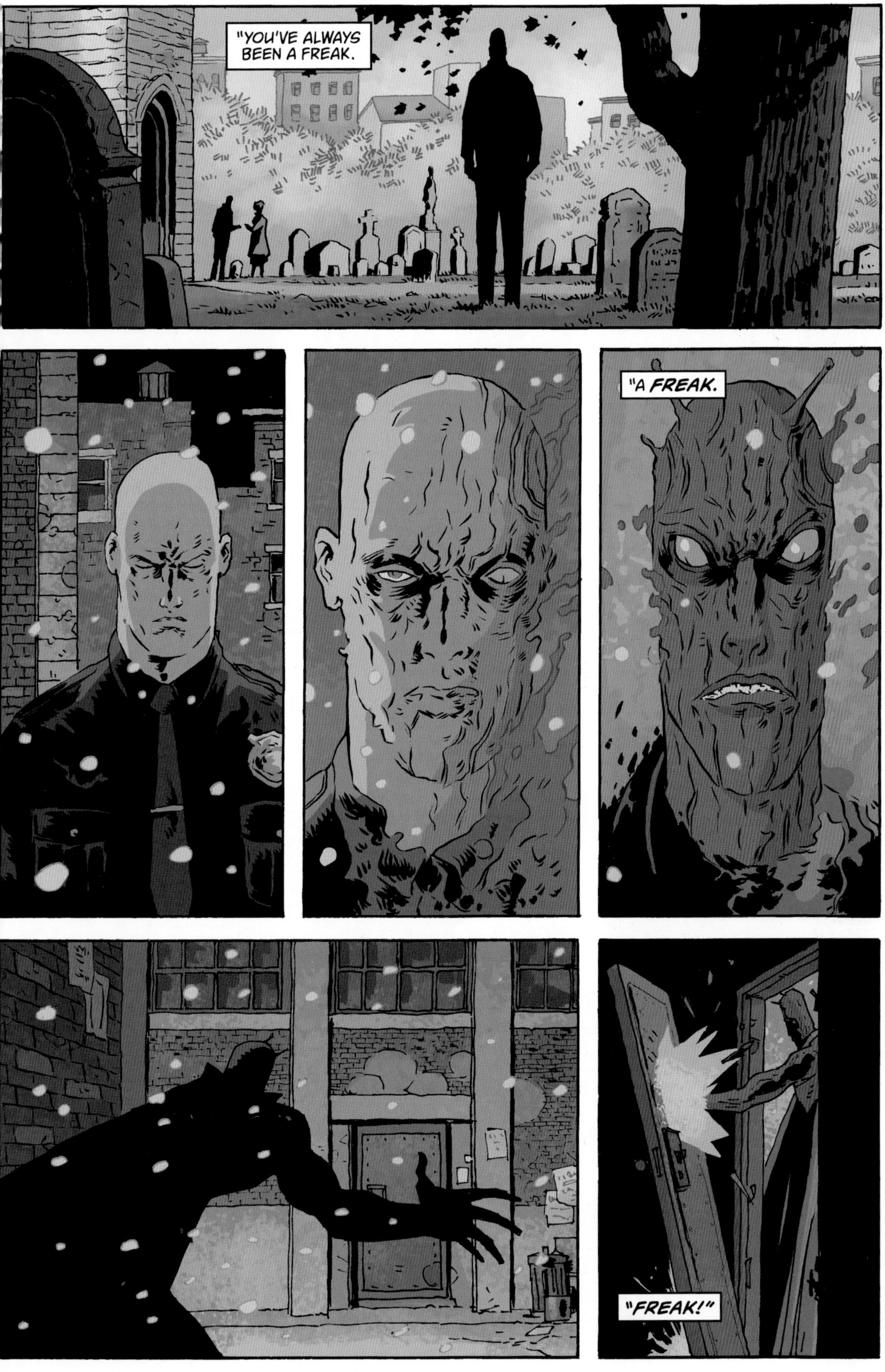
"YOU'VE ALWAYS BEEN A FREAK.
"A FREAK.
"FREAK!"

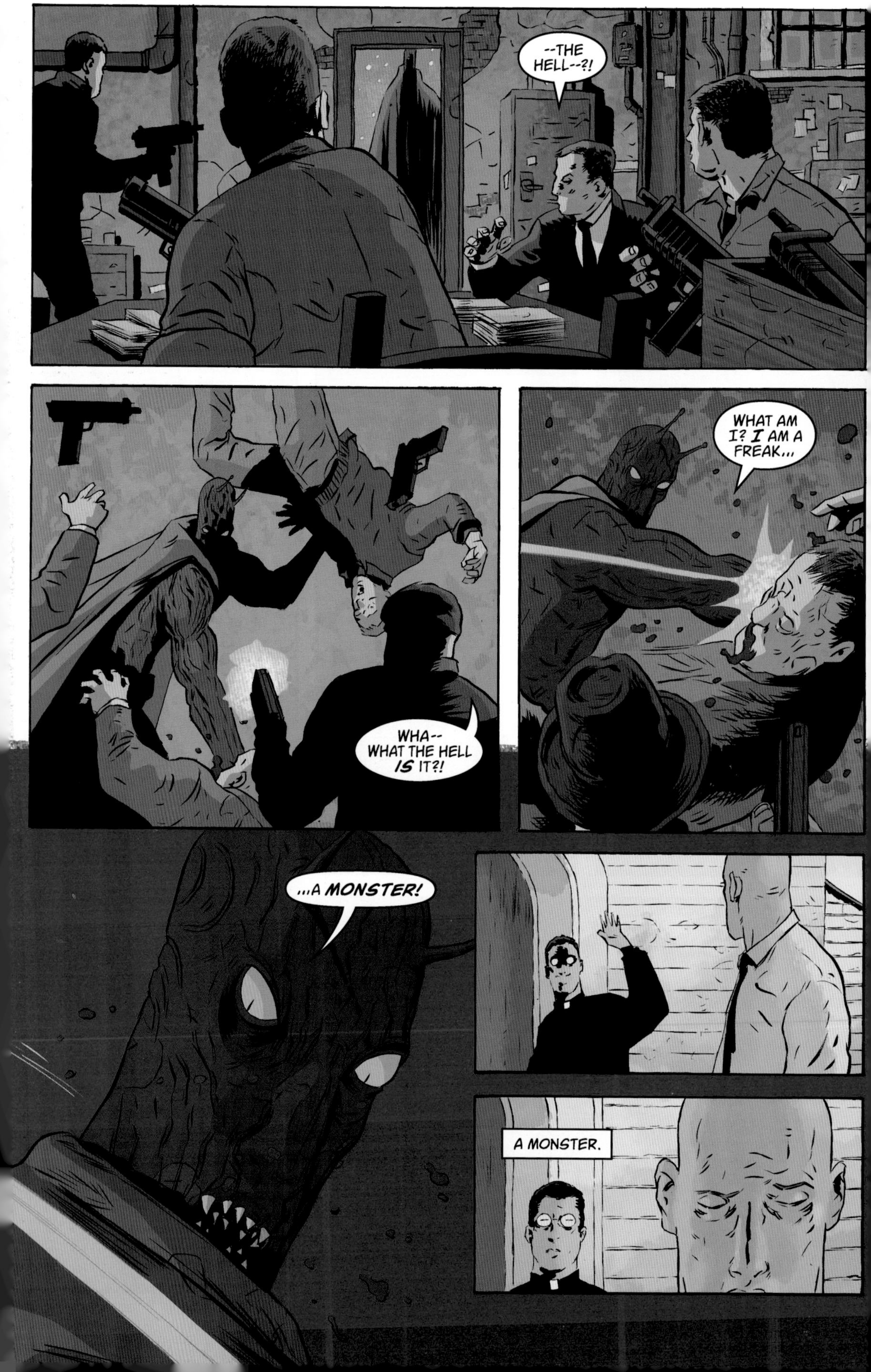
--THE HELL--?!
WHA-- WHAT THE HELL IS IT?!
WHAT AM I? I AM A FREAK...
...A MONSTER!
A MONSTER.

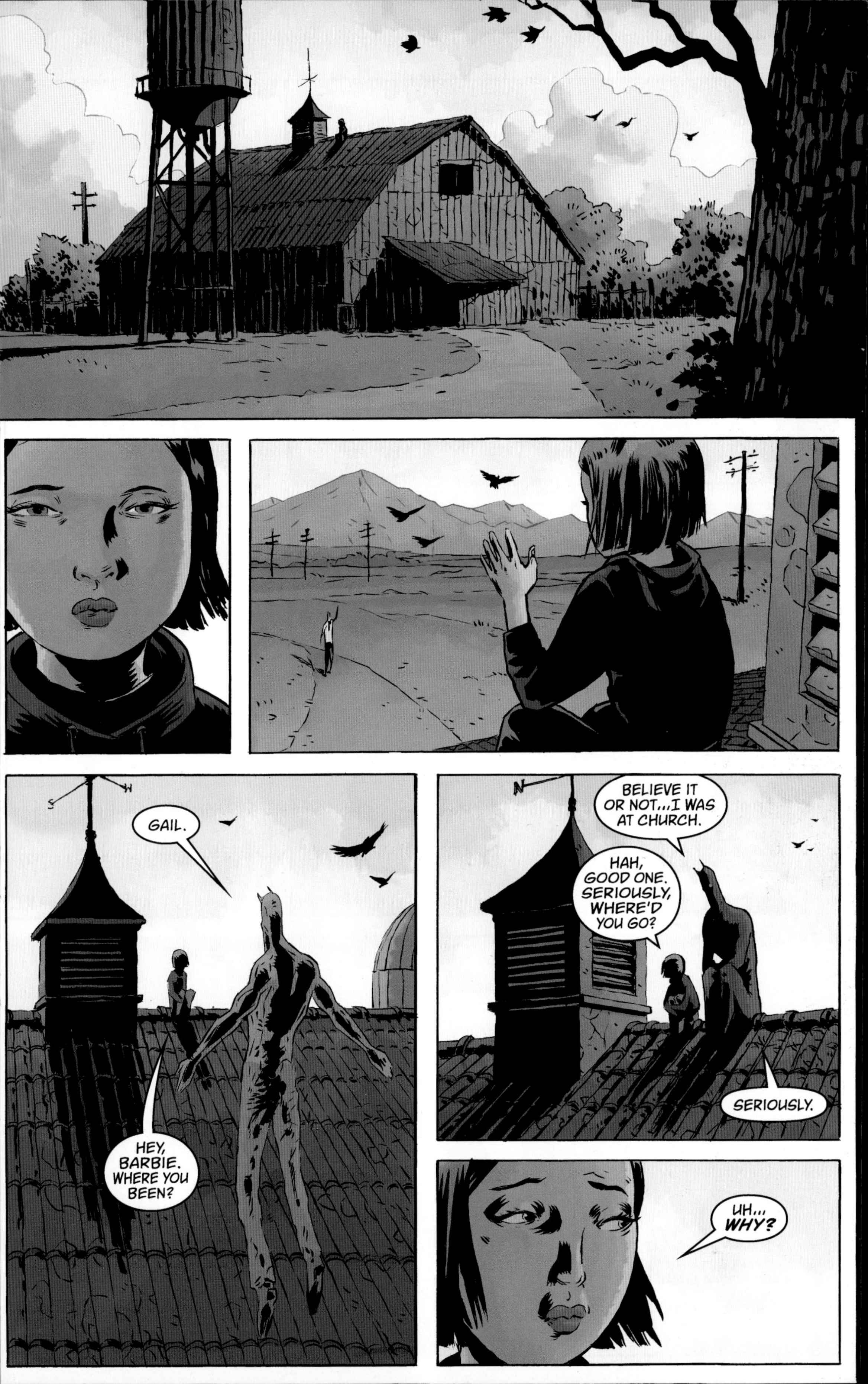
GAIL.
HEY, BARBIE. WHERE YOU BEEN?
BELIEVE IT OR NOT...I WAS AT CHURCH.
HAH, GOOD ONE. SERIOUSLY, WHERE'D YOU GO?
SERIOUSLY.
UH... WHY?

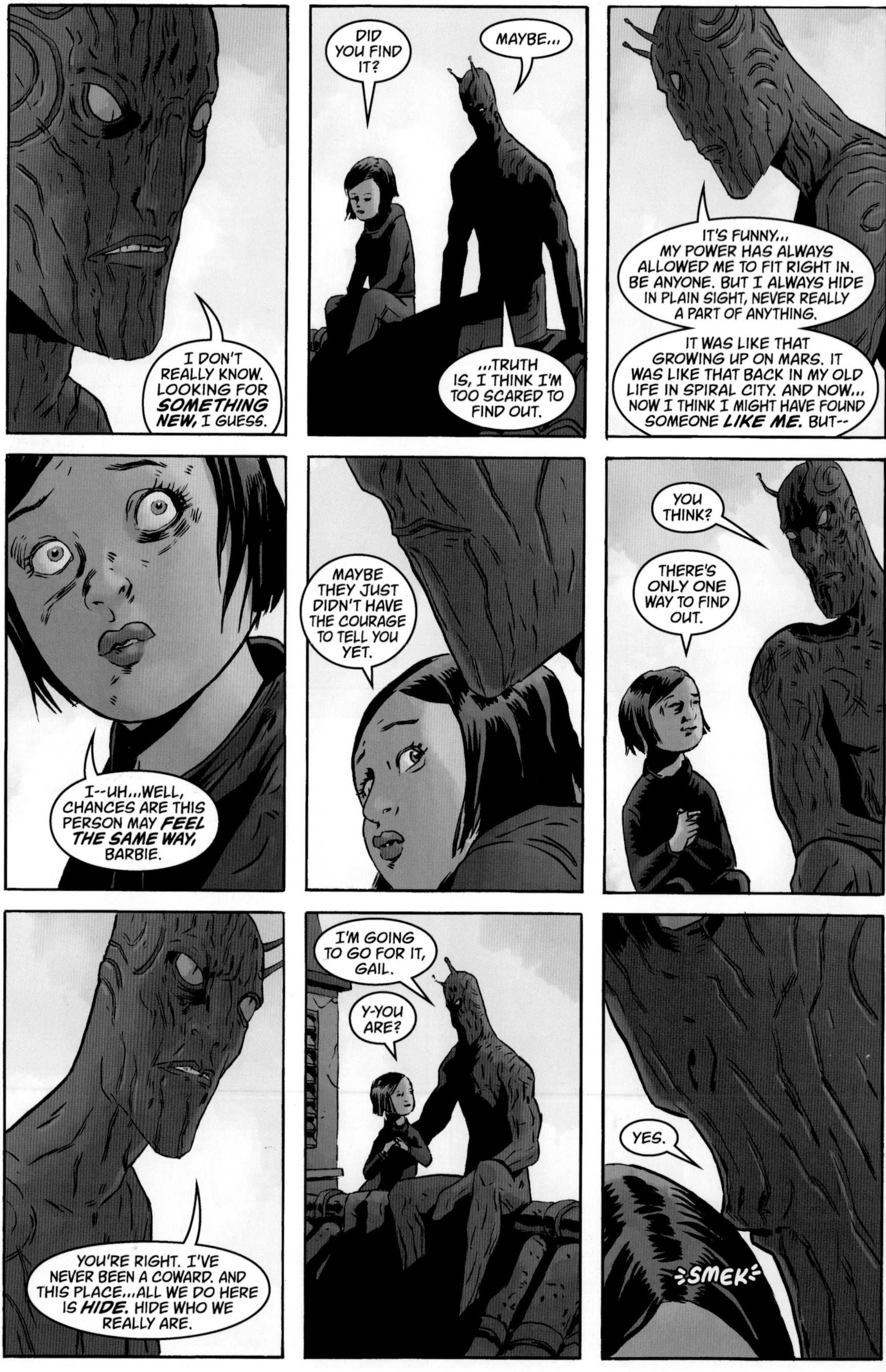
I DON'T REALLY KNOW. LOOKING FOR SOMETHING NEW, I GUESS.
DID YOU FIND IT?
MAYBE...
...TRUTH IS, I THINK I'M TOO SCARED TO FIND OUT.
IT'S FUNNY... MY POWER HAS ALWAYS ALLOWED ME TO FIT RIGHT IN. BE ANYONE. BUT I ALWAYS HIDE IN PLAIN SIGHT, NEVER REALLY A PART OF ANYTHING.
IT WAS LIKE THAT GROWING UP ON MARS. IT WAS LIKE THAT BACK IN MY OLD LIFE IN SPIRAL CITY. AND NOW... NOW I THINK I MIGHT HAVE FOUND SOMEONE LIKE ME. BUT--
I--UH...WELL, CHANCES ARE THIS PERSON MAY FEEL THE SAME WAY, BARBIE.
MAYBE THEY JUST DIDN'T HAVE THE COURAGE TO TELL YOU YET.
YOU THINK?
THERE'S ONLY ONE WAY TO FIND OUT.
YOU'RE RIGHT. I'VE NEVER BEEN A COWARD. AND THIS PLACE...ALL WE DO HERE IS HIDE. HIDE WHO WE REALLY ARE.
I'M GOING TO GO FOR IT, GAIL.
Y-YOU ARE?
YES.
SMEK

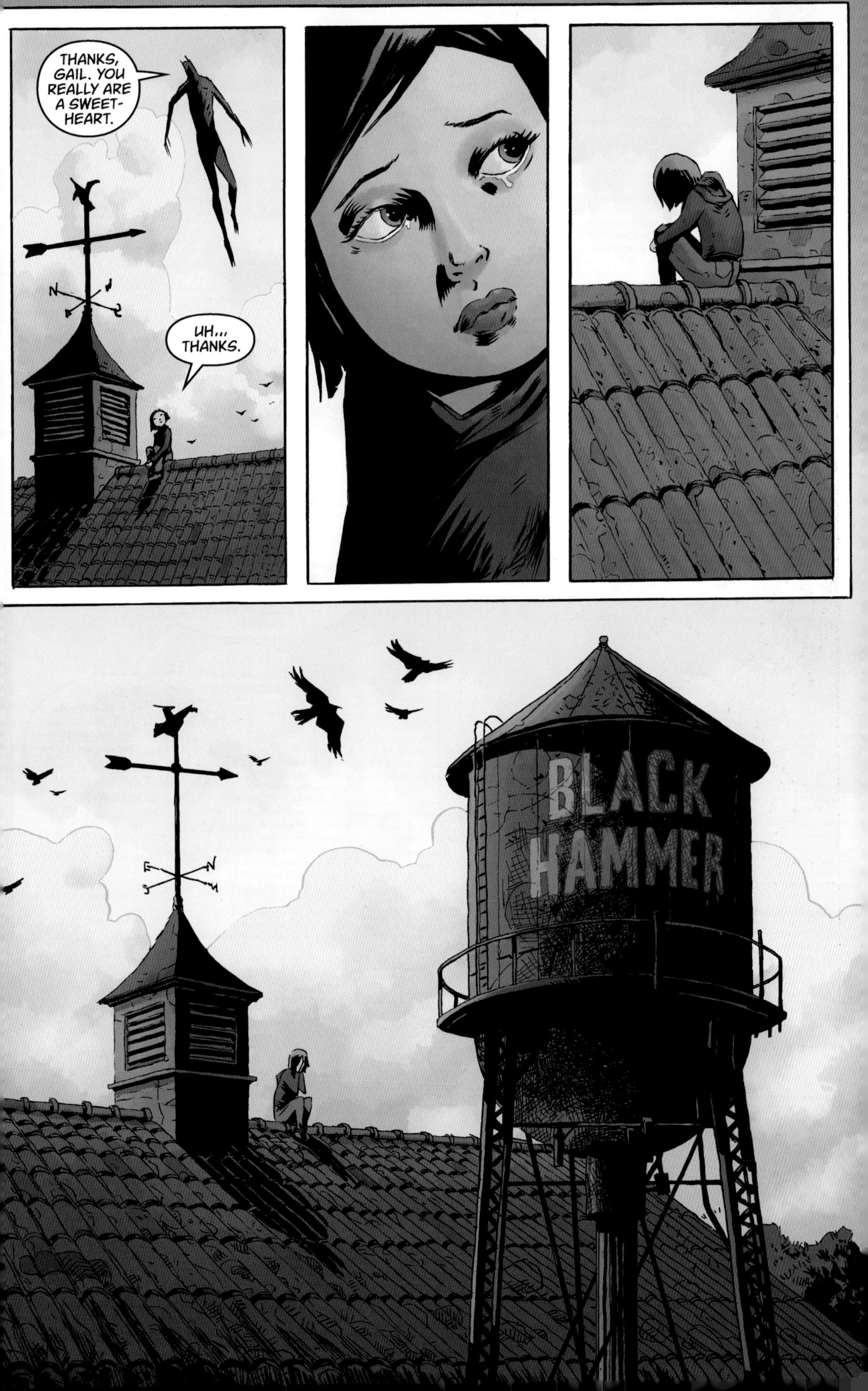
THANKS, GAIL. YOU REALLY ARE A SWEET-HEART.
UH... THANKS.
N
S
E
S
N
W
BLACK HAMMER

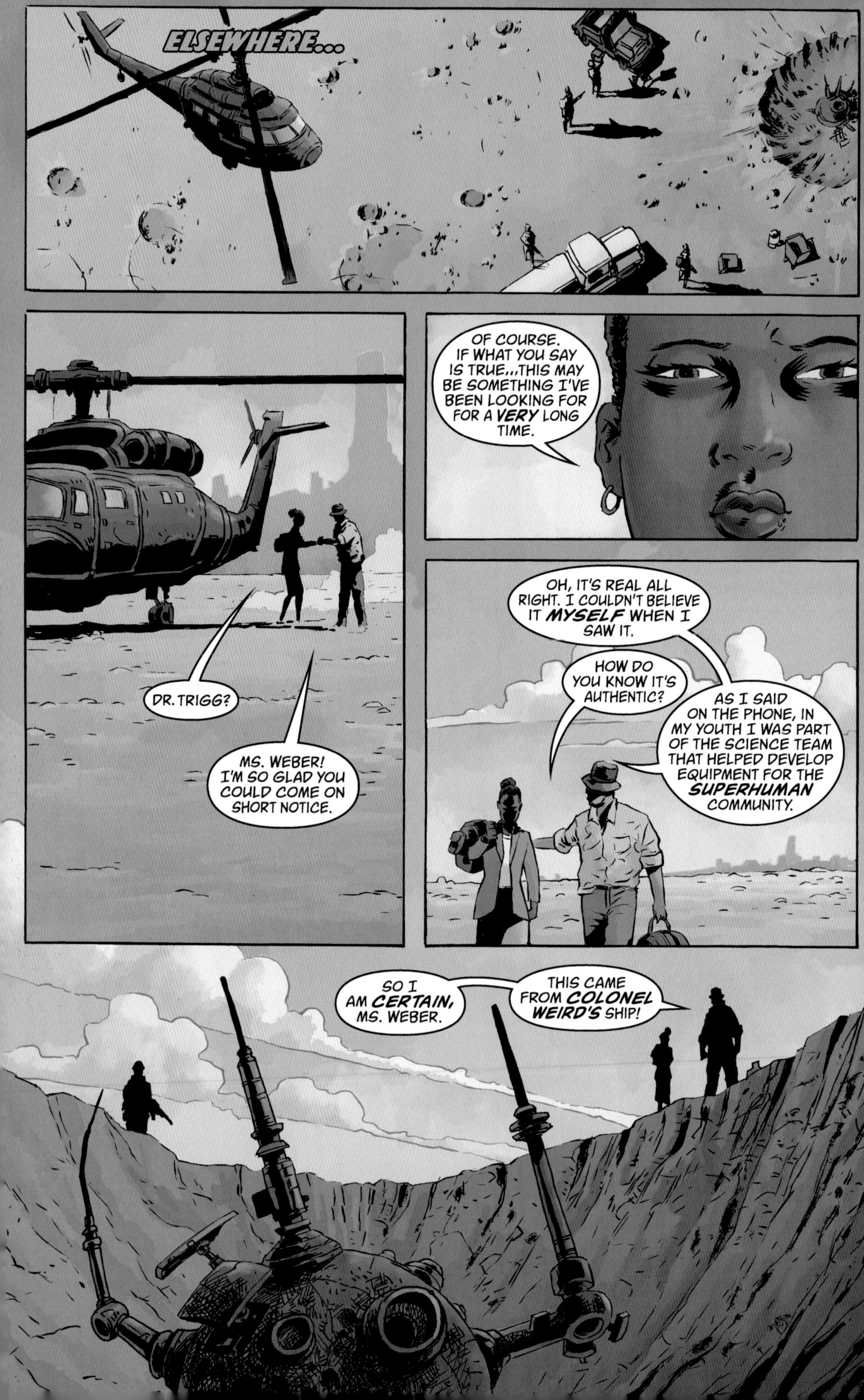

ELSEWHERE...
DR. TRIGG?
MS. WEBER! I'M SO GLAD YOU COULD COME ON SHORT NOTICE.
OF COURSE. IF WHAT YOU SAY IS TRUE...THIS MAY BE SOMETHING I'VE BEEN LOOKING FOR FOR A VERY LONG TIME.
OH, IT'S REAL ALL RIGHT. I COULDN'T BELIEVE IT MYSELF WHEN I SAW IT.
HOW DO YOU KNOW IT'S AUTHENTIC?
AS I SAID ON THE PHONE, IN MY YOUTH I WAS PART OF THE SCIENCE TEAM THAT HELPED DEVELOP EQUIPMENT FOR THE SUPERHUMAN COMMUNITY.
SO I AM CERTAIN, MS. WEBER.
THIS CAME FROM COLONEL WEIRD'S SHIP!

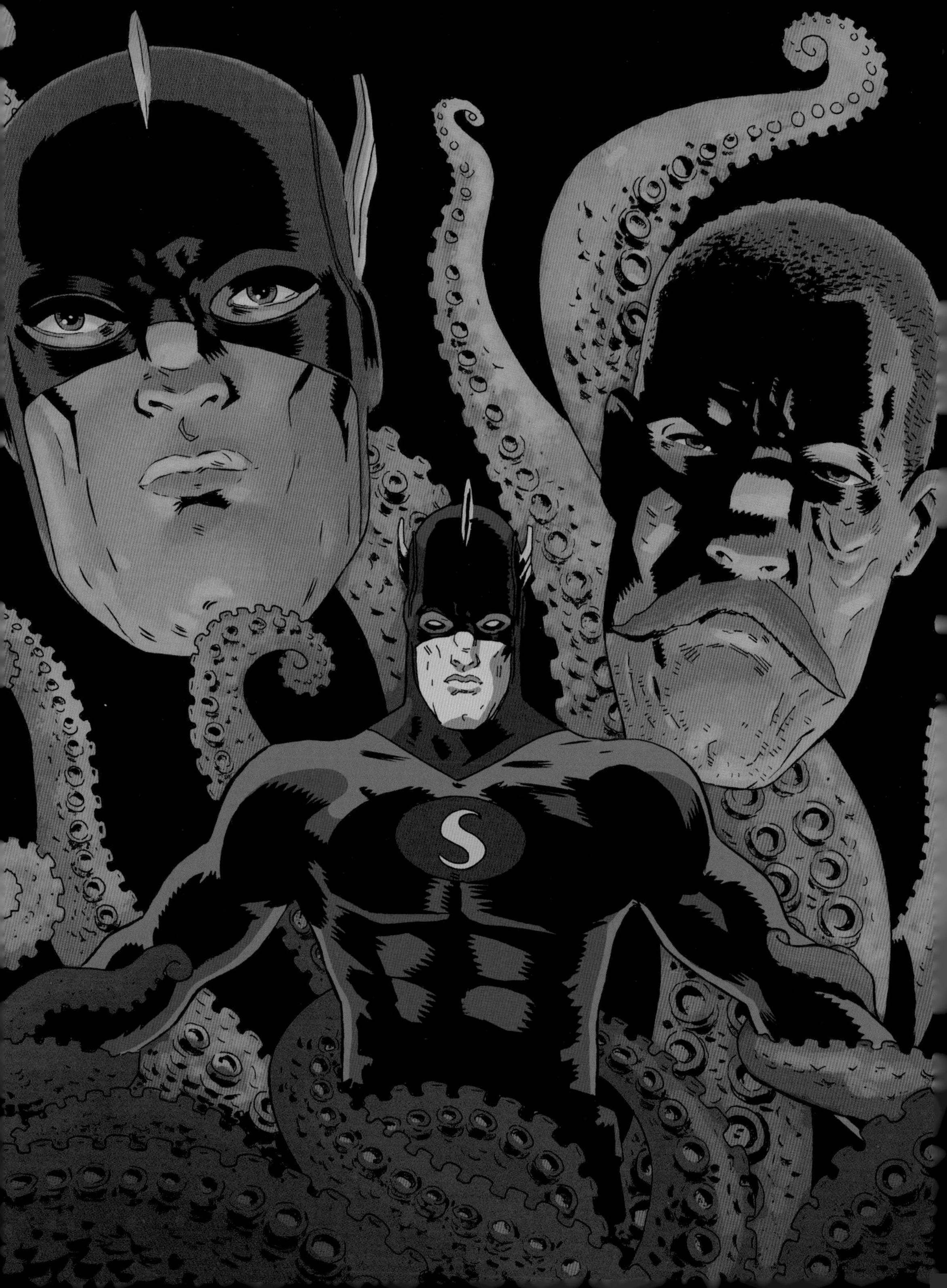

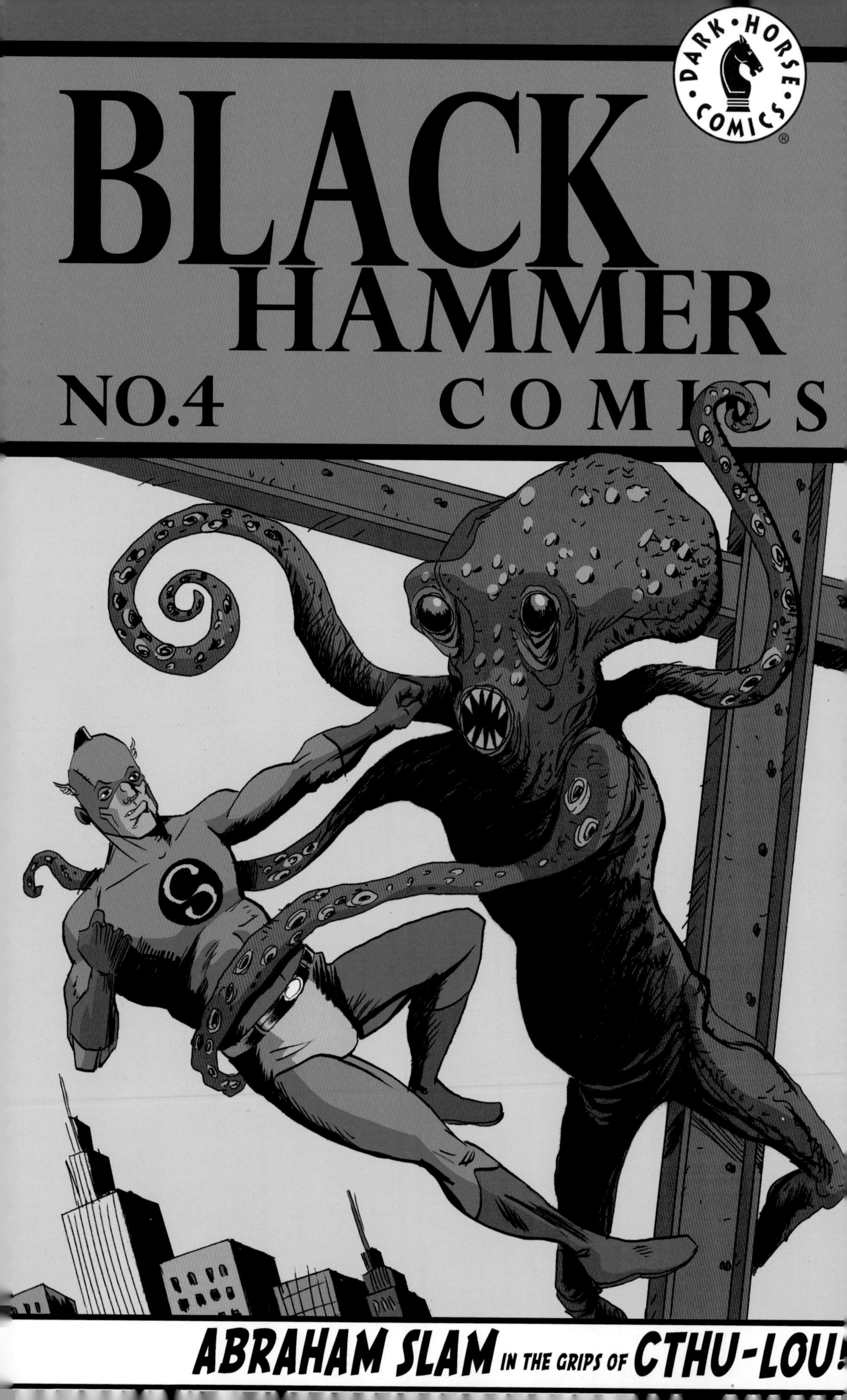
DARK HORSE COMICS
BLACK HAMMER
NO.4
COMICS
ABRAHAM SLAM IN THE GRIPS OF CTHU-LOU!

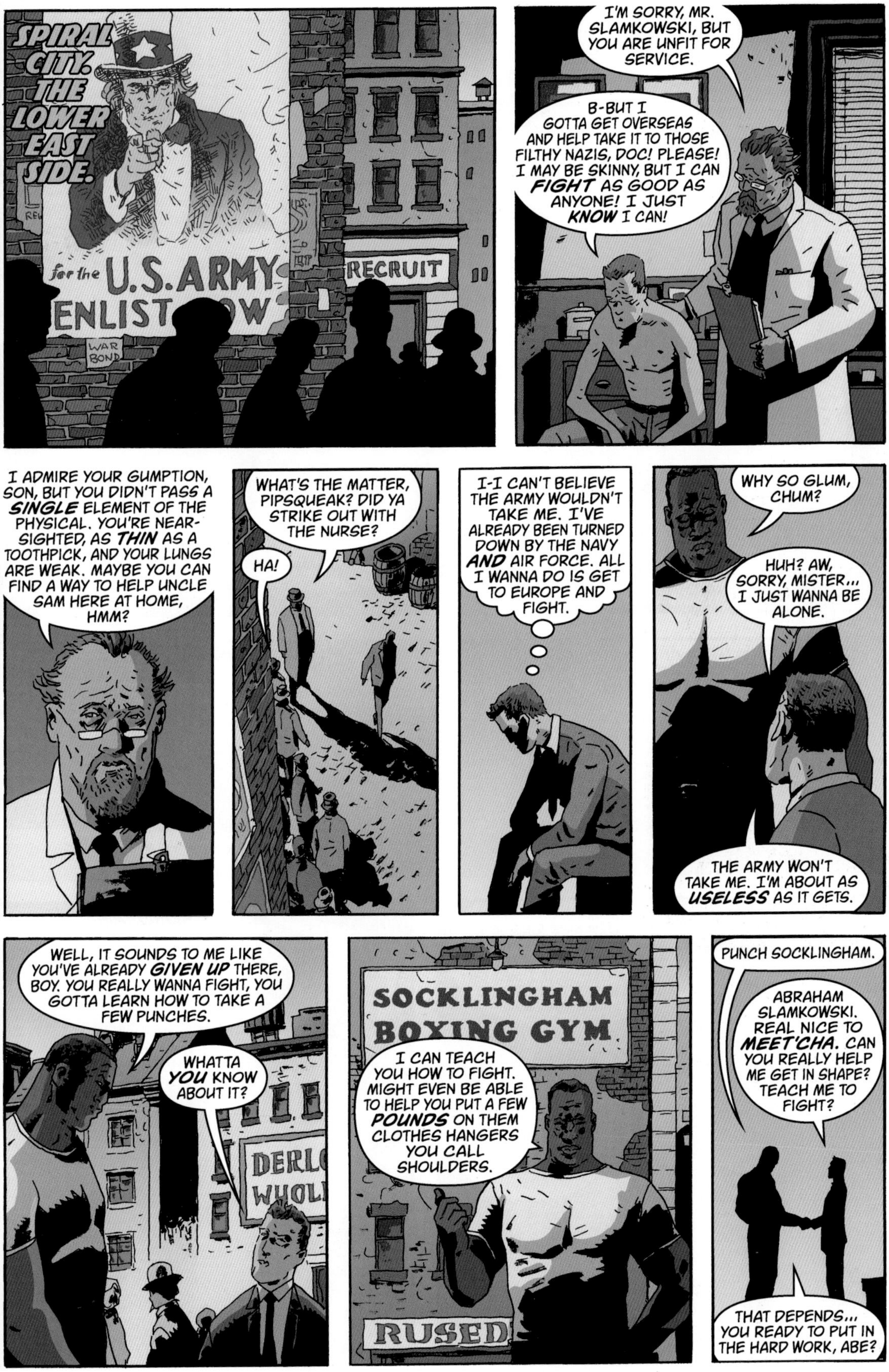
SPIRAL CITY. THE LOWER EAST SIDE.
for the U.S. ARMY ENLIST NOW
WAR BOND
RECRUIT
I'M SORRY, MR. SLAMKOWSKI, BUT YOU ARE UNFIT FOR SERVICE.
B-BUT I GOTTA GET OVERSEAS AND HELP TAKE IT TO THOSE FILTHY NAZIS, DOC! PLEASE! I MAY BE SKINNY, BUT I CAN FIGHT AS GOOD AS ANYONE! I JUST KNOW I CAN!
I ADMIRE YOUR GUMPTION, SON, BUT YOU DIDN'T PASS A SINGLE ELEMENT OF THE PHYSICAL. YOU'RE NEAR-SIGHTED, AS THIN AS A TOOTHPICK, AND YOUR LUNGS ARE WEAK. MAYBE YOU CAN FIND A WAY TO HELP UNCLE SAM HERE AT HOME, HMM?
WHAT'S THE MATTER, PIPSQUEAK? DID YA STRIKE OUT WITH THE NURSE?
HA!
I-I CAN'T BELIEVE THE ARMY WOULDN'T TAKE ME. I'VE ALREADY BEEN TURNED DOWN BY THE NAVY AND AIR FORCE. ALL I WANNA DO IS GET TO EUROPE AND FIGHT.
WHY SO GLUM, CHUM?
HUH? AW, SORRY, MISTER... I JUST WANNA BE ALONE.
THE ARMY WON'T TAKE ME. I'M ABOUT AS USELESS AS IT GETS.
WELL, IT SOUNDS TO ME LIKE YOU'VE ALREADY GIVEN UP THERE, BOY. YOU REALLY WANNA FIGHT, YOU GOTTA LEARN HOW TO TAKE A FEW PUNCHES.
WHATTA YOU KNOW ABOUT IT?
SOCKLINGHAM BOXING GYM
I CAN TEACH YOU HOW TO FIGHT. MIGHT EVEN BE ABLE TO HELP YOU PUT A FEW POUNDS ON THEM CLOTHES HANGERS YOU CALL SHOULDERS.
RUSED
PUNCH SOCKLINGHAM.
ABRAHAM SLAMKOWSKI. REAL NICE TO MEET'CHA. CAN YOU REALLY HELP ME GET IN SHAPE? TEACH ME TO FIGHT?
THAT DEPENDS... YOU READY TO PUT IN THE HARD WORK, ABE?

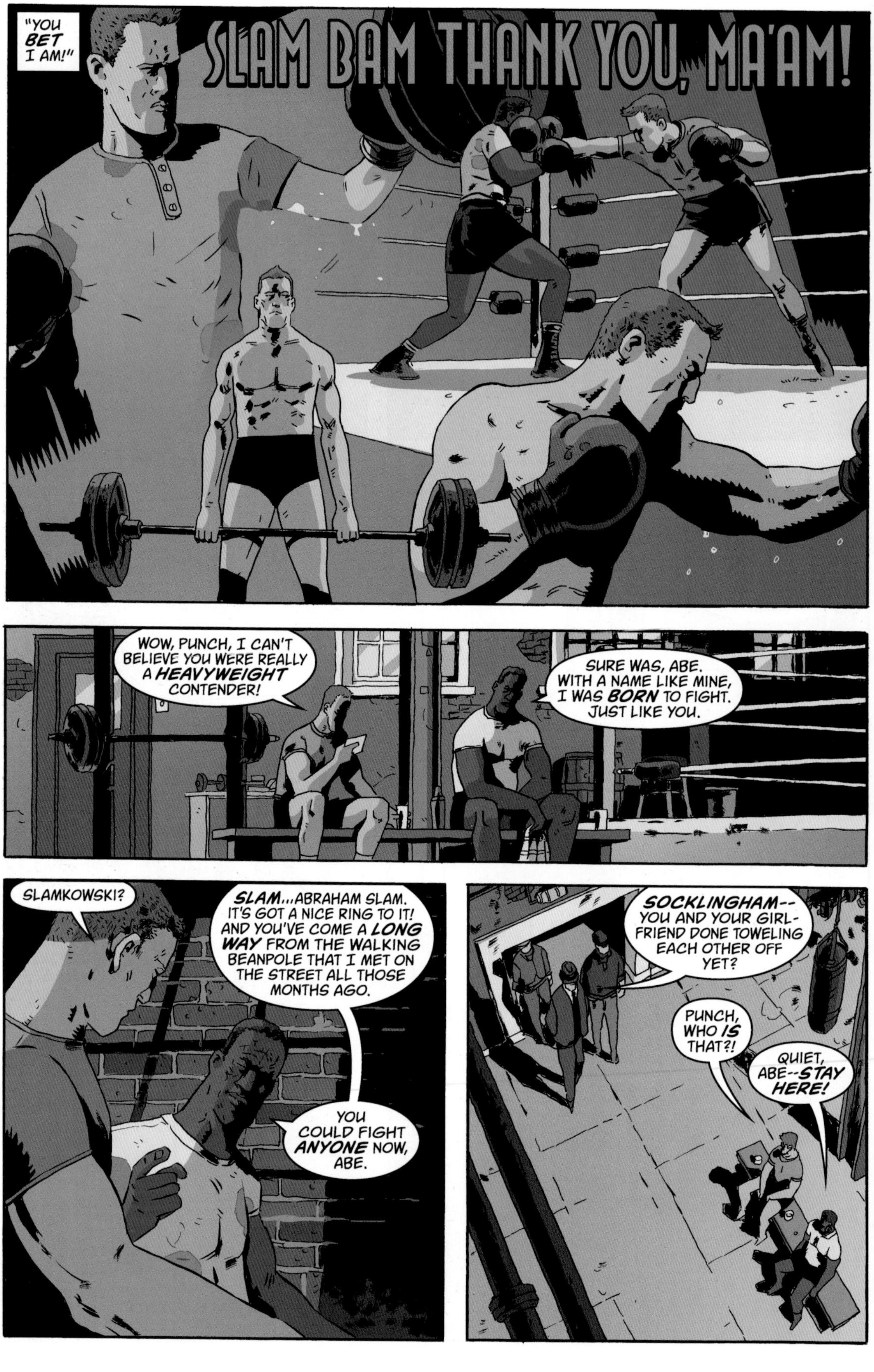
"YOU BET I AM!"
SLAM BAM THANK YOU, MA'AM!
WOW, PUNCH, I CAN'T BELIEVE YOU WERE REALLY A HEAVYWEIGHT CONTENDER!
SURE WAS, ABE. WITH A NAME LIKE MINE, I WAS BORN TO FIGHT. JUST LIKE YOU.
SLAMKOWSKI?
SLAM...ABRAHAM SLAM. IT'S GOT A NICE RING TO IT! AND YOU'VE COME A LONG WAY FROM THE WALKING BEANPOLE THAT I MET ON THE STREET ALL THOSE MONTHS AGO.
YOU COULD FIGHT ANYONE NOW, ABE.
SOCKLINGHAM--YOU AND YOUR GIRL-FRIEND DONE TOWELING EACH OTHER OFF YET?
PUNCH, WHO IS THAT?!
QUIET, ABE--STAY HERE!

TELL MR. OLSEN I'LL HAVE THE MONEY NEXT *FRIDAY*. I GUARANTEE IT!

YOUR WORD IS *MUD* AROUND HERE, SOCKLING-HAM!

PUNCH?

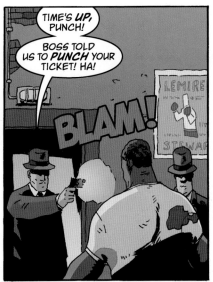

TIME'S *UP*, PUNCH!

BOSS TOLD US TO *PUNCH* YOUR TICKET! HA!

BLAM!

PUNCH!!!

AND WHAT DO WE HAVE *HERE*? PUNCH'S LITTLE GIRLFRIEND GOT SOMETHING TO SAY?

CAN'T LEAVE NO WITNESSES, OTTER!

YOU ROTTEN *BASTARDS*!

THWAP!

YOU'LL NEVER GET AWAY WITH THIS!

POW!

HOLD ON, PUNCH! I'LL CALL AN AMBULANCE!

T-TOO LATE, ABE--BUT NOT FOR YOU...

WH-WHATTA YOU MEAN?

YOU GOT MORE *HEART* THAN ANYONE I'VE EVER SEEN, KID. NEVER STOP...N-NEVER STOP FIGHTING...

PUNCH IS RIGHT...MAYBE I MISSED OUT ON THE FIGHT OVERSEAS, BUT THIS JUST PROVES THERE'S STILL PLENTY I CAN DO BACK HERE AT *HOME*.

I'LL USE MY TRAINING TO TRACK DOWN THIS NEFARIOUS *MR. OLSEN* AND ALL THE OTHER THUGS LIKE HIM THAT ARE TAKING OVER SPIRAL CITY...

...BUT NOT AS *ABE SLAMKOWSKI*. NO, CRIMINALS AND NO-GOODERS WILL COME TO FEAR ME BY *ANOTHER* NAME...

ABRAHAM SLAM!

YO! EARTH TO ABE!

HUH?

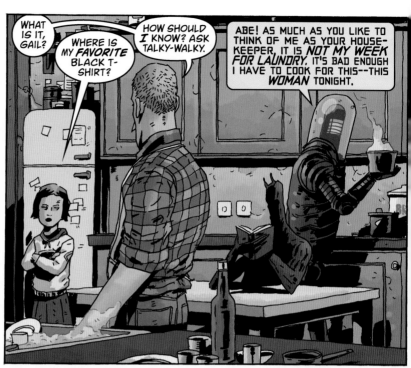

WHAT IS IT, GAIL?

WHERE IS MY *FAVORITE* BLACK T-SHIRT?

HOW SHOULD *I* KNOW? ASK TALKY-WALKY.

ABE! AS MUCH AS YOU LIKE TO THINK OF ME AS YOUR HOUSE-KEEPER, IT IS *NOT MY WEEK FOR LAUNDRY.* IT'S BAD ENOUGH I HAVE TO COOK FOR THIS--THIS *WOMAN* TONIGHT.

SHE'S NOT JUST SOME WOMAN, TALKY--THIS IS *TAMMY TRUEHEART* WE'RE TALKING ABOUT...ABE'S MAIN SQUEEZE. HIS SWEETHEART. SHE MIGHT EVEN BE *THE ONE*, RIGHT, ABRAHAM?

I MEAN, NONE OF US HAVE EVER BROUGHT ANYONE HOME TO MEET THE FAM BEFORE. THIS IS *BIG!*

ARE YOU TWO GOING STEADY, ABE? DID YOU GIVE HER YOUR HOMECOMING PIN? ARE YOU GOING TO PROM TOGETHER?

I'M GLAD YOU FIND THIS *AMUSING*, BARBIE.

THE WAR OF THE WORLD

THE WAR OF THE WORLDS

HG WELLS

OH, I DO. I REALLY, *REALLY* DO.

YOUR T-SHIRT IS PROBABLY IN THE PILE IN THE BASEMENT, GAIL. YOU'LL HAVE TO CLEAN IT YOURSELF. AND REMEMBER, DINNER IS AT SIX! *DO NOT BE LATE!*

WHATEVER...

...LIKE I CARE WHAT *TITTY TAMMY HOSE BAG* THINKS.

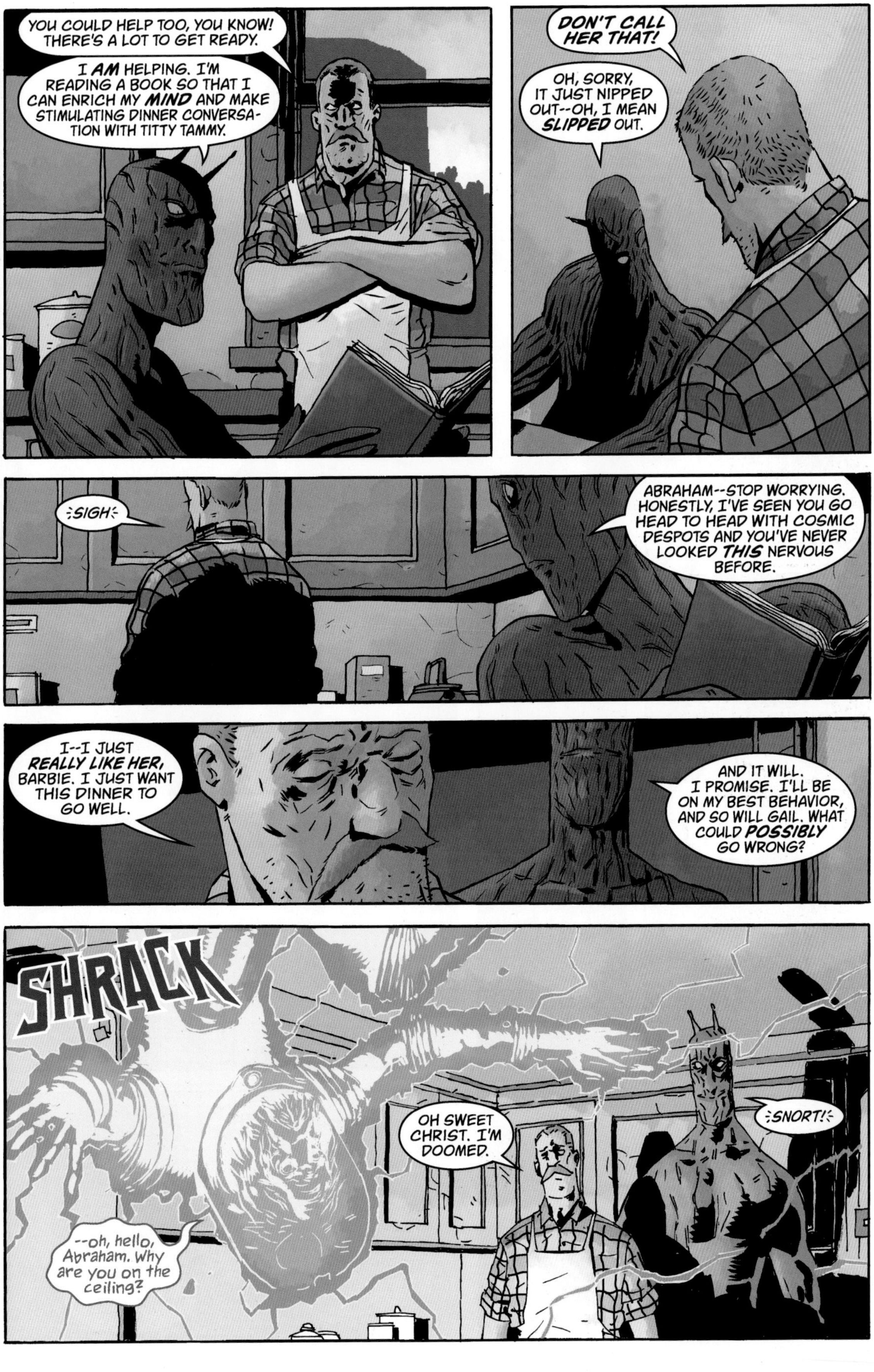
YOU COULD HELP TOO, YOU KNOW! THERE'S A LOT TO GET READY.
I AM HELPING. I'M READING A BOOK SO THAT I CAN ENRICH MY MIND AND MAKE STIMULATING DINNER CONVERSATION WITH TITTY TAMMY.
DON'T CALL HER THAT!
OH, SORRY, IT JUST NIPPED OUT--OH, I MEAN SLIPPED OUT.
SIGH
ABRAHAM--STOP WORRYING. HONESTLY, I'VE SEEN YOU GO HEAD TO HEAD WITH COSMIC DESPOTS AND YOU'VE NEVER LOOKED THIS NERVOUS BEFORE.
I--I JUST REALLY LIKE HER, BARBIE. I JUST WANT THIS DINNER TO GO WELL.
AND IT WILL. I PROMISE. I'LL BE ON MY BEST BEHAVIOR, AND SO WILL GAIL. WHAT COULD POSSIBLY GO WRONG?
SHRACK
OH SWEET CHRIST. I'M DOOMED.
SNORT!
--oh, hello, Abraham. Why are you on the ceiling?

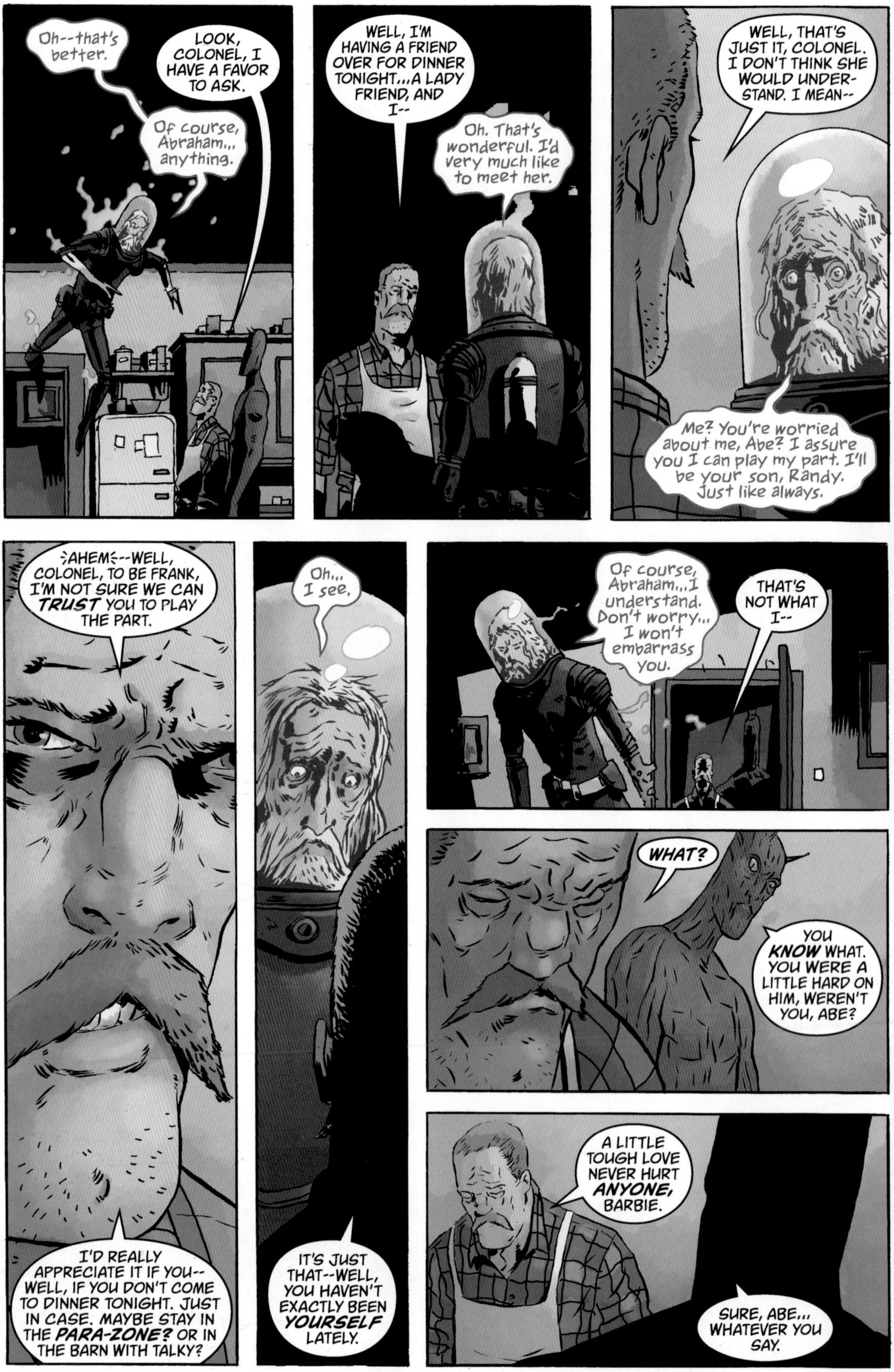
Oh--that's better.
LOOK, COLONEL, I HAVE A FAVOR TO ASK.
Of course, Abraham... anything.
WELL, I'M HAVING A FRIEND OVER FOR DINNER TONIGHT... A LADY FRIEND, AND I--
Oh. That's wonderful. I'd very much like to meet her.
WELL, THAT'S JUST IT, COLONEL. I DON'T THINK SHE WOULD UNDERSTAND. I MEAN--
Me? You're worried about me, Abe? I assure you I can play my part. I'll be your son, Randy. Just like always.
AHEM--WELL, COLONEL, TO BE FRANK, I'M NOT SURE WE CAN ***TRUST*** YOU TO PLAY THE PART.
I'D REALLY APPRECIATE IT IF YOU--WELL, IF YOU DON'T COME TO DINNER TONIGHT. JUST IN CASE. MAYBE STAY IN THE ***PARA-ZONE?*** OR IN THE BARN WITH TALKY?
Oh... I see.
IT'S JUST THAT--WELL, YOU HAVEN'T EXACTLY BEEN ***YOURSELF*** LATELY.
Of course, Abraham... I understand. Don't worry... I won't embarrass you.
THAT'S NOT WHAT I--
WHAT?
YOU ***KNOW*** WHAT. YOU WERE A LITTLE HARD ON HIM, WEREN'T YOU, ABE?
A LITTLE TOUGH LOVE NEVER HURT ***ANYONE,*** BARBIE.
SURE, ABE... WHATEVER YOU SAY.

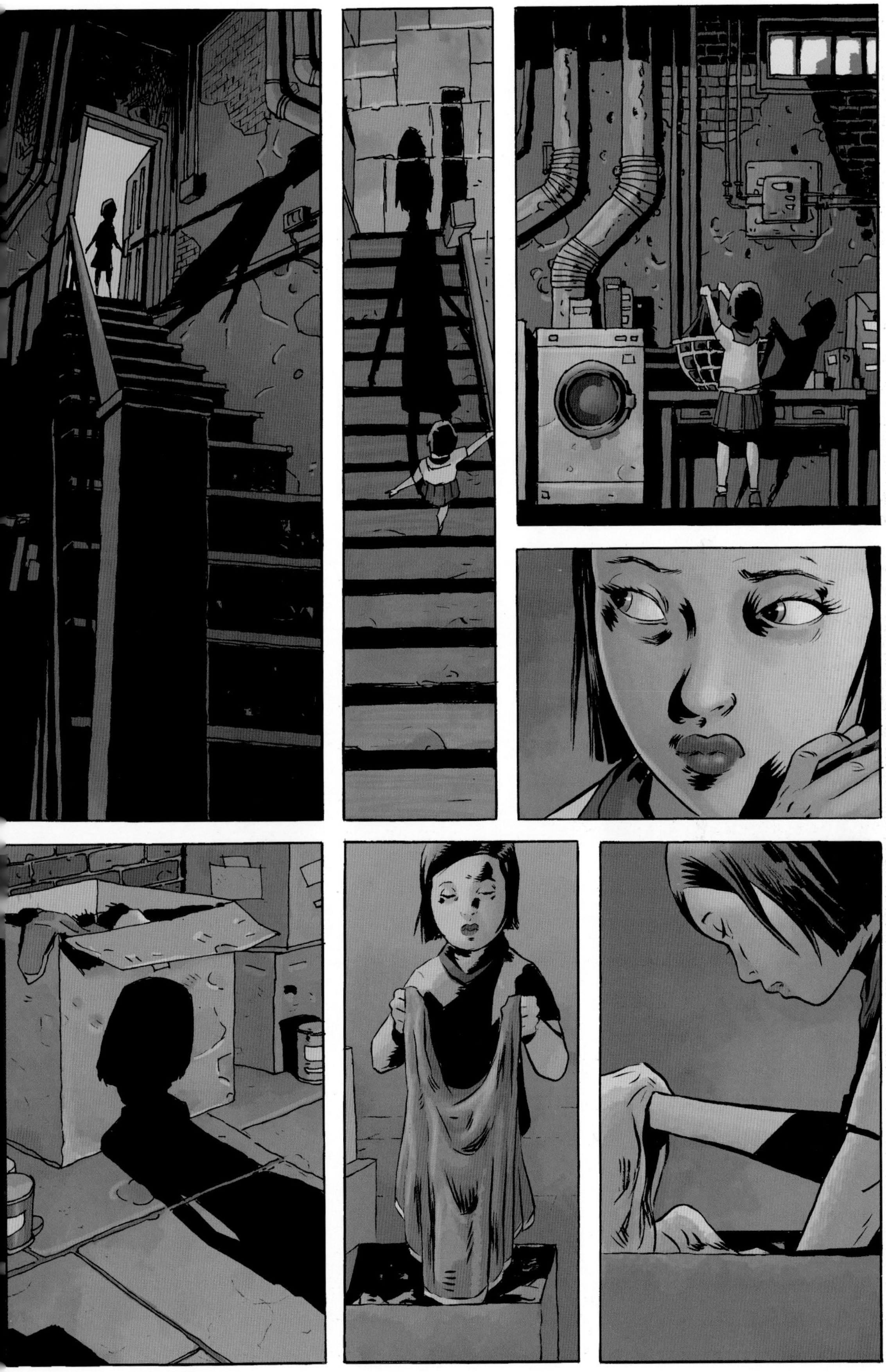

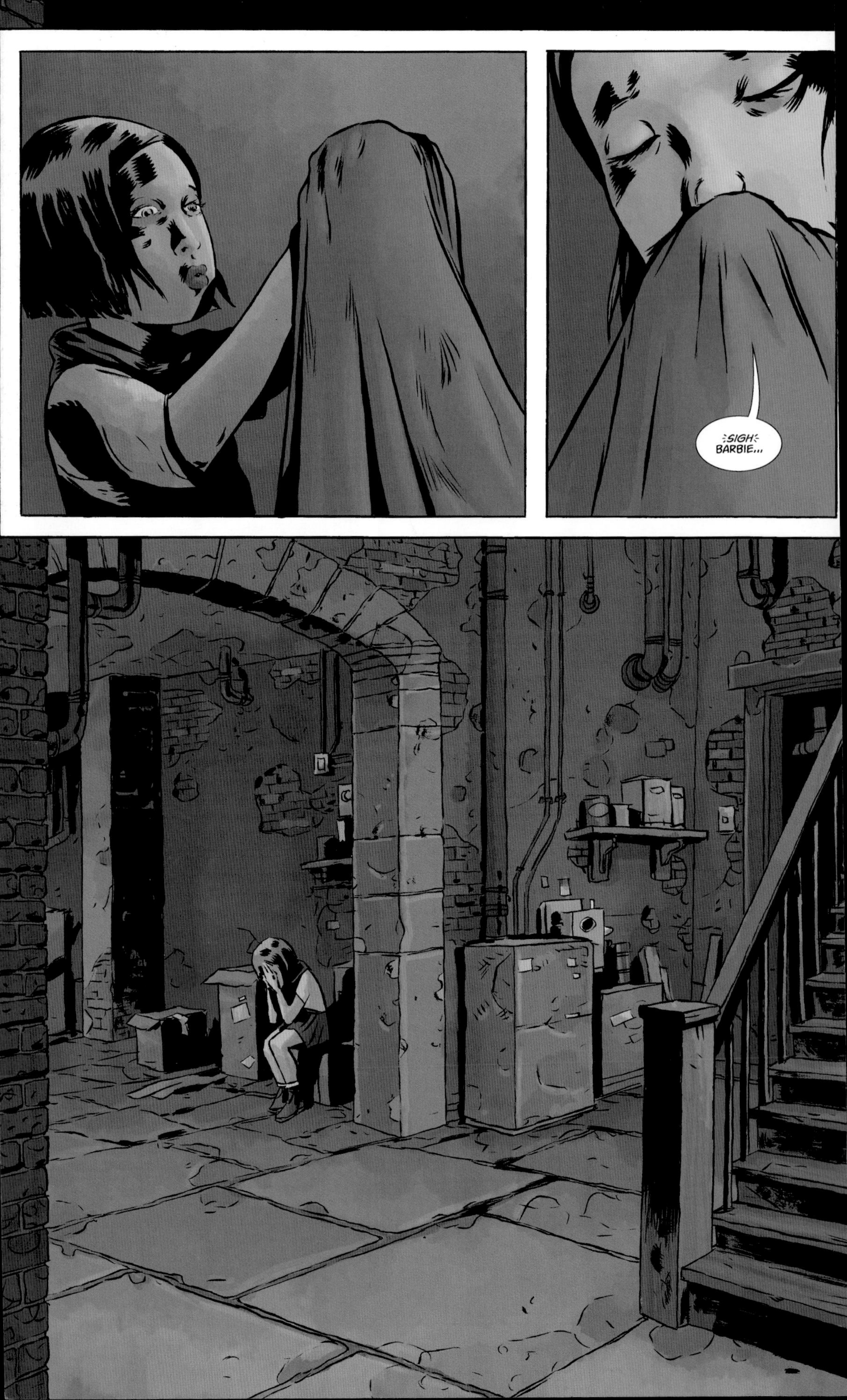
SIGH BARBIE...

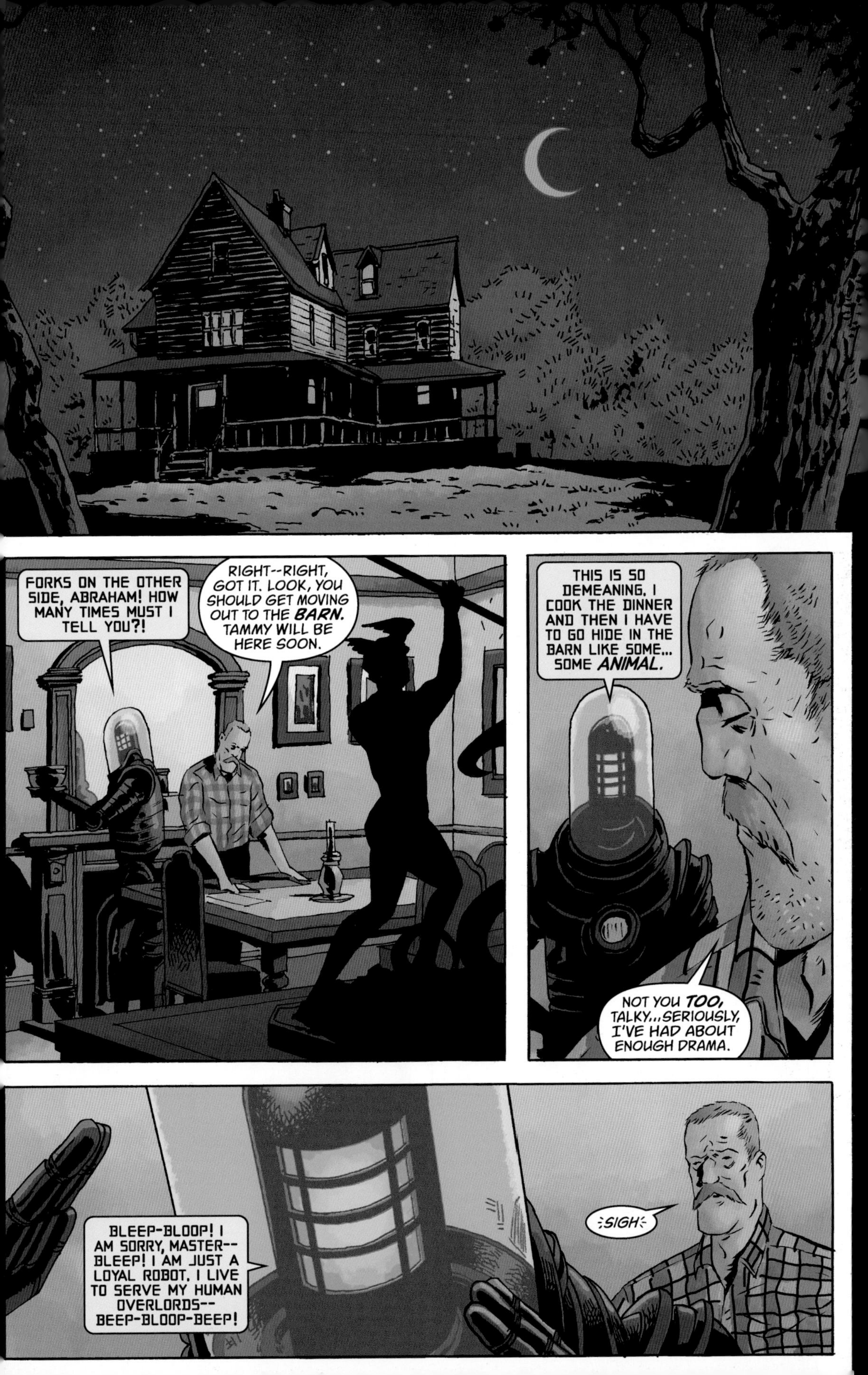
FORKS ON THE OTHER SIDE, ABRAHAM! HOW MANY TIMES MUST I TELL YOU?!
RIGHT--RIGHT, GOT IT. LOOK, YOU SHOULD GET MOVING OUT TO THE BARN. TAMMY WILL BE HERE SOON.
THIS IS SO DEMEANING. I COOK THE DINNER AND THEN I HAVE TO GO HIDE IN THE BARN LIKE SOME... SOME ANIMAL.
NOT YOU TOO, TALKY...SERIOUSLY, I'VE HAD ABOUT ENOUGH DRAMA.
BLEEP-BLOOP! I AM SORRY, MASTER-- BLEEP! I AM JUST A LOYAL ROBOT. I LIVE TO SERVE MY HUMAN OVERLORDS-- BEEP-BLOOP-BEEP!
SIGH

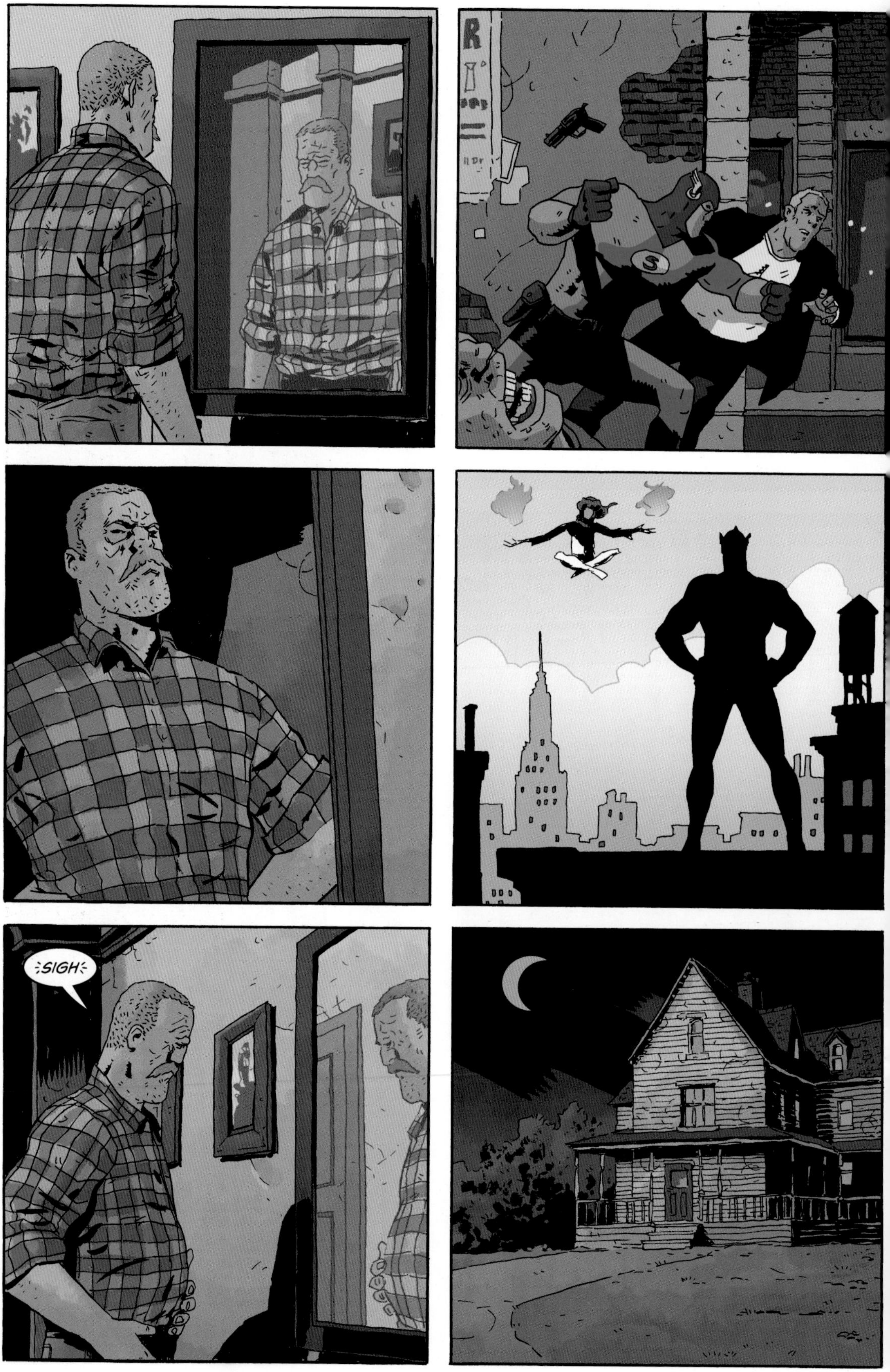
SIGH

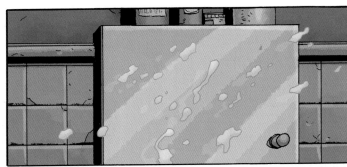

SHRACK

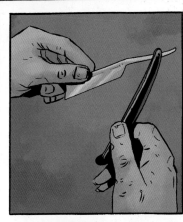

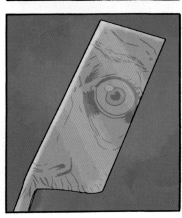

KNOCK
KNOCK

HEY THERE, BEAUTIFUL.

HEY, YOU OLD CHARMER. I BROUGHT PIE. APPLE.

YOU ARE A GOOD ONE, TAMMY TRUEHEART. COME IN.

RELAX, ABE. *I'M* THE ONE WHO'S SUPPOSED TO BE NERVOUS.

HEH. SORRY.

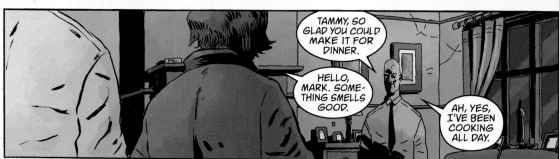

TAMMY, SO GLAD YOU COULD MAKE IT FOR DINNER.

HELLO, MARK. SOMETHING SMELLS GOOD.

AH, YES, I'VE BEEN COOKING ALL DAY.

≥AHEM≤ SO, UH, HAVE YOU SEEN GAIL, MARK? SHE SHOULD BE DOWN HERE BY NOW.

I THINK SHE WAS JUST--

I'M RIGHT *HERE*, GRANDPA.

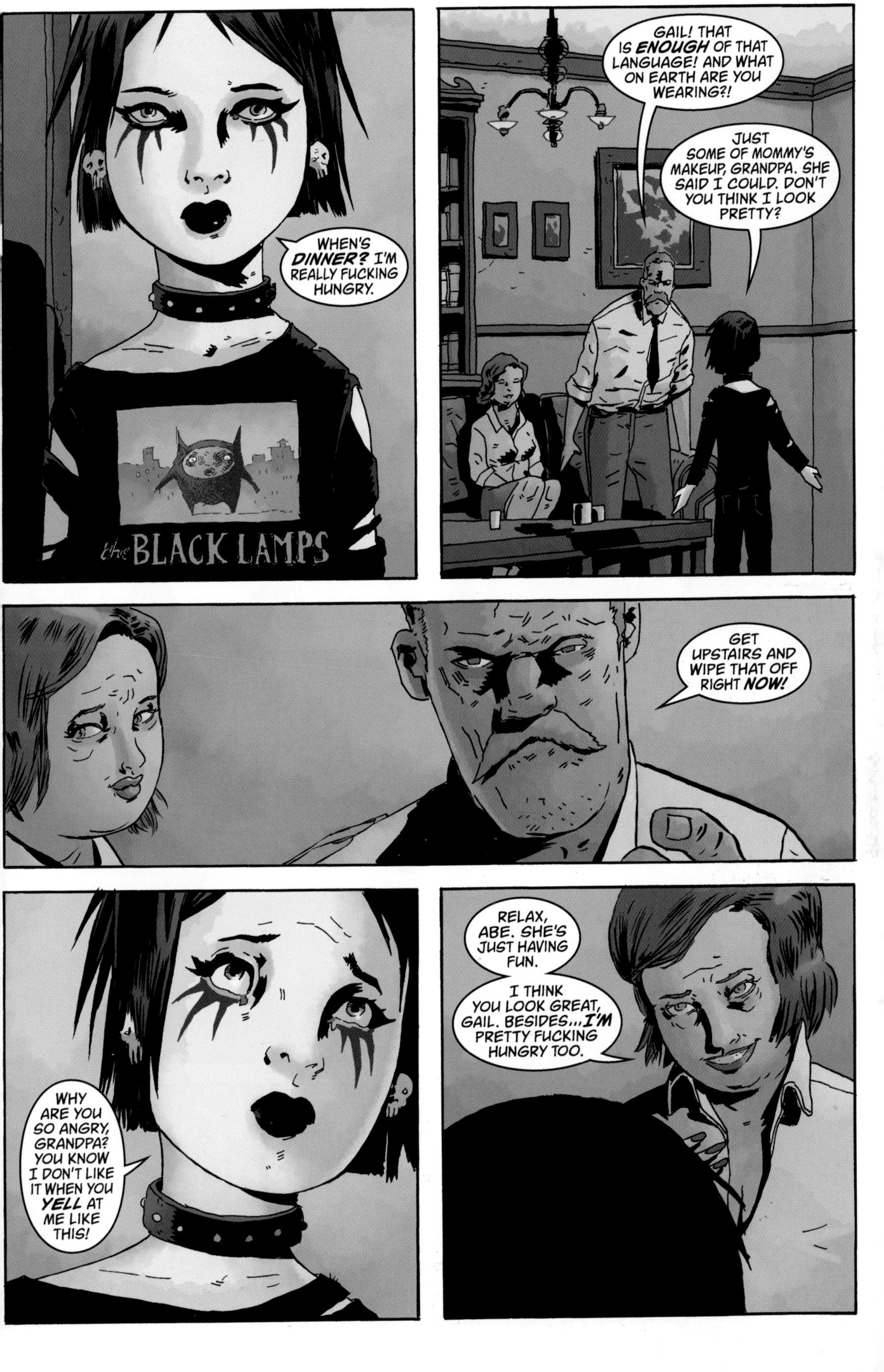
WHEN'S **DINNER?** I'M REALLY FUCKING HUNGRY.
the BLACK LAMPS
GAIL! THAT IS **ENOUGH** OF THAT LANGUAGE! AND WHAT ON EARTH ARE YOU WEARING?!
JUST SOME OF MOMMY'S MAKEUP, GRANDPA. SHE SAID I COULD. DON'T YOU THINK I LOOK PRETTY?
GET UPSTAIRS AND WIPE THAT OFF RIGHT **NOW!**
WHY ARE YOU SO ANGRY, GRANDPA? YOU KNOW I DON'T LIKE IT WHEN YOU **YELL** AT ME LIKE THIS!
RELAX, ABE. SHE'S JUST HAVING FUN.
I THINK YOU LOOK GREAT, GAIL. BESIDES... **I'M** PRETTY FUCKING HUNGRY TOO.

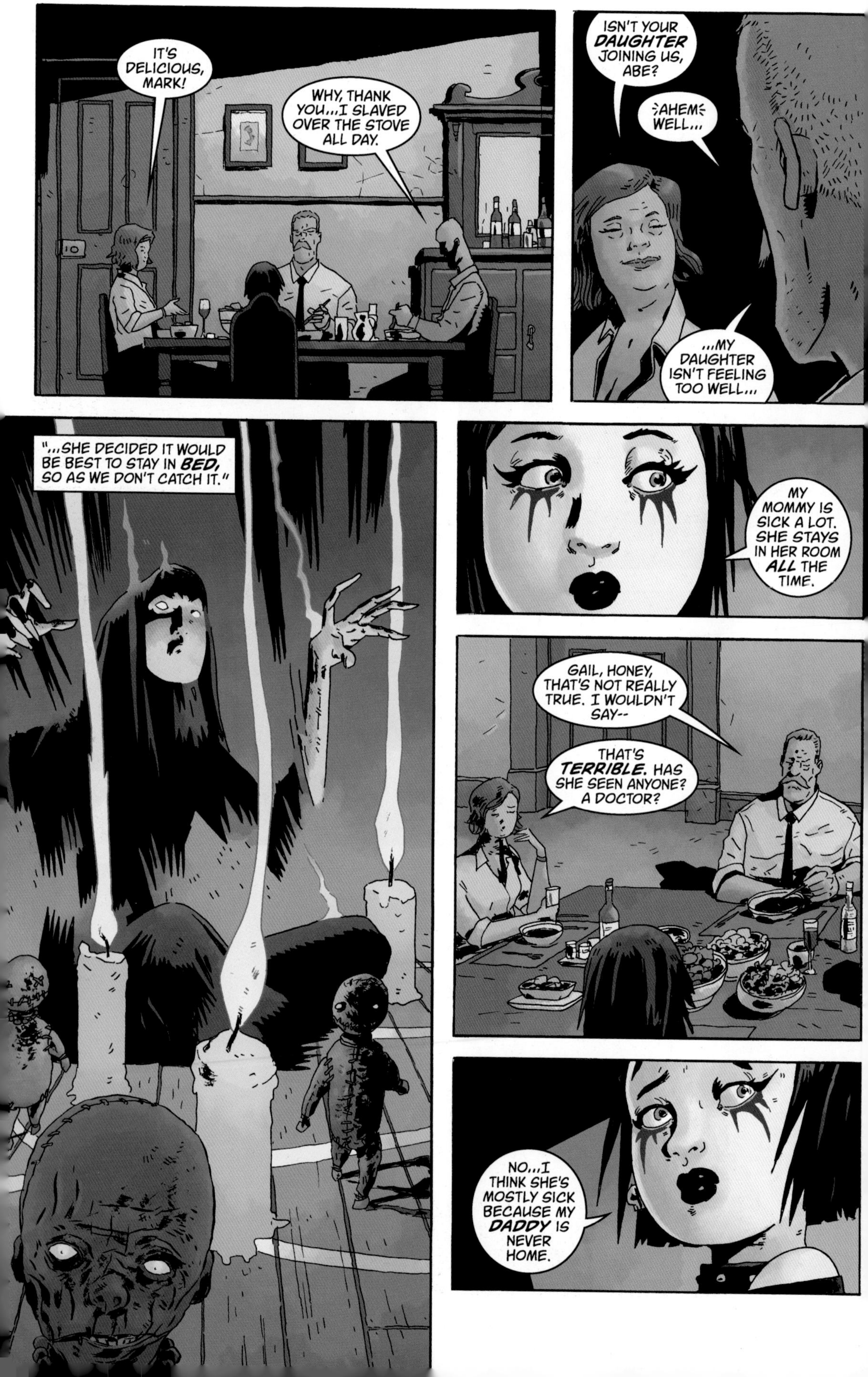
IT'S DELICIOUS, MARK!
WHY, THANK YOU...I SLAVED OVER THE STOVE ALL DAY.
ISN'T YOUR DAUGHTER JOINING US, ABE?
AHEM WELL...
...MY DAUGHTER ISN'T FEELING TOO WELL...
"...SHE DECIDED IT WOULD BE BEST TO STAY IN BED, SO AS WE DON'T CATCH IT."
MY MOMMY IS SICK A LOT. SHE STAYS IN HER ROOM ALL THE TIME.
GAIL, HONEY, THAT'S NOT REALLY TRUE. I WOULDN'T SAY--
THAT'S TERRIBLE. HAS SHE SEEN ANYONE? A DOCTOR?
NO...I THINK SHE'S MOSTLY SICK BECAUSE MY DADDY IS NEVER HOME.

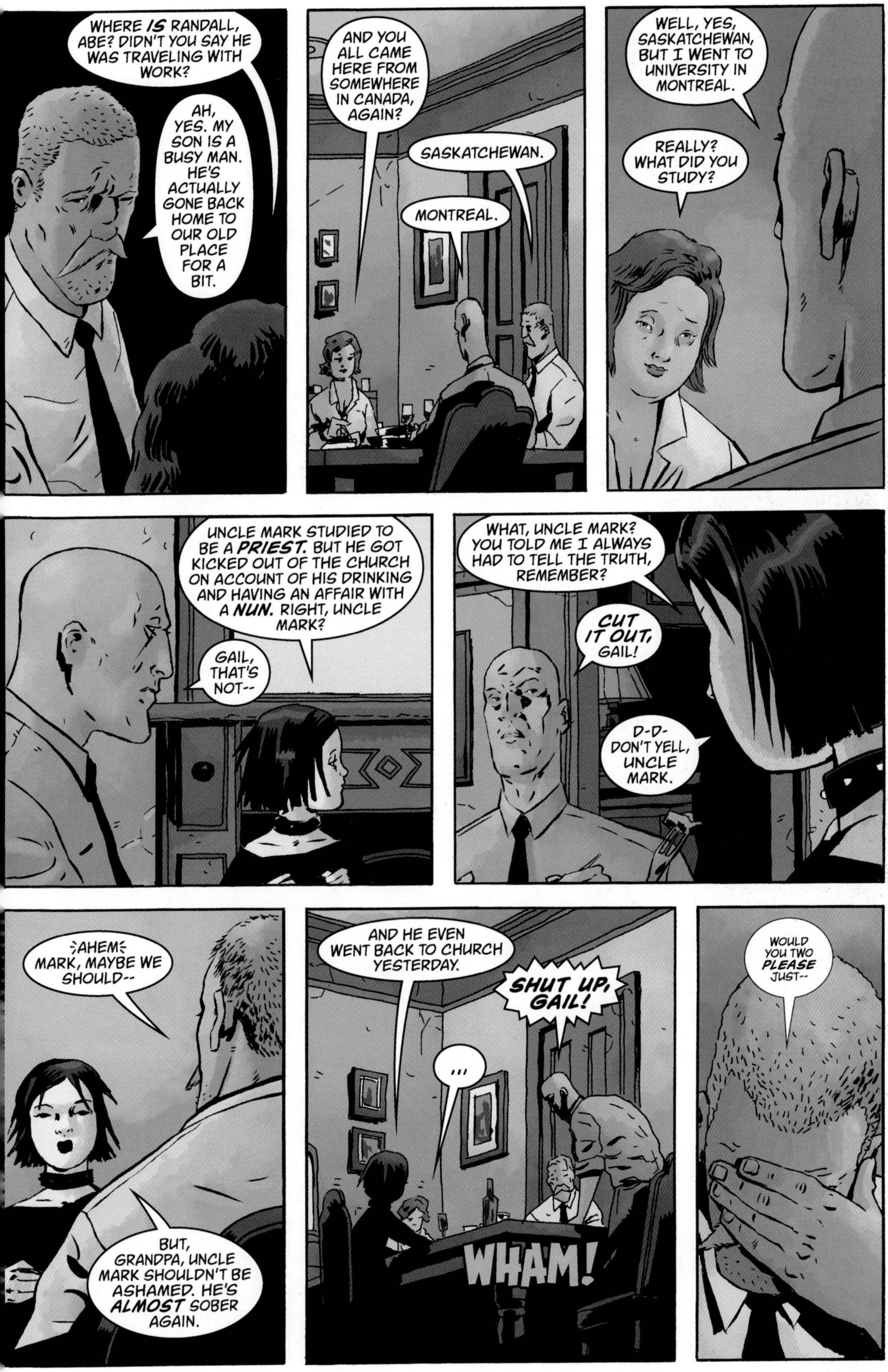

WHERE IS RANDALL, ABE? DIDN'T YOU SAY HE WAS TRAVELING WITH WORK?
AH, YES. MY SON IS A BUSY MAN. HE'S ACTUALLY GONE BACK HOME TO OUR OLD PLACE FOR A BIT.
AND YOU ALL CAME HERE FROM SOMEWHERE IN CANADA, AGAIN?
SASKATCHEWAN.
MONTREAL.
WELL, YES, SASKATCHEWAN, BUT I WENT TO UNIVERSITY IN MONTREAL.
REALLY? WHAT DID YOU STUDY?
UNCLE MARK STUDIED TO BE A PRIEST. BUT HE GOT KICKED OUT OF THE CHURCH ON ACCOUNT OF HIS DRINKING AND HAVING AN AFFAIR WITH A NUN. RIGHT, UNCLE MARK?
GAIL, THAT'S NOT--
WHAT, UNCLE MARK? YOU TOLD ME I ALWAYS HAD TO TELL THE TRUTH, REMEMBER?
CUT IT OUT, GAIL!
D-D-DON'T YELL, UNCLE MARK.
AHEM MARK, MAYBE WE SHOULD--
BUT, GRANDPA, UNCLE MARK SHOULDN'T BE ASHAMED. HE'S ALMOST SOBER AGAIN.
AND HE EVEN WENT BACK TO CHURCH YESTERDAY.
SHUT UP, GAIL!
...
WHAM!
WOULD YOU TWO PLEASE JUST--

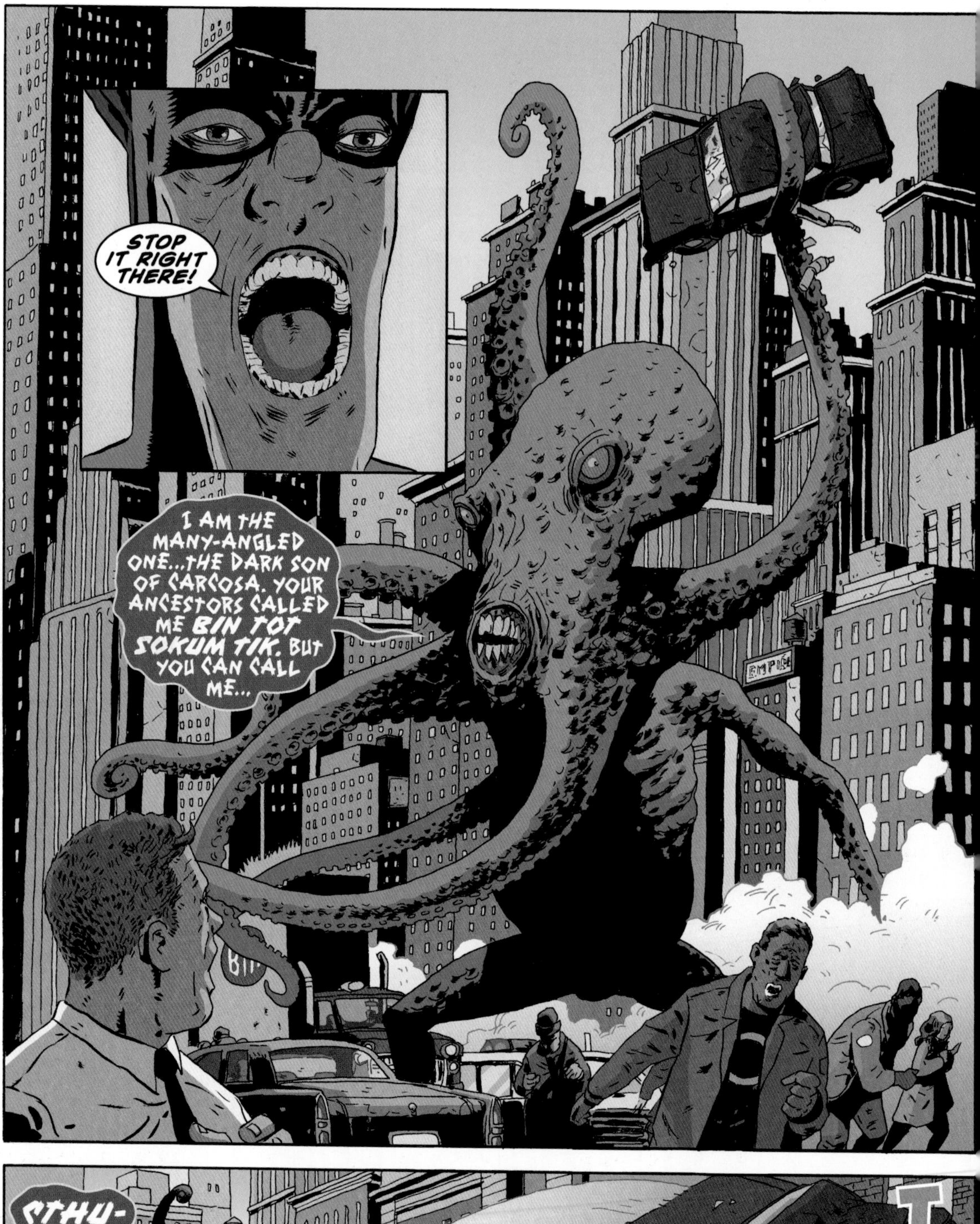
STOP IT RIGHT THERE!
I AM THE MANY-ANGLED ONE...THE DARK SON OF CARCOSA. YOUR ANCESTORS CALLED ME BIN TOT SOKUM TIK. BUT YOU CAN CALL ME...
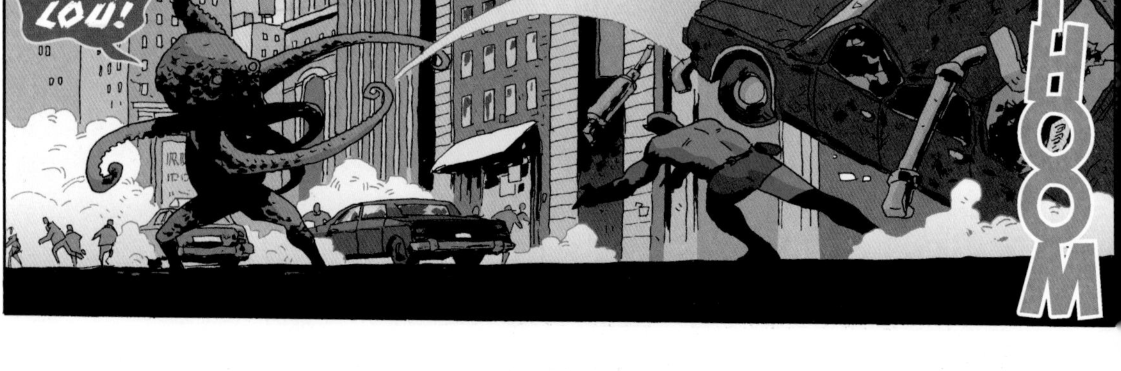
CTHU-LOU!
THOOM

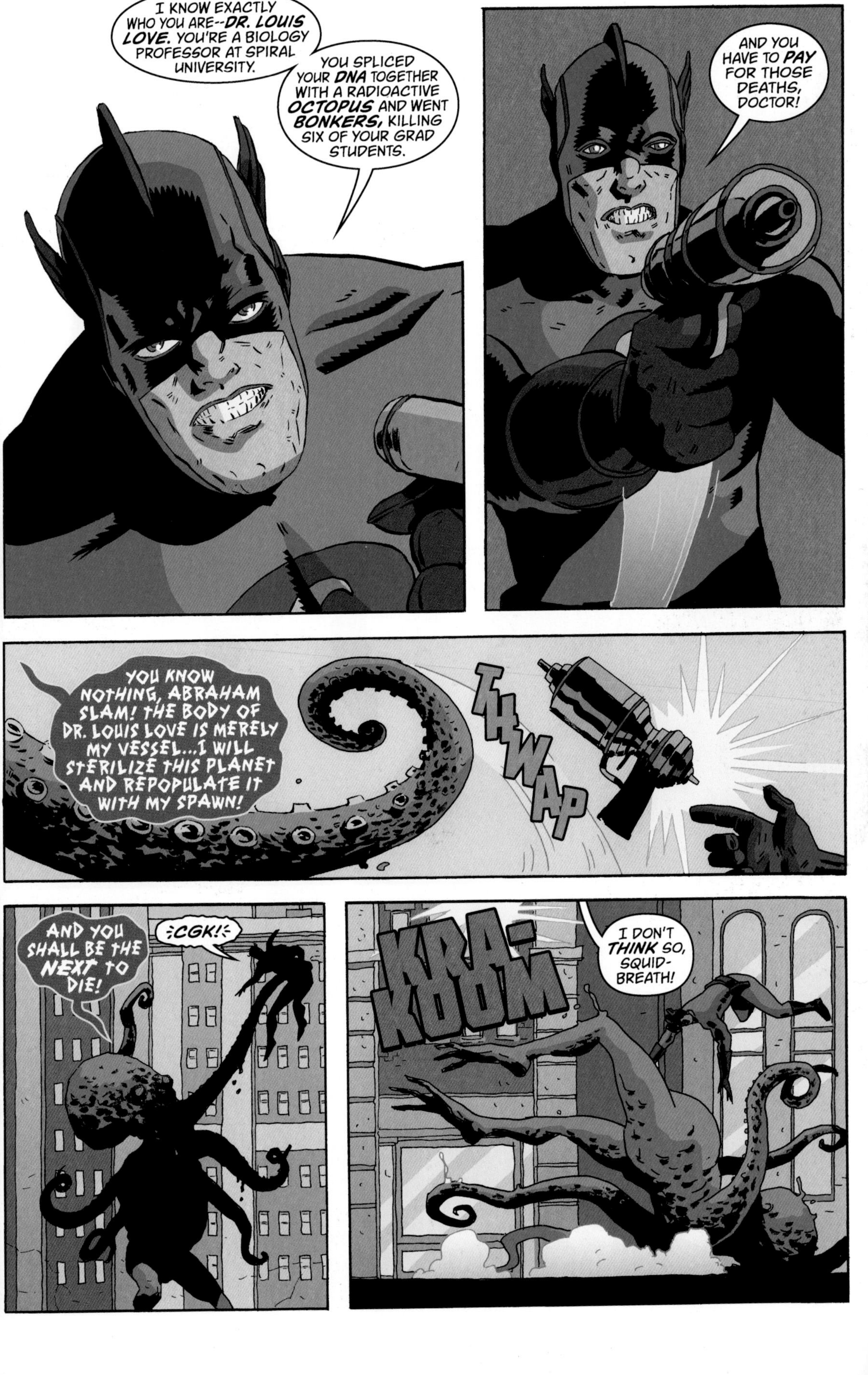

I KNOW EXACTLY WHO YOU ARE--DR. LOUIS LOVE. YOU'RE A BIOLOGY PROFESSOR AT SPIRAL UNIVERSITY.
YOU SPLICED YOUR DNA TOGETHER WITH A RADIOACTIVE OCTOPUS AND WENT BONKERS, KILLING SIX OF YOUR GRAD STUDENTS.
AND YOU HAVE TO PAY FOR THOSE DEATHS, DOCTOR!
YOU KNOW NOTHING, ABRAHAM SLAM! THE BODY OF DR. LOUIS LOVE IS MERELY MY VESSEL...I WILL STERILIZE THIS PLANET AND REPOPULATE IT WITH MY SPAWN!
THWAP
AND YOU SHALL BE THE NEXT TO DIE!
CGK!
KRA-KOOM
I DON'T THINK SO, SQUID-BREATH!

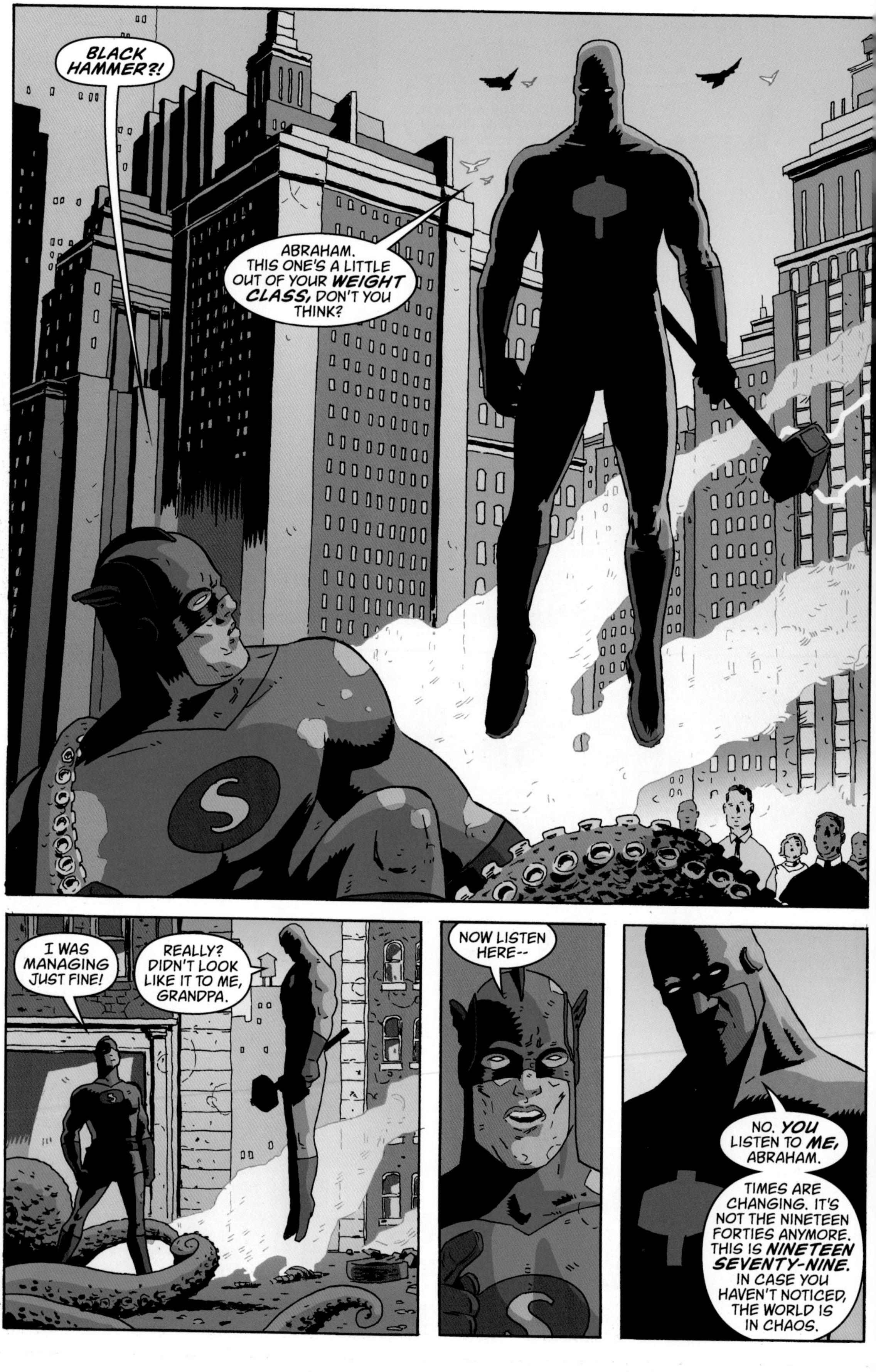
BLACK HAMMER?!
ABRAHAM. THIS ONE'S A LITTLE OUT OF YOUR WEIGHT CLASS, DON'T YOU THINK?
I WAS MANAGING JUST FINE!
REALLY? DIDN'T LOOK LIKE IT TO ME, GRANDPA.
NOW LISTEN HERE--
NO. YOU LISTEN TO ME, ABRAHAM.
TIMES ARE CHANGING. IT'S NOT THE NINETEEN FORTIES ANYMORE. THIS IS NINETEEN SEVENTY-NINE. IN CASE YOU HAVEN'T NOTICED, THE WORLD IS IN CHAOS.

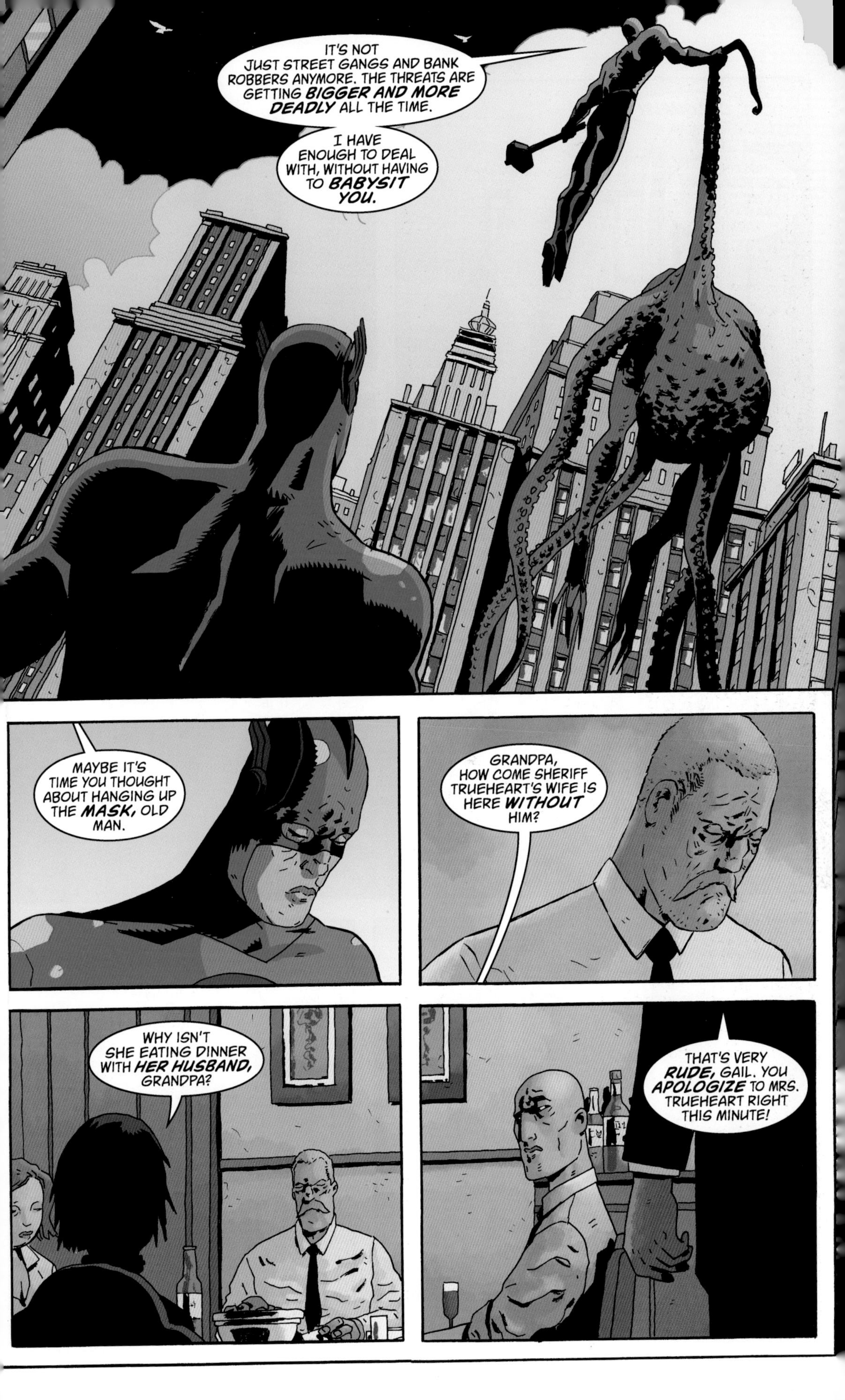
IT'S NOT JUST STREET GANGS AND BANK ROBBERS ANYMORE. THE THREATS ARE GETTING BIGGER AND MORE DEADLY ALL THE TIME.
I HAVE ENOUGH TO DEAL WITH, WITHOUT HAVING TO BABYSIT YOU.
MAYBE IT'S TIME YOU THOUGHT ABOUT HANGING UP THE MASK, OLD MAN.
GRANDPA, HOW COME SHERIFF TRUEHEART'S WIFE IS HERE WITHOUT HIM?
WHY ISN'T SHE EATING DINNER WITH HER HUSBAND, GRANDPA?
THAT'S VERY RUDE, GAIL. YOU APOLOGIZE TO MRS. TRUEHEART RIGHT THIS MINUTE!

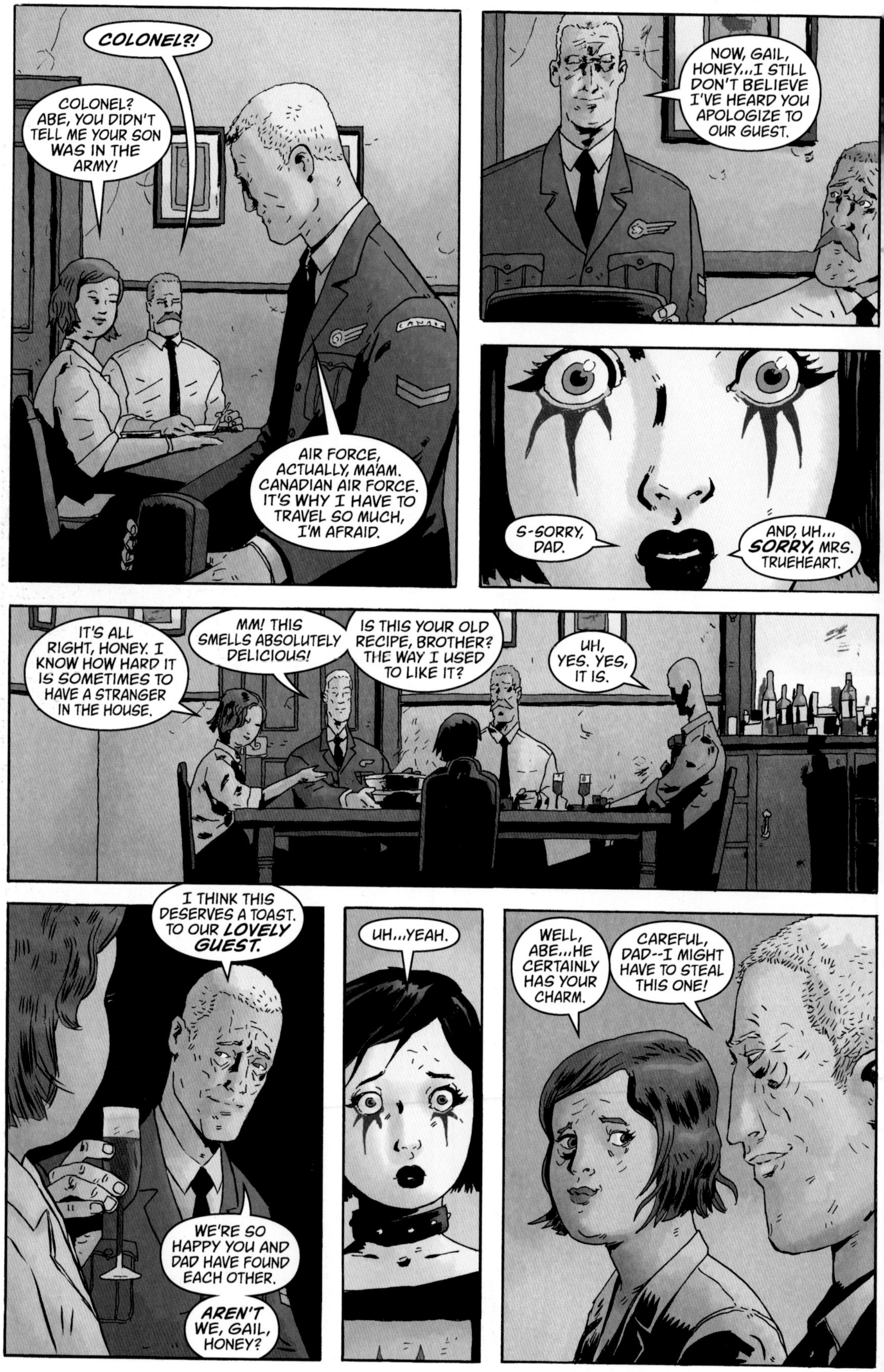

COLONEL?!
COLONEL? ABE, YOU DIDN'T TELL ME YOUR SON WAS IN THE ARMY!
AIR FORCE, ACTUALLY, MA'AM. CANADIAN AIR FORCE. IT'S WHY I HAVE TO TRAVEL SO MUCH, I'M AFRAID.
NOW, GAIL, HONEY...I STILL DON'T BELIEVE I'VE HEARD YOU APOLOGIZE TO OUR GUEST.
S-SORRY, DAD.
AND, UH... SORRY, MRS. TRUEHEART.
IT'S ALL RIGHT, HONEY. I KNOW HOW HARD IT IS SOMETIMES TO HAVE A STRANGER IN THE HOUSE.
MM! THIS SMELLS ABSOLUTELY DELICIOUS!
IS THIS YOUR OLD RECIPE, BROTHER? THE WAY I USED TO LIKE IT?
UH, YES. YES, IT IS.
I THINK THIS DESERVES A TOAST. TO OUR LOVELY GUEST.
WE'RE SO HAPPY YOU AND DAD HAVE FOUND EACH OTHER.
AREN'T WE, GAIL, HONEY?
UH...YEAH.
WELL, ABE...HE CERTAINLY HAS YOUR CHARM.
CAREFUL, DAD--I MIGHT HAVE TO STEAL THIS ONE!

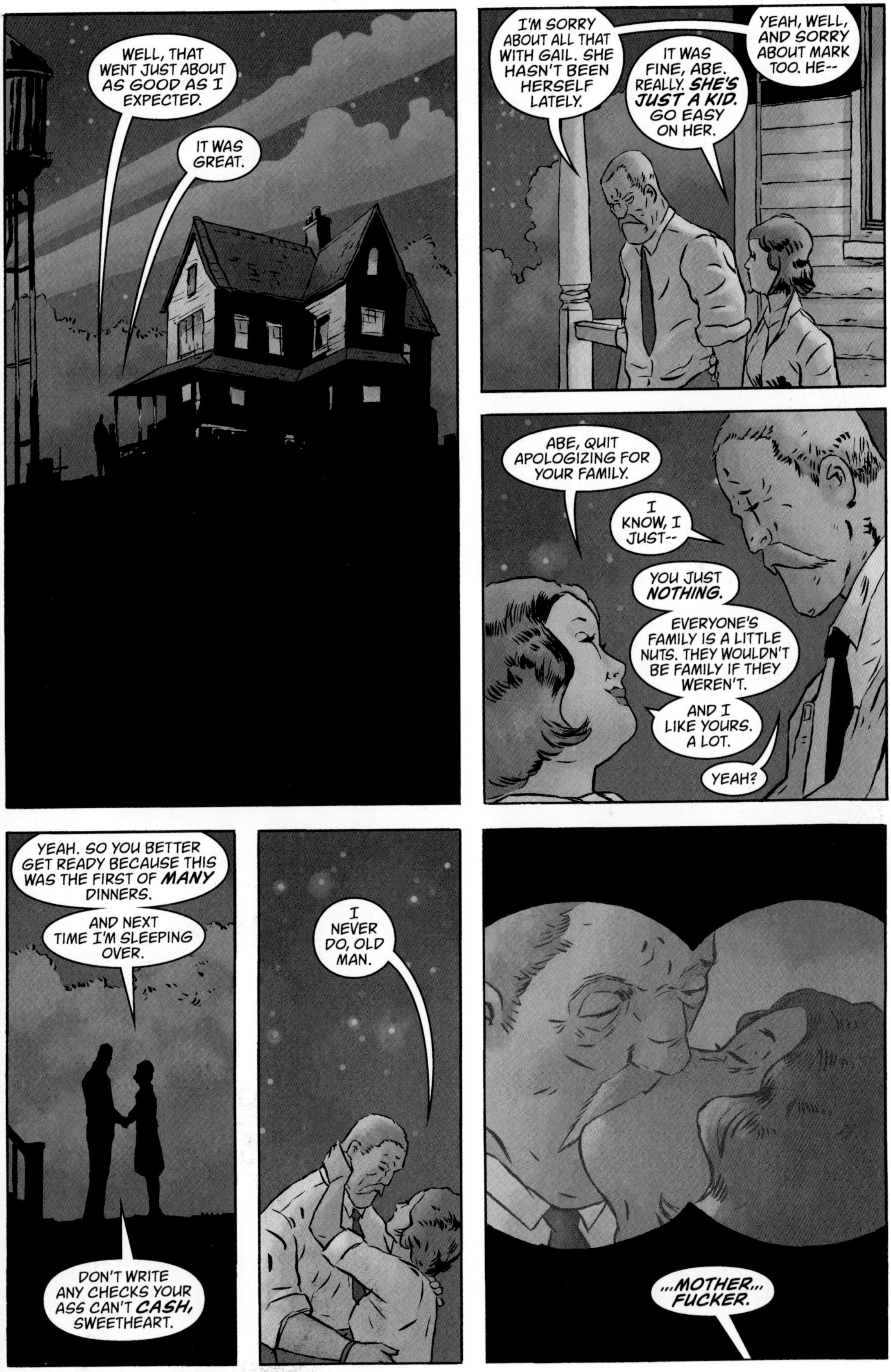
WELL, THAT WENT JUST ABOUT AS GOOD AS I EXPECTED.
IT WAS GREAT.
I'M SORRY ABOUT ALL THAT WITH GAIL. SHE HASN'T BEEN HERSELF LATELY.
IT WAS FINE, ABE. REALLY. SHE'S JUST A KID. GO EASY ON HER.
YEAH, WELL, AND SORRY ABOUT MARK TOO. HE--
ABE, QUIT APOLOGIZING FOR YOUR FAMILY.
I KNOW, I JUST--
YOU JUST NOTHING.
EVERYONE'S FAMILY IS A LITTLE NUTS. THEY WOULDN'T BE FAMILY IF THEY WEREN'T.
AND I LIKE YOURS. A LOT.
YEAH?
YEAH. SO YOU BETTER GET READY BECAUSE THIS WAS THE FIRST OF MANY DINNERS.
AND NEXT TIME I'M SLEEPING OVER.
DON'T WRITE ANY CHECKS YOUR ASS CAN'T CASH, SWEETHEART.
I NEVER DO, OLD MAN.
...MOTHER... FUCKER.

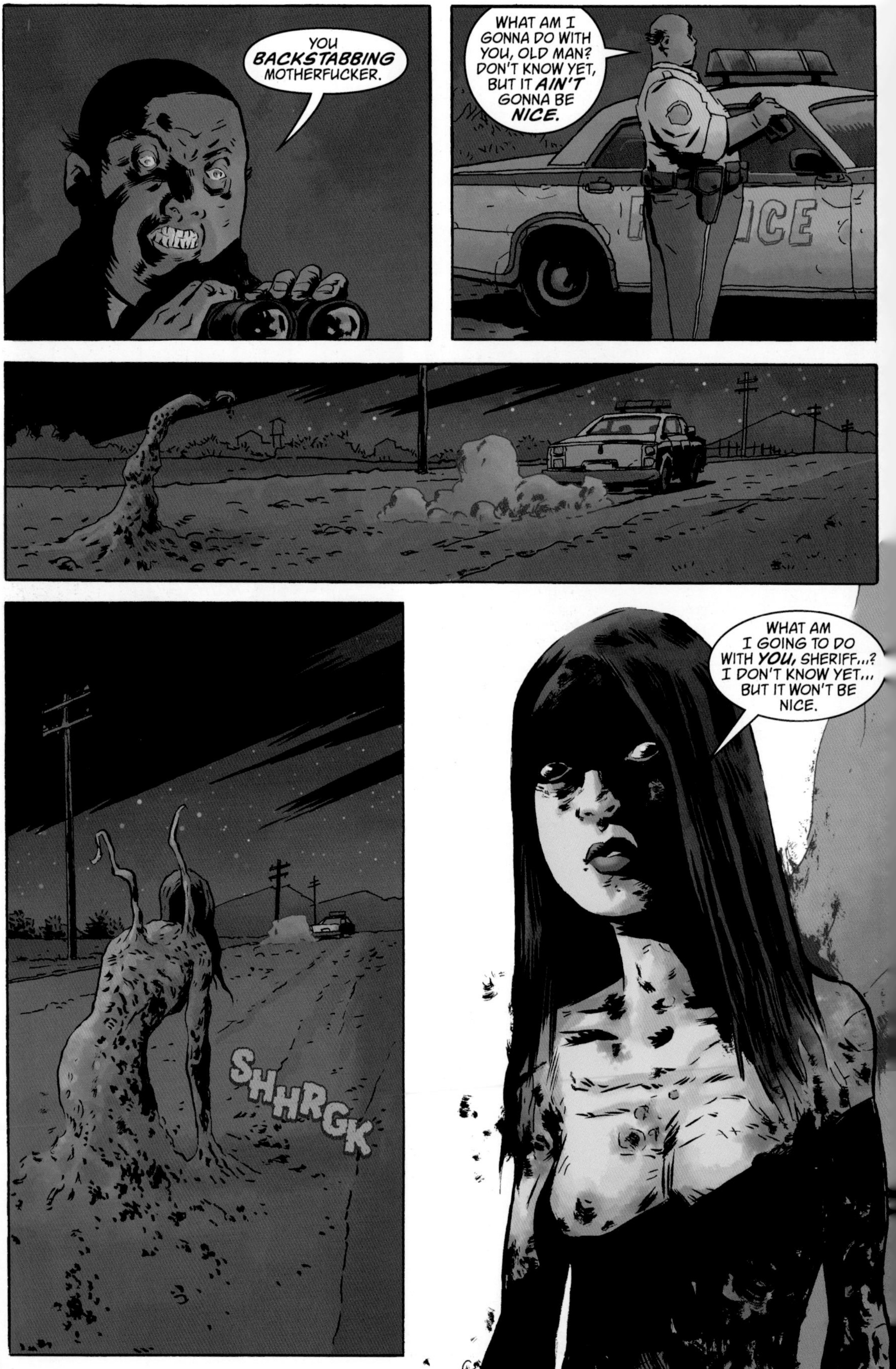
YOU BACKSTABBING MOTHERFUCKER.
WHAT AM I GONNA DO WITH YOU, OLD MAN? DON'T KNOW YET, BUT IT AIN'T GONNA BE NICE.
SHHRGK
WHAT AM I GOING TO DO WITH YOU, SHERIFF...? I DON'T KNOW YET... BUT IT WON'T BE NICE.

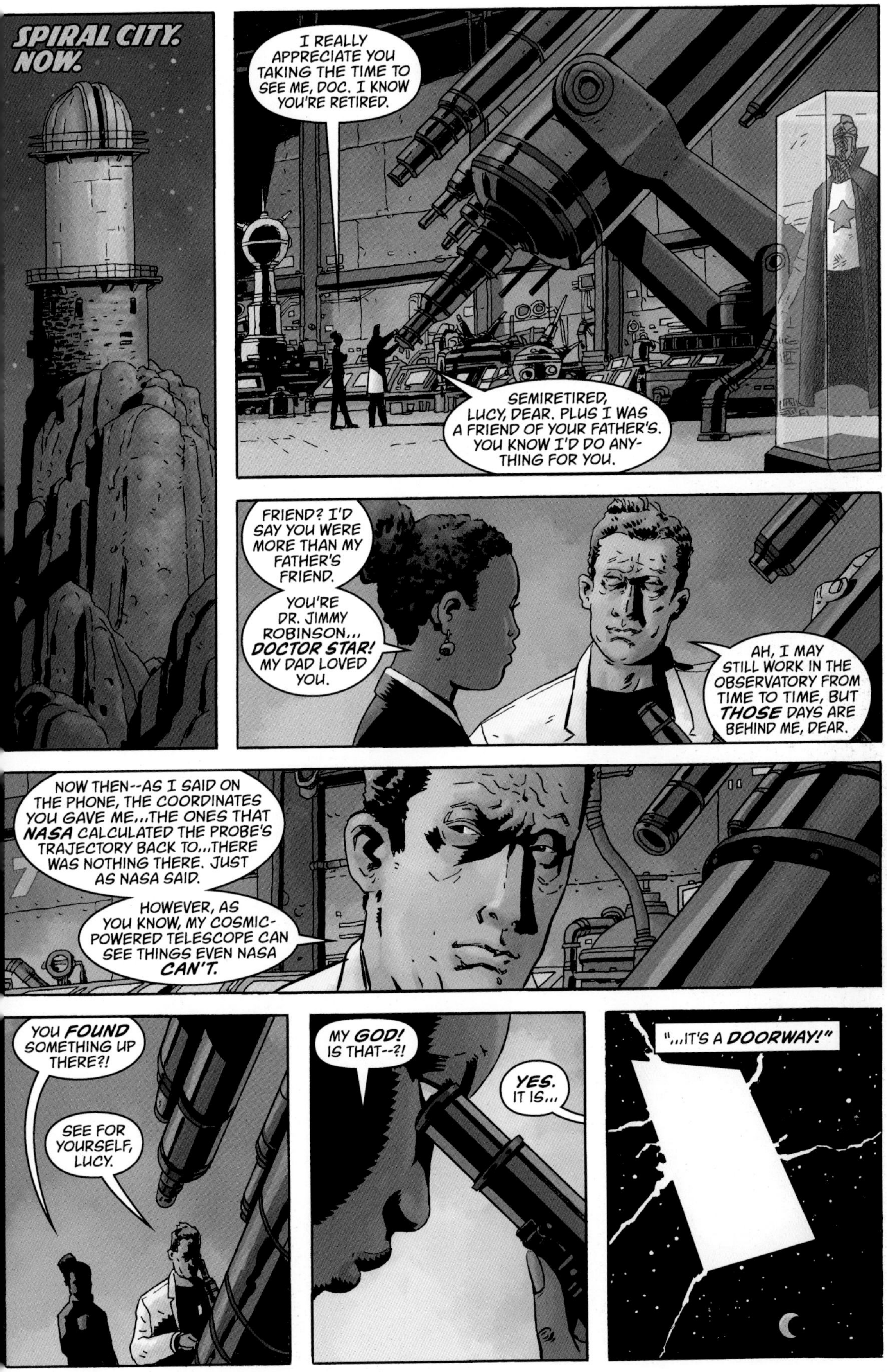
SPIRAL CITY. NOW.
I REALLY APPRECIATE YOU TAKING THE TIME TO SEE ME, DOC. I KNOW YOU'RE RETIRED.
SEMIRETIRED, LUCY, DEAR. PLUS I WAS A FRIEND OF YOUR FATHER'S. YOU KNOW I'D DO ANYTHING FOR YOU.
FRIEND? I'D SAY YOU WERE MORE THAN MY FATHER'S FRIEND.
YOU'RE DR. JIMMY ROBINSON... DOCTOR STAR! MY DAD LOVED YOU.
AH, I MAY STILL WORK IN THE OBSERVATORY FROM TIME TO TIME, BUT THOSE DAYS ARE BEHIND ME, DEAR.
NOW THEN--AS I SAID ON THE PHONE, THE COORDINATES YOU GAVE ME... THE ONES THAT NASA CALCULATED THE PROBE'S TRAJECTORY BACK TO... THERE WAS NOTHING THERE. JUST AS NASA SAID.
HOWEVER, AS YOU KNOW, MY COSMIC-POWERED TELESCOPE CAN SEE THINGS EVEN NASA CAN'T.
YOU FOUND SOMETHING UP THERE?!
SEE FOR YOURSELF, LUCY.
MY GOD! IS THAT--?!
YES. IT IS...
"...IT'S A DOORWAY!"

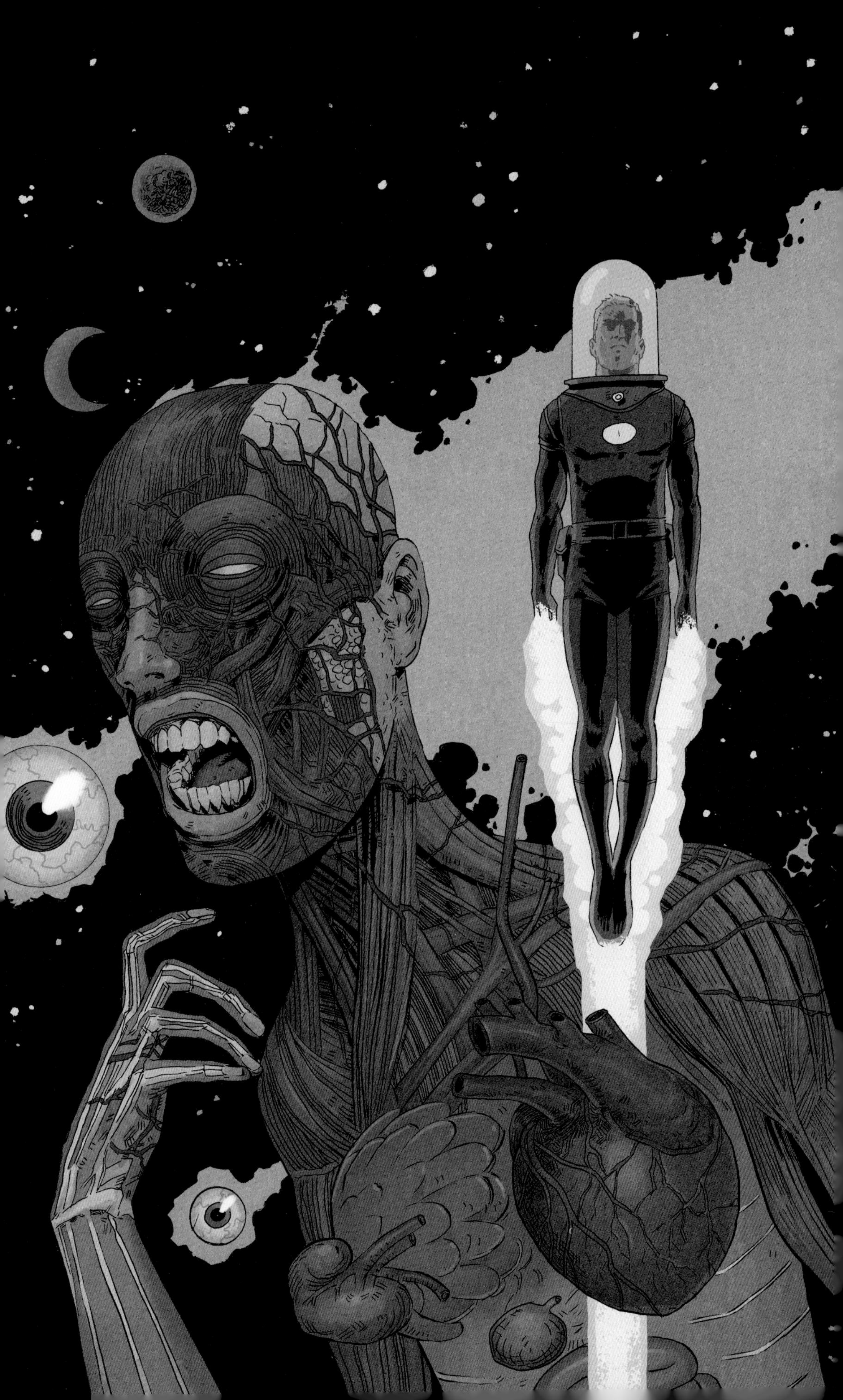

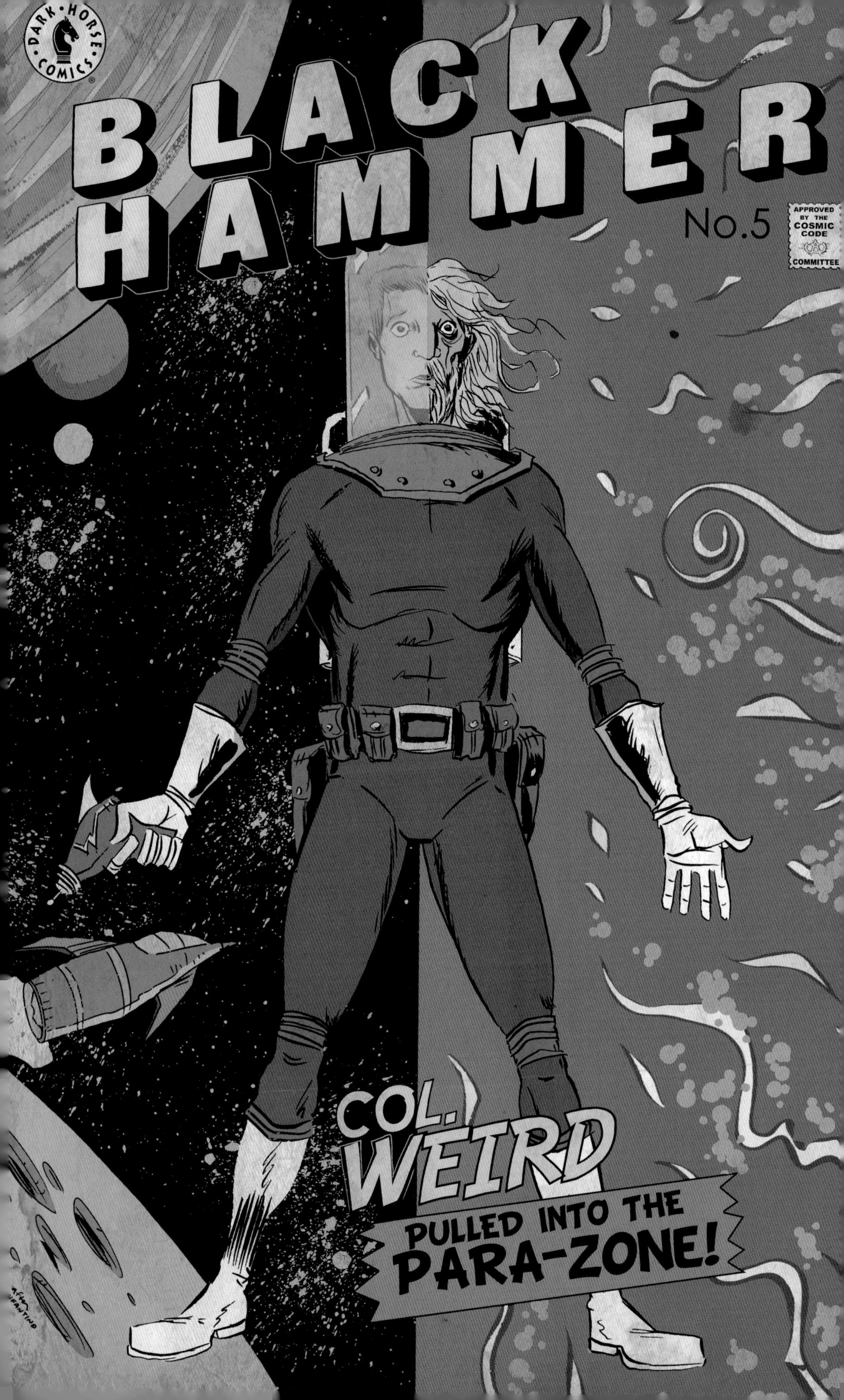
DARK HORSE COMICS
BLACK HAMMER
No.5
APPROVED BY THE COSMIC CODE COMMITTEE
COL. WEIRD
PULLED INTO THE PARA-ZONE!

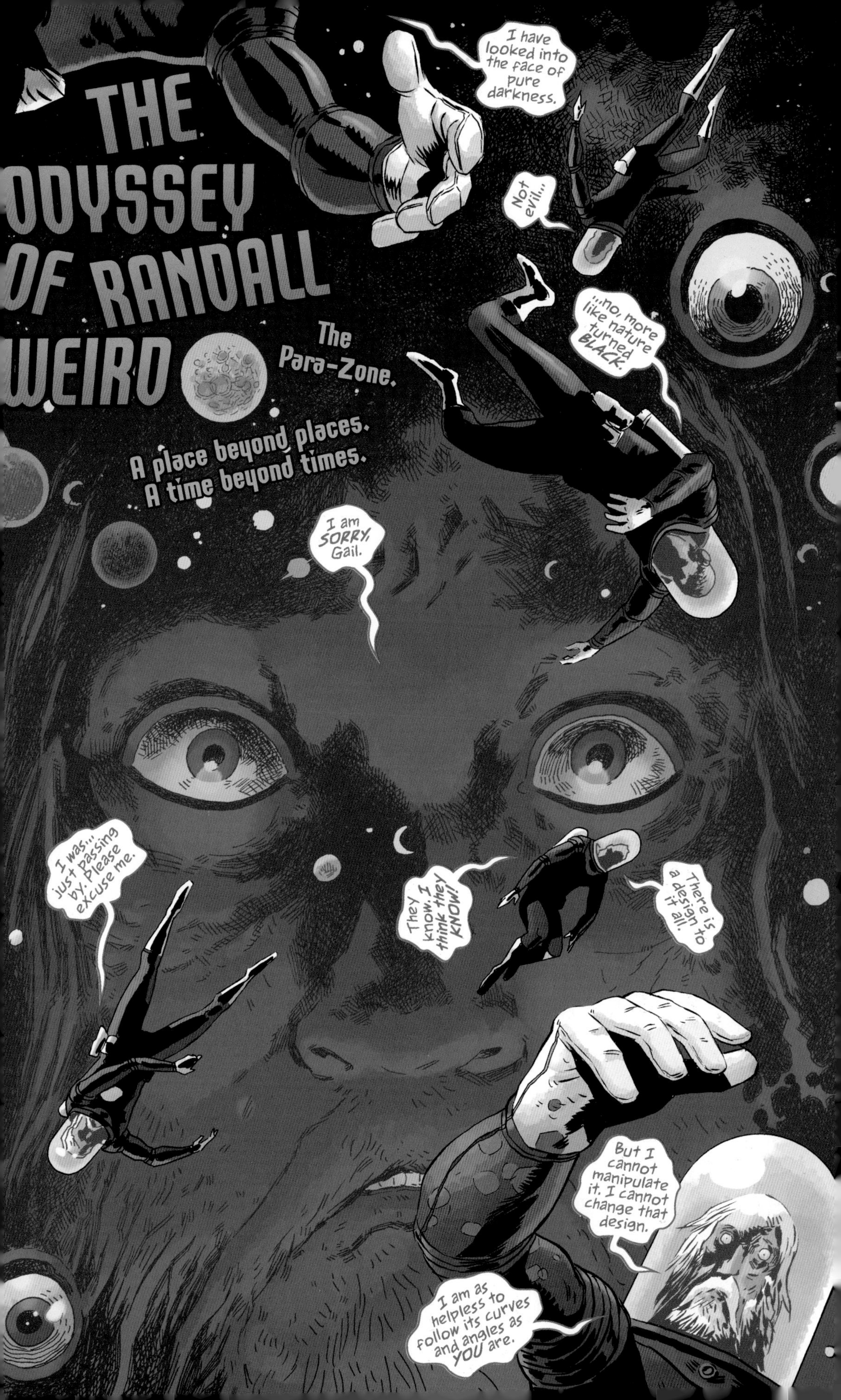

THE ODYSSEY OF RANDALL WEIRD
The Para-Zone.
A place beyond places. A time beyond times.
I have looked into the face of pure darkness.
Not evil...
...no, more like nature turned BLACK.
I am SORRY, Gail.
I was... just passing by. Please excuse me.
They know. I think they KNOW!
There is a design to it all.
But I cannot manipulate it. I cannot change that design.
I am as helpless to follow its curves and angles as YOU are.

--ALMOST DONE HERE, MISSION CONTROL. SHOULD BE WRAPPING THINGS UP AND HEADING *BACK* WITHIN THE HOUR.

THAT MAY BE A RATHER GENEROUS ESTIMATE, COLONEL. MY SENSORS ARE PICKING UP UNKNOWN LIFE FORMS, APPROACHING *FAST*!

I THOUGHT THE ALIEN RACE ON THIS PLANET WAS *EXTINCT*, TALKY?!

∇⋅ナパ┼ムム┐.!!

SO DID I, COLONEL. IT SEEMS NASA'S INTEL WAS INCORRECT.

LET'S *DO* SOMETHING ABOUT THAT, *SHALL* WE, OL' CHUM?

K-ZAP

ZZZOW

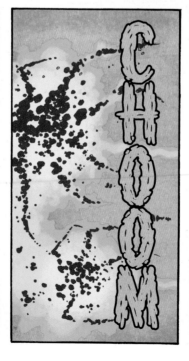

CHOOM

ALMOST SEEMED LIKE THEY WERE TRYING TO PUSH US *BACK* FROM THAT CAVE. I WONDER WHAT THEY'RE HIDING IN THERE?

--ALMOST DONE HERE, MISSION CONTROL. SHOULD BE WRAPPING THINGS UP AND HEADING *BACK* WITHIN THE HOUR.

THAT MAY BE A RATHER GENEROUS ESTIMATE, COLONEL. MY SENSORS ARE PICKING UP UNKNOWN LIFE FORMS, APPROACHING *FAST!*

I THOUGHT THE ALIEN RACE ON THIS PLANET WAS *EXTINCT,* TALKY?!

∇·ᚮᛁᛚᛏᛁᚺᚴ.!!

SO DID I, COLONEL. IT SEEMS NASA'S INTEL WAS INCORRECT.

LET'S *DO* SOMETHING ABOUT THAT, *SHALL* WE, OL' CHUM?

K-ZAP

ZZZOW

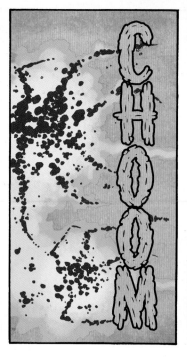

CHOOOM

ALMOST SEEMED LIKE THEY WERE TRYING TO PUSH US *BACK* FROM THAT CAVE. I WONDER WHAT THEY'RE HIDING IN THERE?

A CRUDE CAVE DRAWING, COLONEL, SHOULD I RECORD IT AND SEND THE IMAGE BACK TO MISSION CONTROL ON EARTH?

YES, BUT I DON'T THINK IT'S JUST A DRAWING, *TALKY-WALKY*...I THINK IT'S A MAP!

NASA, THIS IS COLONEL RANDALL WEIRD. WE HAVE FOUND WHAT APPEARS TO BE A STAR CHART ON *VIRIUS-6.* REQUESTING PERMISSION TO INVESTIGATE FURTHER.

:KTZZ: *AFFIRMATIVE,* COLONEL. REQUEST GRANTED.

--BUT YOU BETTER MAKE IT BACK HERE BEFORE *NEW YEAR'S.* I DON'T INTEND TO BRING IN 1956 ALONE.

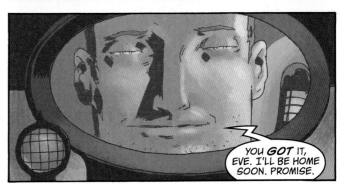

YOU *GOT* IT, EVE. I'LL BE HOME SOON. PROMISE.

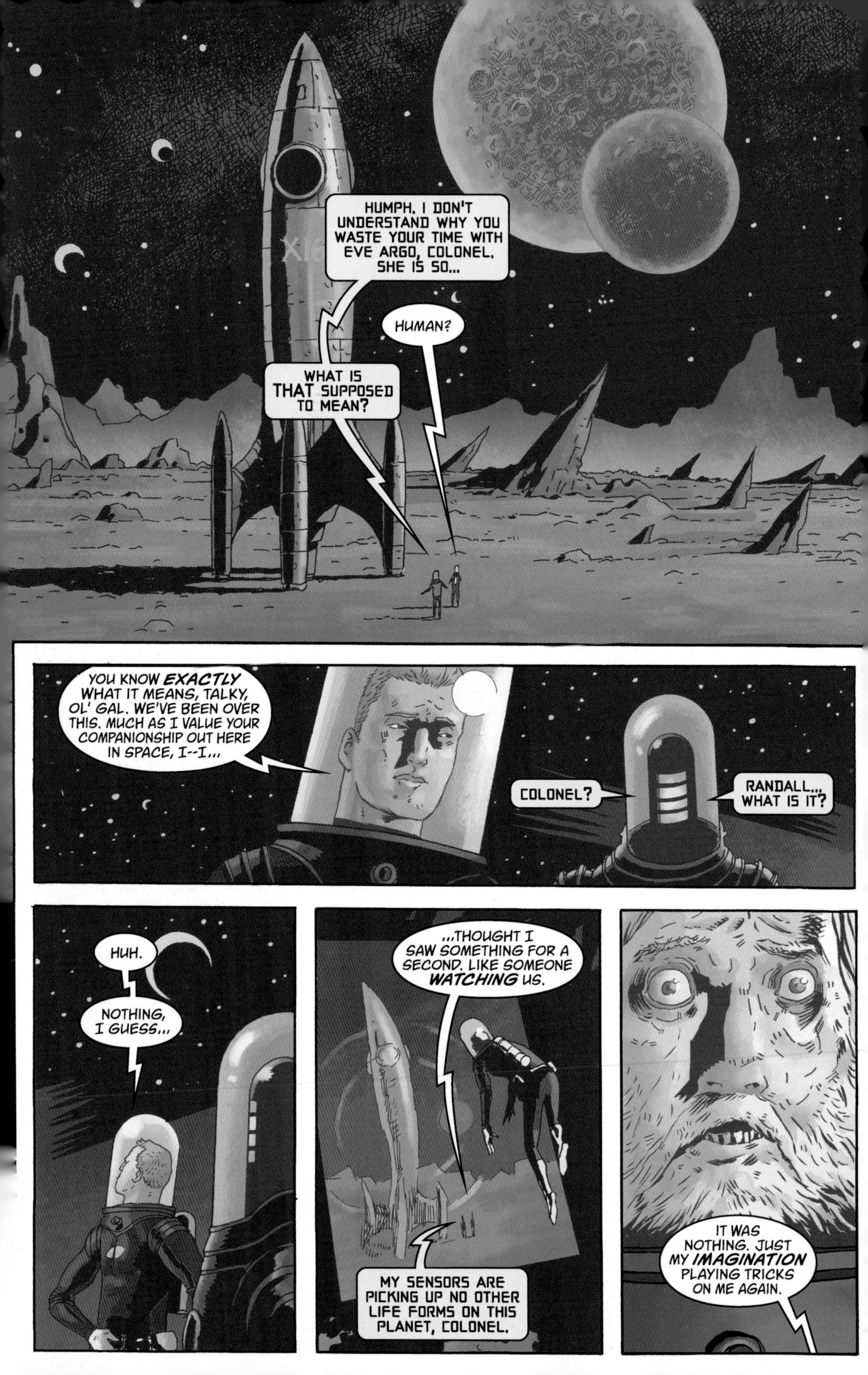
HUMPH. I DON'T UNDERSTAND WHY YOU WASTE YOUR TIME WITH EVE ARGO, COLONEL. SHE IS SO...
HUMAN?
WHAT IS THAT SUPPOSED TO MEAN?
YOU KNOW EXACTLY WHAT IT MEANS, TALKY, OL' GAL. WE'VE BEEN OVER THIS. MUCH AS I VALUE YOUR COMPANIONSHIP OUT HERE IN SPACE, I--I...
COLONEL?
RANDALL... WHAT IS IT?
HUH.
NOTHING, I GUESS...
...THOUGHT I SAW SOMETHING FOR A SECOND. LIKE SOMEONE WATCHING US.
MY SENSORS ARE PICKING UP NO OTHER LIFE FORMS ON THIS PLANET, COLONEL.
IT WAS NOTHING. JUST MY IMAGINATION PLAYING TRICKS ON ME AGAIN.

LET'S GET *GOING*, WALKY. I WANT TO INVESTIGATE THAT MAP AND THEN GO HOME!

...Madame Dragonfly...I--I *DO NOT* like it in here.

There are--too many rooms.

MORE THAN YOU KNOW, COLONEL WEIRD. AND I'VE TOLD YOU BEFORE. IF YOU DON'T LIKE IT, THEN DON'T POP IN HERE LIKE THIS. IT'S CREEPY.

You're creepy.

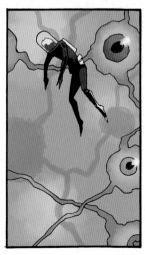

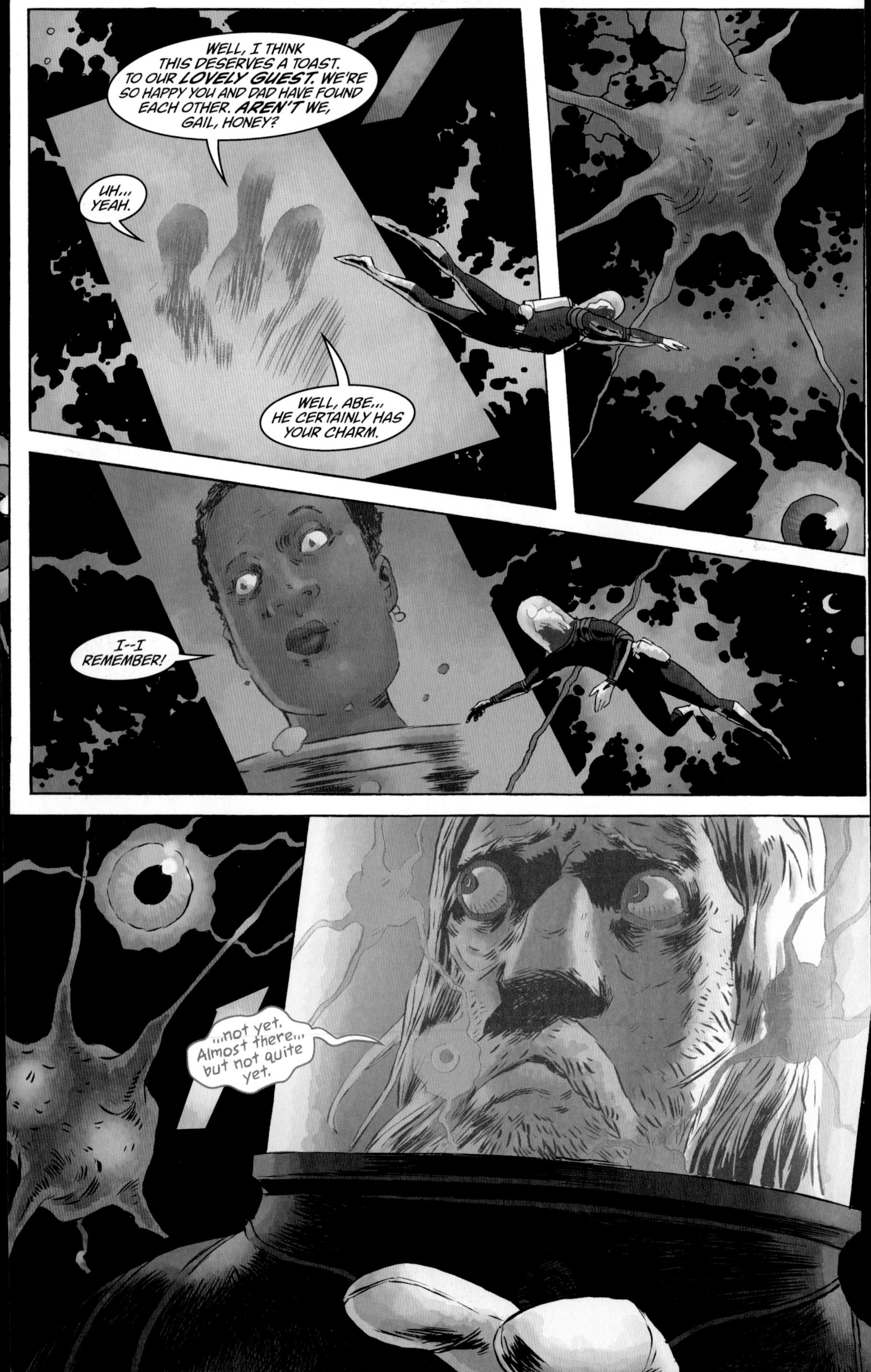
WELL, I THINK THIS DESERVES A TOAST. TO OUR LOVELY GUEST. WE'RE SO HAPPY YOU AND DAD HAVE FOUND EACH OTHER. AREN'T WE, GAIL, HONEY?
UH... YEAH.
WELL, ABE... HE CERTAINLY HAS YOUR CHARM.
I--I REMEMBER!
...not yet. Almost there... but not quite yet.

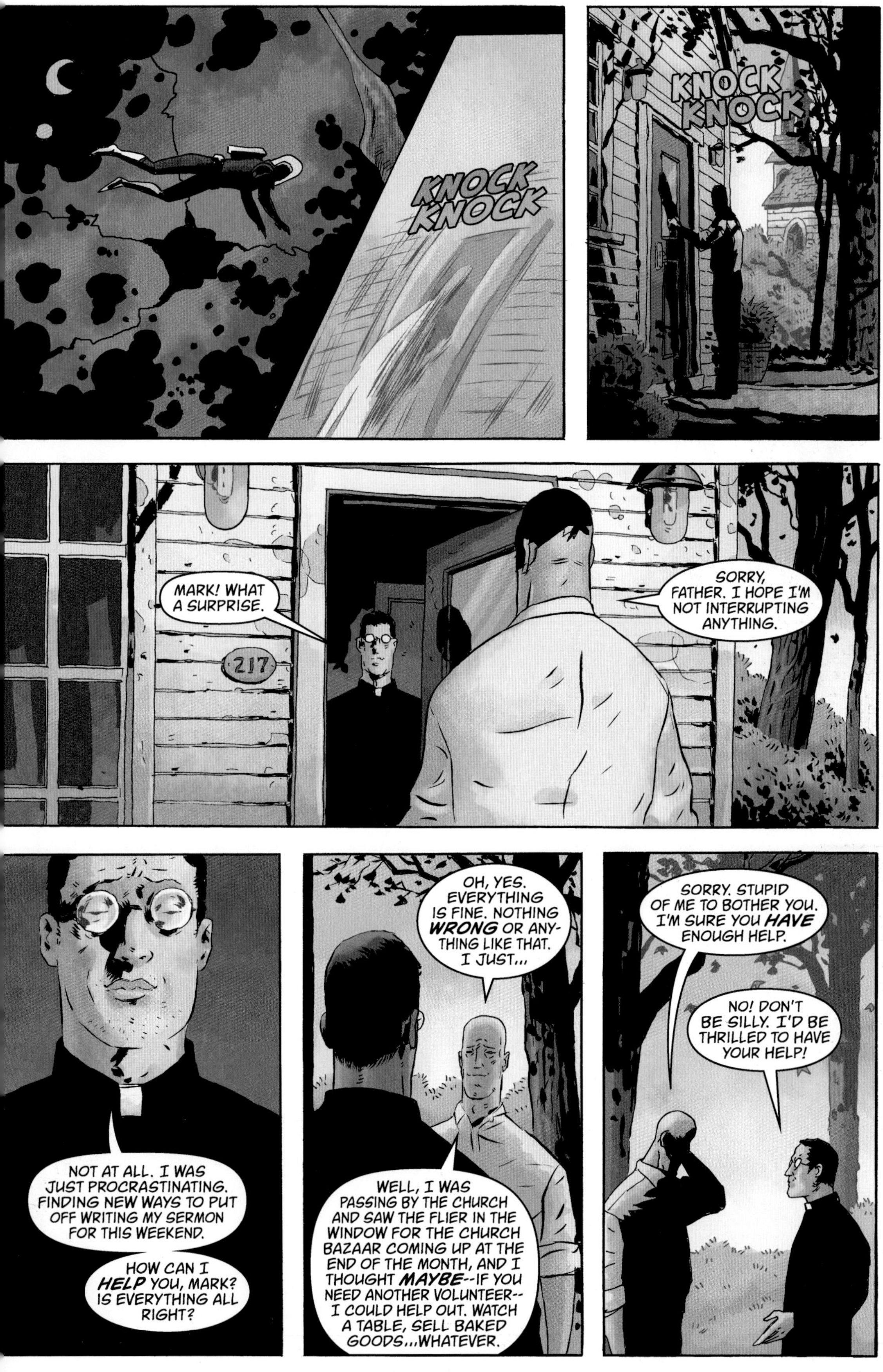
KNOCK KNOCK
KNOCK KNOCK
MARK! WHAT A SURPRISE.
SORRY, FATHER. I HOPE I'M NOT INTERRUPTING ANYTHING.
NOT AT ALL. I WAS JUST PROCRASTINATING. FINDING NEW WAYS TO PUT OFF WRITING MY SERMON FOR THIS WEEKEND.
HOW CAN I **HELP** YOU, MARK? IS EVERYTHING ALL RIGHT?
OH, YES. EVERYTHING IS FINE. NOTHING **WRONG** OR ANYTHING LIKE THAT. I JUST...
WELL, I WAS PASSING BY THE CHURCH AND SAW THE FLIER IN THE WINDOW FOR THE CHURCH BAZAAR COMING UP AT THE END OF THE MONTH, AND I THOUGHT **MAYBE**--IF YOU NEED ANOTHER VOLUNTEER--I COULD HELP OUT. WATCH A TABLE, SELL BAKED GOODS...WHATEVER.
SORRY. STUPID OF ME TO BOTHER YOU. I'M SURE YOU **HAVE** ENOUGH HELP.
NO! DON'T BE SILLY. I'D BE THRILLED TO HAVE YOUR HELP!

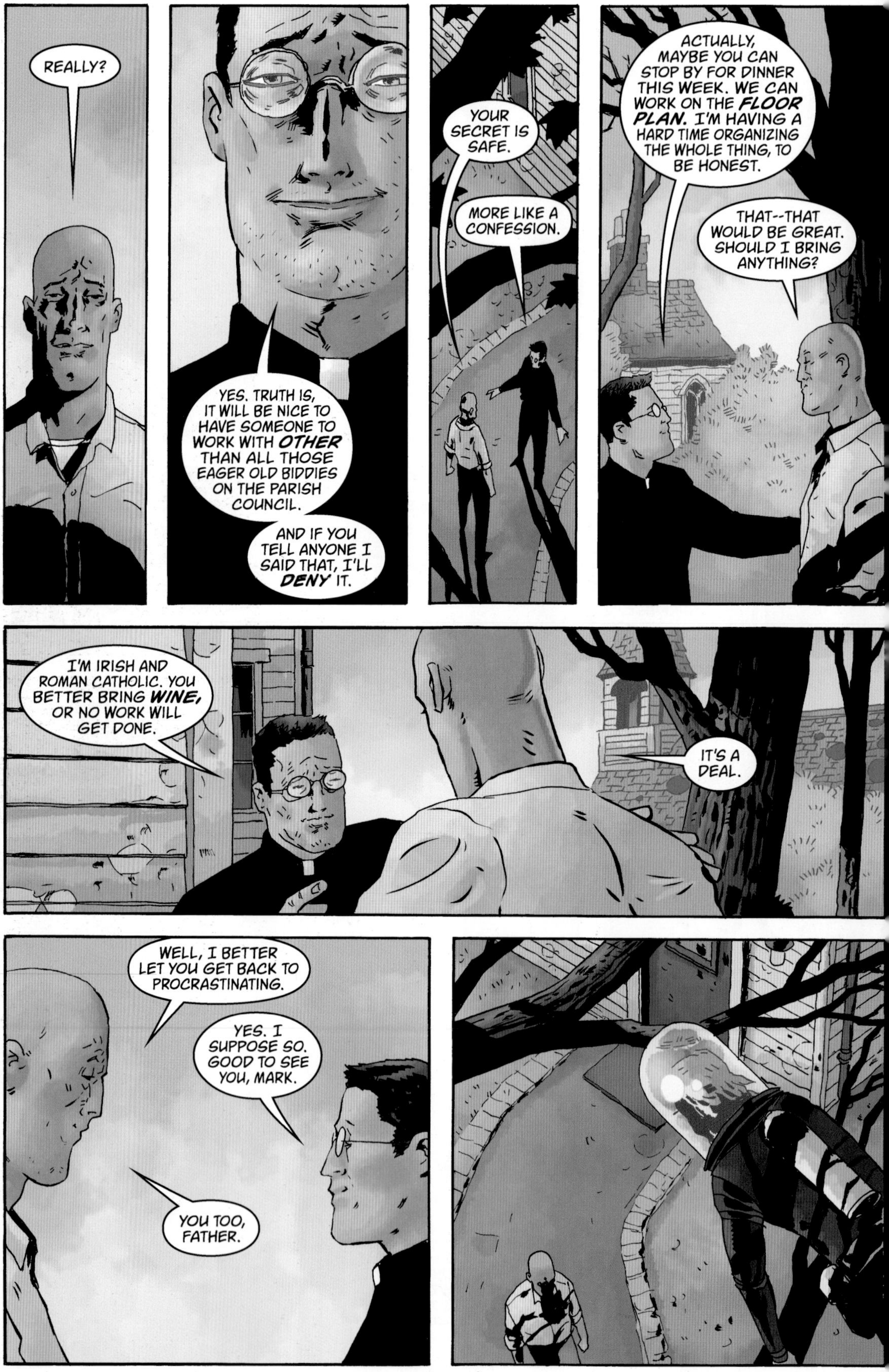
REALLY?
YES. TRUTH IS, IT WILL BE NICE TO HAVE SOMEONE TO WORK WITH OTHER THAN ALL THOSE EAGER OLD BIDDIES ON THE PARISH COUNCIL.
AND IF YOU TELL ANYONE I SAID THAT, I'LL DENY IT.
YOUR SECRET IS SAFE.
MORE LIKE A CONFESSION.
ACTUALLY, MAYBE YOU CAN STOP BY FOR DINNER THIS WEEK. WE CAN WORK ON THE FLOOR PLAN. I'M HAVING A HARD TIME ORGANIZING THE WHOLE THING, TO BE HONEST.
THAT--THAT WOULD BE GREAT. SHOULD I BRING ANYTHING?
I'M IRISH AND ROMAN CATHOLIC. YOU BETTER BRING WINE, OR NO WORK WILL GET DONE.
IT'S A DEAL.
WELL, I BETTER LET YOU GET BACK TO PROCRASTINATING.
YES. I SUPPOSE SO. GOOD TO SEE YOU, MARK.
YOU TOO, FATHER.

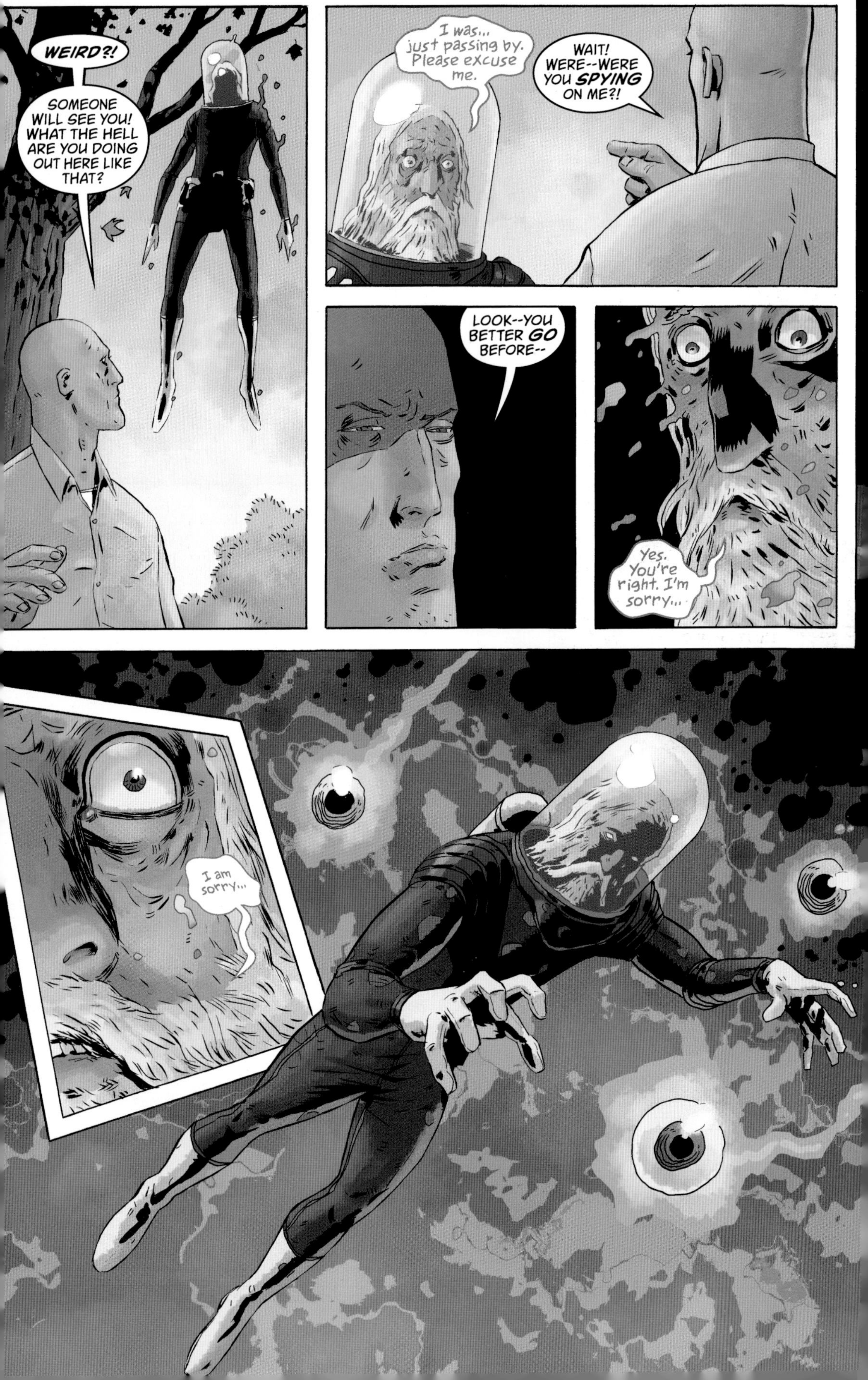
WEIRD?!
SOMEONE WILL SEE YOU! WHAT THE HELL ARE YOU DOING OUT HERE LIKE THAT?
I was... just passing by. Please excuse me.
WAIT! WERE--WERE YOU SPYING ON ME?!
LOOK--YOU BETTER GO BEFORE--
Yes. You're right. I'm sorry...
I am sorry...

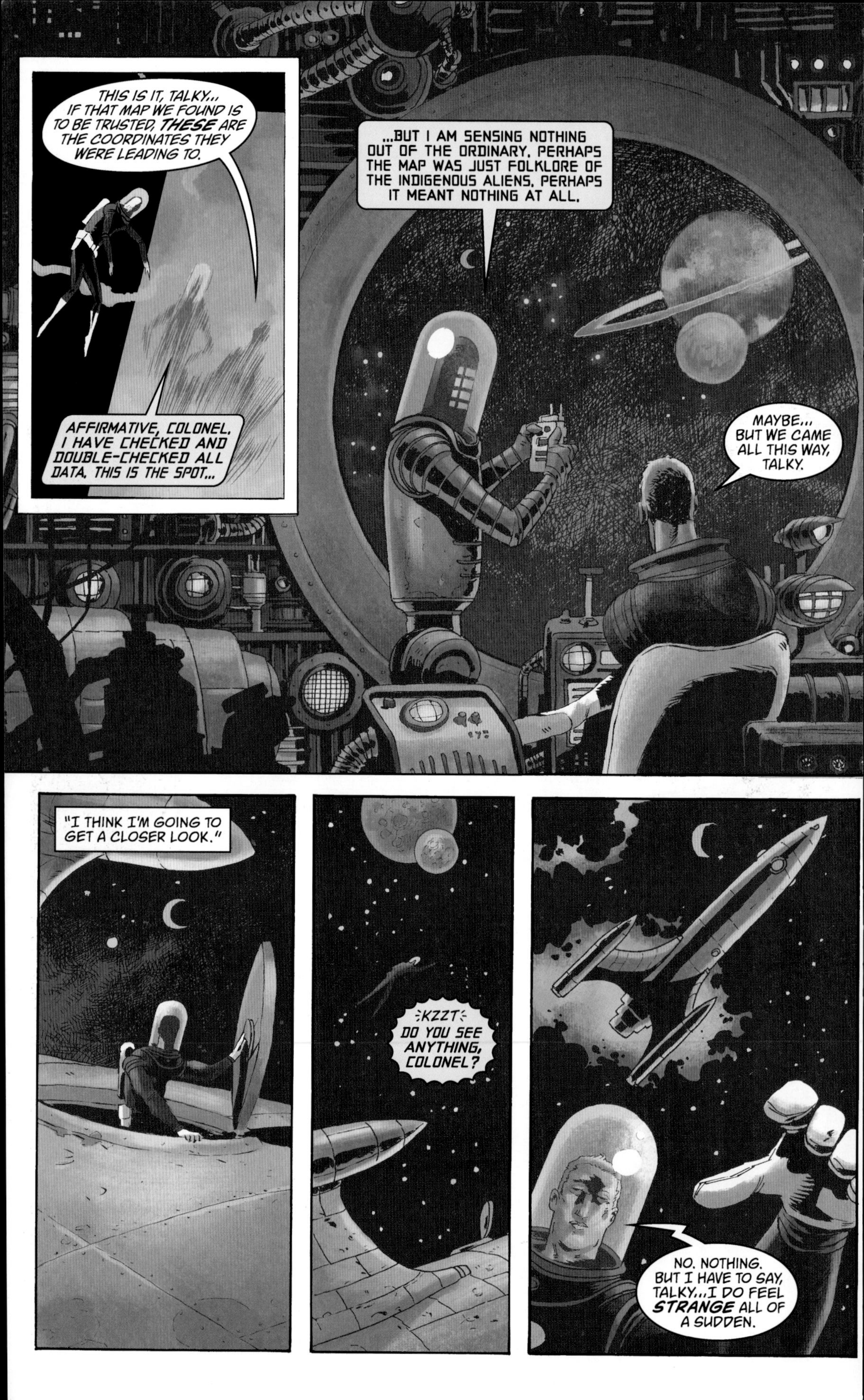
THIS IS IT, TALKY... IF THAT MAP WE FOUND IS TO BE TRUSTED, THESE ARE THE COORDINATES THEY WERE LEADING TO.
AFFIRMATIVE, COLONEL. I HAVE CHECKED AND DOUBLE-CHECKED ALL DATA. THIS IS THE SPOT...
...BUT I AM SENSING NOTHING OUT OF THE ORDINARY. PERHAPS THE MAP WAS JUST FOLKLORE OF THE INDIGENOUS ALIENS. PERHAPS IT MEANT NOTHING AT ALL.
MAYBE... BUT WE CAME ALL THIS WAY, TALKY.
"I THINK I'M GOING TO GET A CLOSER LOOK."
KZZT DO YOU SEE ANYTHING, COLONEL?
NO. NOTHING. BUT I HAVE TO SAY, TALKY... I DO FEEL STRANGE ALL OF A SUDDEN.

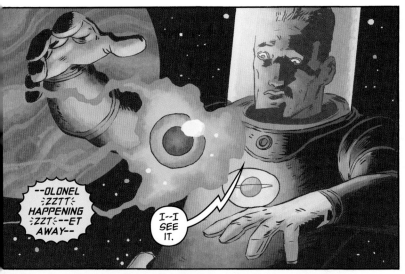

--OLONEL ᙒZZTᙒ HAPPENING ᙒZZTᙒ --ET AWAY--

I--I SEE IT.

IT--IT'S A *DOORWAY!*

--NOT A GOOD IDEA ᙒKZZTᙒ

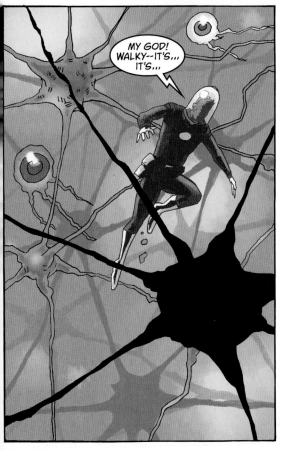

MY GOD! WALKY--IT'S.... IT'S....

WHO... WHO ARE *YOU?*

I am *YOU.*

WHAT?! THE PANEL IS *CLOSING,* TALKY! *NO!*

SHRRRKZZ

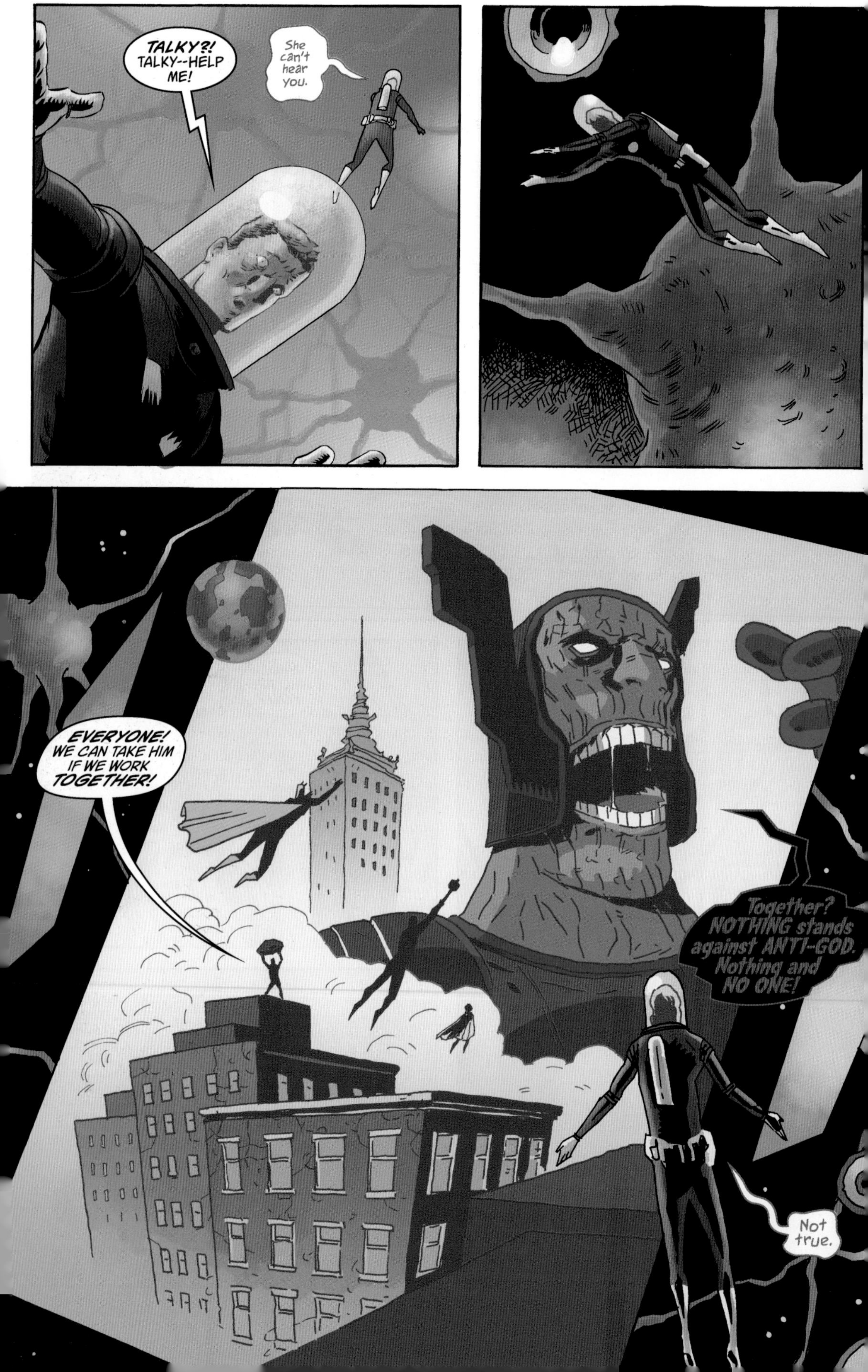
TALKY?! TALKY--HELP ME!
She can't hear you.
EVERYONE! WE CAN TAKE HIM IF WE WORK TOGETHER!
Together? NOTHING stands against ANTI-GOD. Nothing and NO ONE!
Not true.

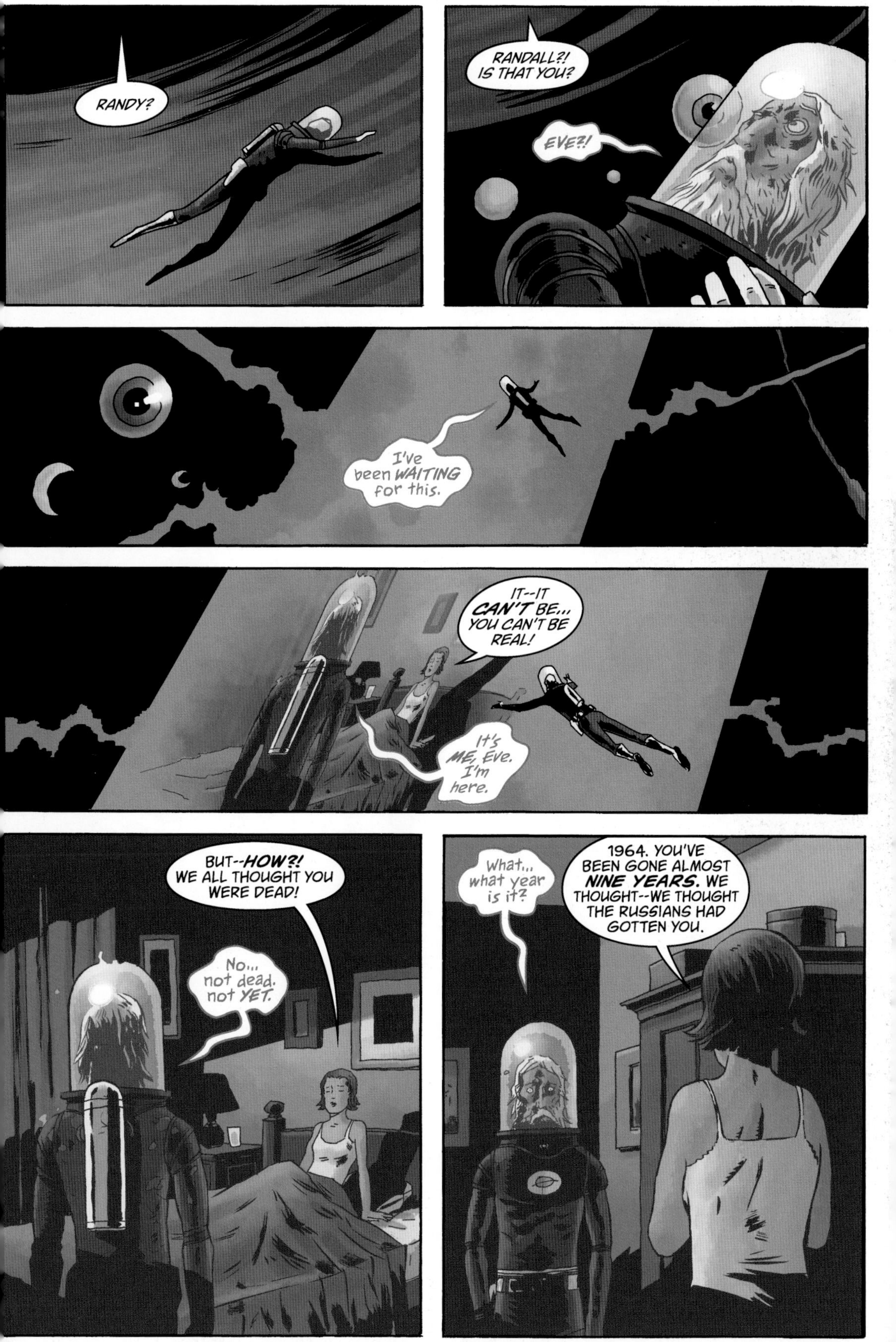
RANDY?
RANDALL?! IS THAT YOU?
EVE?!
I've been WAITING for this.
IT--IT CAN'T BE... YOU CAN'T BE REAL!
It's ME, Eve. I'm here.
BUT--HOW?! WE ALL THOUGHT YOU WERE DEAD!
No... not dead. not YET.
What... what year is it?
1964. YOU'VE BEEN GONE ALMOST NINE YEARS. WE THOUGHT--WE THOUGHT THE RUSSIANS HAD GOTTEN YOU.

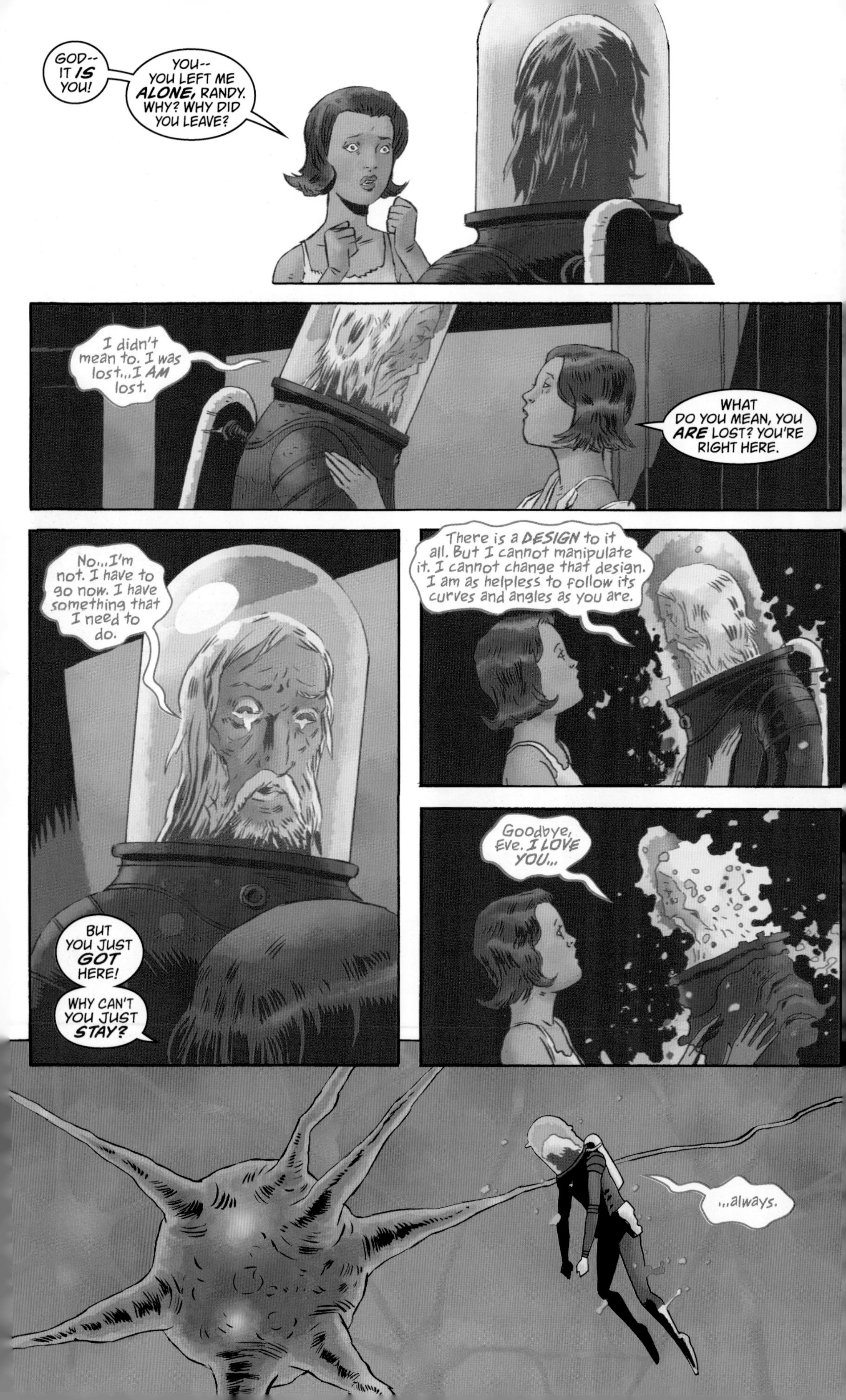

GOD-- IT IS YOU!
YOU-- YOU LEFT ME ALONE, RANDY. WHY? WHY DID YOU LEAVE?
I didn't mean to. I was lost...I AM lost.
WHAT DO YOU MEAN, YOU ARE LOST? YOU'RE RIGHT HERE.
No...I'm not. I have to go now. I have something that I need to do.
BUT YOU JUST GOT HERE!
WHY CAN'T YOU JUST STAY?
There is a DESIGN to it all. But I cannot manipulate it. I cannot change that design. I am as helpless to follow its curves and angles as you are.
Goodbye, Eve. I LOVE YOU...
...always.

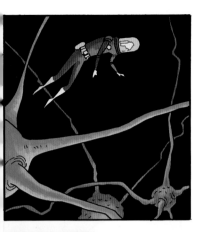

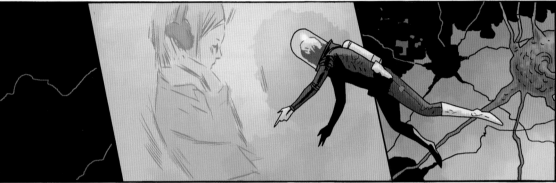

AAHHH!!

WHAT ARE YOU *DOING?!* YOU *CAN'T* JUST POP INTO MY *ROOM* LIKE THAT! WHAT IF I WAS *NAKED* OR SOMETHING, YOU *PERV?!*

But you were not.

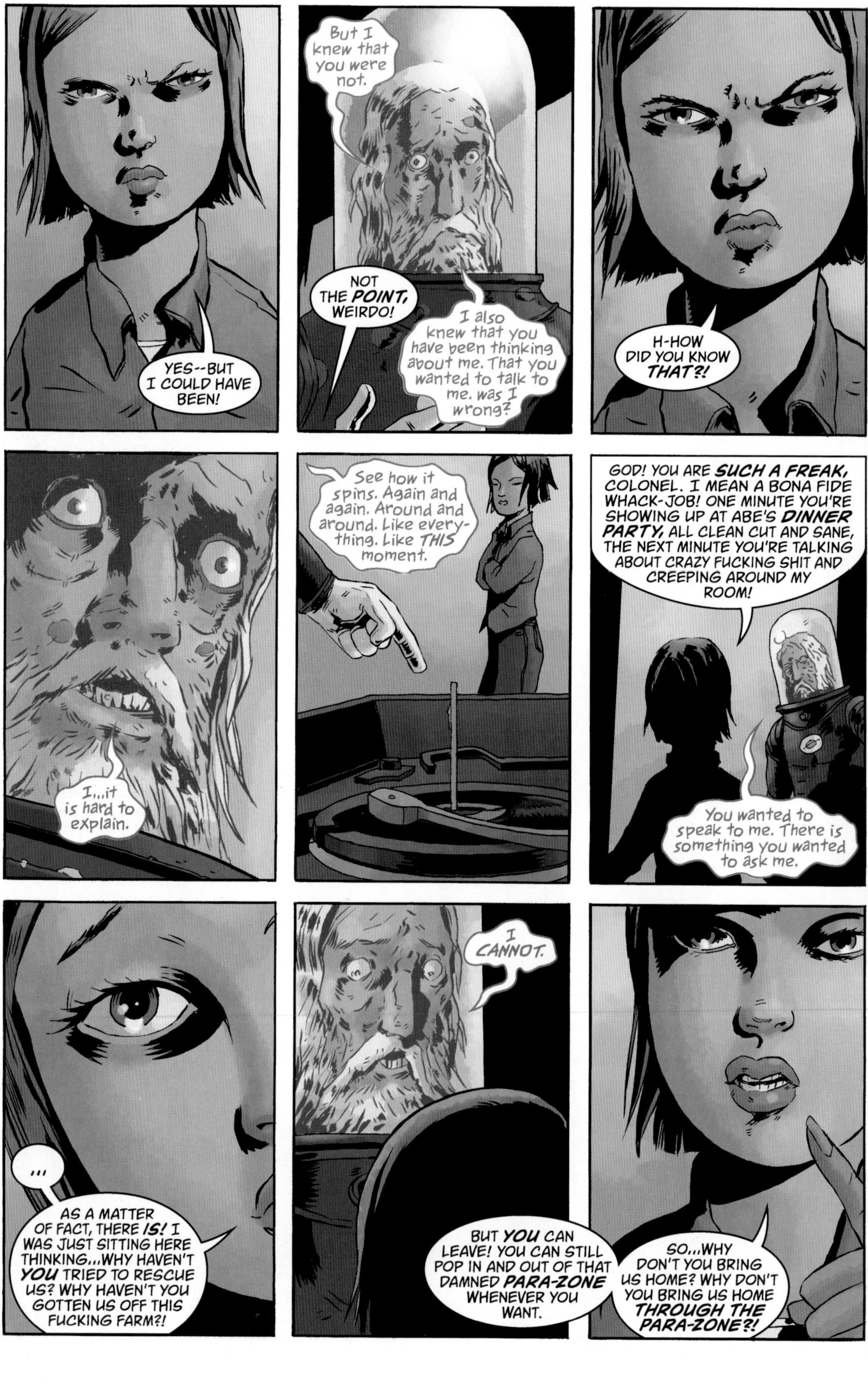

YES--BUT I COULD HAVE BEEN!
But I knew that you were not.
NOT THE POINT, WEIRDO!
I also knew that you have been thinking about me. That you wanted to talk to me. Was I wrong?
H-HOW DID YOU KNOW THAT?!
I...it is hard to explain.
See how it spins. Again and again. Around and around. Like everything. Like THIS moment.
GOD! YOU ARE SUCH A FREAK, COLONEL. I MEAN A BONA FIDE WHACK-JOB! ONE MINUTE YOU'RE SHOWING UP AT ABE'S DINNER PARTY, ALL CLEAN CUT AND SANE, THE NEXT MINUTE YOU'RE TALKING ABOUT CRAZY FUCKING SHIT AND CREEPING AROUND MY ROOM!
You wanted to speak to me. There is something you wanted to ask me.
...
AS A MATTER OF FACT, THERE IS! I WAS JUST SITTING HERE THINKING...WHY HAVEN'T YOU TRIED TO RESCUE US? WHY HAVEN'T YOU GOTTEN US OFF THIS FUCKING FARM?!
I CANNOT.
BUT YOU CAN LEAVE! YOU CAN STILL POP IN AND OUT OF THAT DAMNED PARA-ZONE WHENEVER YOU WANT.
SO...WHY DON'T YOU BRING US HOME? WHY DON'T YOU BRING US HOME THROUGH THE PARA-ZONE?!

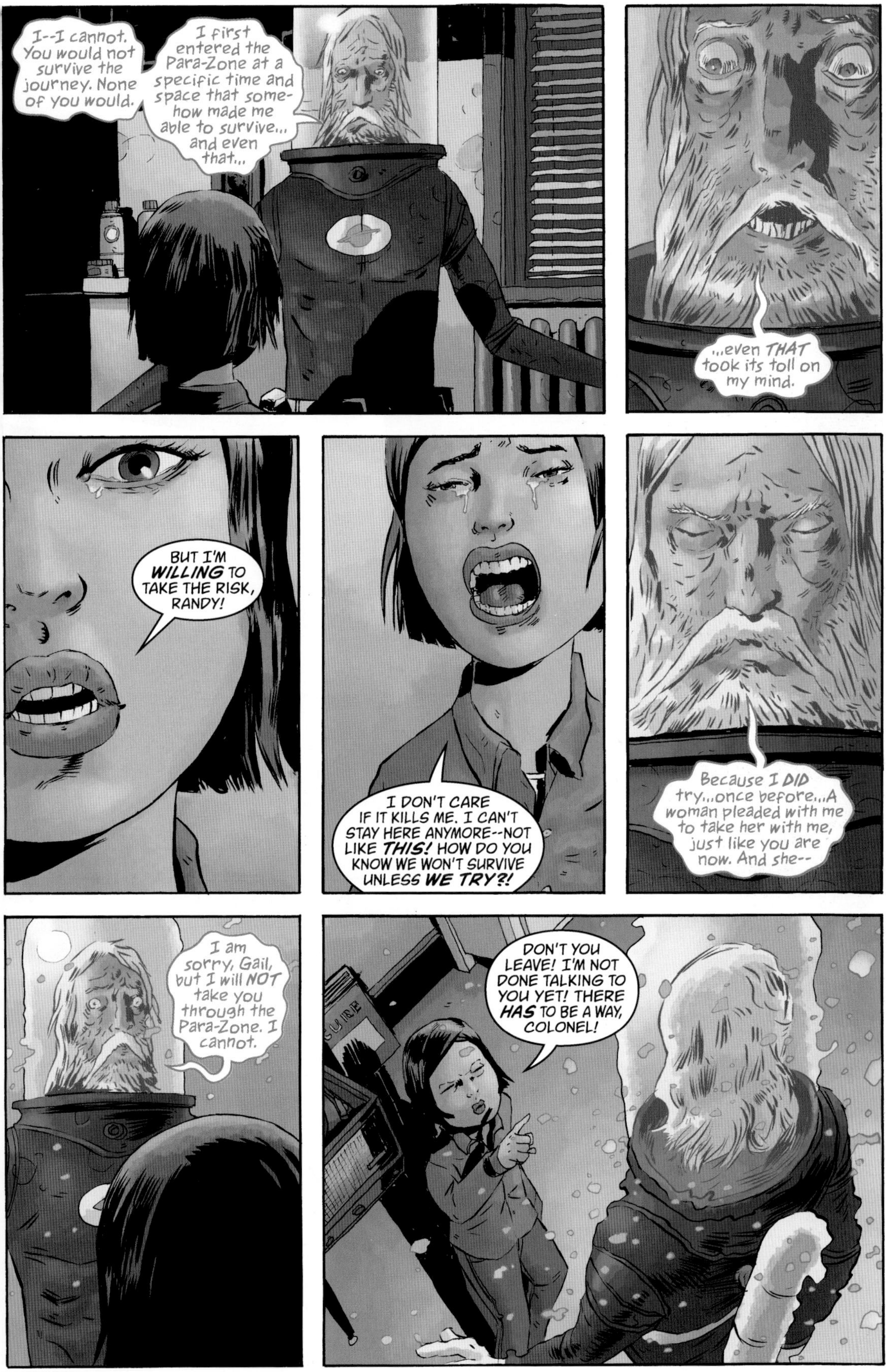
I--I cannot. You would not survive the journey. None of you would.
I first entered the Para-Zone at a specific time and space that somehow made me able to survive... and even that...
...even THAT took its toll on my mind.
BUT I'M WILLING TO TAKE THE RISK, RANDY!
I DON'T CARE IF IT KILLS ME. I CAN'T STAY HERE ANYMORE--NOT LIKE THIS! HOW DO YOU KNOW WE WON'T SURVIVE UNLESS WE TRY?!
Because I DID try...once before...A woman pleaded with me to take her with me, just like you are now. And she--
I am sorry, Gail, but I will NOT take you through the Para-Zone. I cannot.
DON'T YOU LEAVE! I'M NOT DONE TALKING TO YOU YET! THERE HAS TO BE A WAY, COLONEL!

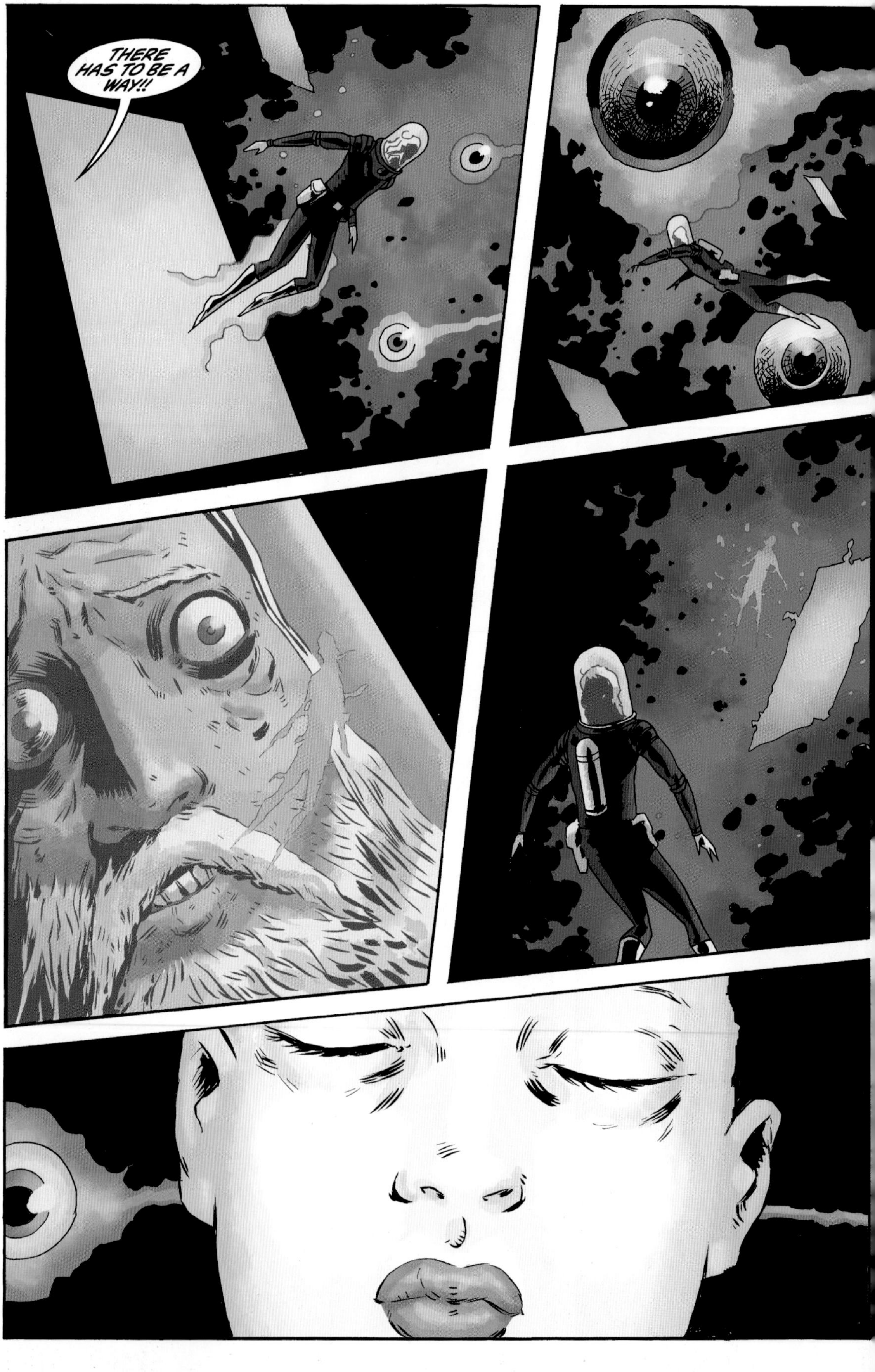
THERE HAS TO BE A WAY!!

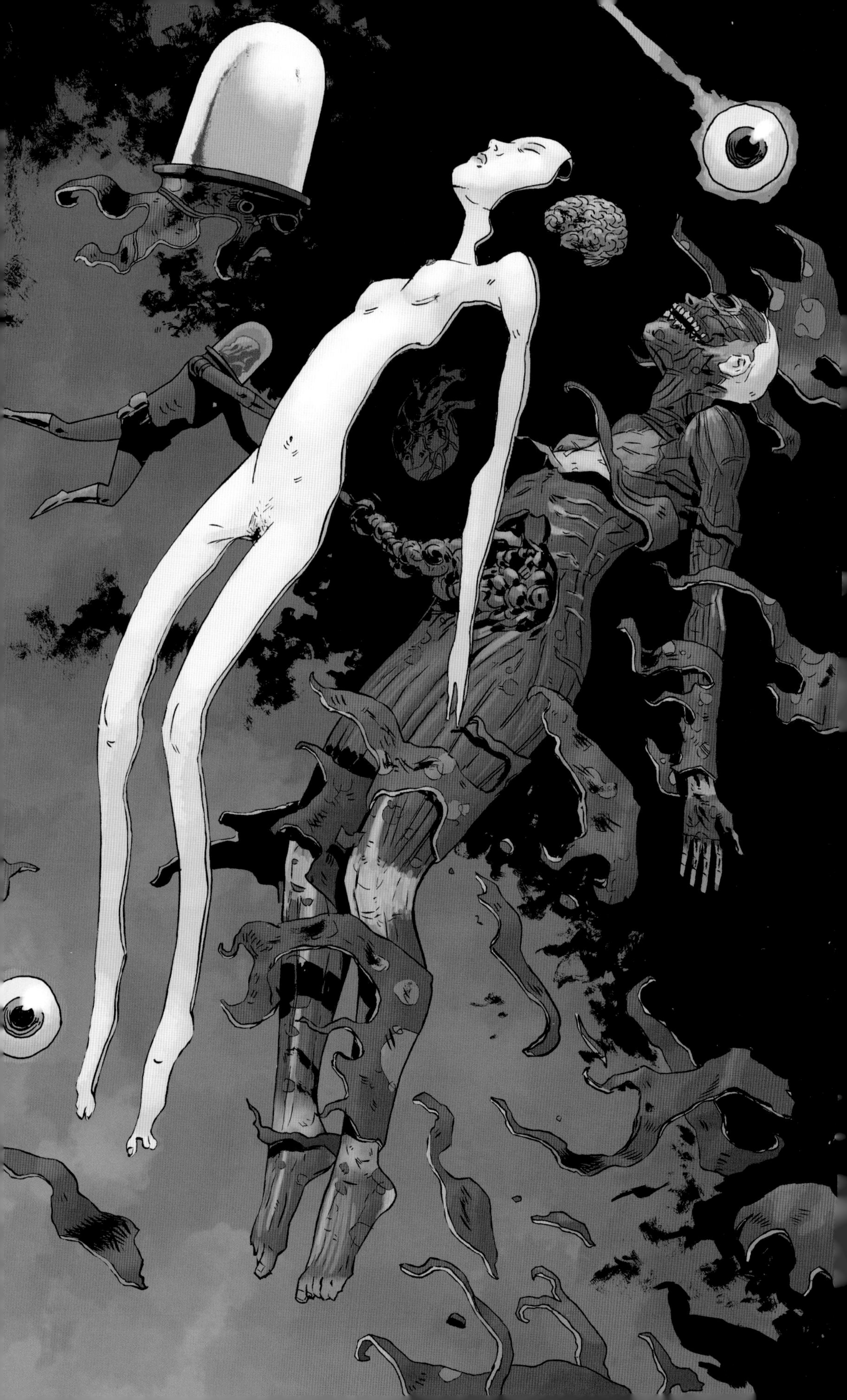

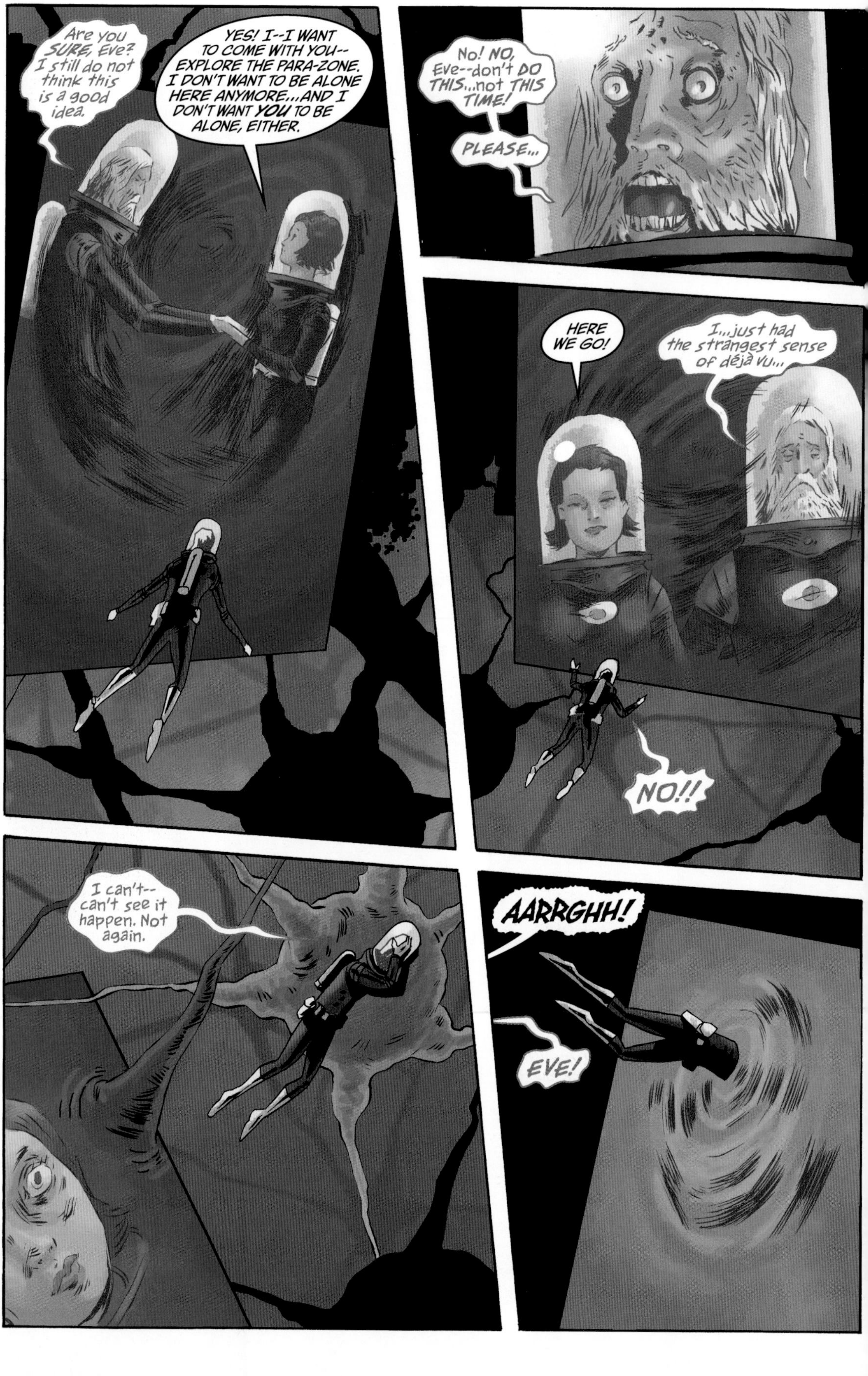
Are you SURE, Eve? I still do not think this is a good idea.
YES! I--I WANT TO COME WITH YOU--EXPLORE THE PARA-ZONE. I DON'T WANT TO BE ALONE HERE ANYMORE...AND I DON'T WANT YOU TO BE ALONE, EITHER.
No! NO, Eve--don't DO THIS...not THIS TIME!
PLEASE...
HERE WE GO!
I...just had the strangest sense of déjà vu...
NO!!
I can't--can't see it happen. Not again.
AARRGHH!
EVE!

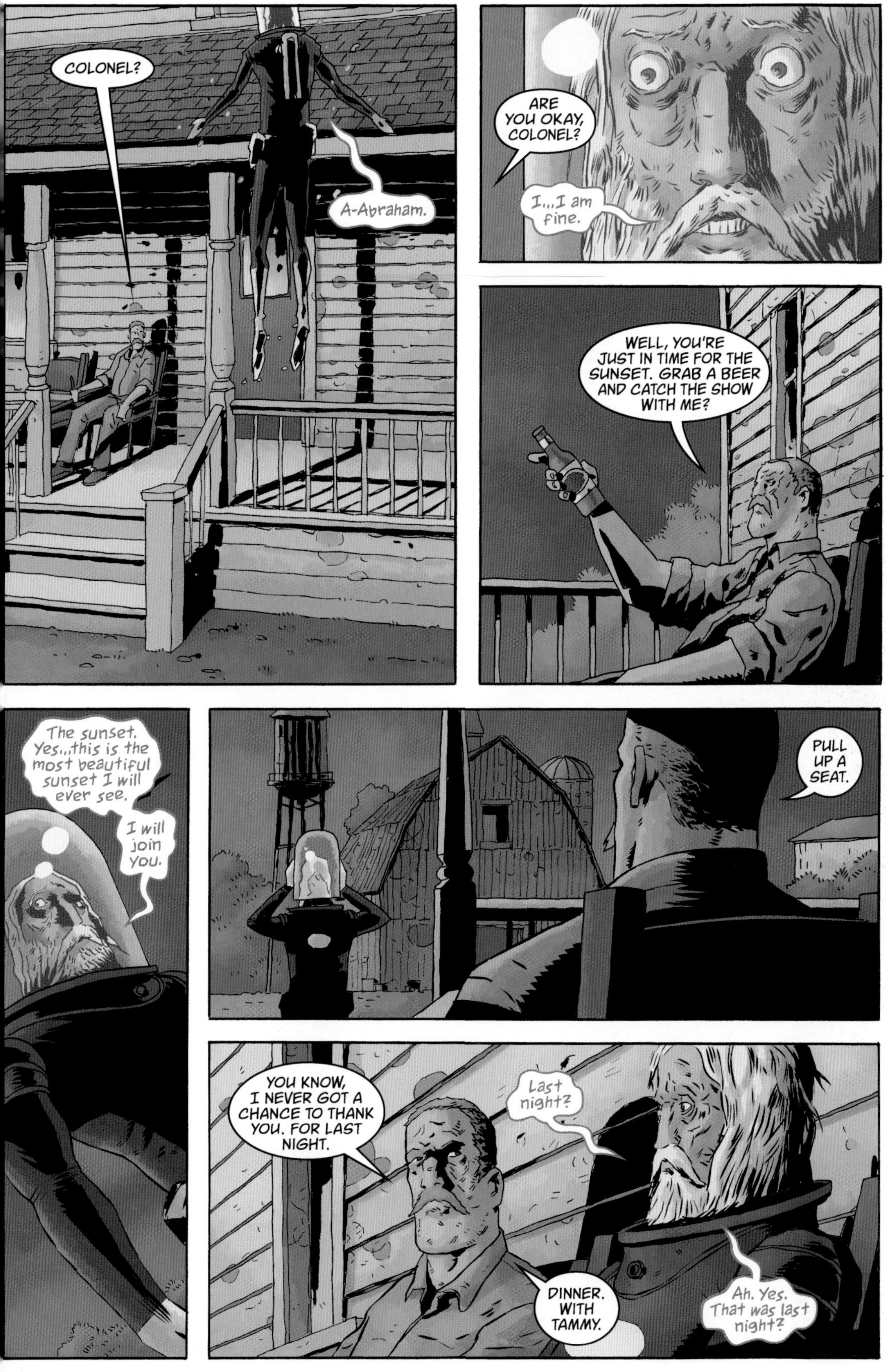
COLONEL?
A-Abraham.
ARE YOU OKAY, COLONEL?
I...I am fine.
WELL, YOU'RE JUST IN TIME FOR THE SUNSET. GRAB A BEER AND CATCH THE SHOW WITH ME?
The sunset. Yes...this is the most beautiful sunset I will ever see.
I will join you.
PULL UP A SEAT.
YOU KNOW, I NEVER GOT A CHANCE TO THANK YOU. FOR LAST NIGHT.
Last night?
DINNER. WITH TAMMY.
Ah. Yes. That was last night?

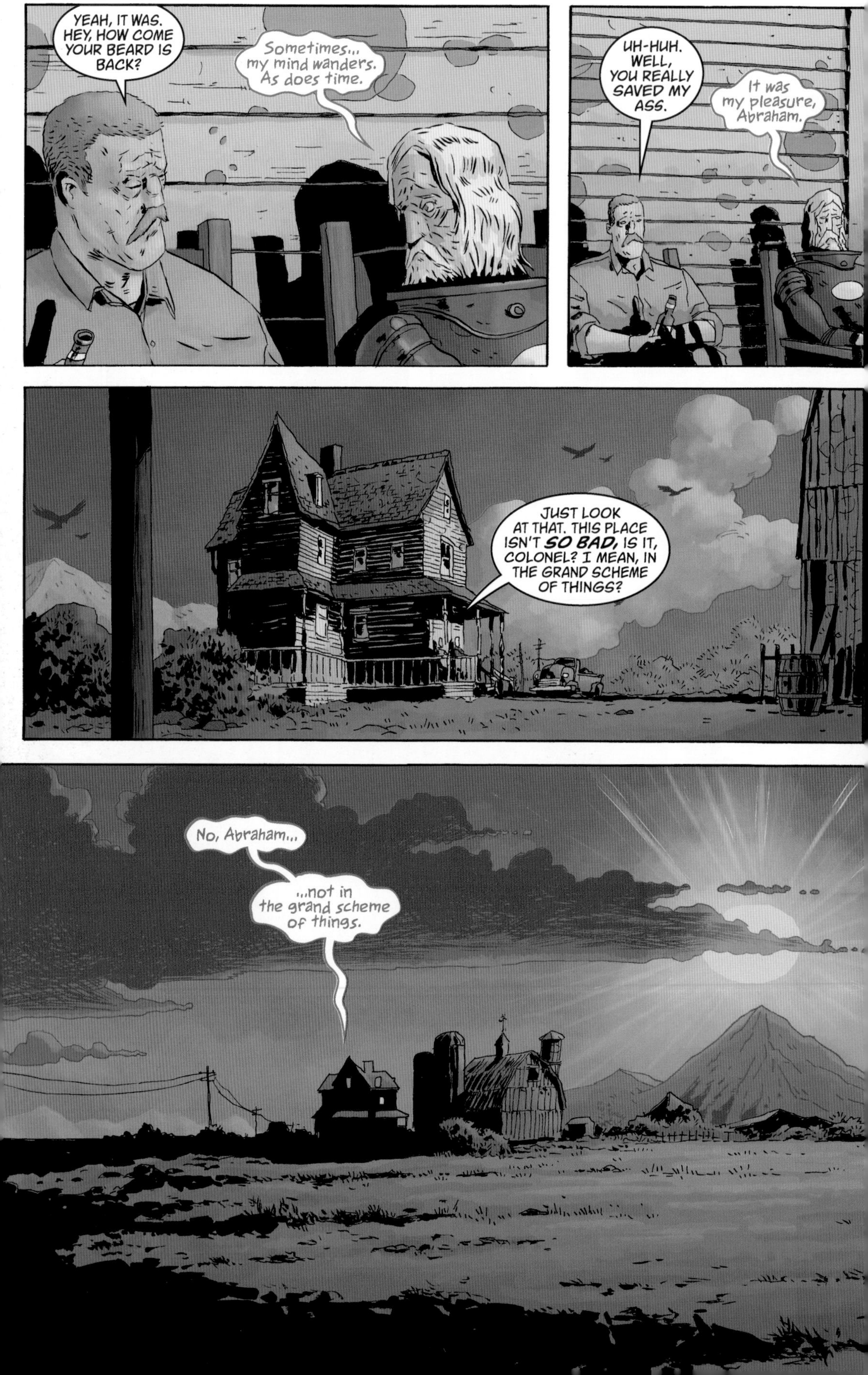

YEAH, IT WAS. HEY, HOW COME YOUR BEARD IS BACK?
Sometimes... my mind wanders. As does time.
UH-HUH. WELL, YOU REALLY SAVED MY ASS.
It was my pleasure, Abraham.
JUST LOOK AT THAT. THIS PLACE ISN'T **SO BAD,** IS IT, COLONEL? I MEAN, IN THE GRAND SCHEME OF THINGS?
No, Abraham...
...not in the grand scheme of things.

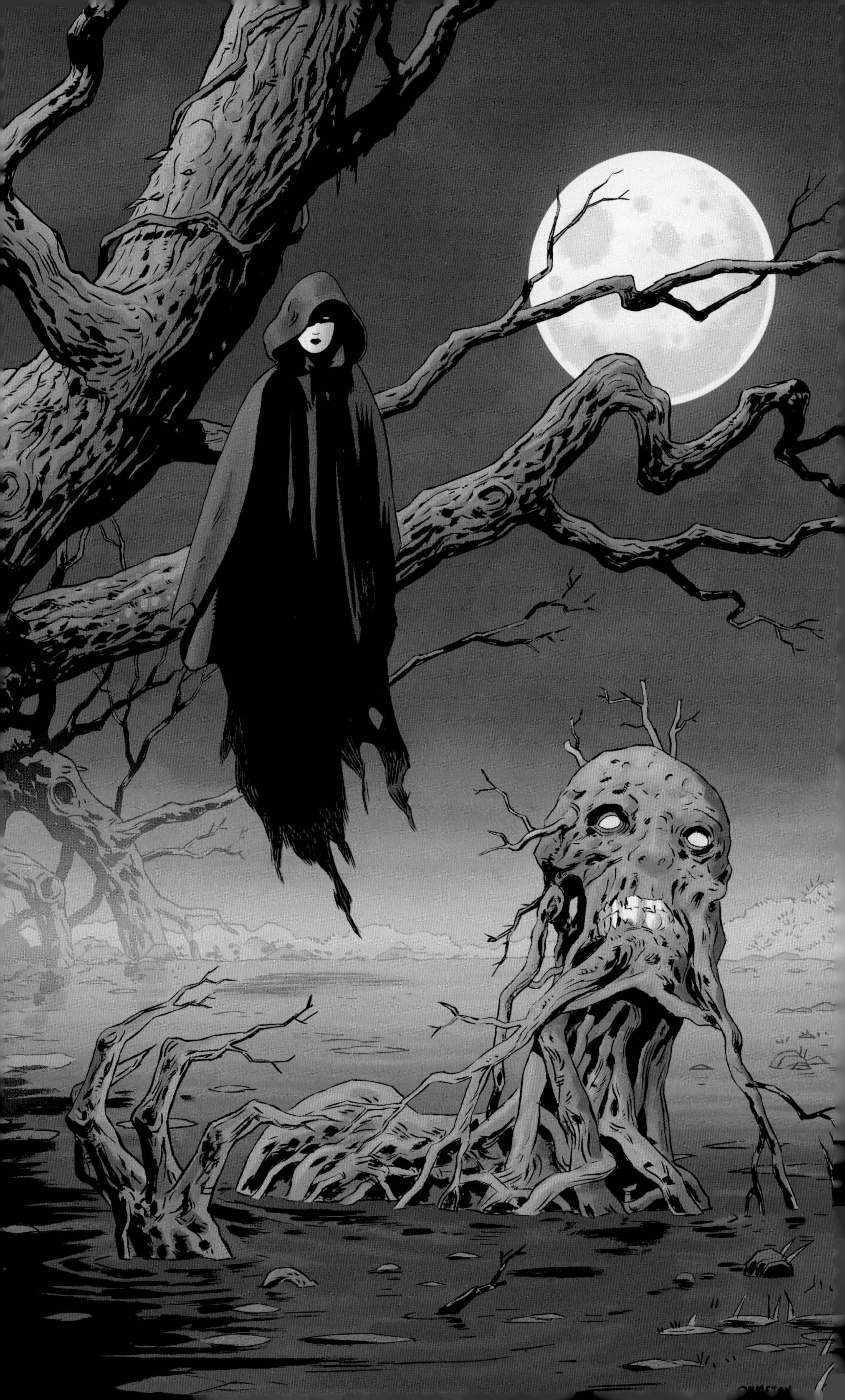

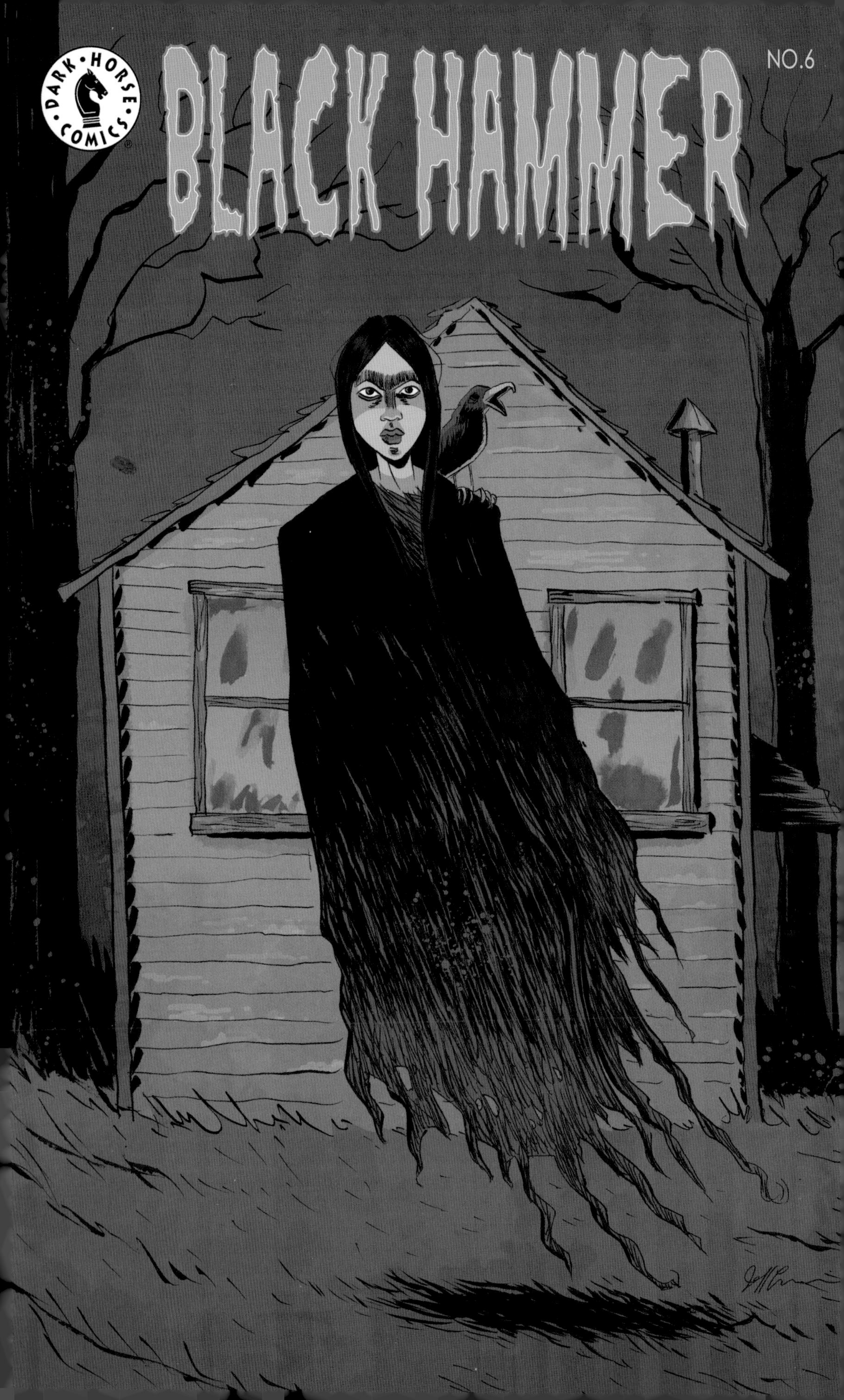
DARK HORSE COMICS
BLACK HAMMER
NO.6

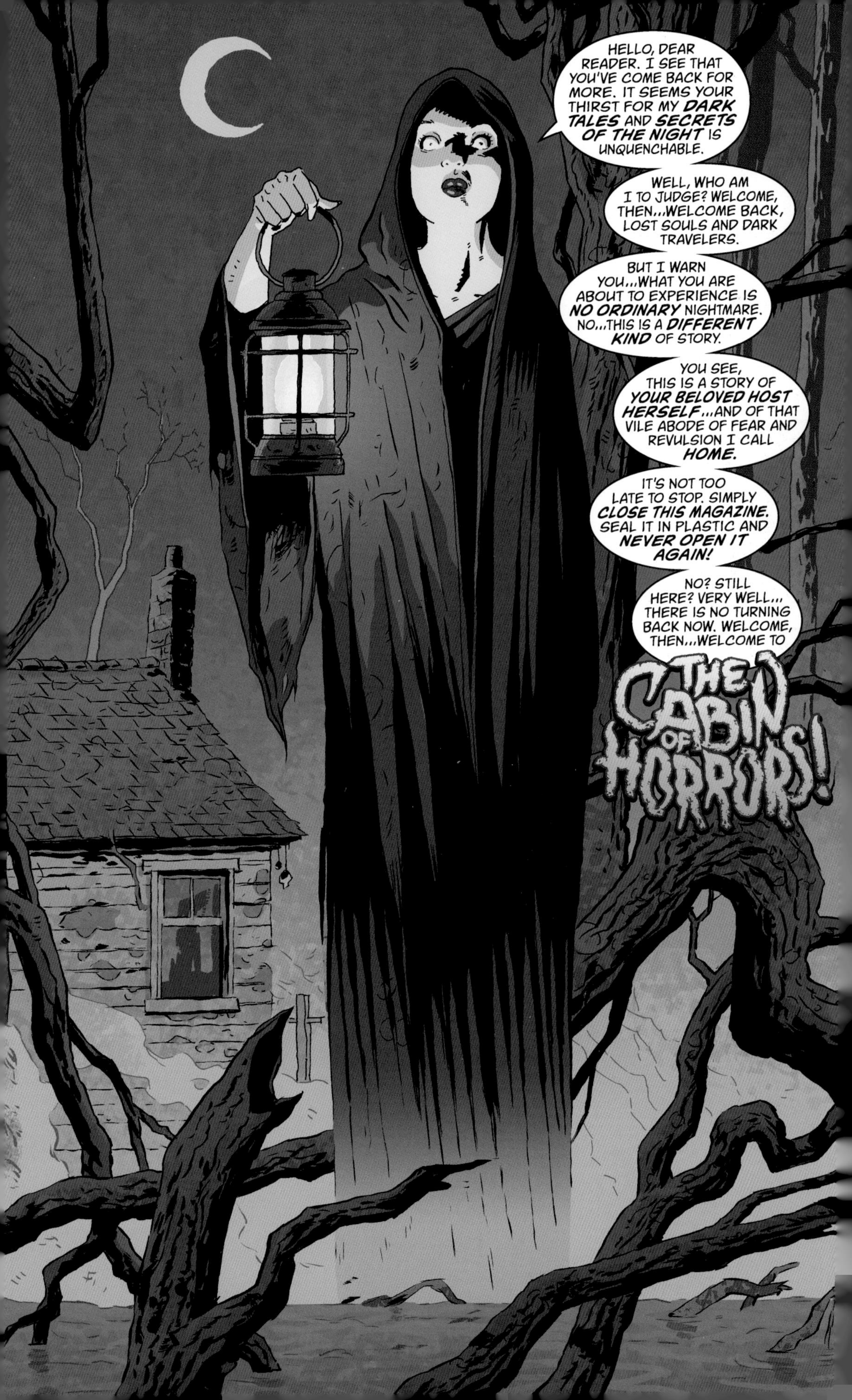
HELLO, DEAR READER. I SEE THAT YOU'VE COME BACK FOR MORE. IT SEEMS YOUR THIRST FOR MY DARK TALES AND SECRETS OF THE NIGHT IS UNQUENCHABLE.
WELL, WHO AM I TO JUDGE? WELCOME, THEN...WELCOME BACK, LOST SOULS AND DARK TRAVELERS.
BUT I WARN YOU...WHAT YOU ARE ABOUT TO EXPERIENCE IS NO ORDINARY NIGHTMARE. NO...THIS IS A DIFFERENT KIND OF STORY.
YOU SEE, THIS IS A STORY OF YOUR BELOVED HOST HERSELF...AND OF THAT VILE ABODE OF FEAR AND REVULSION I CALL HOME.
IT'S NOT TOO LATE TO STOP. SIMPLY CLOSE THIS MAGAZINE. SEAL IT IN PLASTIC AND NEVER OPEN IT AGAIN!
NO? STILL HERE? VERY WELL... THERE IS NO TURNING BACK NOW. WELCOME, THEN...WELCOME TO
THE CABIN OF HORRORS!

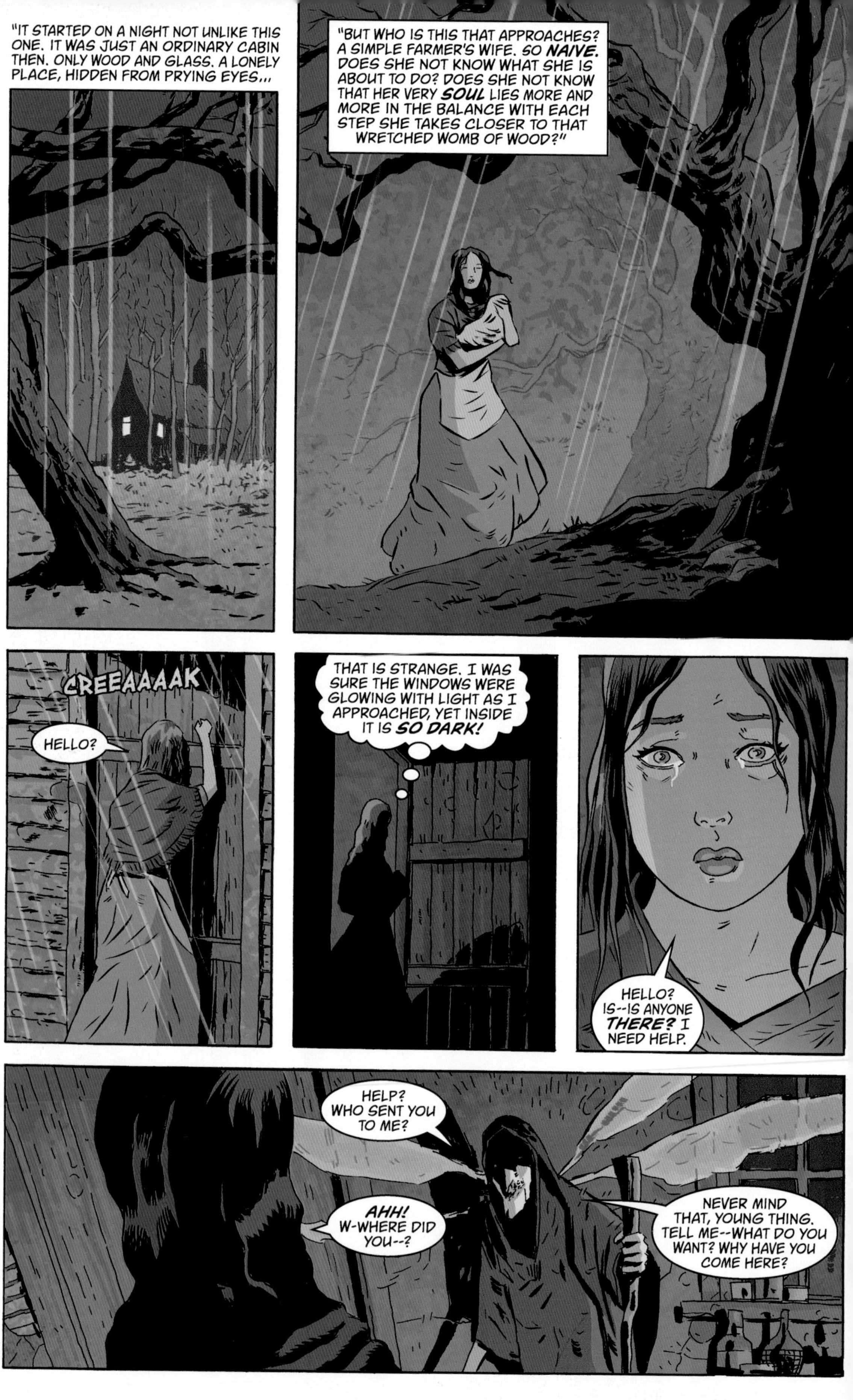
"IT STARTED ON A NIGHT NOT UNLIKE THIS ONE. IT WAS JUST AN ORDINARY CABIN THEN. ONLY WOOD AND GLASS. A LONELY PLACE, HIDDEN FROM PRYING EYES...
"BUT WHO IS THIS THAT APPROACHES? A SIMPLE FARMER'S WIFE. SO NAIVE. DOES SHE NOT KNOW WHAT SHE IS ABOUT TO DO? DOES SHE NOT KNOW THAT HER VERY SOUL LIES MORE AND MORE IN THE BALANCE WITH EACH STEP SHE TAKES CLOSER TO THAT WRETCHED WOMB OF WOOD?"
CREEAAAAK
HELLO?
THAT IS STRANGE. I WAS SURE THE WINDOWS WERE GLOWING WITH LIGHT AS I APPROACHED, YET INSIDE IT IS SO DARK!
HELLO? IS--IS ANYONE THERE? I NEED HELP.
HELP? WHO SENT YOU TO ME?
AHH! W-WHERE DID YOU--?
NEVER MIND THAT, YOUNG THING. TELL ME--WHAT DO YOU WANT? WHY HAVE YOU COME HERE?

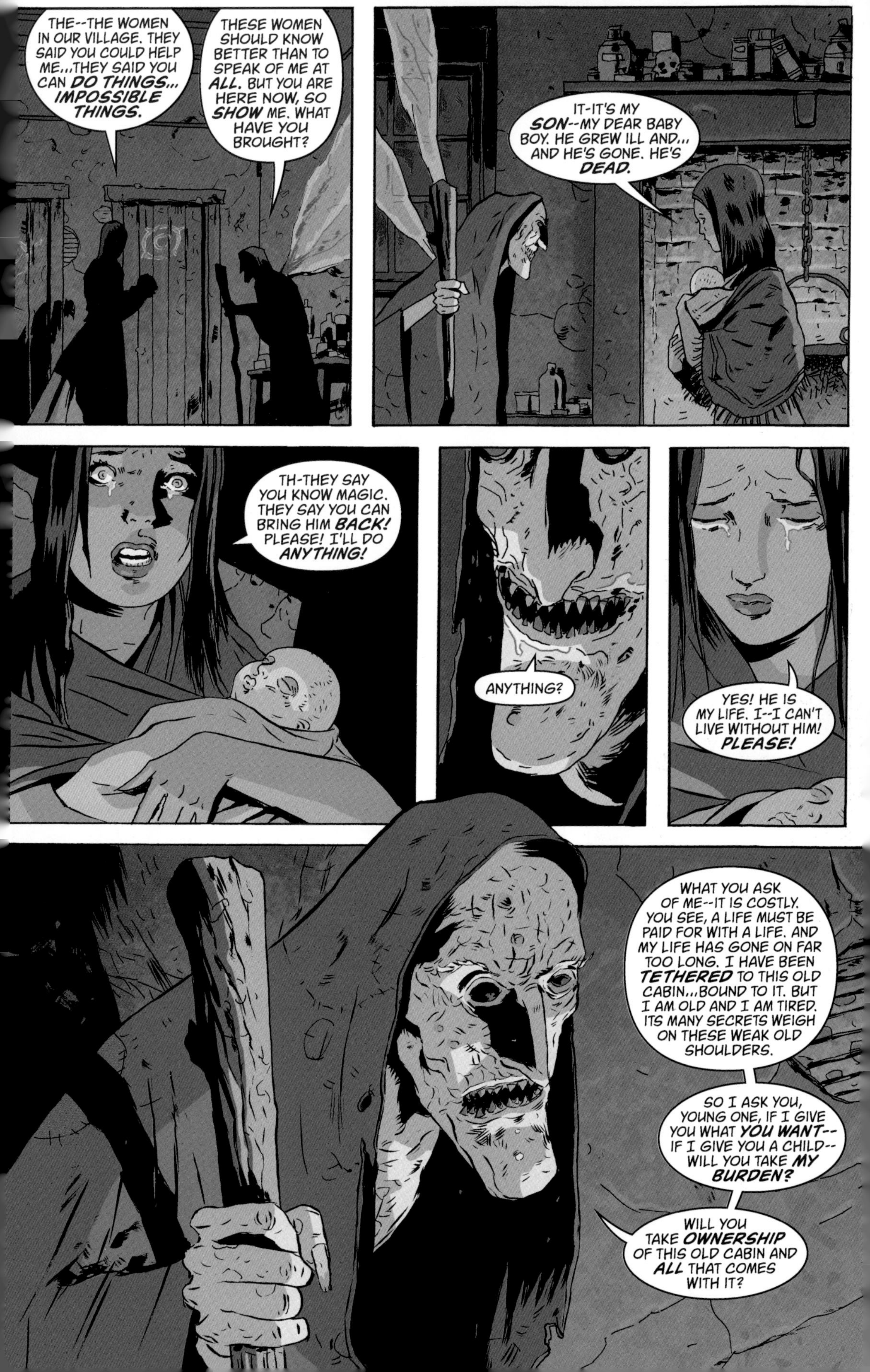
THE--THE WOMEN IN OUR VILLAGE. THEY SAID YOU COULD HELP ME...THEY SAID YOU CAN DO THINGS... IMPOSSIBLE THINGS.
THESE WOMEN SHOULD KNOW BETTER THAN TO SPEAK OF ME AT ALL. BUT YOU ARE HERE NOW, SO SHOW ME. WHAT HAVE YOU BROUGHT?
IT-IT'S MY SON--MY DEAR BABY BOY. HE GREW ILL AND... AND HE'S GONE. HE'S DEAD.
TH-THEY SAY YOU KNOW MAGIC. THEY SAY YOU CAN BRING HIM BACK! PLEASE! I'LL DO ANYTHING!
ANYTHING?
YES! HE IS MY LIFE. I--I CAN'T LIVE WITHOUT HIM! PLEASE!
WHAT YOU ASK OF ME--IT IS COSTLY. YOU SEE, A LIFE MUST BE PAID FOR WITH A LIFE. AND MY LIFE HAS GONE ON FAR TOO LONG. I HAVE BEEN TETHERED TO THIS OLD CABIN...BOUND TO IT. BUT I AM OLD AND I AM TIRED. ITS MANY SECRETS WEIGH ON THESE WEAK OLD SHOULDERS.
SO I ASK YOU, YOUNG ONE, IF I GIVE YOU WHAT YOU WANT-- IF I GIVE YOU A CHILD-- WILL YOU TAKE MY BURDEN?
WILL YOU TAKE OWNERSHIP OF THIS OLD CABIN AND ALL THAT COMES WITH IT?

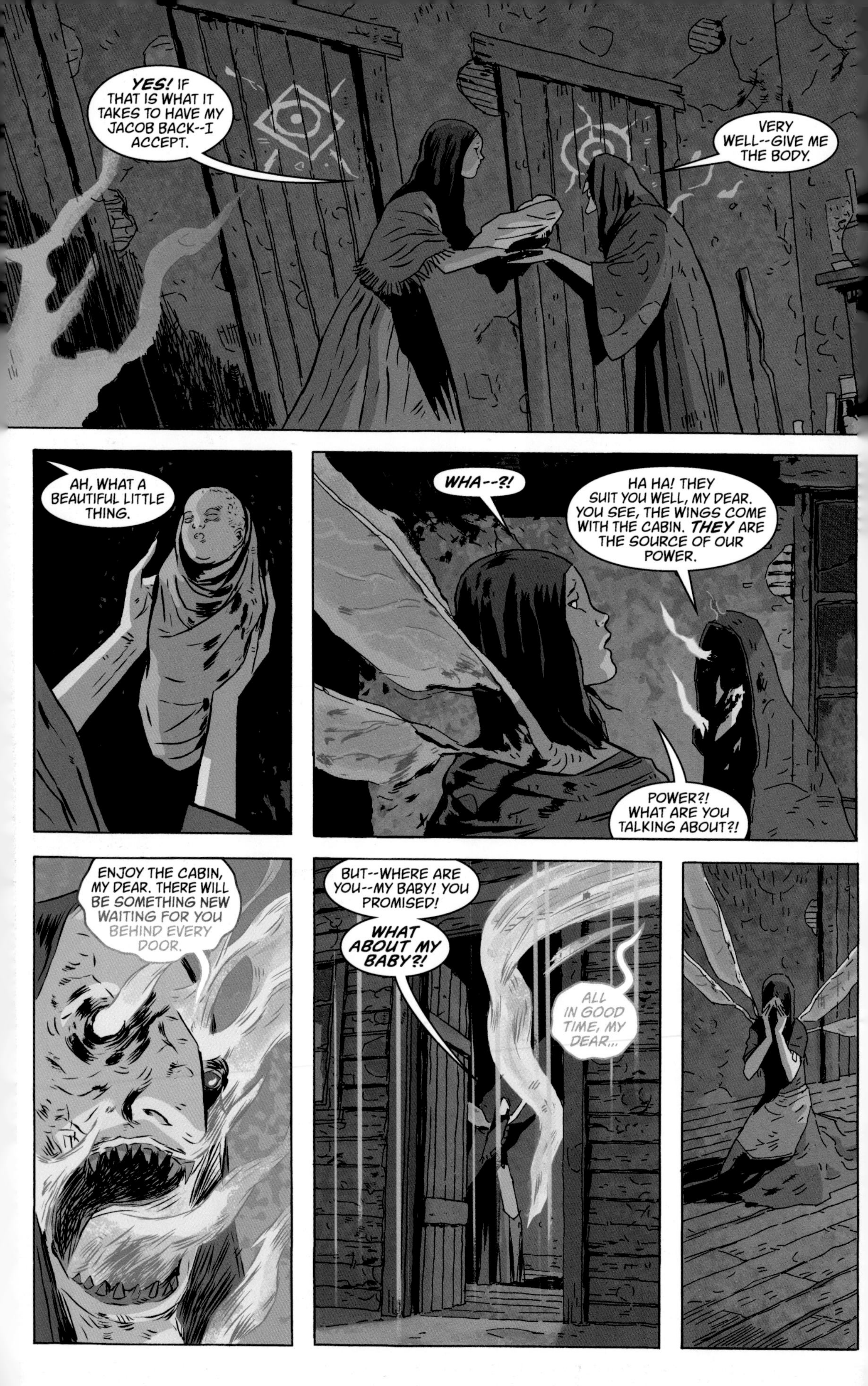
YES! IF THAT IS WHAT IT TAKES TO HAVE MY JACOB BACK--I ACCEPT.
VERY WELL--GIVE ME THE BODY.
AH, WHAT A BEAUTIFUL LITTLE THING.
WHA--?!
HA HA! THEY SUIT YOU WELL, MY DEAR. YOU SEE, THE WINGS COME WITH THE CABIN. THEY ARE THE SOURCE OF OUR POWER.
POWER?! WHAT ARE YOU TALKING ABOUT?!
ENJOY THE CABIN, MY DEAR. THERE WILL BE SOMETHING NEW WAITING FOR YOU BEHIND EVERY DOOR.
BUT--WHERE ARE YOU--MY BABY! YOU PROMISED!
WHAT ABOUT MY BABY?!
ALL IN GOOD TIME, MY DEAR...

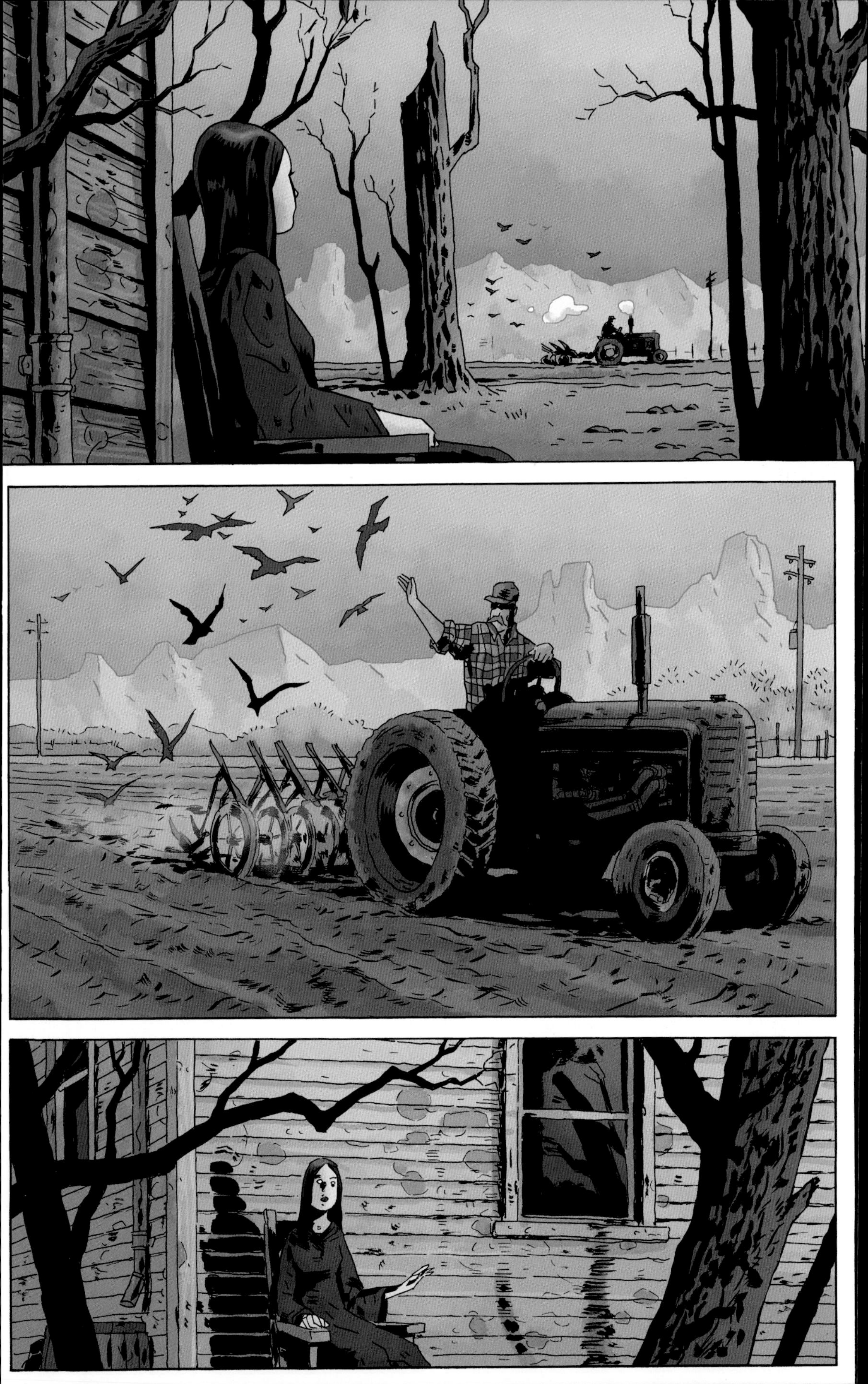

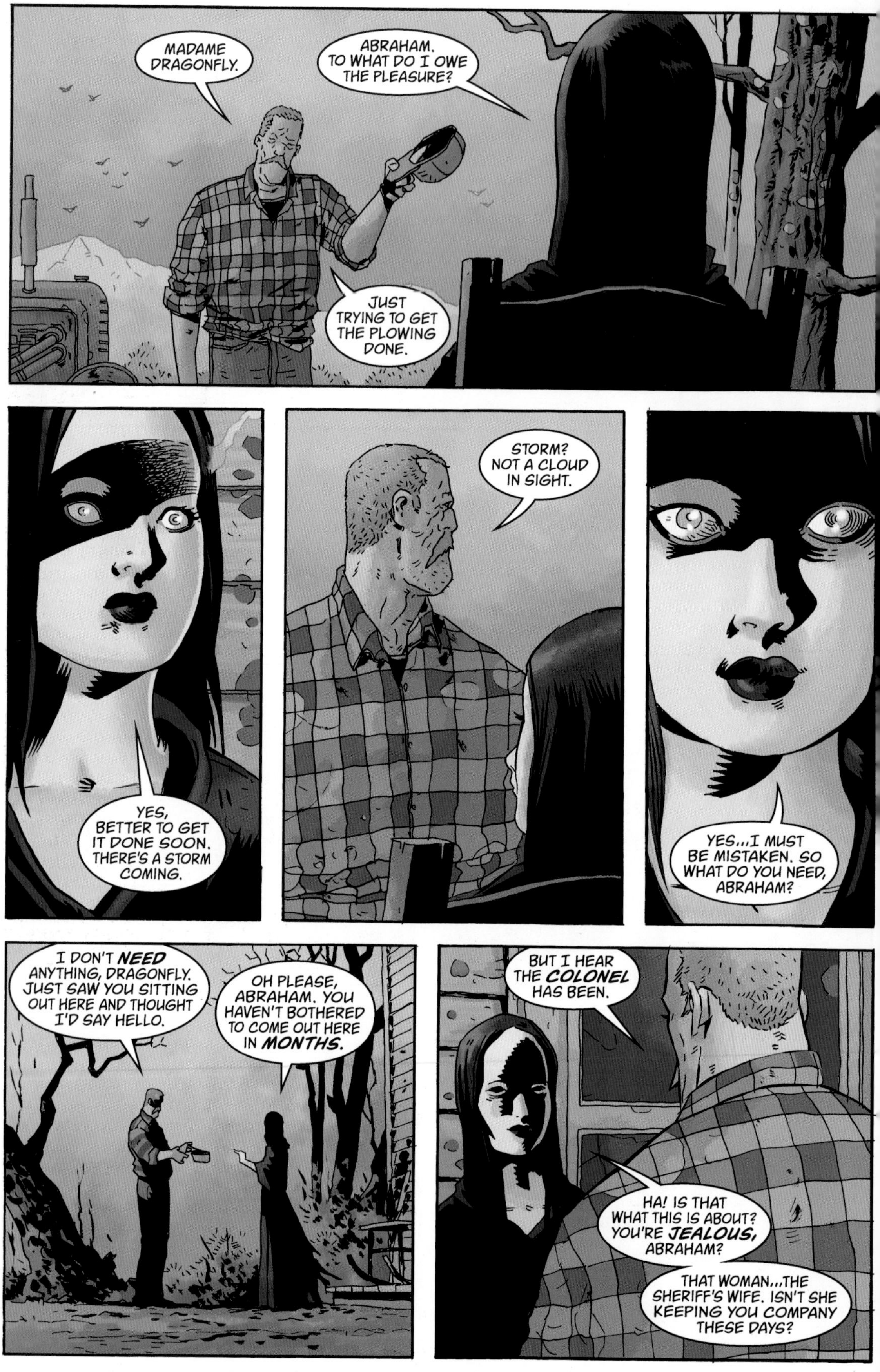
MADAME DRAGONFLY.
ABRAHAM. TO WHAT DO I OWE THE PLEASURE?
JUST TRYING TO GET THE PLOWING DONE.
YES, BETTER TO GET IT DONE SOON. THERE'S A STORM COMING.
STORM? NOT A CLOUD IN SIGHT.
YES...I MUST BE MISTAKEN. SO WHAT DO YOU NEED, ABRAHAM?
I DON'T NEED ANYTHING, DRAGONFLY. JUST SAW YOU SITTING OUT HERE AND THOUGHT I'D SAY HELLO.
OH PLEASE, ABRAHAM. YOU HAVEN'T BOTHERED TO COME OUT HERE IN MONTHS.
BUT I HEAR THE COLONEL HAS BEEN.
HA! IS THAT WHAT THIS IS ABOUT? YOU'RE JEALOUS, ABRAHAM?
THAT WOMAN...THE SHERIFF'S WIFE. ISN'T SHE KEEPING YOU COMPANY THESE DAYS?

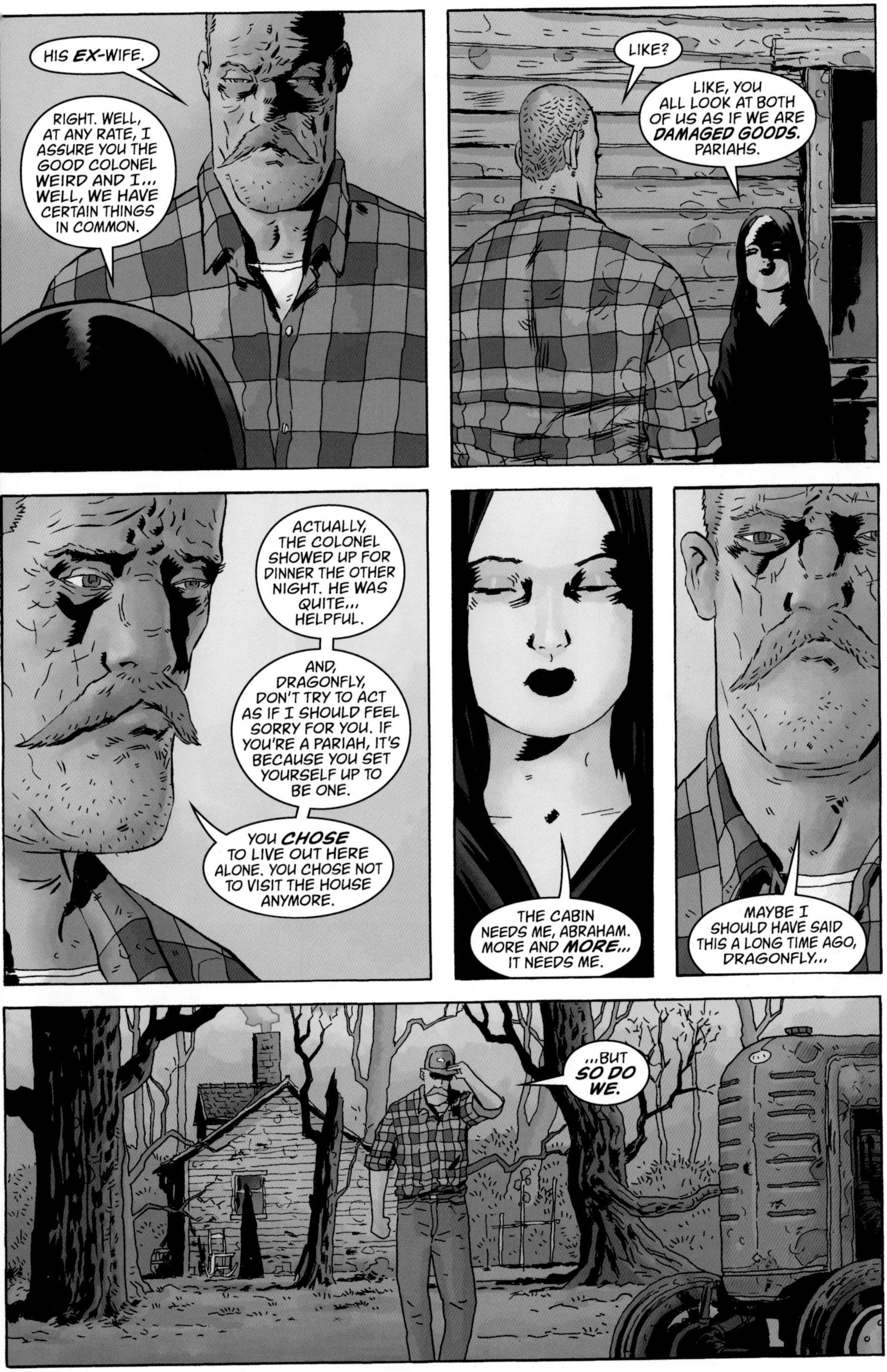
HIS EX-WIFE.
RIGHT. WELL, AT ANY RATE, I ASSURE YOU THE GOOD COLONEL WEIRD AND I... WELL, WE HAVE CERTAIN THINGS IN COMMON.
LIKE?
LIKE, YOU ALL LOOK AT BOTH OF US AS IF WE ARE DAMAGED GOODS. PARIAHS.
ACTUALLY, THE COLONEL SHOWED UP FOR DINNER THE OTHER NIGHT. HE WAS QUITE... HELPFUL.
AND, DRAGONFLY, DON'T TRY TO ACT AS IF I SHOULD FEEL SORRY FOR YOU. IF YOU'RE A PARIAH, IT'S BECAUSE YOU SET YOURSELF UP TO BE ONE.
YOU CHOSE TO LIVE OUT HERE ALONE. YOU CHOSE NOT TO VISIT THE HOUSE ANYMORE.
THE CABIN NEEDS ME, ABRAHAM. MORE AND MORE... IT NEEDS ME.
MAYBE I SHOULD HAVE SAID THIS A LONG TIME AGO, DRAGONFLY...
...BUT SO DO WE.

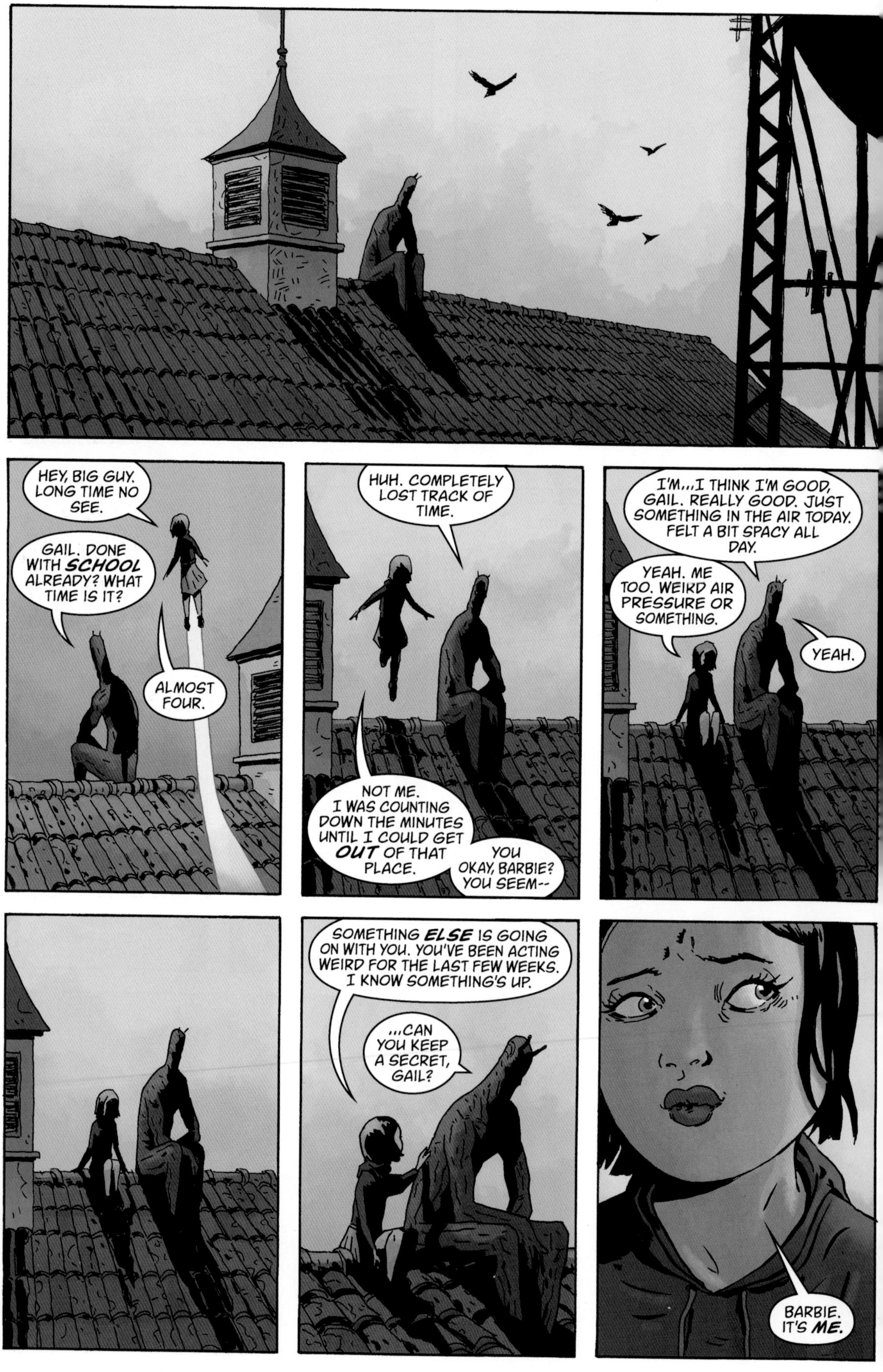
HEY, BIG GUY. LONG TIME NO SEE.
GAIL. DONE WITH SCHOOL ALREADY? WHAT TIME IS IT?
ALMOST FOUR.
HUH. COMPLETELY LOST TRACK OF TIME.
NOT ME. I WAS COUNTING DOWN THE MINUTES UNTIL I COULD GET OUT OF THAT PLACE.
YOU OKAY, BARBIE? YOU SEEM--
I'M...I THINK I'M GOOD, GAIL. REALLY GOOD. JUST SOMETHING IN THE AIR TODAY. FELT A BIT SPACY ALL DAY.
YEAH. ME TOO. WEIRD AIR PRESSURE OR SOMETHING.
YEAH.
SOMETHING ELSE IS GOING ON WITH YOU. YOU'VE BEEN ACTING WEIRD FOR THE LAST FEW WEEKS. I KNOW SOMETHING'S UP.
...CAN YOU KEEP A SECRET, GAIL?
BARBIE. IT'S ME.

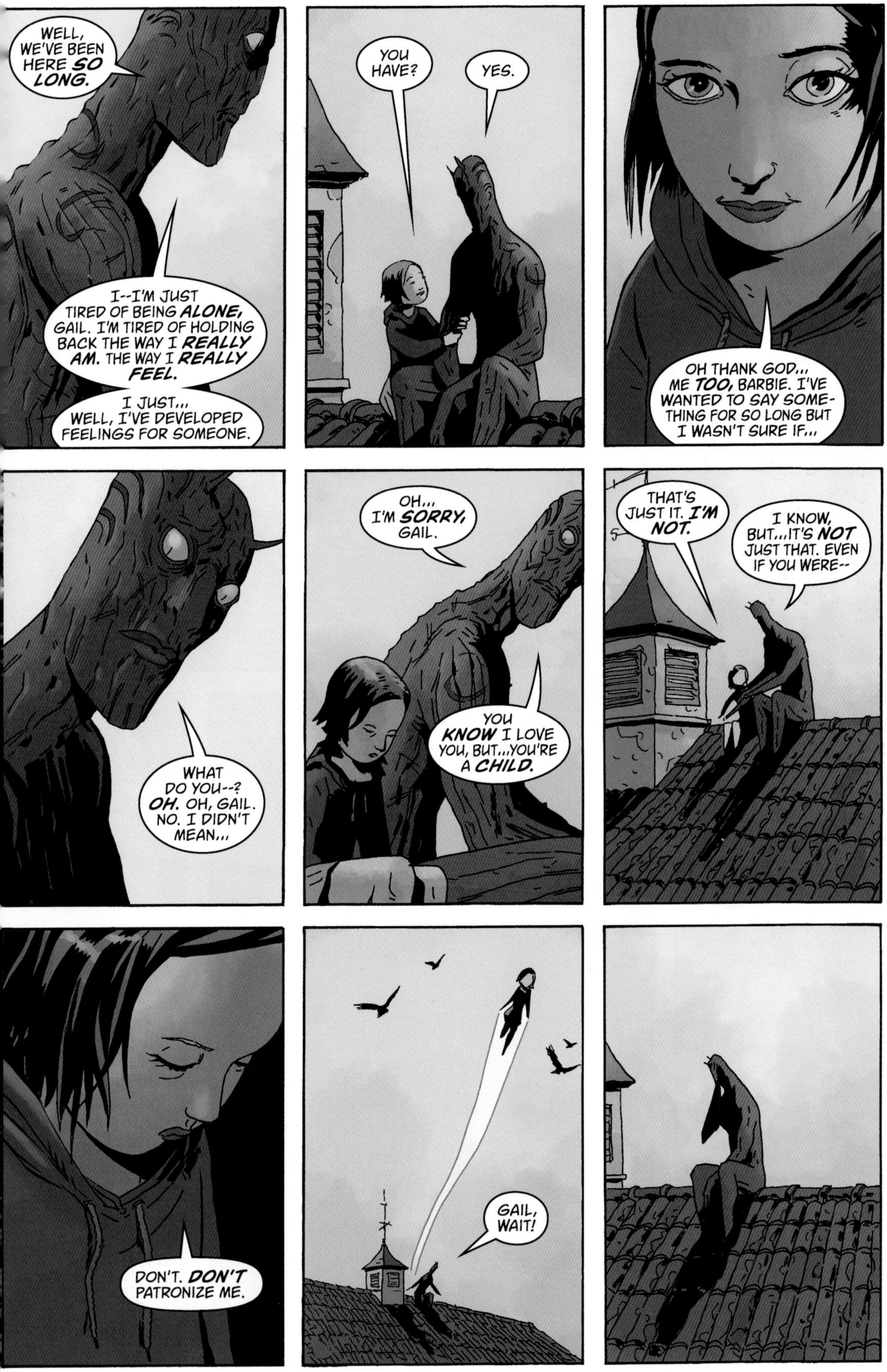
WELL, WE'VE BEEN HERE SO LONG.
I--I'M JUST TIRED OF BEING ALONE, GAIL. I'M TIRED OF HOLDING BACK THE WAY I REALLY AM. THE WAY I REALLY FEEL.
I JUST... WELL, I'VE DEVELOPED FEELINGS FOR SOMEONE.
YOU HAVE?
YES.
OH THANK GOD... ME TOO, BARBIE. I'VE WANTED TO SAY SOMETHING FOR SO LONG BUT I WASN'T SURE IF...
WHAT DO YOU--? OH. OH, GAIL. NO. I DIDN'T MEAN...
OH... I'M SORRY, GAIL.
YOU KNOW I LOVE YOU, BUT...YOU'RE A CHILD.
THAT'S JUST IT. I'M NOT.
I KNOW, BUT...IT'S NOT JUST THAT. EVEN IF YOU WERE--
DON'T. DON'T PATRONIZE ME.
GAIL, WAIT!

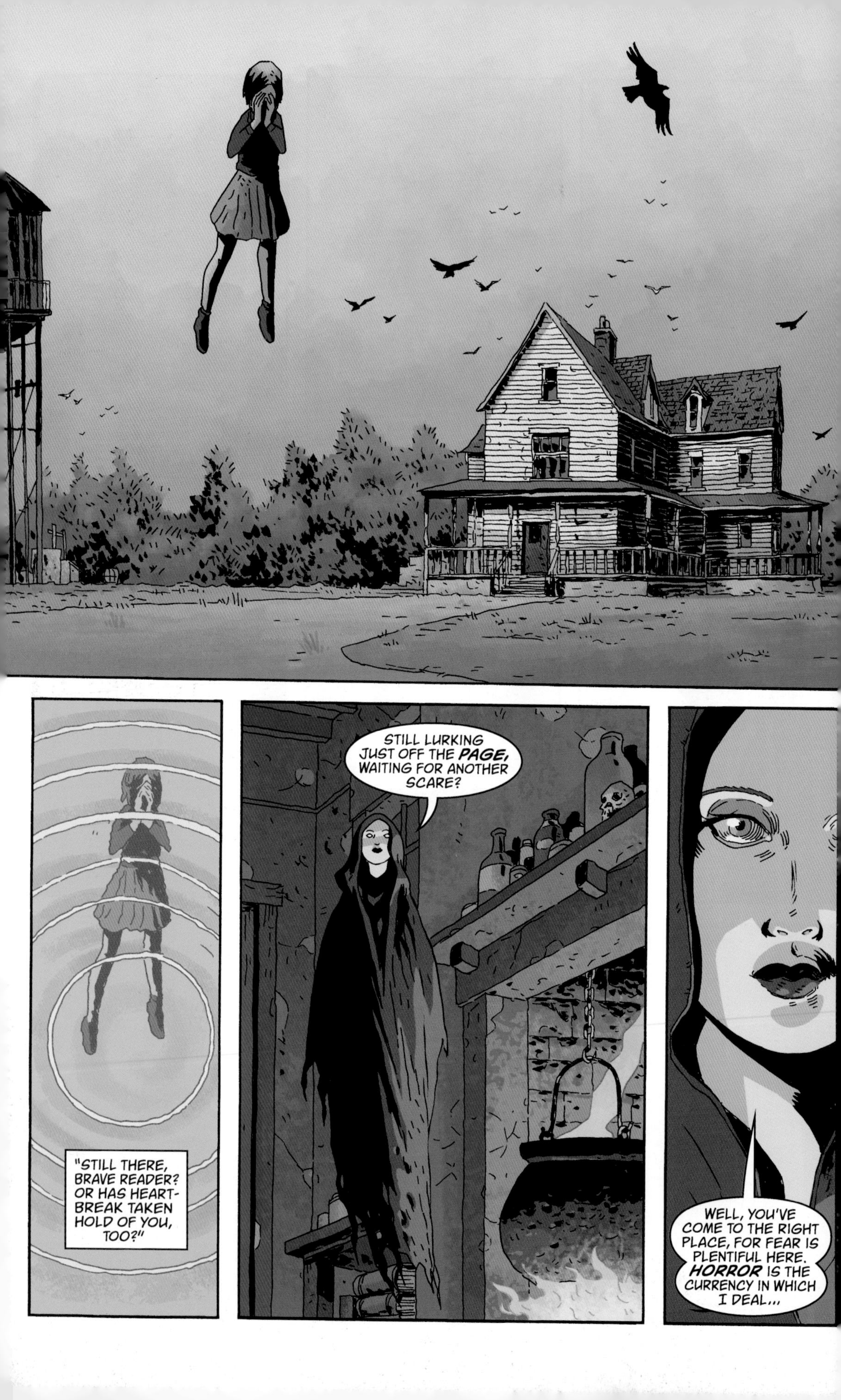
"STILL THERE, BRAVE READER? OR HAS HEART-BREAK TAKEN HOLD OF YOU, TOO?"
STILL LURKING JUST OFF THE *PAGE,* WAITING FOR ANOTHER SCARE?
WELL, YOU'VE COME TO THE RIGHT PLACE, FOR FEAR IS PLENTIFUL HERE. *HORROR* IS THE CURRENCY IN WHICH I DEAL...

"WHEN WE LAST MET, I TOLD YOU A TALE OF LONG AGO. *THIS* PARABLE OF PAIN IS MUCH FRESHER...NEARLY ONE HUNDRED YEARS AFTER THE OLD WITCH PROMISED YOUR FAITHFUL HOST HER HEART'S DESIRE, AND INSTEAD LEFT HER WITH A *BURDEN* IN THE SHAPE OF A CABIN."

KRA-KOOM

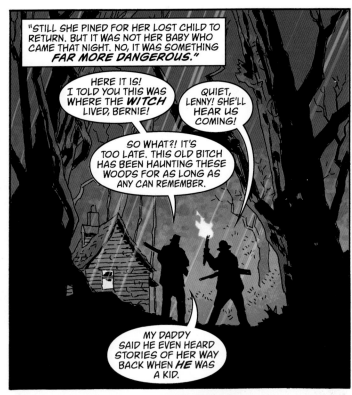

"STILL SHE PINED FOR HER LOST CHILD TO RETURN. BUT IT WAS NOT HER BABY WHO CAME THAT NIGHT. NO, IT WAS SOMETHING *FAR MORE DANGEROUS.*"

HERE IT IS! I TOLD YOU THIS WAS WHERE THE *WITCH* LIVED, BERNIE!

QUIET, LENNY! SHE'LL HEAR US COMING!

SO WHAT?! IT'S TOO LATE. THIS OLD BITCH HAS BEEN HAUNTING THESE WOODS FOR AS LONG AS ANY CAN REMEMBER.

MY DADDY SAID HE EVEN HEARD STORIES OF HER WAY BACK WHEN *HE* WAS A KID.

WHO *DARES* APPROACH *MY CABIN* WITHOUT AN INVITA- TION?!

WE--WE DON'T WANT NO TROUBLE. WE WANT THE KIDS--THE *MISSING KIDS.* WE KNOW YOU HAVE 'EM!

THERE ARE CHILDREN MISSING? I'M SORRY, I DIDN'T REALIZE--PERHAPS I CAN HELP?

STAY BACK, YOU LYING WHORE! YOU GOT THEM *IN THERE,* DON'T YOU?!

THERE ARE *MANY THINGS* HIDING IN THIS OLD CABIN, BUT I ASSURE YOU, CHILDREN ARE *NOT* AMONG THEM.

NOW, I WARN YOU...*DO NOT THREATEN ME AGAIN.*

COME ON, LEN, MAYBE WE SHOULD GO. THIS AIN'T RIGHT.

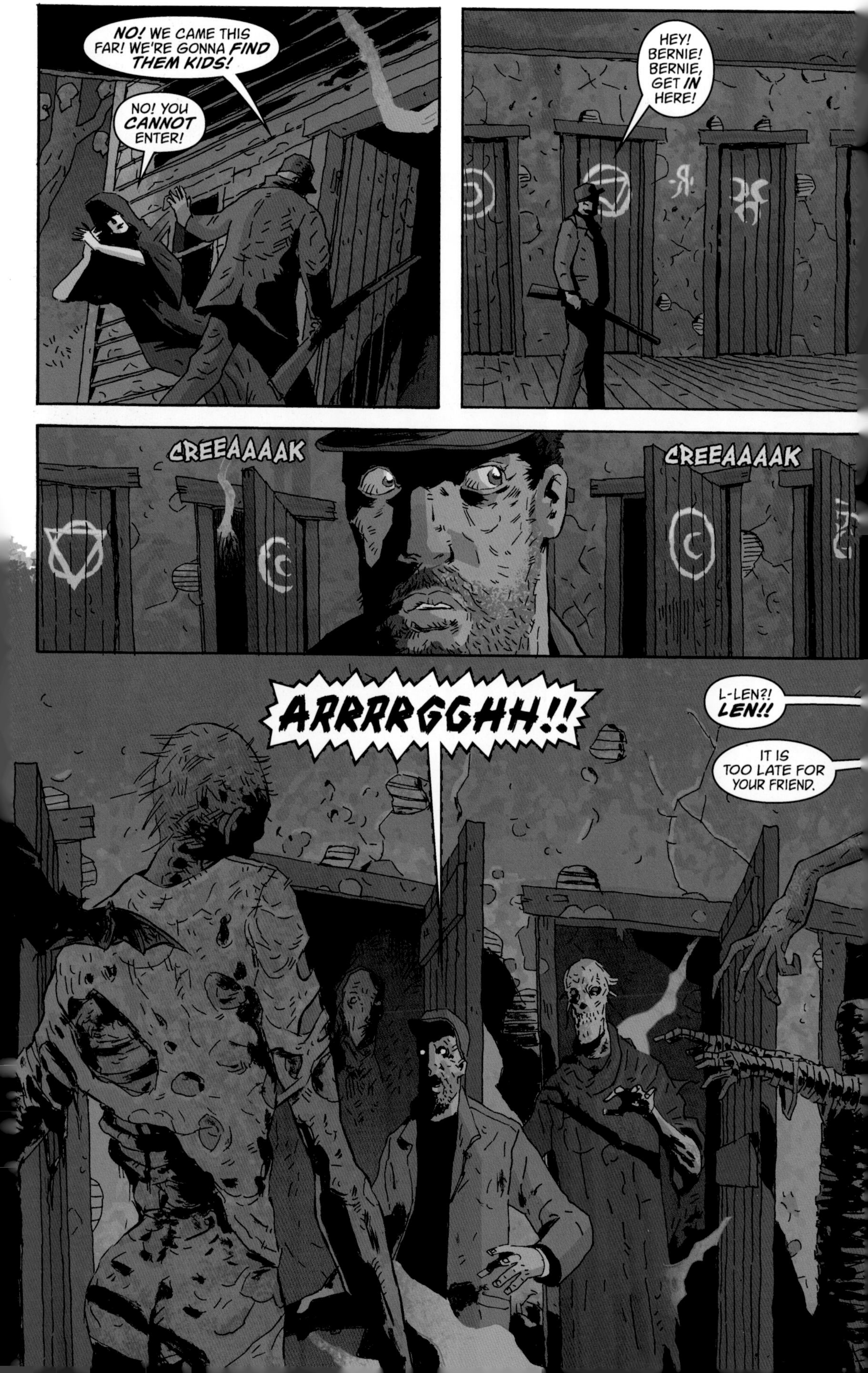
NO! WE CAME THIS FAR! WE'RE GONNA FIND THEM KIDS!
NO! YOU CANNOT ENTER!
HEY! BERNIE! BERNIE, GET IN HERE!
CREEAAAAK
CREEAAAAK
ARRRRGGHH!!
L-LEN?! LEN!!
IT IS TOO LATE FOR YOUR FRIEND.

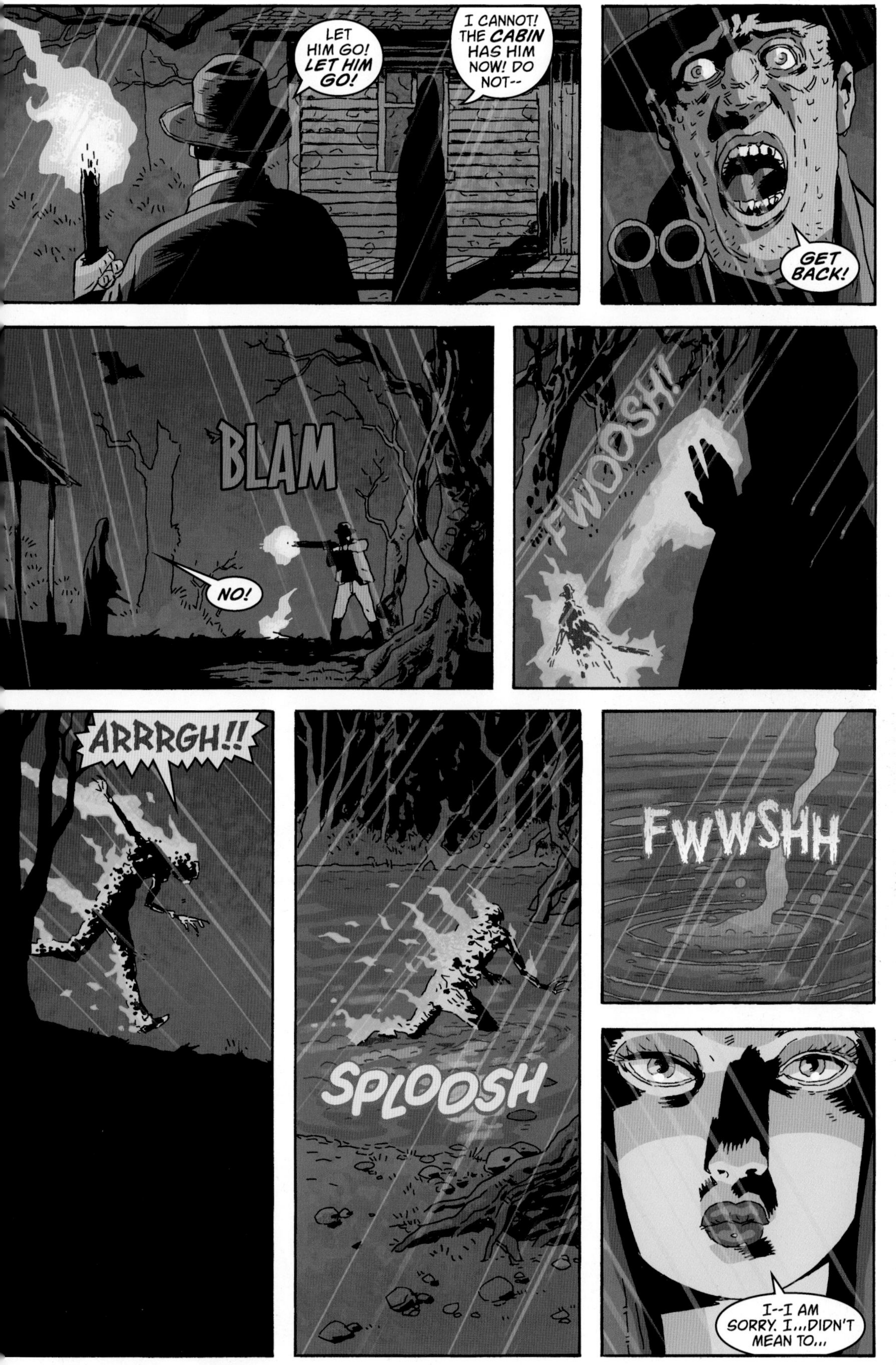
LET HIM GO! LET HIM GO!
I CANNOT! THE CABIN HAS HIM NOW! DO NOT--
GET BACK!
BLAM
NO!
FWOOSH!
ARRRGH!!
SPLOOSH
FWWSHH
I--I AM SORRY. I...DIDN'T MEAN TO...

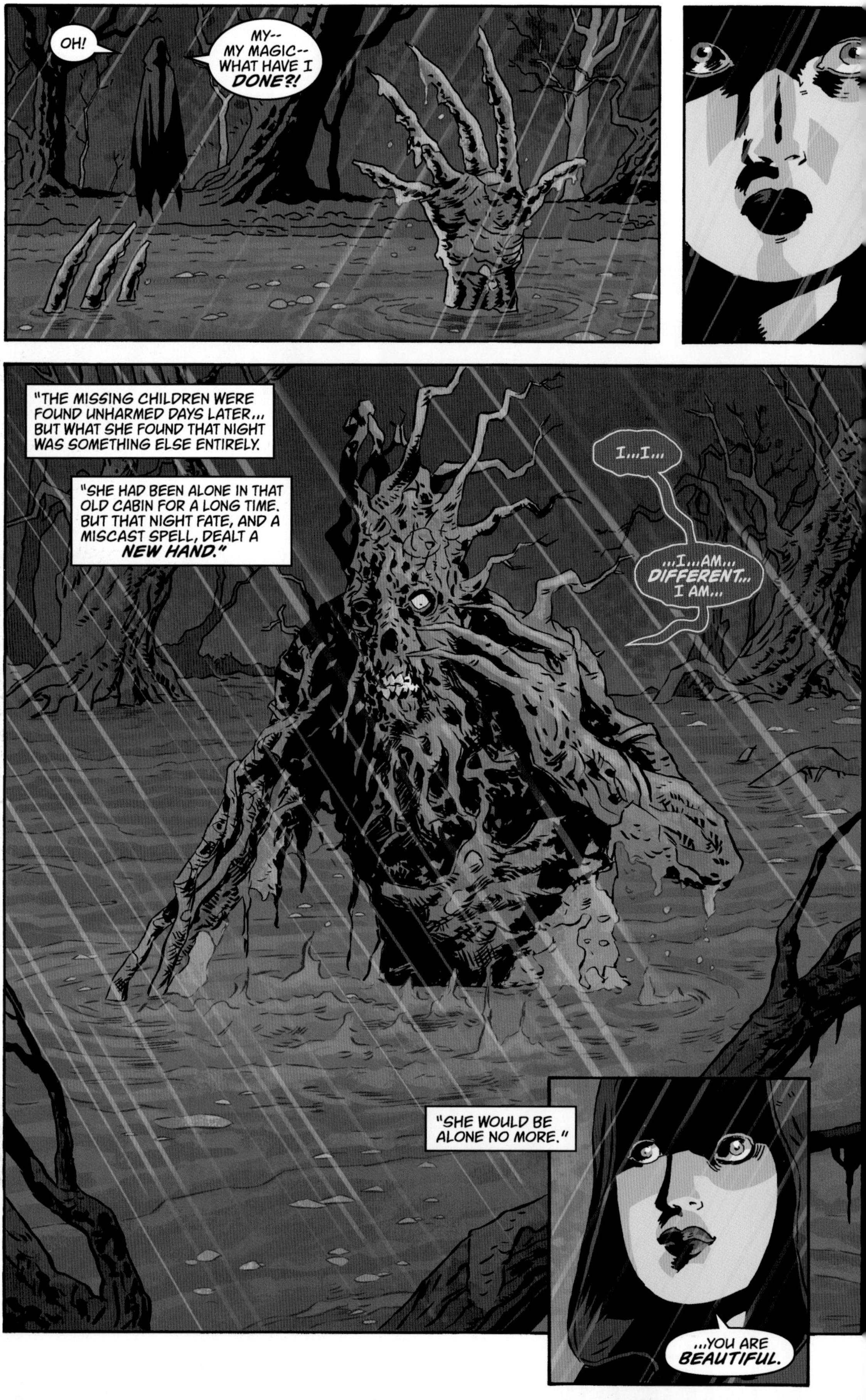
OH!
MY-- MY MAGIC-- WHAT HAVE I DONE?!
"THE MISSING CHILDREN WERE FOUND UNHARMED DAYS LATER... BUT WHAT SHE FOUND THAT NIGHT WAS SOMETHING ELSE ENTIRELY.
"SHE HAD BEEN ALONE IN THAT OLD CABIN FOR A LONG TIME. BUT THAT NIGHT FATE, AND A MISCAST SPELL, DEALT A NEW HAND."
I...I...
...I...AM... DIFFERENT... I AM...
"SHE WOULD BE ALONE NO MORE."
...YOU ARE BEAUTIFUL.

HEY, BEAUTIFUL.

ABE! I THOUGHT YOU WERE WORKING ALL DAY?

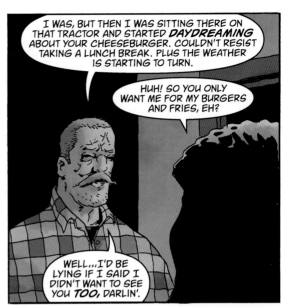

I WAS, BUT THEN I WAS SITTING THERE ON THAT TRACTOR AND STARTED *DAYDREAMING* ABOUT YOUR CHEESEBURGER. COULDN'T RESIST TAKING A LUNCH BREAK. PLUS THE WEATHER IS STARTING TO TURN.

HUH! SO YOU ONLY WANT ME FOR MY BURGERS AND FRIES, EH?

WELL...I'D BE LYING IF I SAID I DIDN'T WANT TO SEE YOU *TOO*, DARLIN'.

I HAD A REAL NICE TIME AT DINNER THE OTHER NIGHT.

YEAH, THAT WAS ALL RIGHT, WASN'T IT?

SURE WAS.

YOU KNOW, ABE, I BEEN *THINKING*...YOU SAID YOU'D BE DONE IN THE FIELDS IN ANOTHER WEEK OR TWO, AND I GOT A VACATION WEEK SAVED UP...WHAT DO YOU THINK ABOUT GETTING OUT OF TOWN?

I....UH....

WELL. THAT IS *NOT* THE REACTION I EXPECTED.

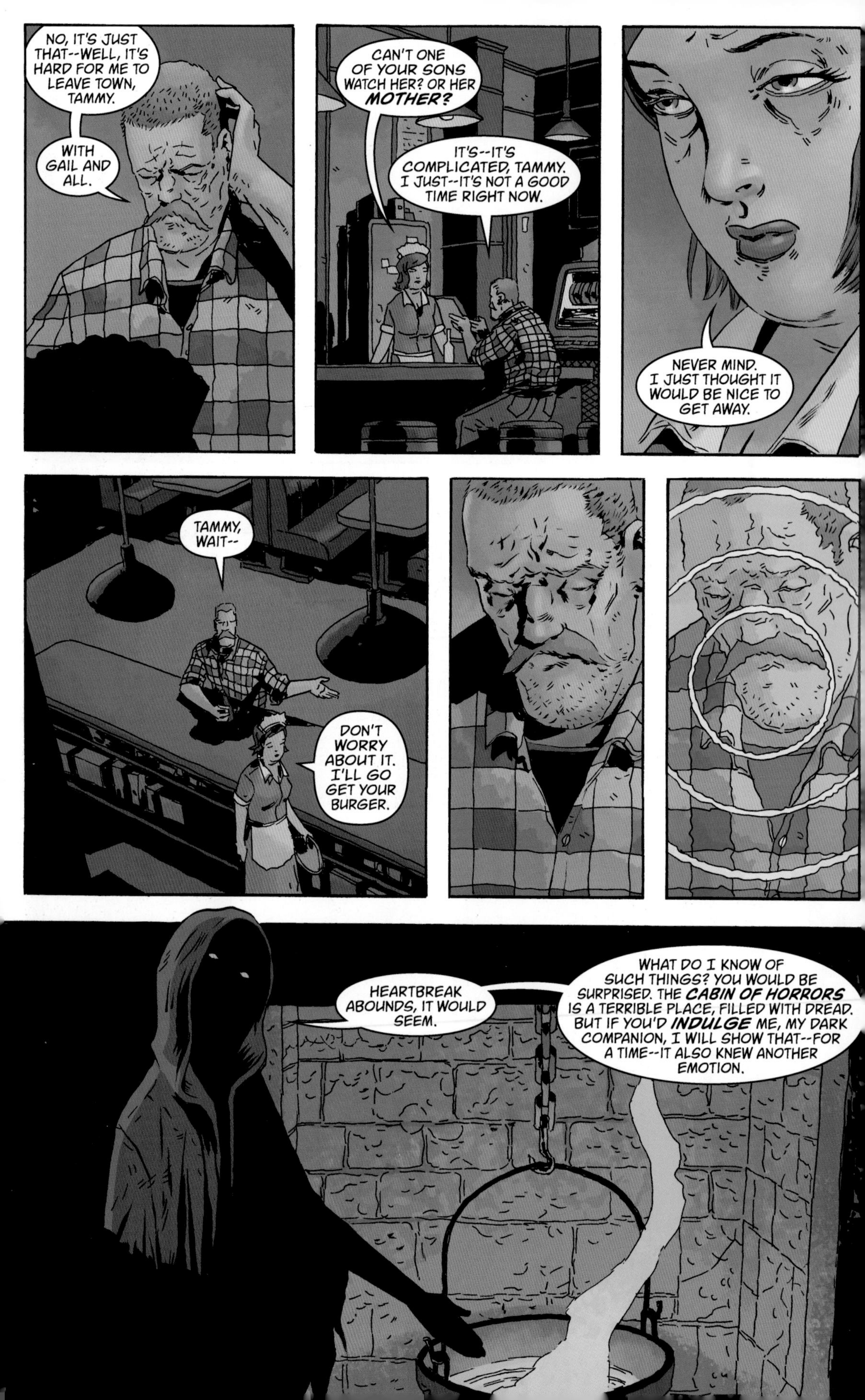
NO, IT'S JUST THAT--WELL, IT'S HARD FOR ME TO LEAVE TOWN, TAMMY.
WITH GAIL AND ALL.
CAN'T ONE OF YOUR SONS WATCH HER? OR HER **MOTHER?**
IT'S--IT'S COMPLICATED, TAMMY. I JUST--IT'S NOT A GOOD TIME RIGHT NOW.
NEVER MIND. I JUST THOUGHT IT WOULD BE NICE TO GET AWAY.
TAMMY, WAIT--
DON'T WORRY ABOUT IT. I'LL GO GET YOUR BURGER.
HEARTBREAK ABOUNDS, IT WOULD SEEM.
WHAT DO I KNOW OF SUCH THINGS? YOU WOULD BE SURPRISED. THE **CABIN OF HORRORS** IS A TERRIBLE PLACE, FILLED WITH DREAD. BUT IF YOU'D **INDULGE** ME, MY DARK COMPANION, I WILL SHOW THAT--FOR A TIME--IT ALSO KNEW ANOTHER EMOTION.

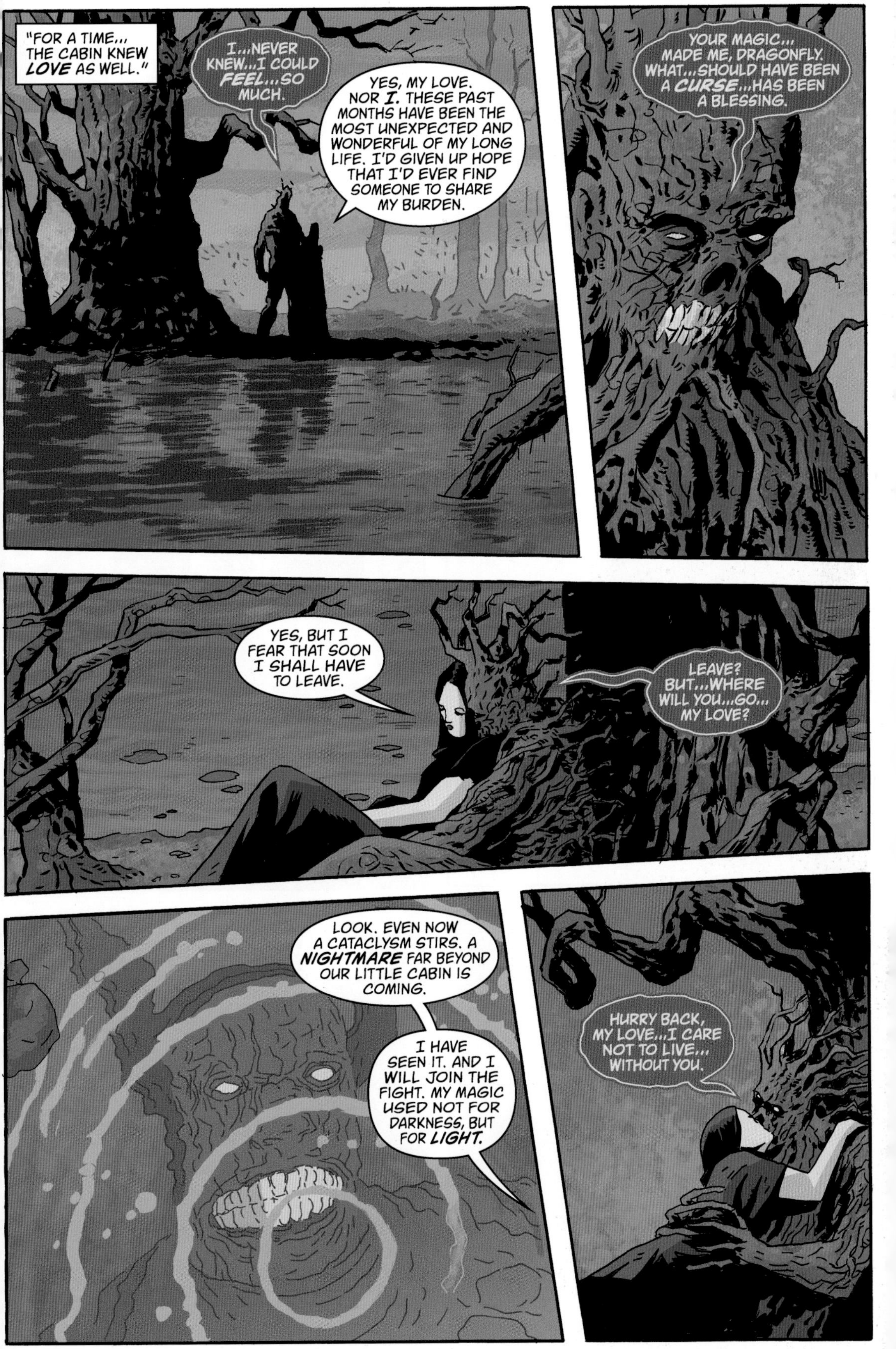
"FOR A TIME... THE CABIN KNEW LOVE AS WELL."
I...NEVER KNEW...I COULD FEEL...SO MUCH.
YES, MY LOVE. NOR I. THESE PAST MONTHS HAVE BEEN THE MOST UNEXPECTED AND WONDERFUL OF MY LONG LIFE. I'D GIVEN UP HOPE THAT I'D EVER FIND SOMEONE TO SHARE MY BURDEN.
YOUR MAGIC... MADE ME, DRAGONFLY. WHAT...SHOULD HAVE BEEN A CURSE...HAS BEEN A BLESSING.
YES, BUT I FEAR THAT SOON I SHALL HAVE TO LEAVE.
LEAVE? BUT...WHERE WILL YOU...GO... MY LOVE?
LOOK. EVEN NOW A CATACLYSM STIRS. A NIGHTMARE FAR BEYOND OUR LITTLE CABIN IS COMING.
I HAVE SEEN IT. AND I WILL JOIN THE FIGHT. MY MAGIC USED NOT FOR DARKNESS, BUT FOR LIGHT.
HURRY BACK, MY LOVE...I CARE NOT TO LIVE... WITHOUT YOU.

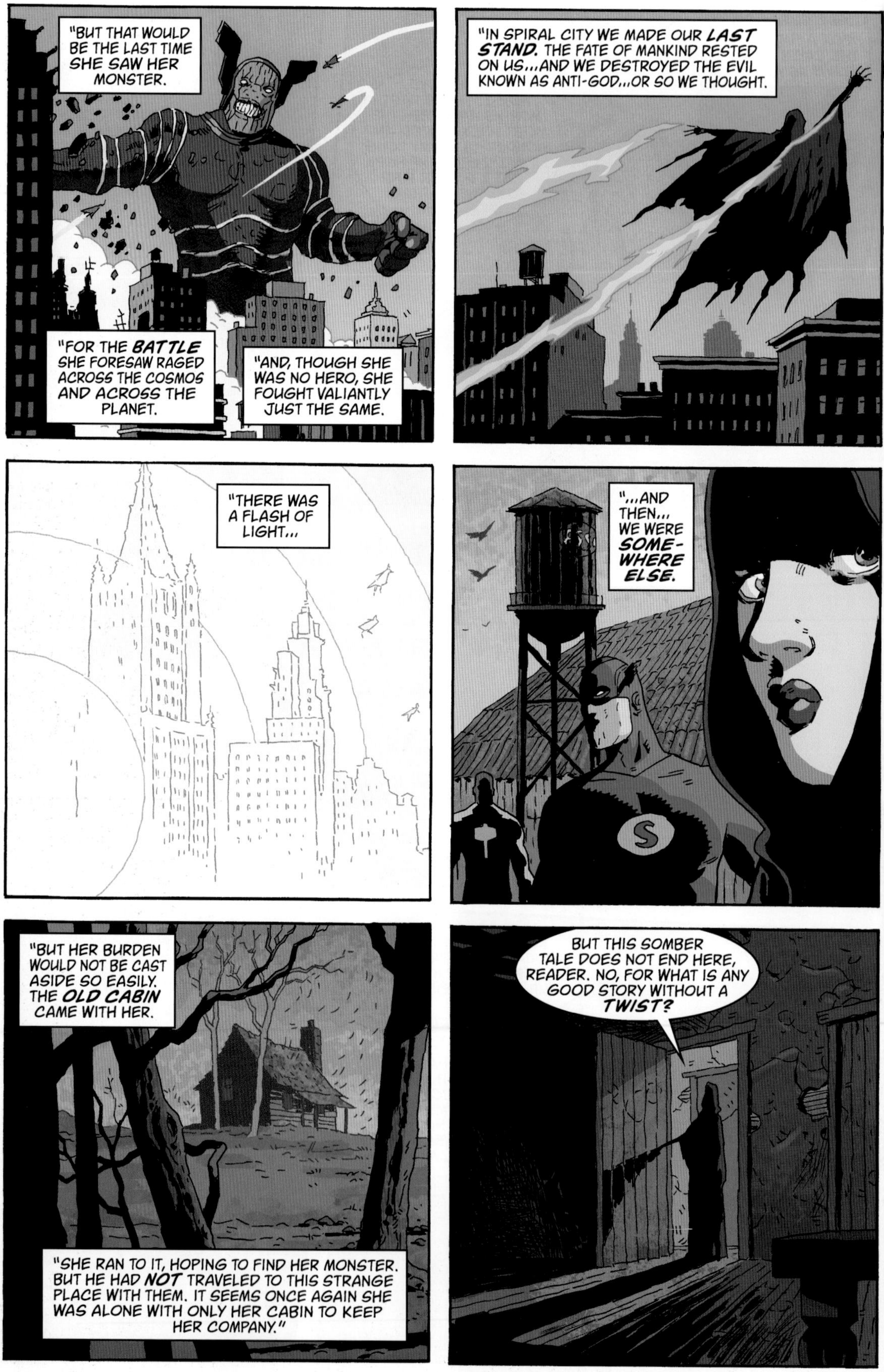
"BUT THAT WOULD BE THE LAST TIME SHE SAW HER MONSTER.
"FOR THE BATTLE SHE FORESAW RAGED ACROSS THE COSMOS AND ACROSS THE PLANET.
"AND, THOUGH SHE WAS NO HERO, SHE FOUGHT VALIANTLY JUST THE SAME.
"IN SPIRAL CITY WE MADE OUR LAST STAND. THE FATE OF MANKIND RESTED ON US...AND WE DESTROYED THE EVIL KNOWN AS ANTI-GOD...OR SO WE THOUGHT.
"THERE WAS A FLASH OF LIGHT...
"...AND THEN... WE WERE SOME-WHERE ELSE.
"BUT HER BURDEN WOULD NOT BE CAST ASIDE SO EASILY. THE OLD CABIN CAME WITH HER.
"SHE RAN TO IT, HOPING TO FIND HER MONSTER. BUT HE HAD NOT TRAVELED TO THIS STRANGE PLACE WITH THEM. IT SEEMS ONCE AGAIN SHE WAS ALONE WITH ONLY HER CABIN TO KEEP HER COMPANY."
BUT THIS SOMBER TALE DOES NOT END HERE, READER. NO, FOR WHAT IS ANY GOOD STORY WITHOUT A TWIST?

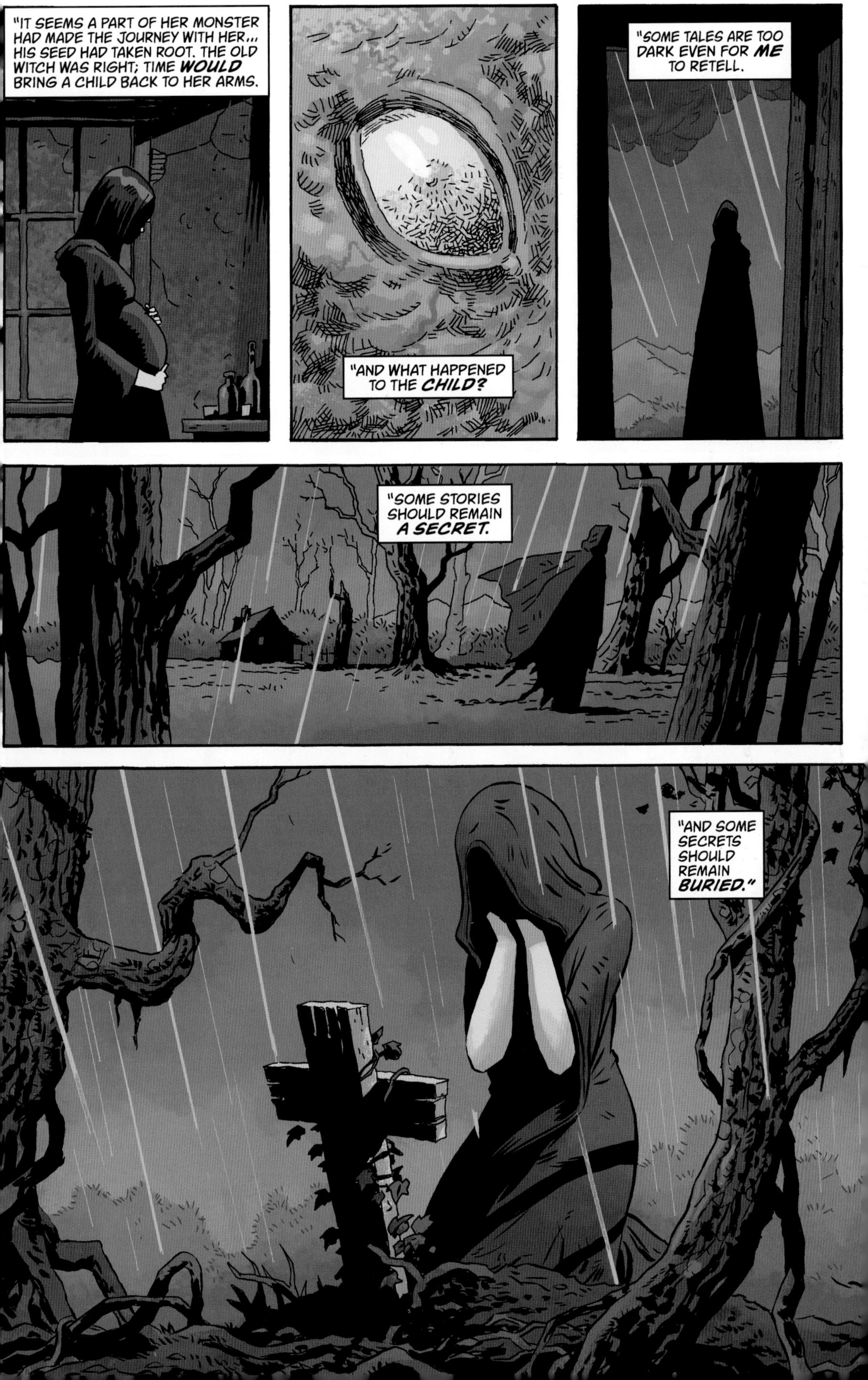
"IT SEEMS A PART OF HER MONSTER HAD MADE THE JOURNEY WITH HER... HIS SEED HAD TAKEN ROOT. THE OLD WITCH WAS RIGHT; TIME **WOULD** BRING A CHILD BACK TO HER ARMS.
"AND WHAT HAPPENED TO THE **CHILD?**
"SOME TALES ARE TOO DARK EVEN FOR **ME** TO RETELL.
"SOME STORIES SHOULD REMAIN **A SECRET.**
"AND SOME SECRETS SHOULD REMAIN **BURIED.**"

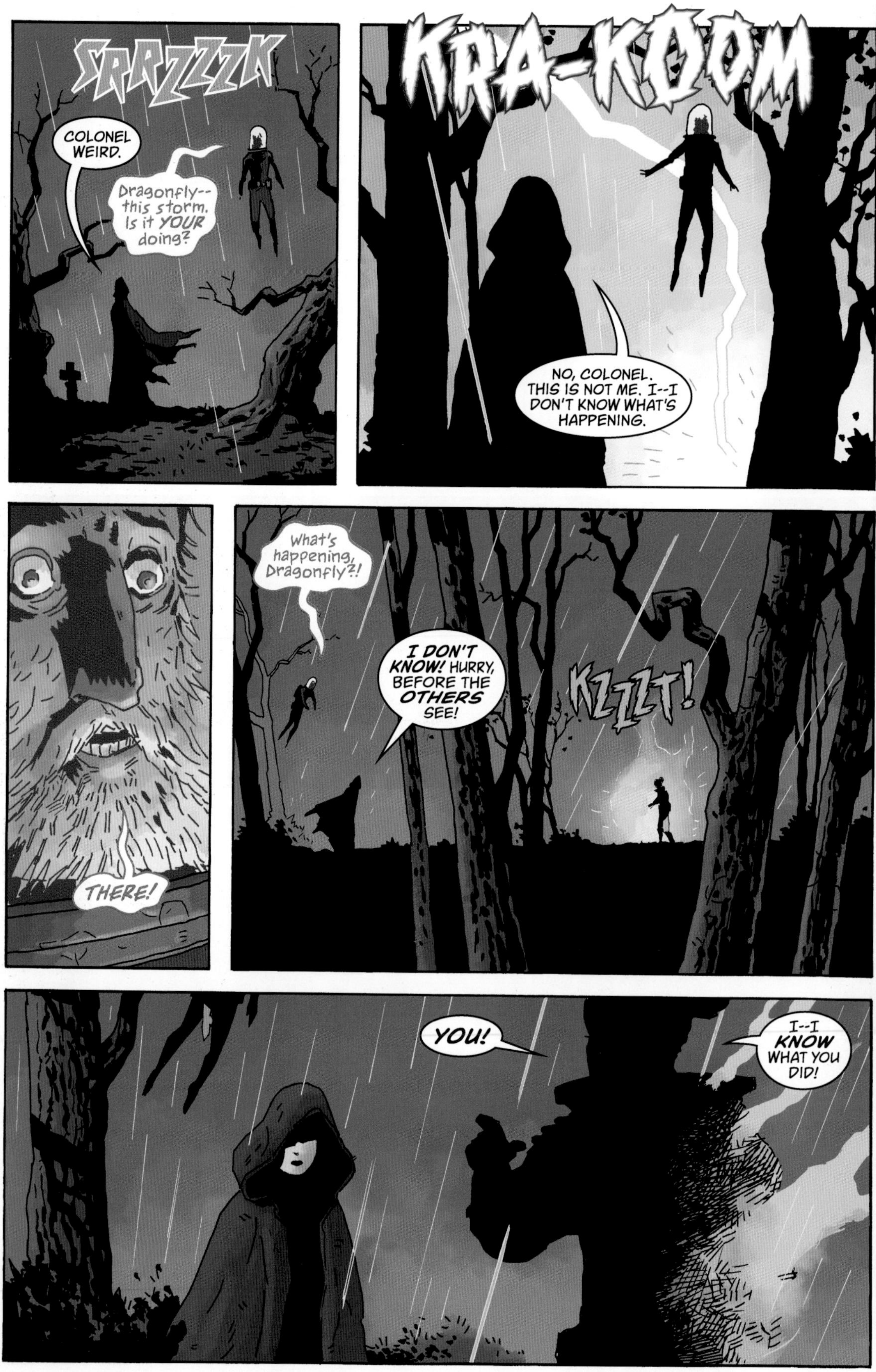
SPRZZZK
COLONEL WEIRD.
Dragonfly-- this storm. Is it YOUR doing?
KRA-KOOM
NO, COLONEL. THIS IS NOT ME. I--I DON'T KNOW WHAT'S HAPPENING.
THERE!
What's happening, Dragonfly?!
I DON'T KNOW! HURRY, BEFORE THE OTHERS SEE!
KZZZT!
YOU!
I--I KNOW WHAT YOU DID!

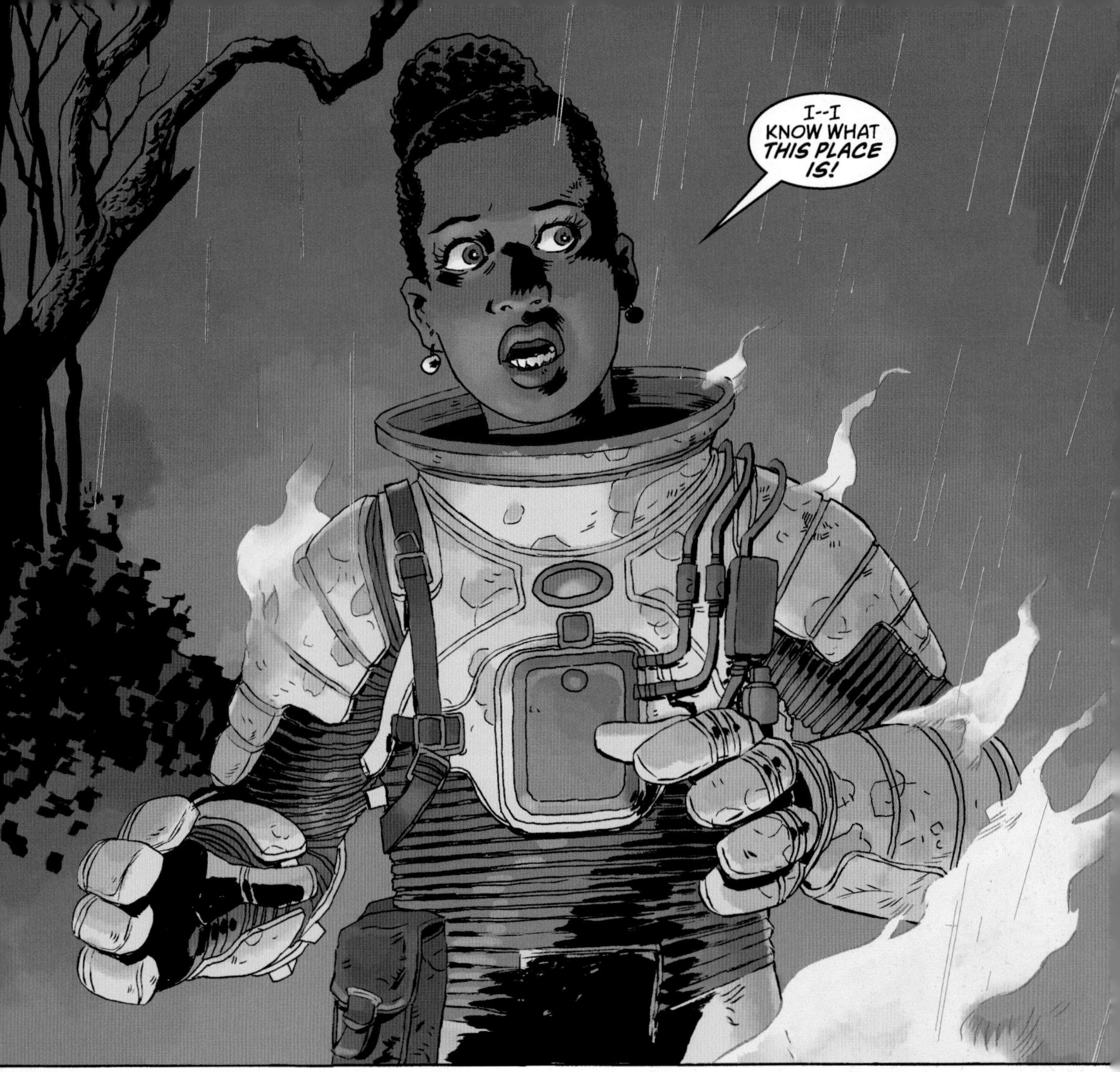
I--I KNOW WHAT THIS PLACE IS!

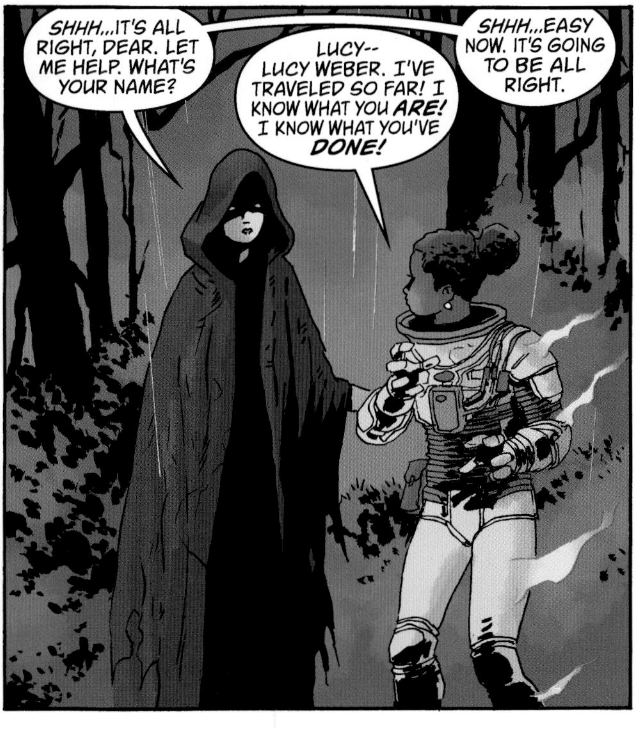
SHHH...IT'S ALL RIGHT, DEAR. LET ME HELP. WHAT'S YOUR NAME?
LUCY-- LUCY WEBER. I'VE TRAVELED SO FAR! I KNOW WHAT YOU ARE! I KNOW WHAT YOU'VE DONE!
SHHH...EASY NOW. IT'S GOING TO BE ALL RIGHT.

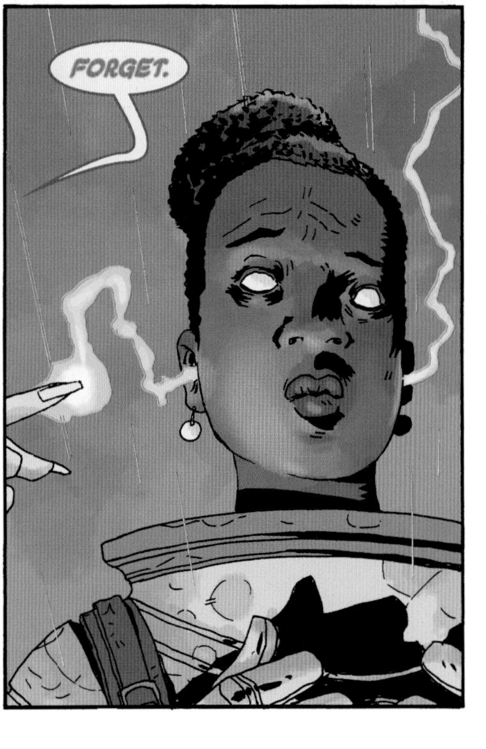
FORGET.

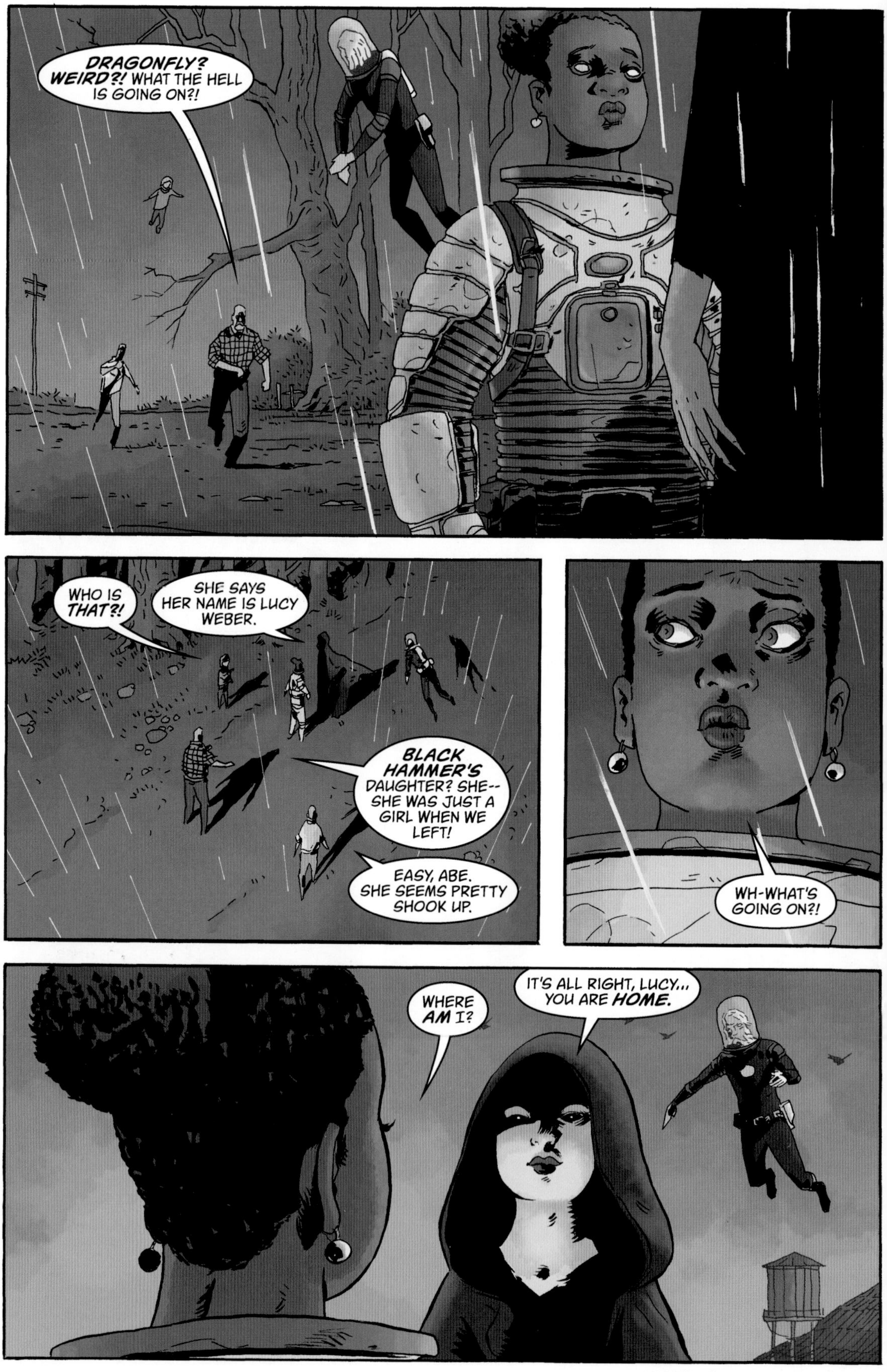
DRAGONFLY? WEIRD?! WHAT THE HELL IS GOING ON?!
WHO IS THAT?!
SHE SAYS HER NAME IS LUCY WEBER.
BLACK HAMMER'S DAUGHTER? SHE-- SHE WAS JUST A GIRL WHEN WE LEFT!
EASY, ABE. SHE SEEMS PRETTY SHOOK UP.
WH-WHAT'S GOING ON?!
WHERE AM I?
IT'S ALL RIGHT, LUCY... YOU ARE HOME.

END OF PART ONE.

THE *REAL* SECRET ORIGINS OF
BLACK HAMMER

It's a bit surreal to be writing an afterword for *Black Hammer* in late 2016 because this story has been with me for a long time and existed in a few different incarnations before becoming the version you just read. I originally conceived the idea for *Black Hammer* back in 2007 or 2008. At that time, I was still working on my debut graphic novel, *Essex County*, for Top Shelf. I was also still working a day job (or night job, as it were) as a line cook here in Toronto. At the time, I never dreamed I could actually make a full-time career out of making comics, and I certainly never thought I would ever write mainstream superhero comics for DC or Marvel.

So, it was under this assumption—that I would never get a chance to write "real" superhero comics—that I started working on *Black Hammer*. It would be my version of superheroes, filtered through everything I liked to do—grounded human stories about family and small towns. Basically, it would be *Essex County* meets superheroes.

I love superheroes. I loved them as a kid. I loved them back in 2007 when I was first working on *Black Hammer*, and I love them now. At the time, when I was working in indie comics, this wasn't really a cool thing to say. Indie cartoonists were supposed to rebel against those *evil, mainstream corporate comics*. Whatever. I just love comics. All comics. Like with any genre, there are good superhero comics and bad ones. Just like there are good indie comics and bad ones. So with *Black Hammer*, I set out to create a love letter to all the superhero comics I loved, but to ground it in the indie sensibilities of the work I was making then.

At the time, I was going to write *and* draw *Black Hammer* myself. One of my copublishers at Top Shelf, Brett Warnock, was friendly with many of the folks in his local Portland comics community, including Diana Schutz, an editor at Dark Horse. Brett mentioned that Diana really liked *Essex County* and suggested I talk to her about potential projects. I pitched *Black Hammer* to Diana and her then–assistant editor Brendan Wright, and they accepted it! I was ecstatic. *Black Hammer* was going to be my next project after *Essex*.

That didn't happen. Instead, a little boy with antlers kept popping up in my sketchbooks, and the next thing I knew I was writing and drawing forty issues of the monthly comic *Sweet Tooth* at DC/Vertigo. And somewhere in there I also started writing "real" superhero comics for DC.

So, *Black Hammer* got sort of pushed to the side. I figured I would get back to it eventually. But I never really did until 2014, when the time was finally right. At that point I had been writing for DC for five or six years and had a completely different perspective of superheroes . . . but I still

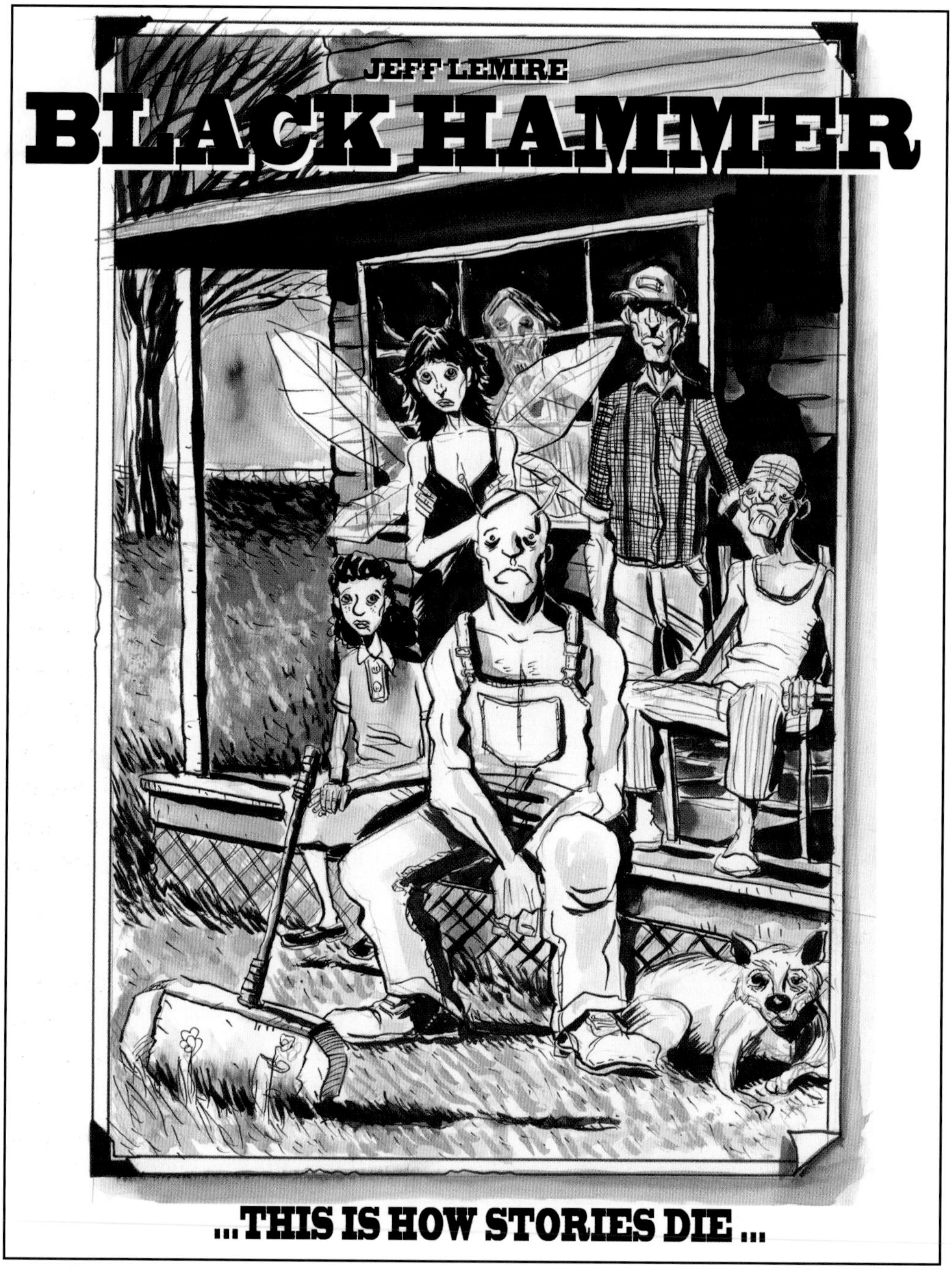
JEFF LEMIRE
BLACK HAMMER
...THIS IS HOW STORIES DIE...

loved them. And I also knew I couldn't draw the book myself if I ever wanted to actually get it off the ground. I was busy drawing other projects. And while I can juggle multiple writing assignments, drawing is extremely labor intensive, and I can only ever draw one book at a time. So drawing it wasn't possible. This led me to the great Dean Ormston.

I had fallen in love with Dean's work years back when he was doing a series called *Books of Magick: Life during Wartime* for Vertigo. And I met Dean in 2011 at the Thought Bubble comics festival in Leeds, UK, near his hometown of Barnsley. I hit it off with Dean right away and expressed my love of his work. We talked about working together at some point. I tried to get Dean hired to do some issues of *Animal Man* at DC with me, but it never panned out. So, when I committed to the idea of writing *Black Hammer* for another artist, I immediately circled back to Dean.

What made Dean perfect for *Black Hammer* was that his art looked nothing like mainstream superhero comics. And I knew that if *Black Hammer* were drawn in a traditional superhero style, it would be at risk of becoming just another superhero book. I wanted it to stand outside of superhero comics and comment on them, not become one of them. So Dean's idiosyncratic style seemed perfect to me. And now that you have read the first six issues of *Black Hammer*, I think you'll agree that I was right. He is perfect for this story. Now I can't imagine ever having done the book with anyone else. *Black Hammer* has become as much Dean's world as it is mine.

And for those who do not know, Dean has had to work through a series of challenges of his own to get this book into your hands. A few weeks after completing work on the first issues, Dean suffered from a brain hemorrhage. Basically, he had a stroke. It took Dean months to recover, with the right side of his body, including his drawing hand, partially paralyzed. After lots of hard work and rehab, Dean is now almost fully recovered and almost back to his regular work schedule. All of this is an incredible testament to Dean's work ethic, his passion for *Black Hammer*, and the fact that he is one of the kindest, most talented, and all around one of the most inspiring and amazing people I've ever had the fortune to work with and call a friend.

When getting this current incarnation of *Black Hammer* off the ground, I went back to Dark Horse. They had shown commitment to my work and to the story long before I was an established name in the industry, so I felt like there was no other place for *Black Hammer* to be. In the years between my original 2008 pitch and the reworking of *Black Hammer*, Diana had left Dark Horse, but Brendan was still there. So Brendan helped get this book off the ground and assembled the incredible creative team Dean and I are lucky enough to work with, letterer Todd Klein and colorist Dave Stewart.

TODD KLEIN!!!!! The 2007 Jeff would *freak out* if he knew he was ever going to be able to work with Todd Klein. I mean, he is a *legend*. He lettered *Sandman*, for god's sake! And Dave Stewart is . . . Well, he is a genius. He has colored so many of my favorite comics and favorite cartoonists. I can't say enough about how much these two talented gentlemen bring to *Black Hammer*. The book would not be what it is without them.

Since starting work on this book, Brendan also left Dark Horse, but his presence remains. And now we are aided by the awesome editorial team of Daniel Chabon and Cardner Clark.

So, this is the secret origin of *Black Hammer*. It's been a long road from 2007 to now, but I could not be more proud of the book.

Oh, one more thing. On the following pages you will see preliminary artwork from Dean and me. Among this material are some of my drawings and character designs from that original 2008 pitch. As part of that pitch I created a mock "encyclopedia" of the characters. I did this in the style of the old DC Comics *Who's Who* series that I loved so much as a kid. (*Hey, Gerard Way, I did this eight years before you did the same thing with* Young Animal, *so there! Just kidding . . . Love* Young Animal.) I even tried to draw each entry in the art style of one of my favorite artists.

But I do want to add a little disclaimer: many of the character descriptions and histories are from an earlier version of the story and no longer resemble the versions that exist today. So in other words, these character designs and histories are not canon.

There are a few fun things to note here. Back in 2008 the character of Abraham Slam was originally going to be much older. Abe was going to be in his eighties or nineties. And there was another cast member called "the Farmer" who was going to be a riff on a Joe Kubert–style DC war hero. When I started working on the series again in 2014 I combined these two characters into the version of Abe that exists today. You'll also notice a couple of other characters, "Time Boy" and "the Horseless Rider," who were riffs on Jack Kirby's Fourth World and Jim Aparo's Spectre. These two characters have not made their way into the pages of *Black Hammer*. At least, not yet.

Anyway, despite being out of date, these early designs and drawings are a part of *Black Hammer's* history, and I hope you enjoy them. And thanks again for reading *Black Hammer*. I hope you stick around, because the story is just getting started.

Jeff Lemire
Toronto, Canada
November 2016

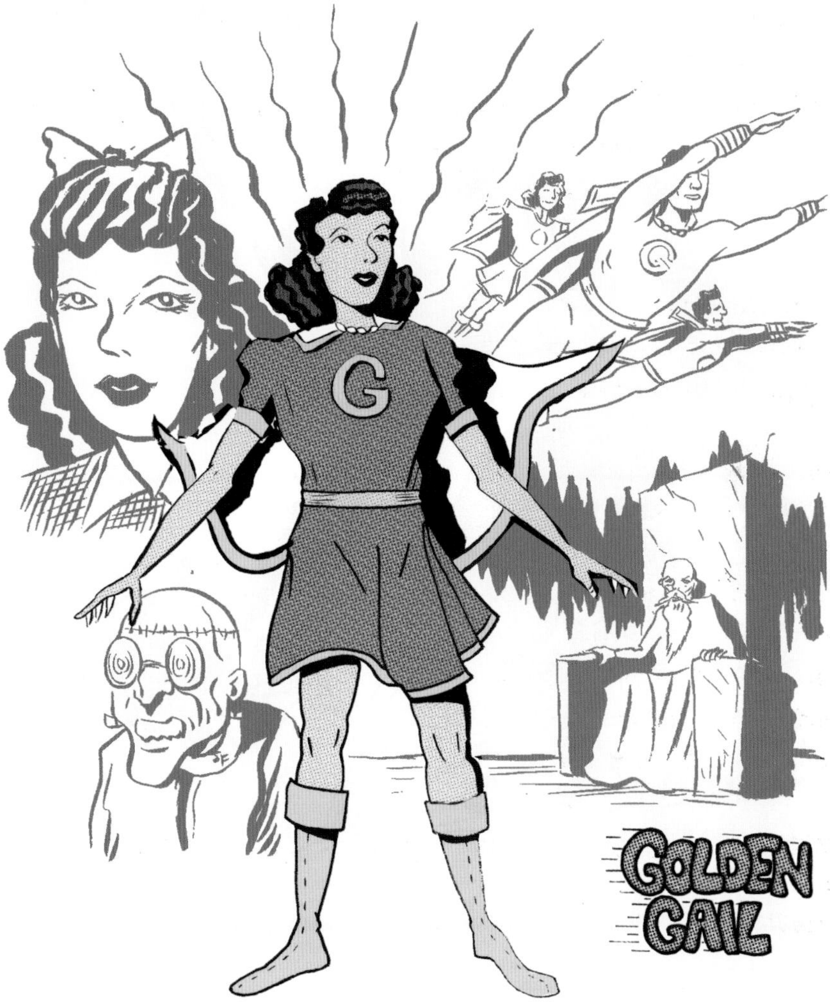

GOLDEN GAIL

PERSONAL DATA

Alter Ego: Gail Garnett
Occupation: Elementary school student
Marital Status: Single
Known Relatives: Mary and Billy Garnett (parents, deceased)
Base of Operations: Spiral City
First Appearance: CAPTAIN GOLDEN ADVENTURES #18
Height: 5'1" *Weight:* 87 lbs.
Eyes: Green *Hair*: Brown

HISTORY

When her parents were killed in an auto accident, Gail Garnett was placed in the Spiral City Orphanage. There she met young Tommy O'Toole, another orphan. The two became quick friends in the often harsh environment of the orphanage.

They ran away together one rainy night, and took refuge in an abandoned subway station. There they found a secret doorway which led them to the lair of the mighty wizard Zafram. With his dying breath, Zafram showered his magical Golden Rays upon the two children, and they soon discovered they could transform into powerful beings by saying his name.

Taking on the names Golden Gail and Captain Golden, the two had many adventures protecting Spiral City. The Golden family soon grew to include Uncle Golden, Cousin Golden, and Captain Golden Jr.

When the mad scientist Dr. Sherlock Frankenstein attacked Spiral City with a giant robot, the entire Golden family was killed except for Gail.

Afterward she found she was trapped in her Golden form and could no longer return to normal. As a result Gail will never age.

POWERS & WEAPONS

Upon speaking the wizard Zafram's name Gail is endowed with super-strength, flight, and invulnerability. She is also a gifted gymnast and hand-to-hand fighter.

Art by Jeff Lemire after C. C. Beck

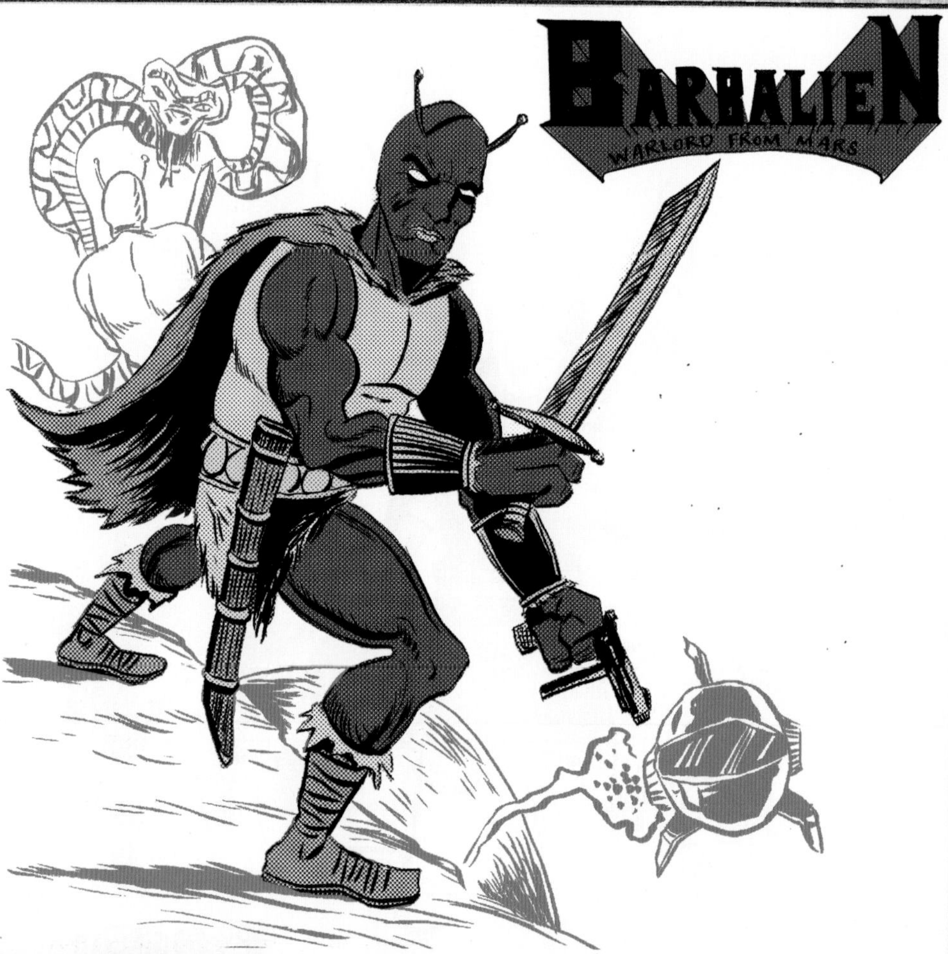
BARBALIEN
WARLORD FROM MARS

PERSONAL DATA

Alter Ego: Markkon Markken
Occupation: None
Marital Status: Widowed
Known Relatives: Syra (wife, deceased)
Group Affiliation: The Un-Squad
Base of Operations: Lost Lands of Earth
First Appearance: BARBALIEN, WARLORD OF MARS #1
Height: 6'5" *Weight:* 300 lbs.
Eyes: Green *Hair*: None

HISTORY

When his home world of Mars became overrun by tyranny and war, gentle scientist Markkon Markken took his wife Syra and left for Earth in an experimental rocket ship. In transit, a Martian fighter squad damaged the vessel, killing Syra. Markkon managed to escape with his life. However, as his spaceship entered Earth's atmosphere, it broke a dimensional barrier and Markkon landed in an alternate plane of reality. This barren version of Earth called the Lost Lands was ruled by an evil sorcerer named Daggus. Ironically, Markkon had landed in a world just like the one he had run from. Enraged by the death of Syra, and the terrible conditions of the Lost Lands, Markkon dubbed himself Barbalien, Warlord of Mars, and began to strike back against the dark forces of Daggus. The people of the Lost Lands soon rallied around Barbalien's uprising. Eventually Barbalien even found love again with the beautiful Princess Gandra. They had a son, named Murkkon. Their love affair however was cut short when he learned that Gandra was really an agent of Daggus. She took Murkkon and returned to Daggus's castle. Here, Daggus used his black magic to rapidly age Murkkon, finally creating a warrior who could match Barbalien. In a final climactic battle, Barbalien stormed Daggus's castle and faced his own son in battle. Barbalien was forced to kill Murkkon, and then killed Daggus as well. With the people of Lost Earth free, he left for space again, determined to return to Mars and free it as he had Earth. Upon returning to his home world, Barbalien found that the entire population had been wiped out by one devasting final war. He was now the sole survivor of Mars. Barbalien returned to Earth, this time landing in the proper dimension. Here he joined the superhero team the Un-Squad for a time and became one of Earth's most powerful and popular superheroes.

POWERS & WEAPONS

Barbalien's Martian biology gives him super strength, speed, and agility. He is also able to jump huge distances. He is able to hold his breath for hours at a time, and his skin is invulnerable to harm. In addition to his superhuman abilities, Barbalien is also an expert at all forms of hand-to-hand combat, and a master swordsman and marksman.

Art by Jeff Lemire after John Buscema

ABRAHAM SLAM

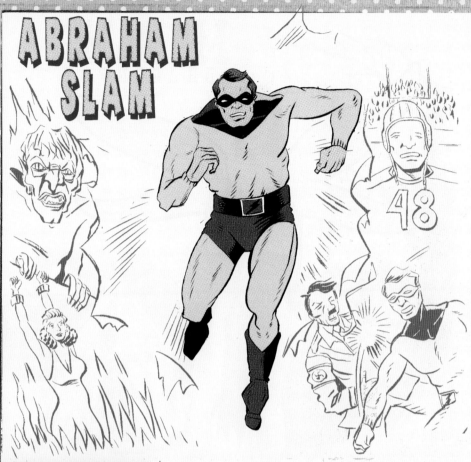

Art by Jeff Lemire after Al Camy

PERSONAL DATA

Alter Ego: Abraham Ezekiel Slam
Occupation: Crime buster
Marital Status: Widowed
Known Relatives: Maureen Slam (wife, deceased)
Base of Operations: Spiral City
First Appearance: MORE FUN ACTION #1
Height: 5'9"   *Weight:* 150 lbs.
Eyes: Brown   *Hair:* Brown

HISTORY

Abraham Ezekiel Slam was born to a poor family in the ghettos of Spiral City at the dawn of the century. Always a feeble boy, Abe often stayed inside his parents' tenement apartment to avoid the often cruel tauntings of the other neighborhood children.

When the boy gangs in the ghetto began to threaten local shop owners, including his father's taxidermy shop, Abe was forced to step in. The puny boy was beaten to within an inch of his life. Afterward, Abe dedicated his young self to getting stronger and learning to protect himself. As he hit his teenage years Abe sprouted up and before long, his robust frame was the envy of the local boys. Abe became a star athlete and pugilist. Attending Spiral City University, he set new records for yards rushed and touchdowns in a single season by a college running back.

After his school years, Abe married Maureen Stein, the girl next door, and moved into a small apartment not unlike the one he grew up in. Disgusted by the crime and local gangs, Abe took it upon himself to fight back. Donning a flamboyant costume and mask, Abe became one of the very first masked avengers in the prewar days. As America rushed off to war, Abe joined the fight abroad, leading a unit of costumed heroes known as the Super All-Stars against Nazi forces. After the war, a new generation of heroes began to emerge in postwar America. Abe decided to retire from superheroics. He opened a tiny butcher shop in Spiral City and worked happily for years. But Abe grew restless, and came out of retirement. Well into his fifties, Abe joined the young new generation of heroes, and shared many adventures with the likes of the Farmer, Investi-Gator, the Prawn, Ms. Metallurgy, and Ghost Spy.

When Maureen passed away from cancer in the '70s, Abe finally hung up the mask for good, leaving behind an incredible legacy.

POWERS & WEAPONS

Though he has no superpowers, Abe Slam was trained well as a fighter and gymnast. He was remarkably strong and tough as well as agile. Abe was a gifted athlete and never backed down from a fight.

MADAME DRAGONFLY

Art by Jeff Lemire after Mike Kaluta

PERSONAL DATA

Alter Ego: Unknown
Occupation: Fortuneteller
Marital Status: Unknown
Known Relatives: None
Base of Operations: Dead Dog Swamps, Louisiana
First Appearance: MANSION OF THE MACABRE #126
Height: 5'9" *Weight:* 110 lbs.
Eyes: Green *Hair:* Black

HISTORY

Very little is known about the origins of the mysterious occult figure and part-time fortuneteller known as Madame Dragonfly. She resides in a small cabin deep in the swamps of Dead Dog, Louisiana. Early in her career, Madame Dragonfly was said to have engaged in a romantic relationship with the monster known as Muck Thing. This, however, has never been proven. Sometime after Muck Thing's apparent death, Madame Dragonfly popped up in New York's Greenwich Village. Here she spent a short period of time acting as a fortune-teller, and amateur stage magician. Recently she has returned to the swamps and can be found lending her special talents in the arcane arts to those in distress.

For a short time Madame Dragonfly was associated with the group of mystical beings known as the Covenant, but more recently seems to work alone. She has shown a knack for "ghost hunting" and has been called upon from time to time to help the superhero community with super-natural crises.

She has been seen with the once-missing space hero Col. Weird on more than one occasion.

POWERS & WEAPONS

Madame Dragonfly is in possession of a number of powerful occult artifacts which lend her a variety of magical abilities. Moreover Madame Dragonfly has strong telekinetic and psychic abilities on her own. She can also produce incredibly powerful illusions.

COL. WEIRD

PERSONAL DATA

Alter Ego: Randel Weird
Occupation: Astronaut
Marital Status: Single
Known Relatives: Douglas Weird (father, deceased), Mary Weird (mother)
Group Affiliation: None
Base of Operations: Moonbase 12
First Appearance: FUTURE TALES #17
Height: 6'0" *Weight:* 175 lbs.
Eyes: Blue *Hair:* Blond

HISTORY

At the dawn of the Space Age, US test pilot Col. Weird volunteered for NASA's first manned flight to the stars. There Weird helped establish and protect Earth's first moon base. In space, Col. Weird embarked on a number of astonishing interstellar adventures. Eventually Weird returned home, a hero. In the early 1970s Weird again volunteered for a deep space mission, this time the rescue mission of a manned crew headed to Mars who had lost contact with Earth. As Weird approached the vessel he encountered something and he too disappeared. He was not seen or heard from for five years until he suddenly reappeared on Earth in the late '70s. He had only a limited understanding of what happened to him, or where he had been all those years. Nonetheless, Weird was changed. He now possessed a number of extranormal abilities and senses, all apparently derived from somewhere he called the Anti-Zone. As time passed however, Weird began to lose his grip on reality, and his sanity slowly faded with it. He now appears only sporadically in a distant, ghost-like state, a shadow of his former self.

POWERS & WEAPONS

Though the full extent of Weird's powers is unknown, he can apparently tele-port incredible distances, phase through solid objects, and tap into something called Anti-Energy which has incredible and destructive properties. In addition, Weird's NASA and Air Force training make him an excellent hand-to-hand combatant and an accomplished pilot.

Art by Jeff Lemire after Murphy Anderson

PERSONAL DATA

Alter Ego: Henry Lacroix
Occupation: Farmer, soldier, adventurer
Marital Status: Single
Known Relatives: Hubert Lacroix
(father, deceased), Mabel Lacroix
(mother, deceased)
Group Affiliation: The Unbelongables
Base of Operations: Northern California
First Appearance: COMBAT TALES #26
Height: 6'0"   *Weight:* 175 lbs.
Eyes: Blue   *Hair:* Gray

HISTORY

Born on a small unassuming ranch in
northern California, Henry Lacroix
seemed like just an average boy. His
father Hubert, however, saw something
special in Henry and helped to foster
his love of math and science. Before
long Henry was considered a prodigy.
When the boom of costumed adven-
turers and masked crime busters hit
the States in the days preceding WWII,
Hubert decided to join in on the action.
He took on the guise of the masked
hero known as the Farmer (see the
Farmer I).

Relying mainly on his fists and his trusty
pitchfork to fight injustice in the rural
communities of the American heartland,
Hubert often found himself in over his
head. Before long Hubert enlisted the
help of his gifted son to help invent a
number of ingenious gadgets to aid his
cause.

Henry soon put on a mask himself and
often joined his father as his sidekick
Farmboy. The Farmer and Farmboy had
a number of high-profile adventures
leading up to the war. They often joined
Spiral City's ace crime buster, Abraham
Slam (see Abraham Slam), to help take
down organized-crime rings in that city.
On a routine patrol one night, the Farmer
and Farmboy were ambushed by their
archfoe, the Cityslicker. Hubert was
mortally wounded and died in young
Henry's arms.

As WWII approached, Henry enlisted in the
armed forces, just like millions of other American
boys. He soon came to epitomize the fighting
man and spirit.
Henry soon found himself donning his father's
mantle, becoming the Fighting Farmer.
As the Fighting Farmer, Henry led a
group of soldiers onto the beaches of
Normandy on D-day, and helped secure the
Allied victory.
After the war Henry retired to the family farm
and lived a quiet life for some time. But when
a new generation of costumed science heroes
emerged in the postwar world, a restless
Henry once again put on his mask, this time
calling himself only the Farmer, thus fully
paying tribute to his father's legacy.
The Farmer became one of the most
respected superheroes in the world.
Around that time, Henry also invented the
giant Tractor which could transform into
a combat-ready robot.
Always putting his allegiance to his country
before his superheroics, the Farmer and
Tractor were a key part of America's
offensive in Vietnam.

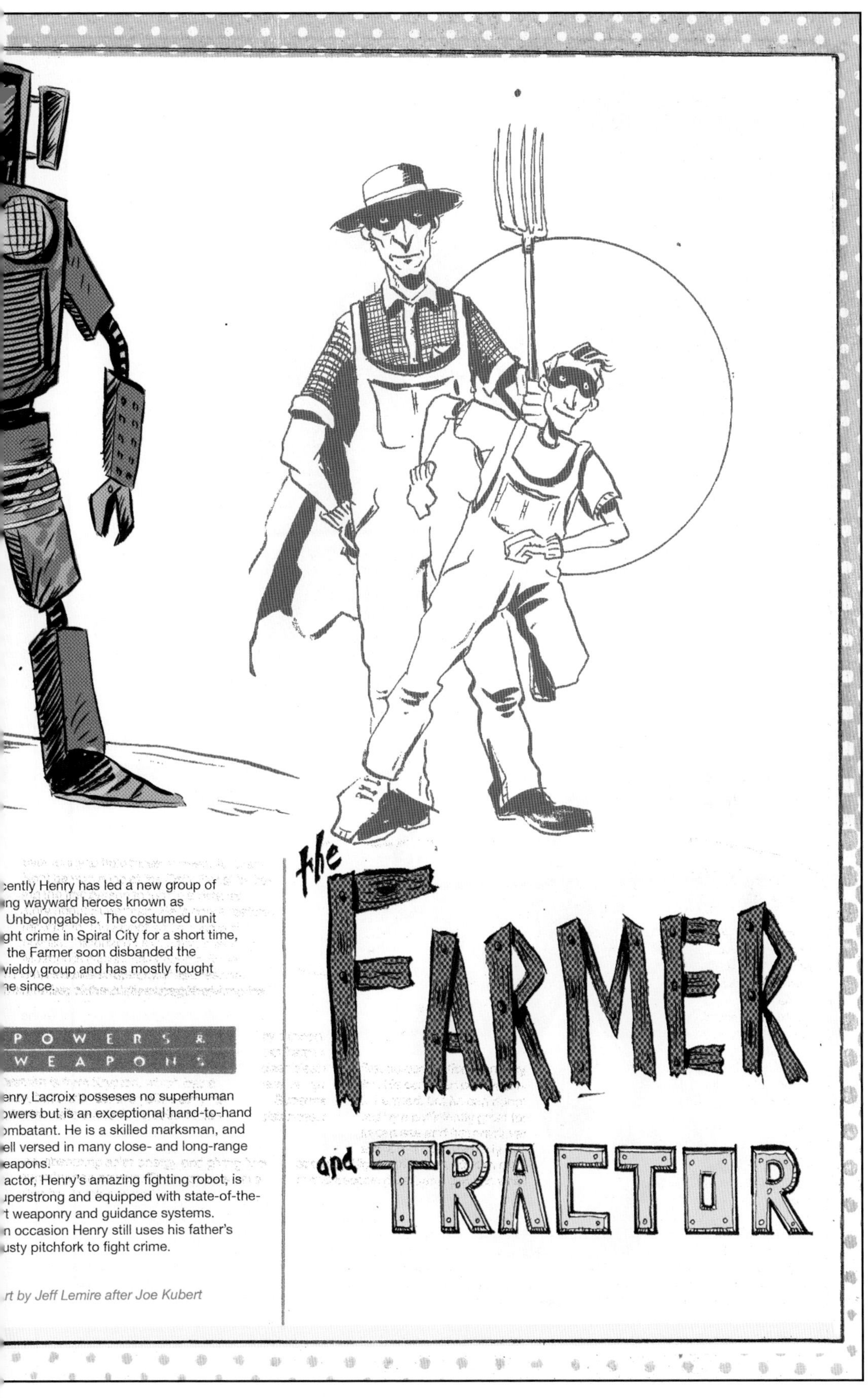

the FARMER and TRACTOR

:ently Henry has led a new group of
ng wayward heroes known as
Unbelongables. The costumed unit
ght crime in Spiral City for a short time,
the Farmer soon disbanded the
vieldy group and has mostly fought
ne since.

POWERS & WEAPONS

enry Lacroix posseses no superhuman
owers but is an exceptional hand-to-hand
ombatant. He is a skilled marksman, and
ell versed in many close- and long-range
eapons.
actor, Henry's amazing fighting robot, is
iperstrong and equipped with state-of-the-
t weaponry and guidance systems.
n occasion Henry still uses his father's
usty pitchfork to fight crime.

rt by Jeff Lemire after Joe Kubert

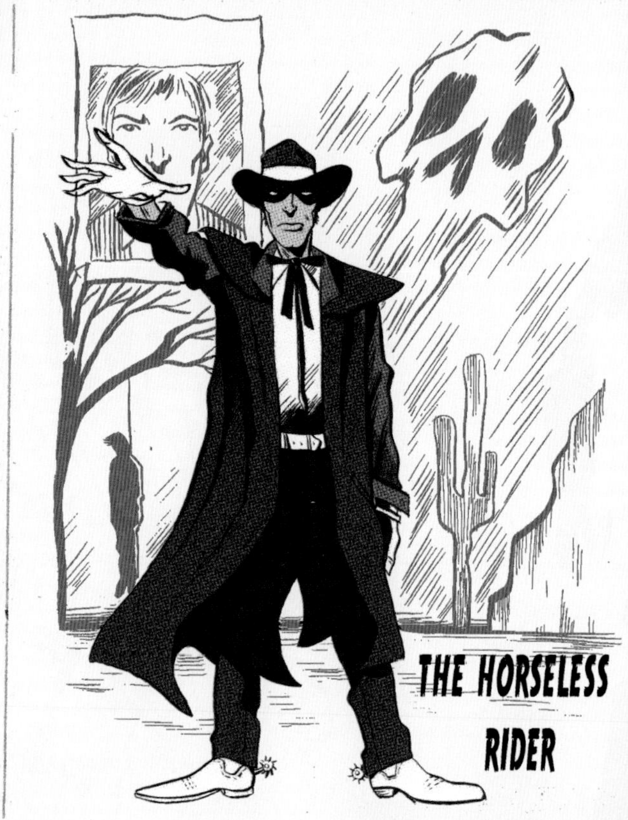
THE HORSELESS RIDER

PERSONAL DATA

Alter Ego: Formerly Jacob Tex
Occupation: Formerly gambler
Marital Status: Single
Known Relatives: None
Base of Operations: Unknown
First Appearance: THE HORSELESS RIDER #1
Height: 6'2" *Weight:* 185 lbs.
Eyes: White *Hair:* White

HISTORY

After murdering and cheating his way across the Old West, gambler Jacob Tex was killed in a drunken saloon brawl and enlisted by God to exact vengeance on the evil men of the Wild West as the haunting "Specter of the Prairies," the Horseless Rider.

In cases where some supernatural or physical threat is involved, the Horseless Rider has been known to appear in the present day, particularly in Spiral City, where he shares an uneasy alliance with many superheroes.

POWERS & WEAPONS

The Horseless Rider's abilities defy all attempts at classification. He seems to be able to appear and vanish at will. At times he has shown the ability to control supernatural energy. He can become intangible, and is impervious to harm.

He often uses his mystical six-shooters to exact vengeance.

Art by Jeff Lemire after Jim Aparo

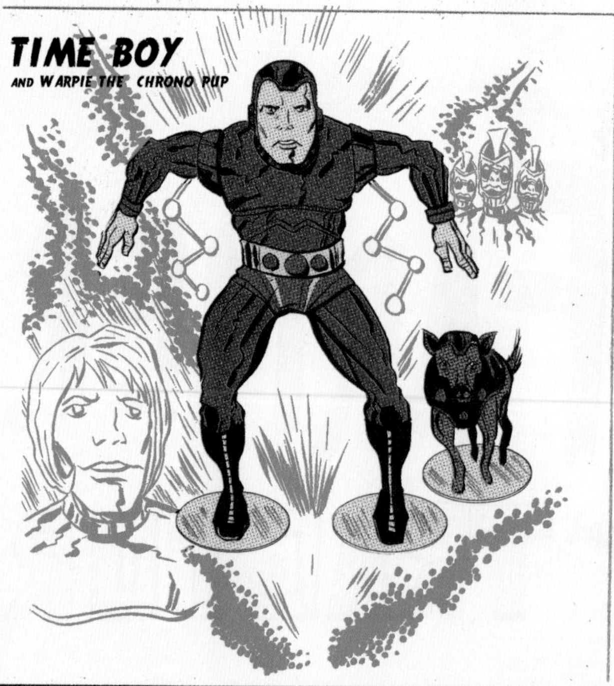
TIME BOY
AND WARPIE THE CHRONO PUP

PERSONAL DATA

Alter Ego: None
Occupation: None
Marital Status: Single
Known Relatives: The High God (father)
Base of Operations: None
First Appearance: YOUNG GODS #1
Height: 5'9" *Weight:* 150 lbs.
Eyes: Blue *Hair:* Black

HISTORY

One of the powerful Young Gods of New Pantheon (see Young Gods), Time Boy is a time-hopping adventurer and space champion. His father is the powerful High God (see High God), and is often sent as New Pantheon's ambassador on Earth.

The cosmic pooch named Warpie is his loyal pet and companion.

POWERS & WEAPONS

Time Boy flies at tremendous speeds and can traverse space and time freely. He can also project blasts of cosmic energy.

Art by Jeff Lemire after Jack Kirby

BLACK HAMMER

SKETCHBOOK

NOTES BY DEAN ORMSTON

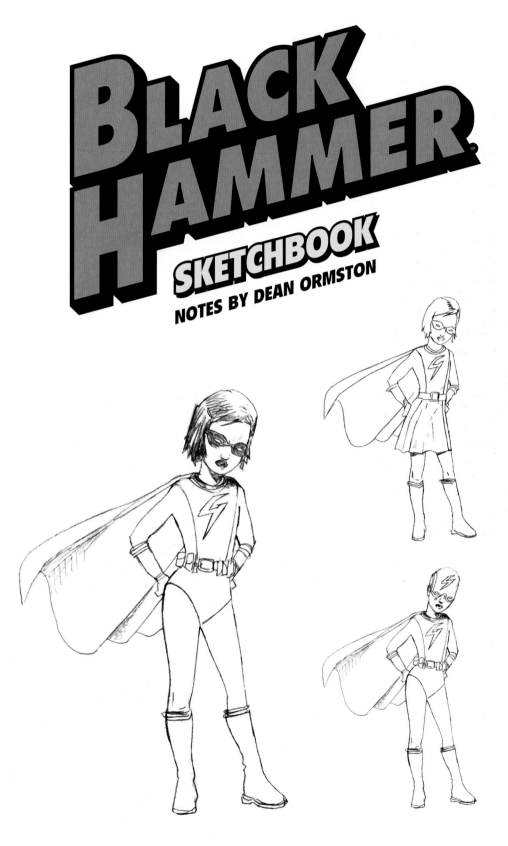

Jeff's original sketches had Gail quite a bit older, but by the time he had written the first issue, Gail was a middle-aged woman stuck in the body of a nine-year-old girl, and a very moody, pissed-off girl indeed. These sketches were done for issue #2, where we get to see Golden Gail's origin and superhero costume, and the final choice was quite similar to Jeff's sketch but adapted to suit a young girl.

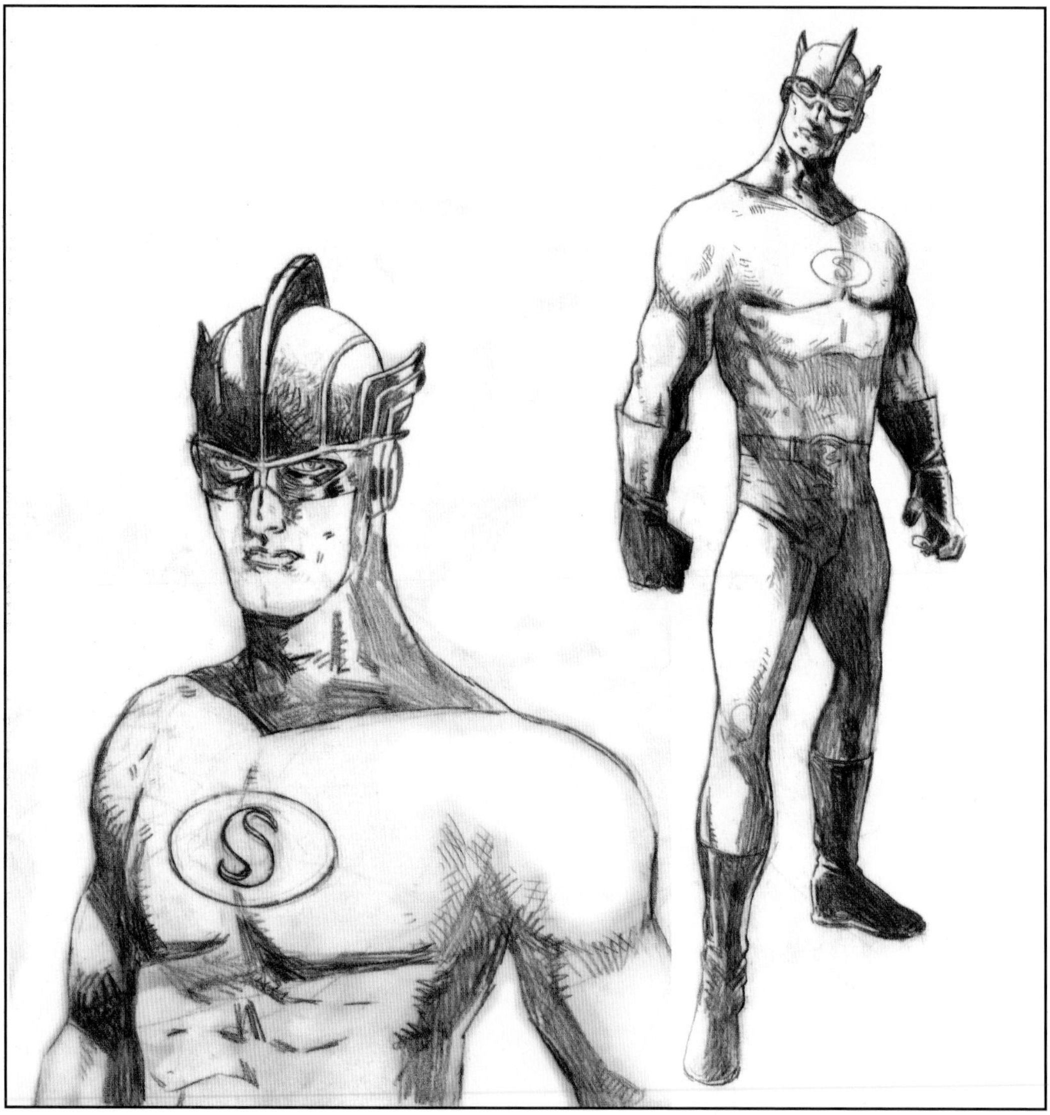

The Abraham Slam sketches were inspired by many Golden Age heroes of comics and film. He's part Captain America, part Batman, and an all-American hero. Although we don't get to see him in costume that much, these sketches were the first ones that I did of Abe. The old and weary Abe we see in the present-day world of *Black Hammer* was actually developed on the first three pages I drew for the book. He grew out of the pages. Abe's costume changes slightly with each era.

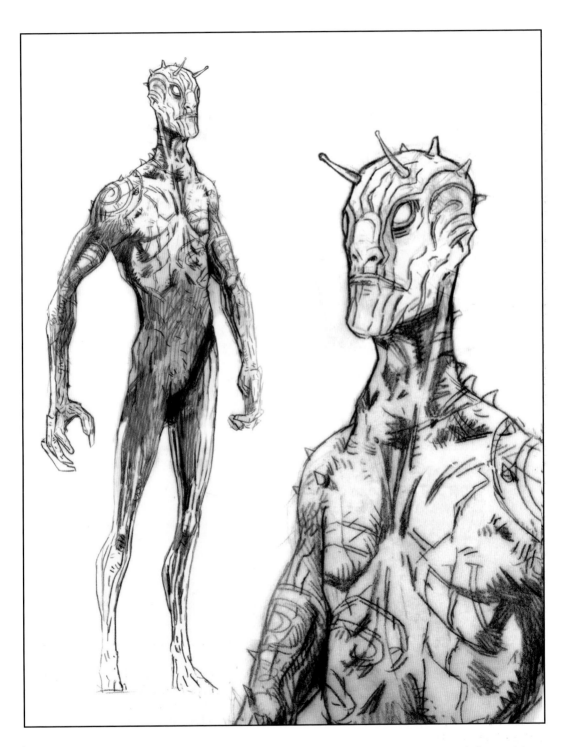

Jeff had quite a strong design for Barbalien. I wanted to keep the same body shape, but to suit the way I draw, I made him almost like a walking tree with heavily lined skin. I also had a bit of inspiration from David Bowie's portrayal of an alien in the movie *The Man Who Fell to Earth*. He has odd-shaped pupils . . . and where are his sex organs?

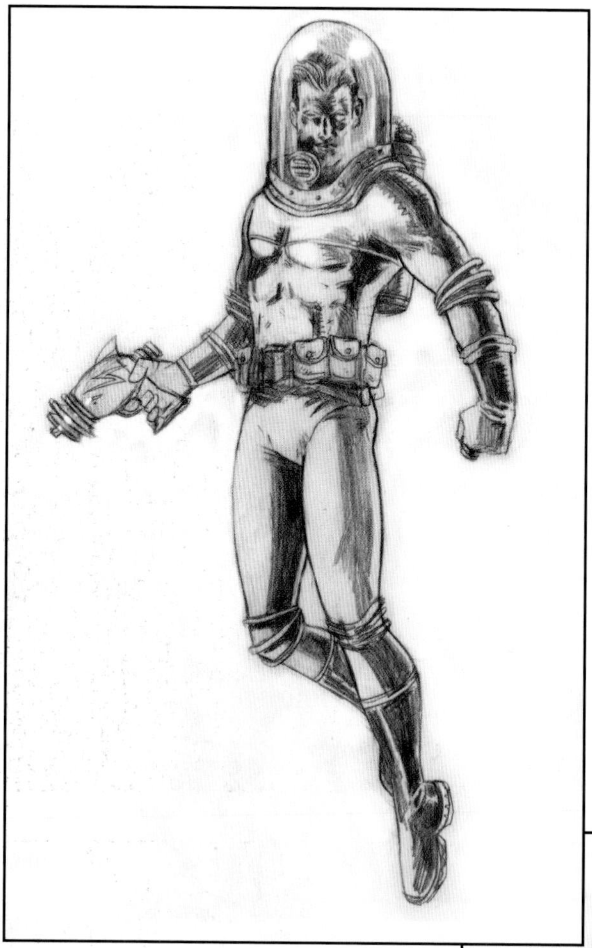

The sketch of the young and sound-of-mind Colonel Weird was inspired by 1950s sci-fi movies and Adam Strange. As you can see from Jeff's original sketches (page 163), both versions of Weird we get to see in *Black Hammer* are quite close to his original designs; there are just a few changes here and there to suit my way of drawing.

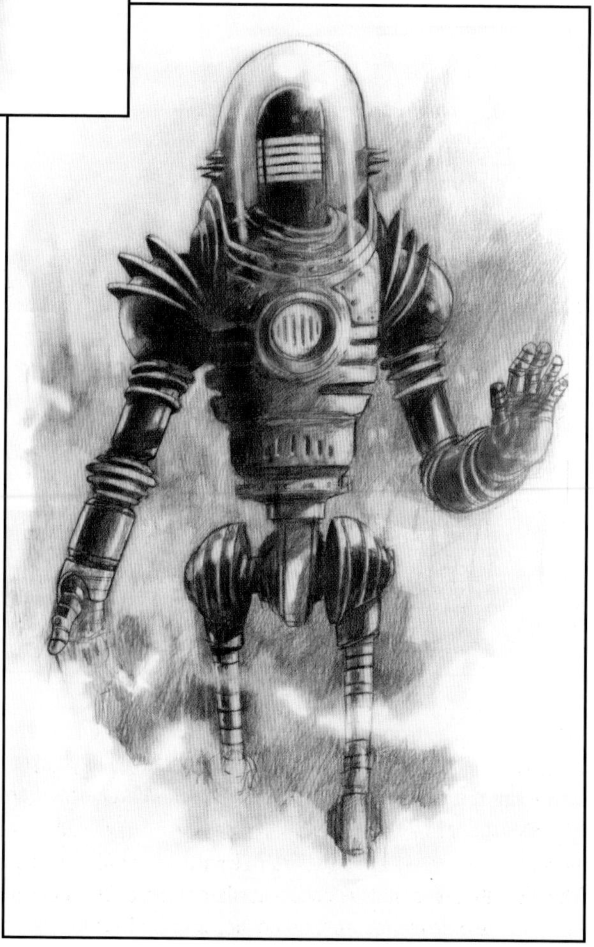

Sitting at the side of my desk is an old tin-plate toy Robby the Robot from *Forbidden Planet*. This was the inspiration for Talky-Walky: pure 1950s robot.

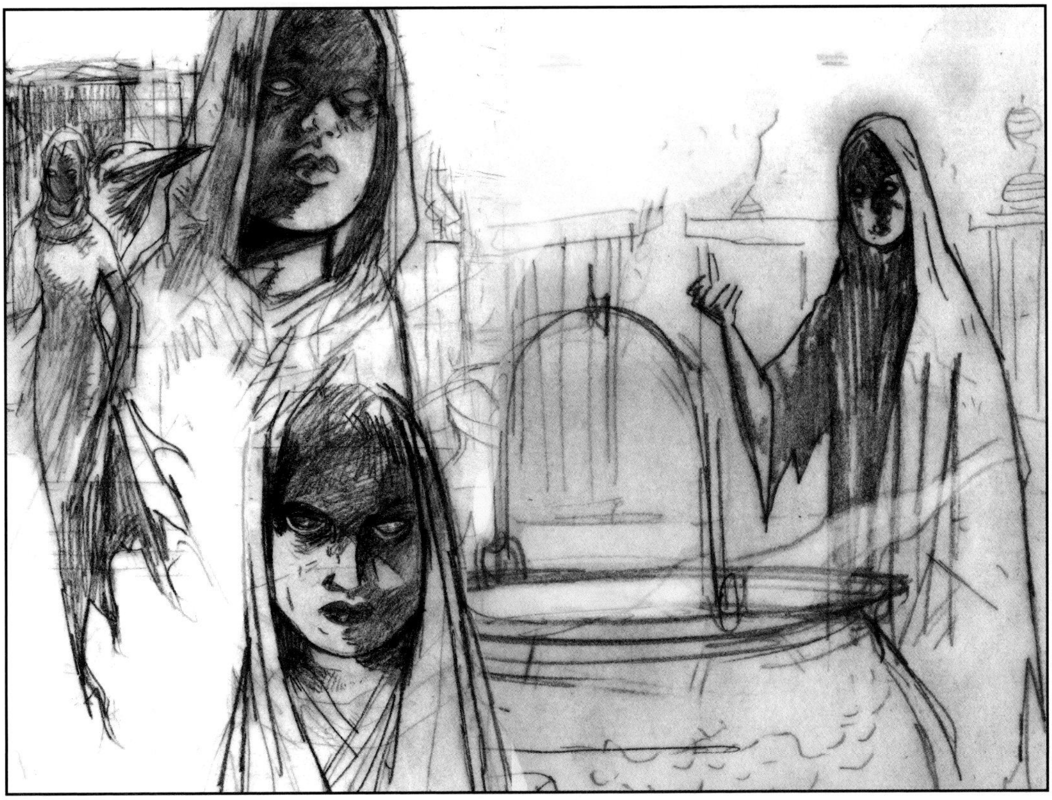

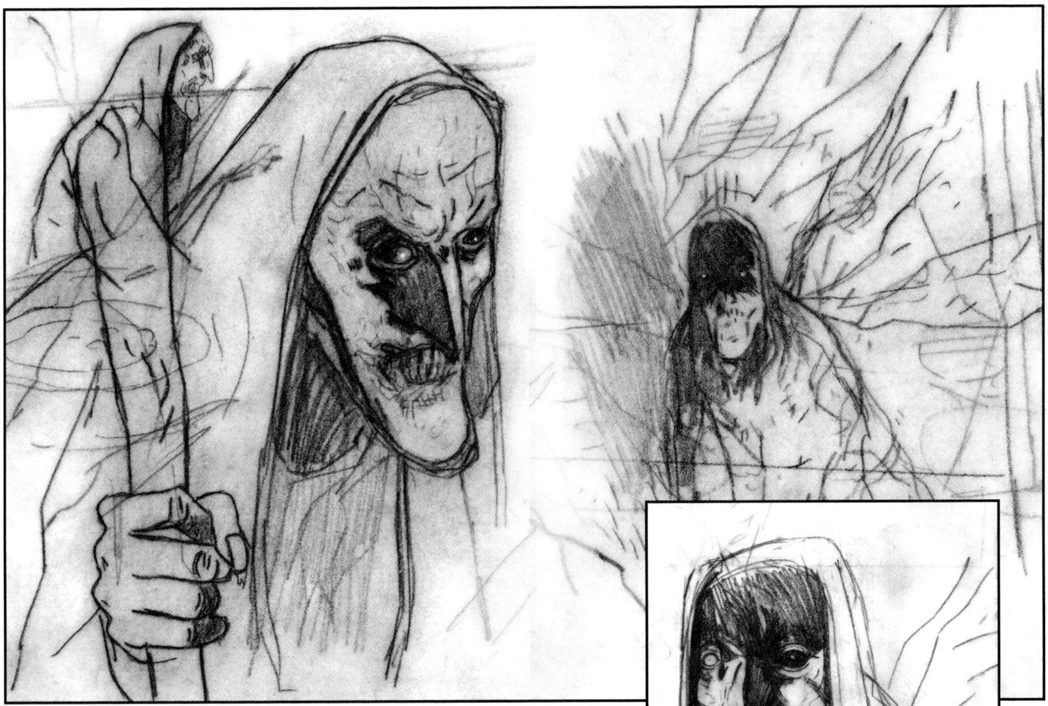

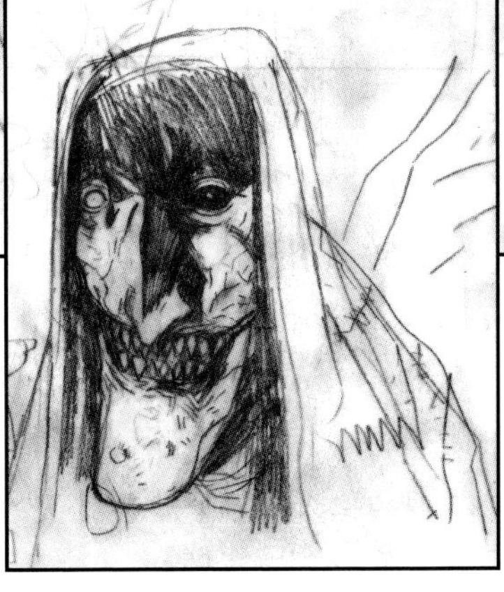

I always seem to be happiest drawing images that are unsettling and creepy. I took the opportunity and the freedom I had been given to make Madame Dragonfly as shadowy as possible—so these early sketches are a departure from Jeff's original designs. The old witch who passes on the burden of the cabin is my love letter to the old witches from EC comics and Graham Ingels.

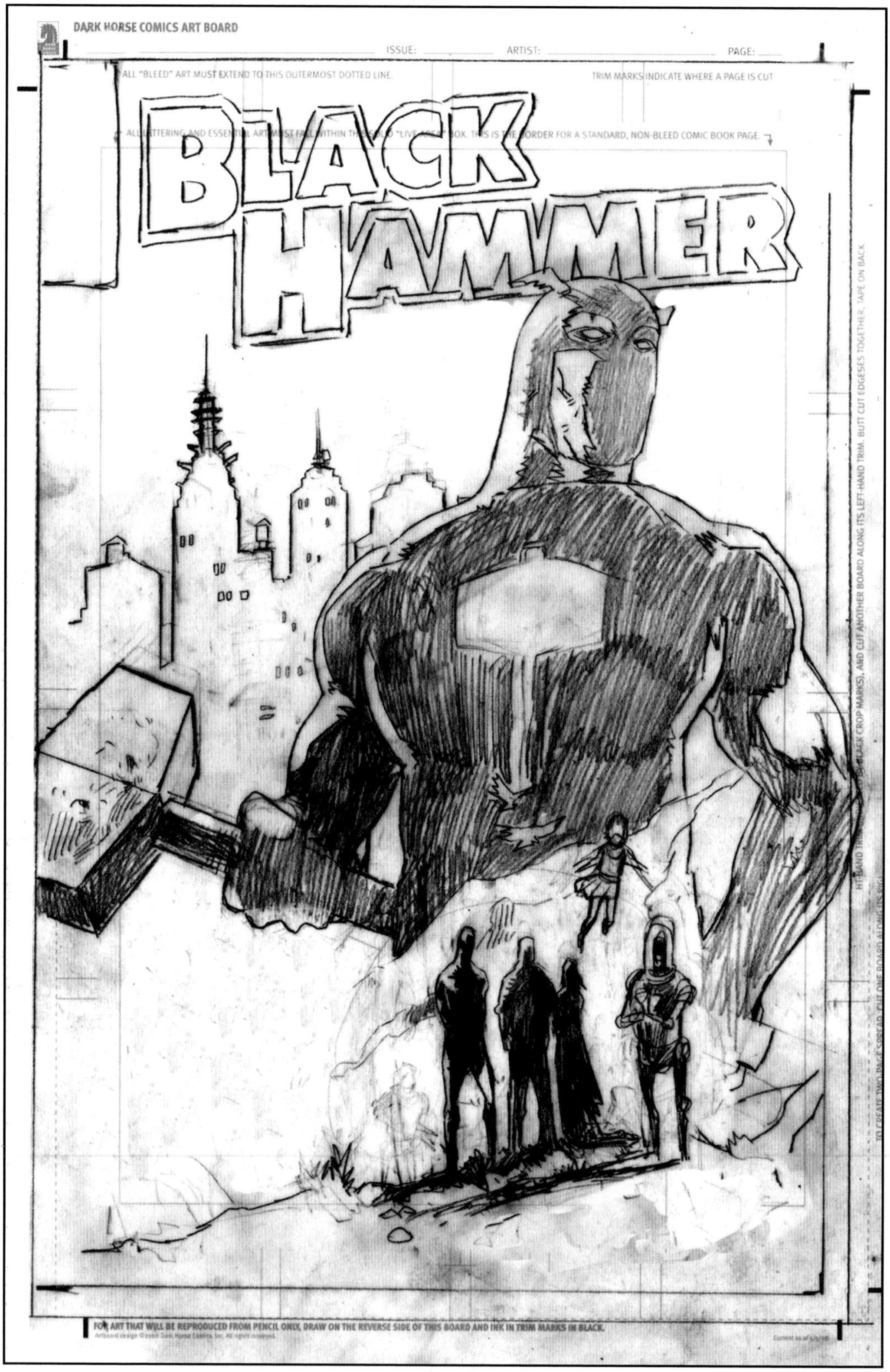
DARK HORSE COMICS ART BOARD
ISSUE:
ARTIST:
PAGE:
ALL "BLEED" ART MUST EXTEND TO THIS OUTERMOST DOTTED LINE.
TRIM MARKS INDICATE WHERE A PAGE IS CUT
BLACK HAMMER
FOR ART THAT WILL BE REPRODUCED FROM PENCIL ONLY, DRAW ON THE REVERSE SIDE OF THIS BOARD AND INK IN TRIM MARKS IN BLACK.

The problem I had with issue #1's cover was how to feature all six main characters and not make it cluttered and uninspiring. It was a difficult and time-consuming struggle but made for a better cover in the end. Jeff suggested showing the whole "family" gathered around the Hammer, and the problem was solved when I decided that Golden Gail should be the main focus. I think the end result turned out a little bit odd: a hint of superhero mixed with a slightly unsettling feel. I drew two finished versions of the cover, inked in different styles.

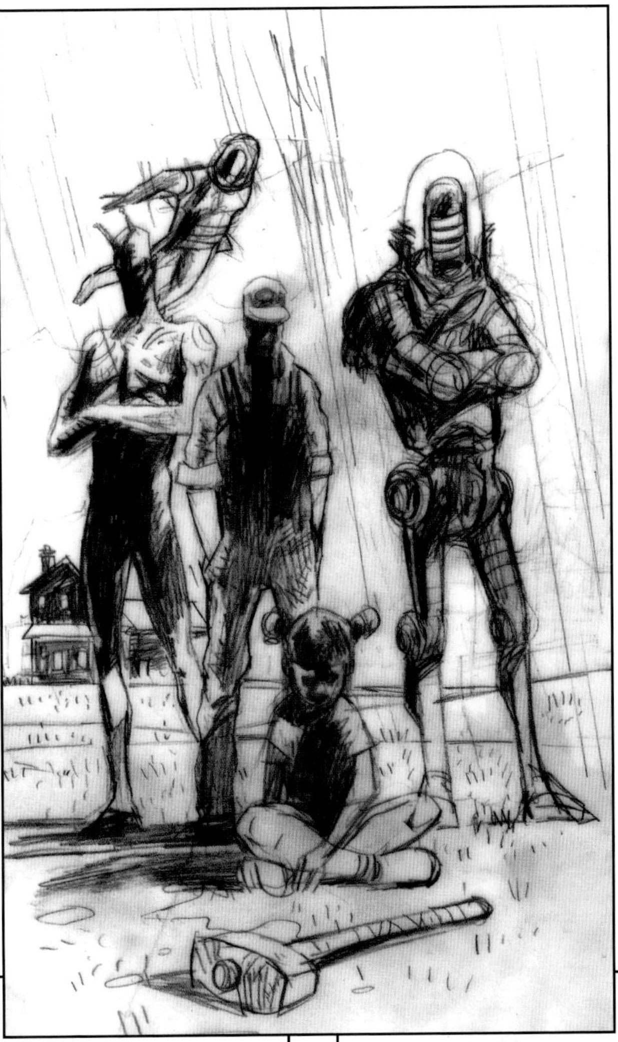
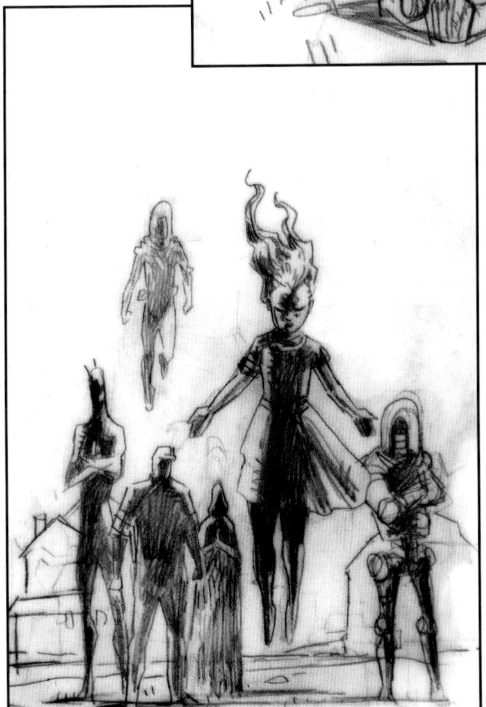
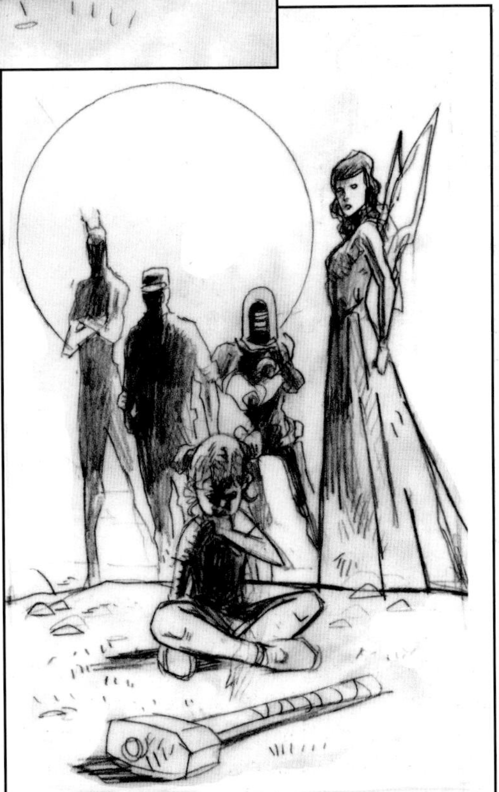

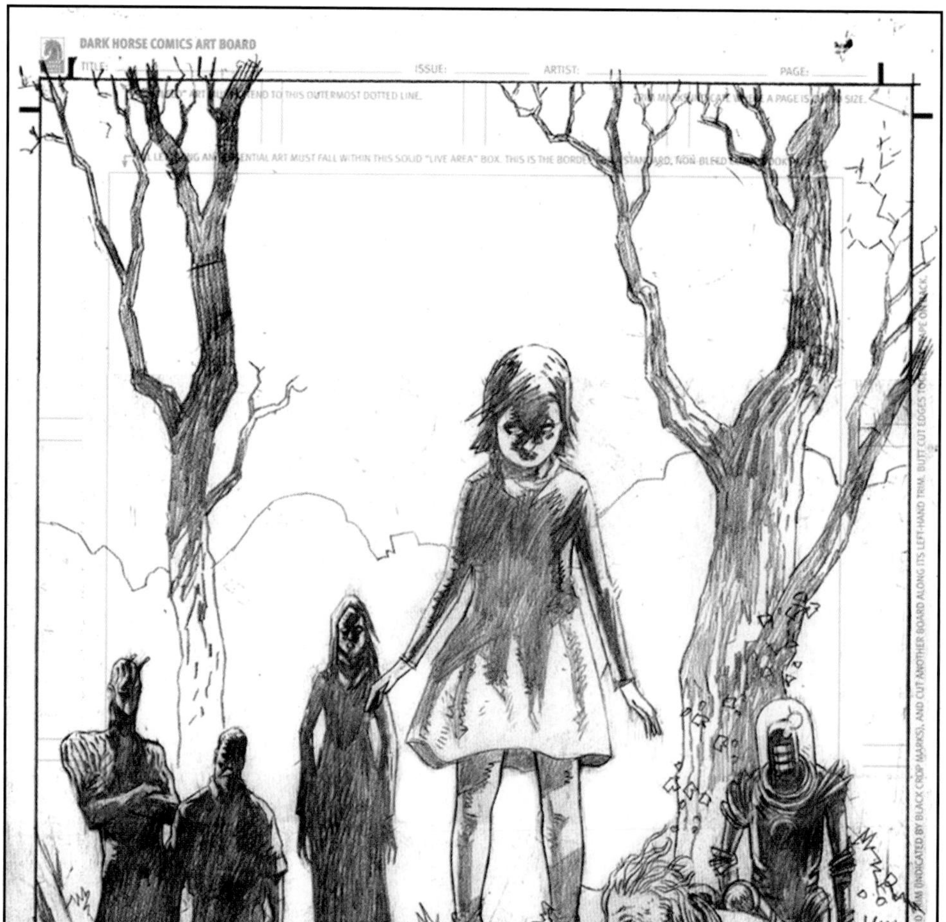
DARK HORSE COMICS ART BOARD
TITLE:
ISSUE:
ARTIST:
PAGE:
FOR ART THAT WILL BE REPRODUCED FROM PENCIL ONLY, DRAW ON THE REVERSE SIDE OF THIS BOARD AND INK IN TR

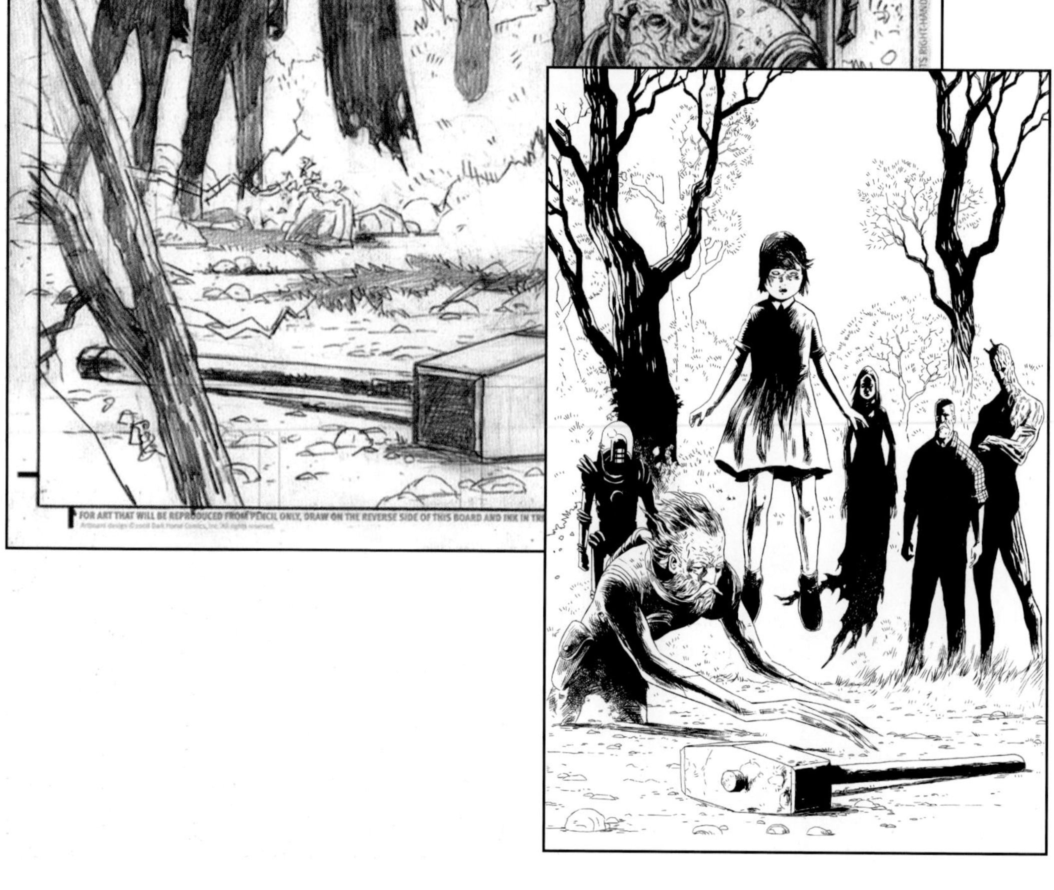

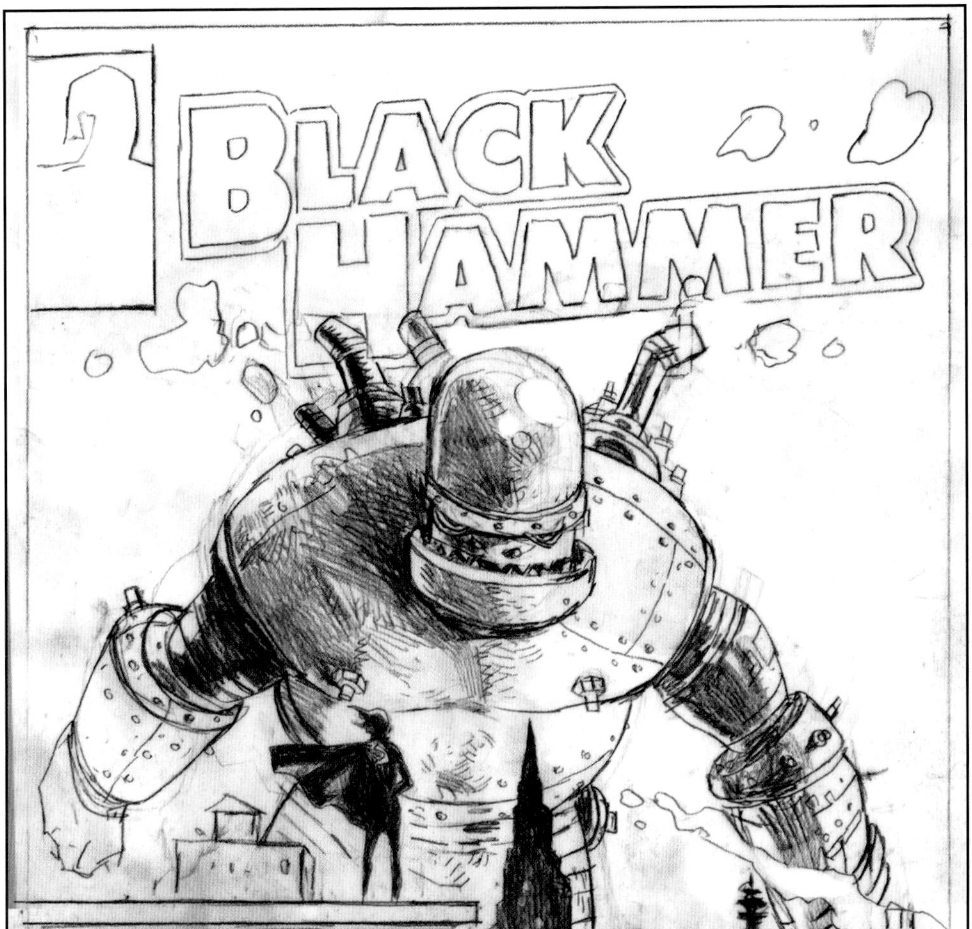
BLACK
HAMMER

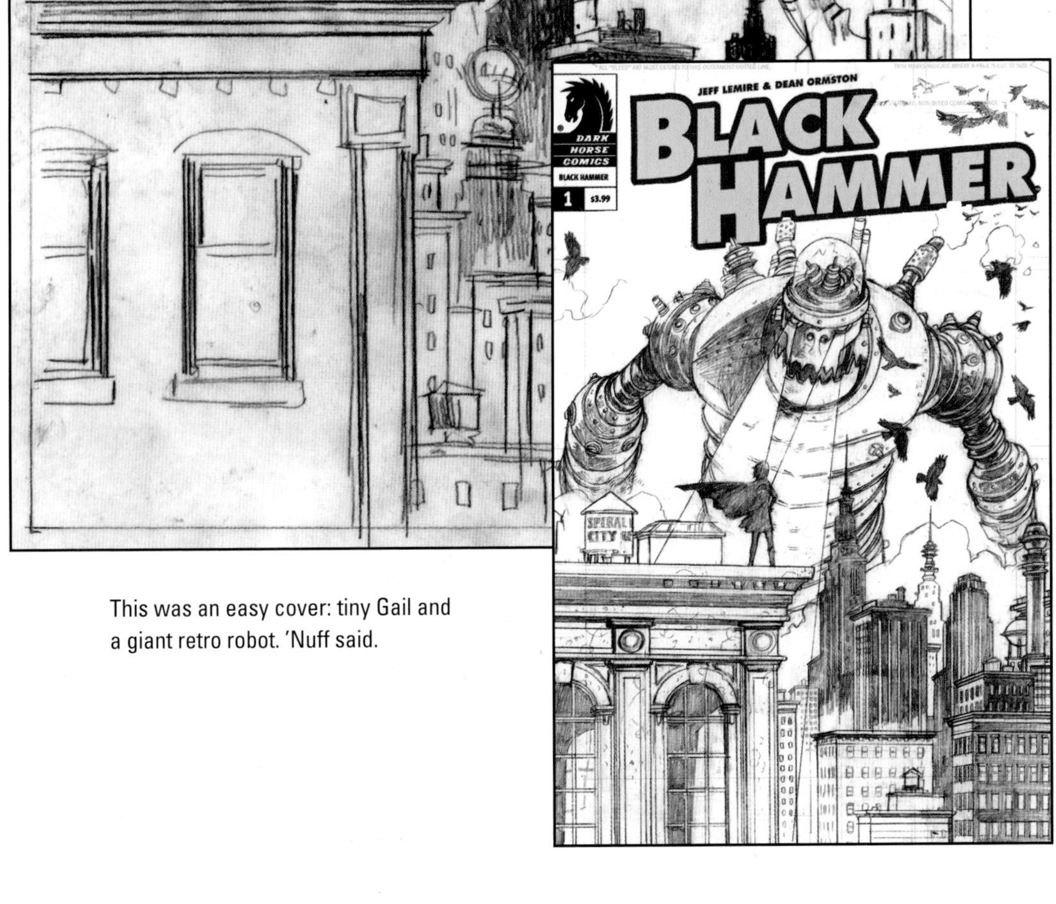
JEFF LEMIRE & DEAN ORMSTON
BLACK
HAMMER
DARK
HORSE
COMICS
BLACK HAMMER
1
$3.99
SPIRAL
CITY

This was an easy cover: tiny Gail and
a giant retro robot. 'Nuff said.

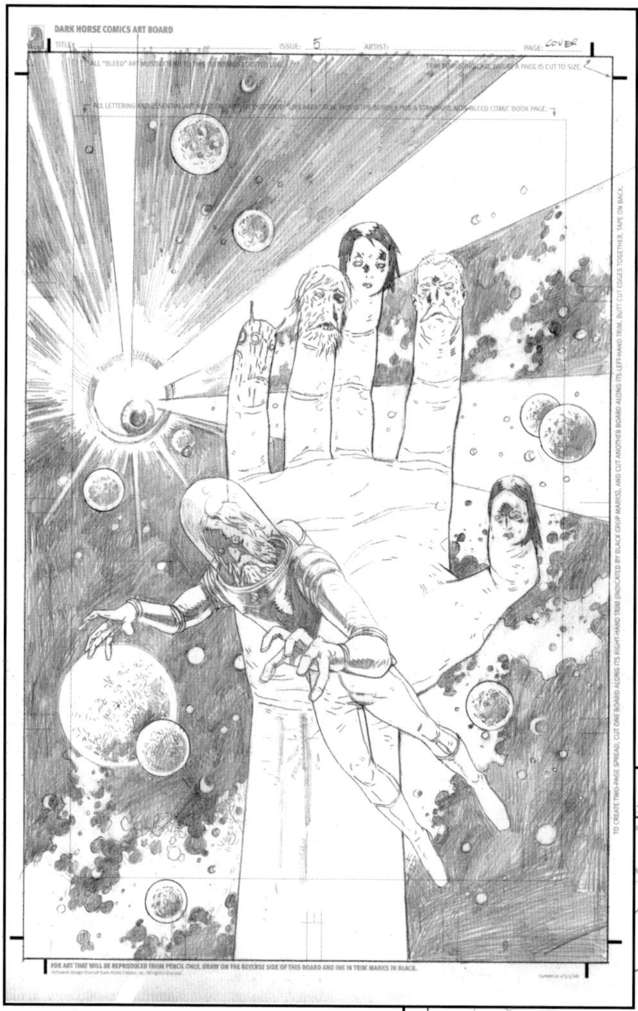
DARK HORSE COMICS ART BOARD
ISSUE: 5
PAGE: COVER
FOR ART THAT WILL BE REPRODUCED FROM PENCIL ONLY, DRAW ON THE REVERSE SIDE OF THIS BOARD AND INK IN TRIM MARKS IN BLACK.

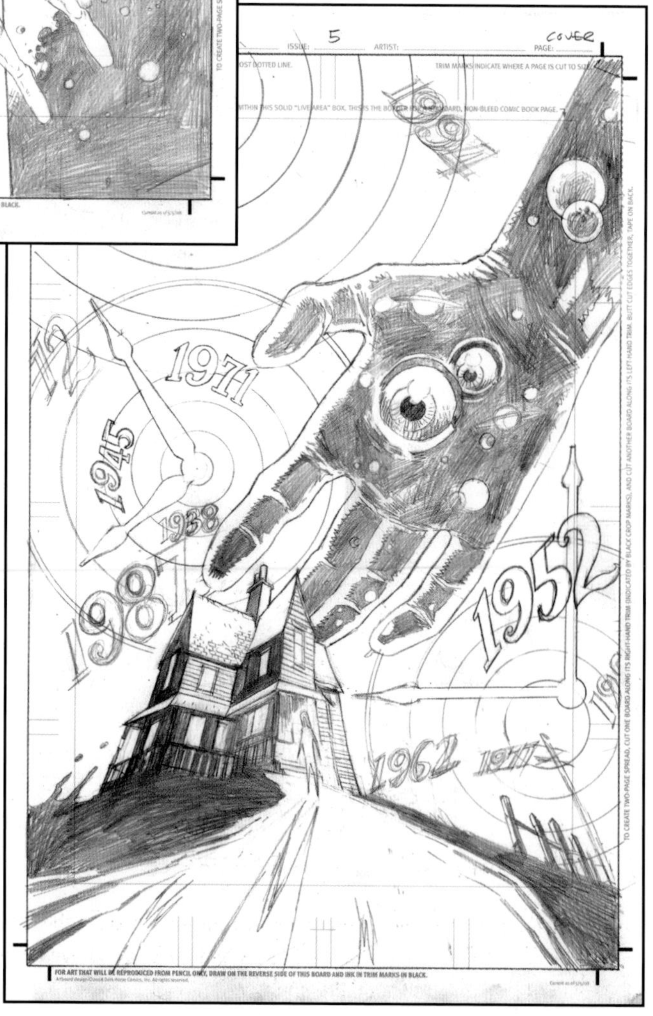
ISSUE: 5
PAGE: COVER
1971
1945
1938
1952
1962
FOR ART THAT WILL BE REPRODUCED FROM PENCIL ONLY, DRAW ON THE REVERSE SIDE OF THIS BOARD AND INK IN TRIM MARKS IN BLACK.

I penciled three different covers for issue #5 . . . I am cursed with indecision! The first version, with the floating dates and *Twilight Zone* clock hands, was a homage to the 1960s Steve Ditko covers, and I still kinda like it. But after working on the interior, I got another idea—the giant hand with little heads—but by the time I had finished the issue I'd decided to use the floating body of Eve. Looking back, each version has elements that I like, and I would have been happy with any as the final cover.

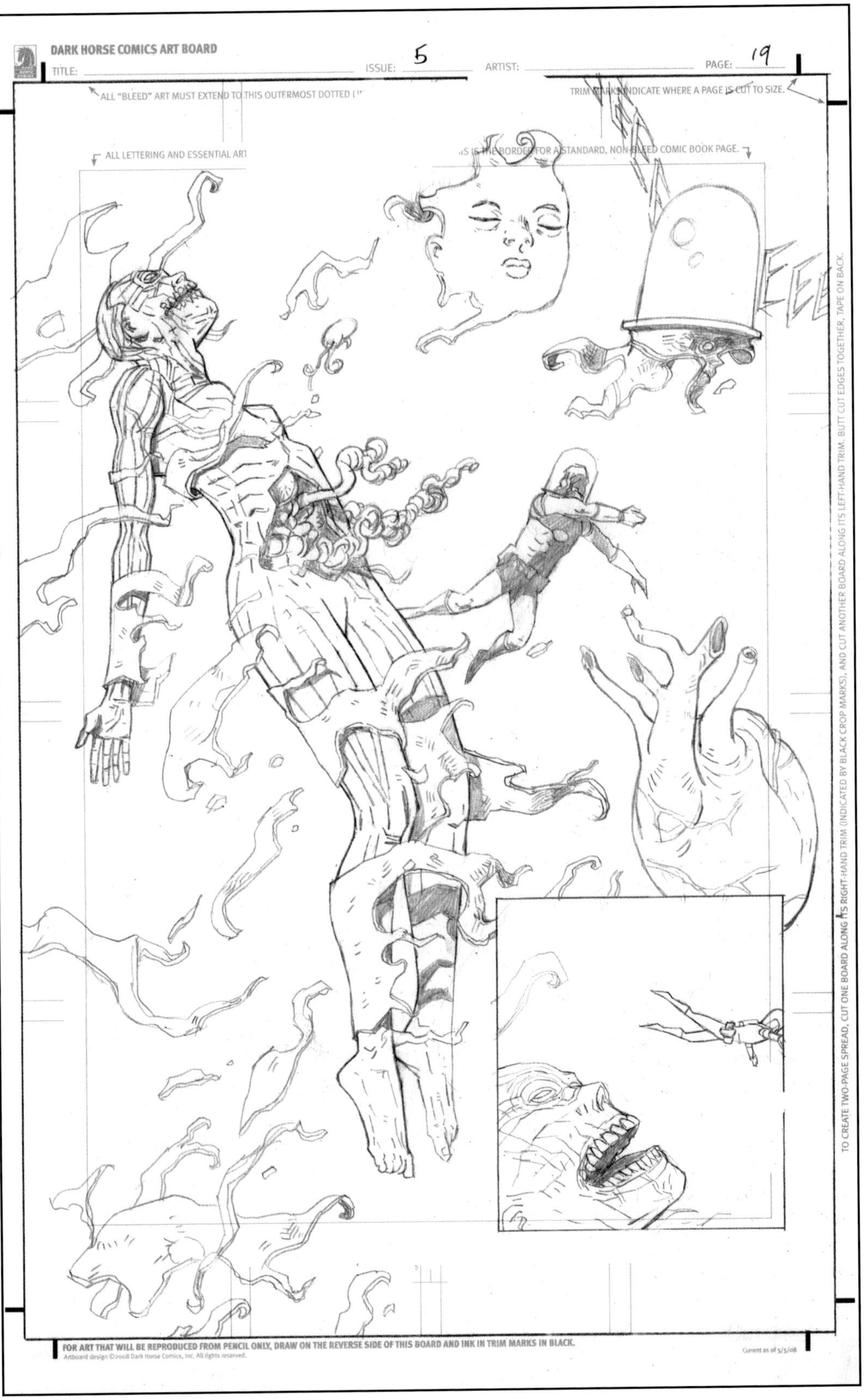
DARK HORSE COMICS ART BOARD
TITLE:
ISSUE: 5
ARTIST:
PAGE: 19
ALL "BLEED" ART MUST EXTEND TO THIS OUTERMOST DOTTED LINE
TRIM MARKS INDICATE WHERE A PAGE IS CUT TO SIZE.
ALL LETTERING AND ESSENTIAL ART
THIS IS THE BORDER FOR A STANDARD, NON-BLEED COMIC BOOK PAGE.
TO CREATE TWO-PAGE SPREAD, CUT ONE BOARD ALONG ITS RIGHT-HAND TRIM (INDICATED BY BLACK CROP MARKS), AND CUT ANOTHER BOARD ALONG ITS LEFT-HAND TRIM. BUTT CUT EDGES TOGETHER, TAPE ON BACK.
FOR ART THAT WILL BE REPRODUCED FROM PENCIL ONLY, DRAW ON THE REVERSE SIDE OF THIS BOARD AND INK IN TRIM MARKS IN BLACK.
Artboard design ©2008 Dark Horse Comics, Inc. All rights reserved.
Current as of 5/5/08

I like this version of issue #5, page 19, but I redrew it to make the story clearer. We needed to see more of Eve's skin floating in front of her skinless body. I had an idea to have a frozen scream curling in and out of view but for some reason didn't do it on the final version.

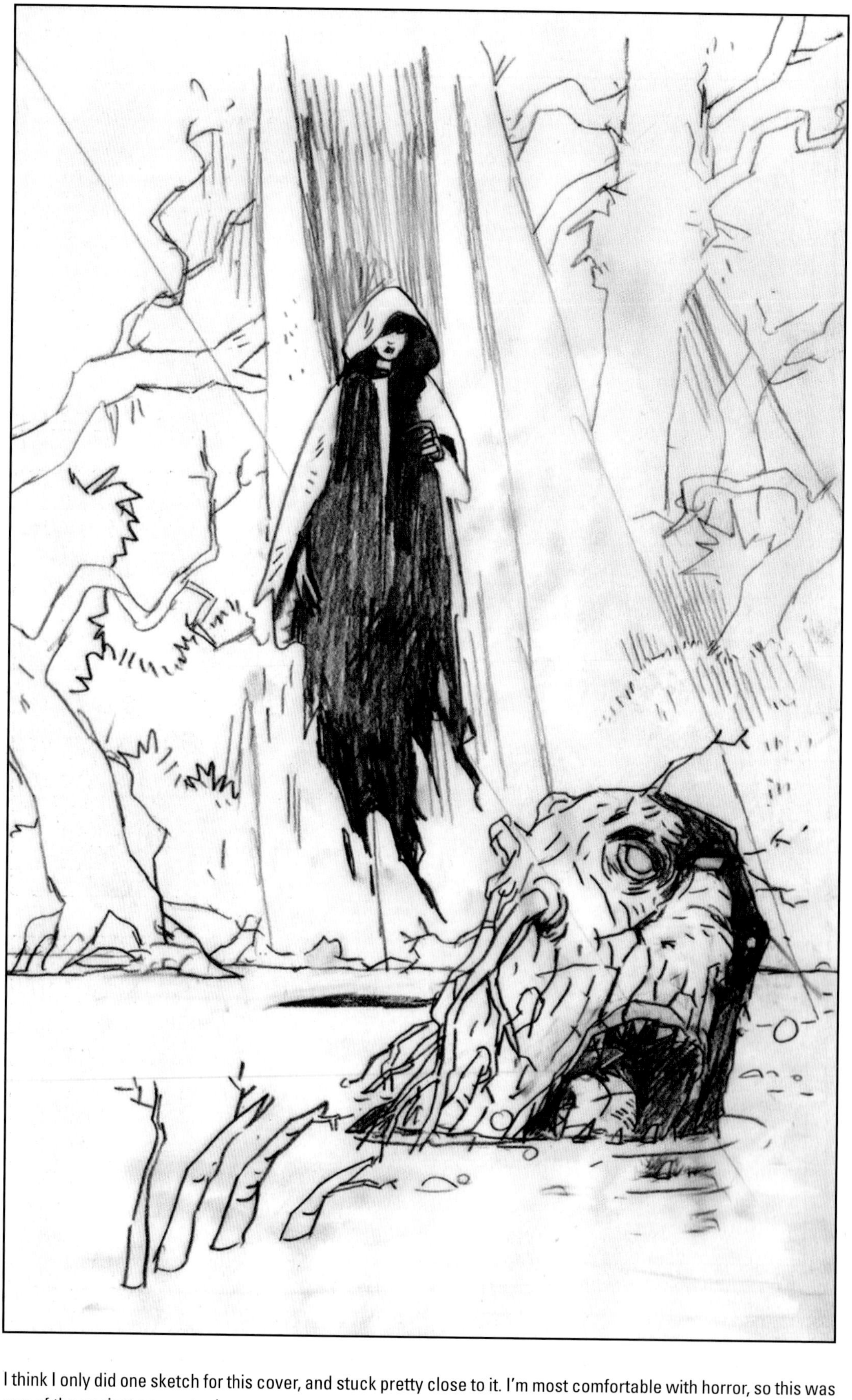

I think I only did one sketch for this cover, and stuck pretty close to it. I'm most comfortable with horror, so this was one of the easiest covers to do.

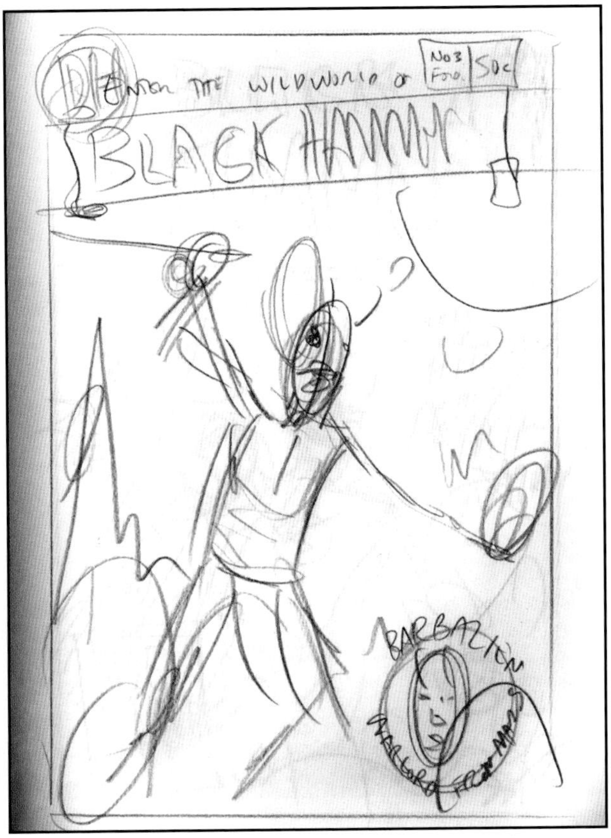
No 3
50¢
BLACK HAMM
BARBALIEN

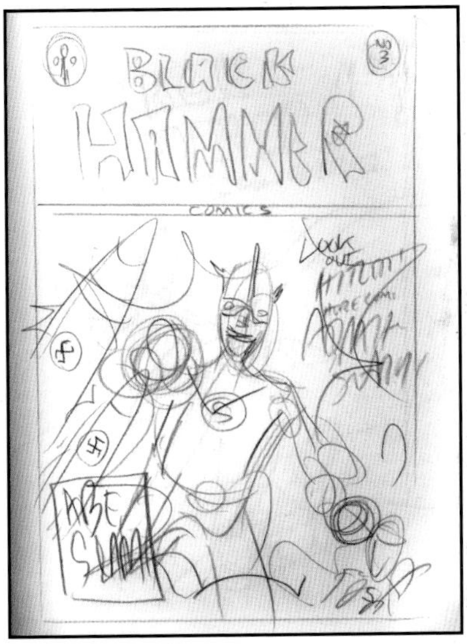
BLACK
HAMMER
COMICS

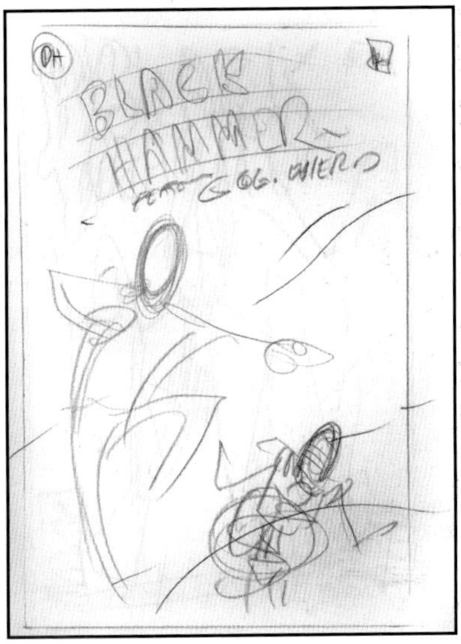
BLACK
HAMMER

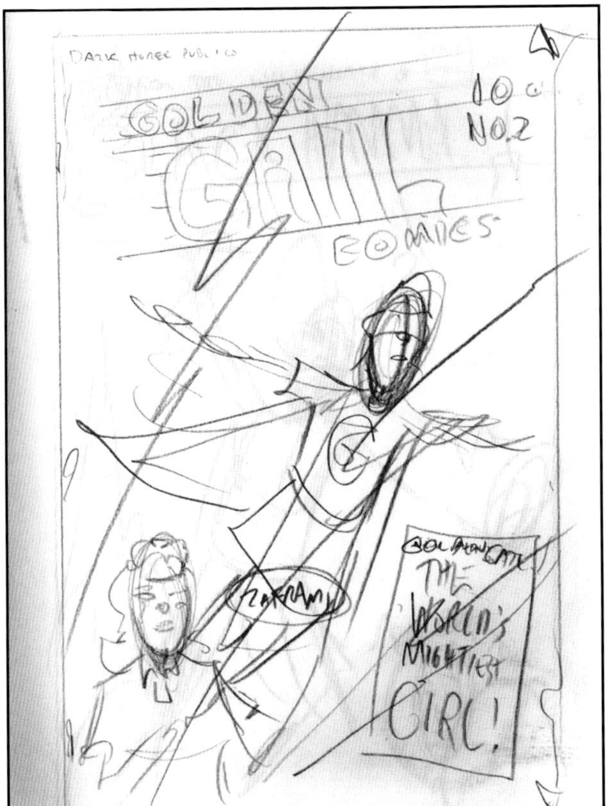
GOLDEN
10¢
No.2
GAIL
COMICS
THE
WORLD'S
MIGHTIEST
GIRL!

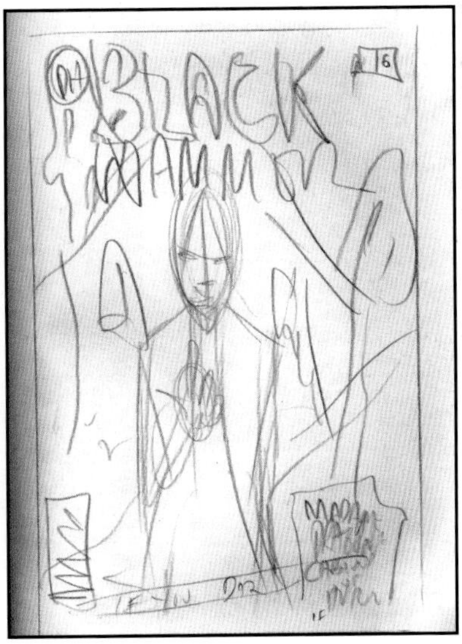
BLACK
6

Variant cover sketches by Jeff for issues #2–#6.

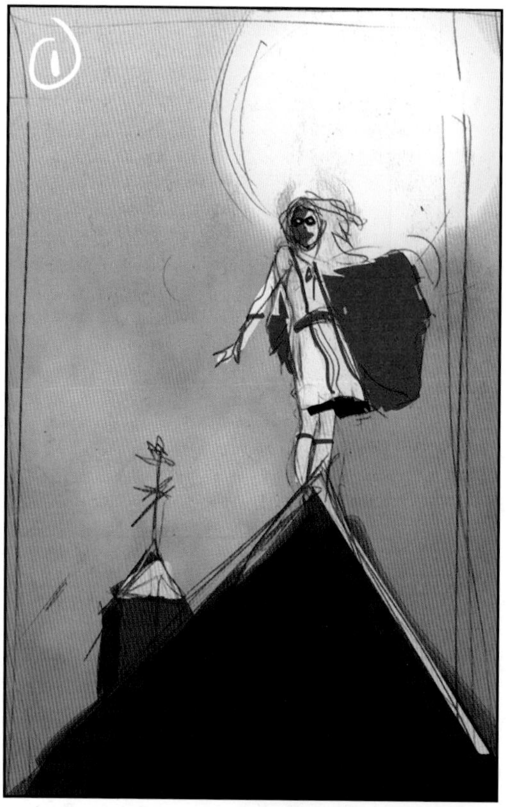
1

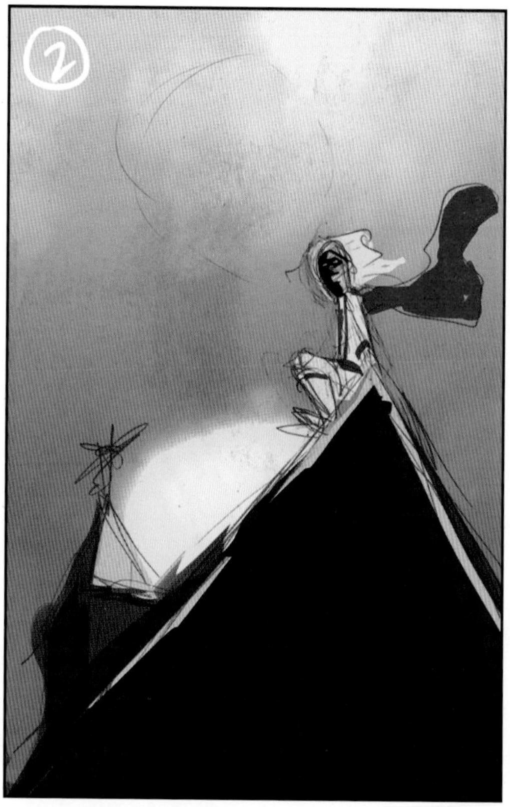
2

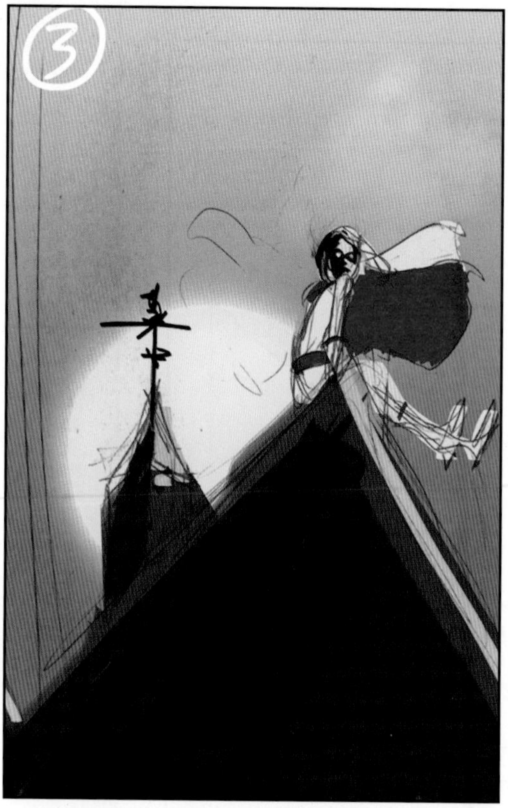
3

This page: Cover sketches by Dustin Nguyen for his SDCC variant.
Facing page: The final cover by Dustin.

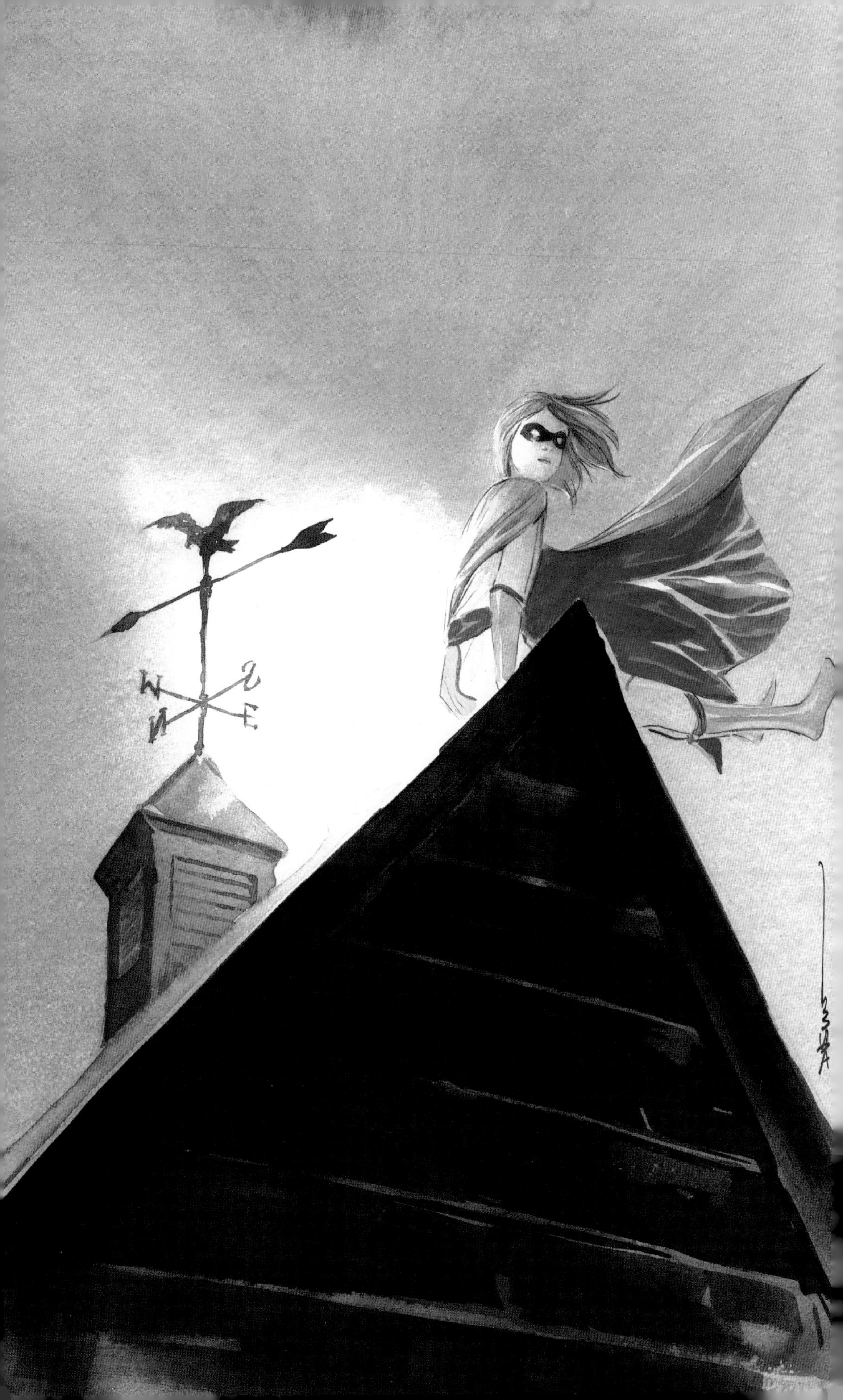
W
E
N

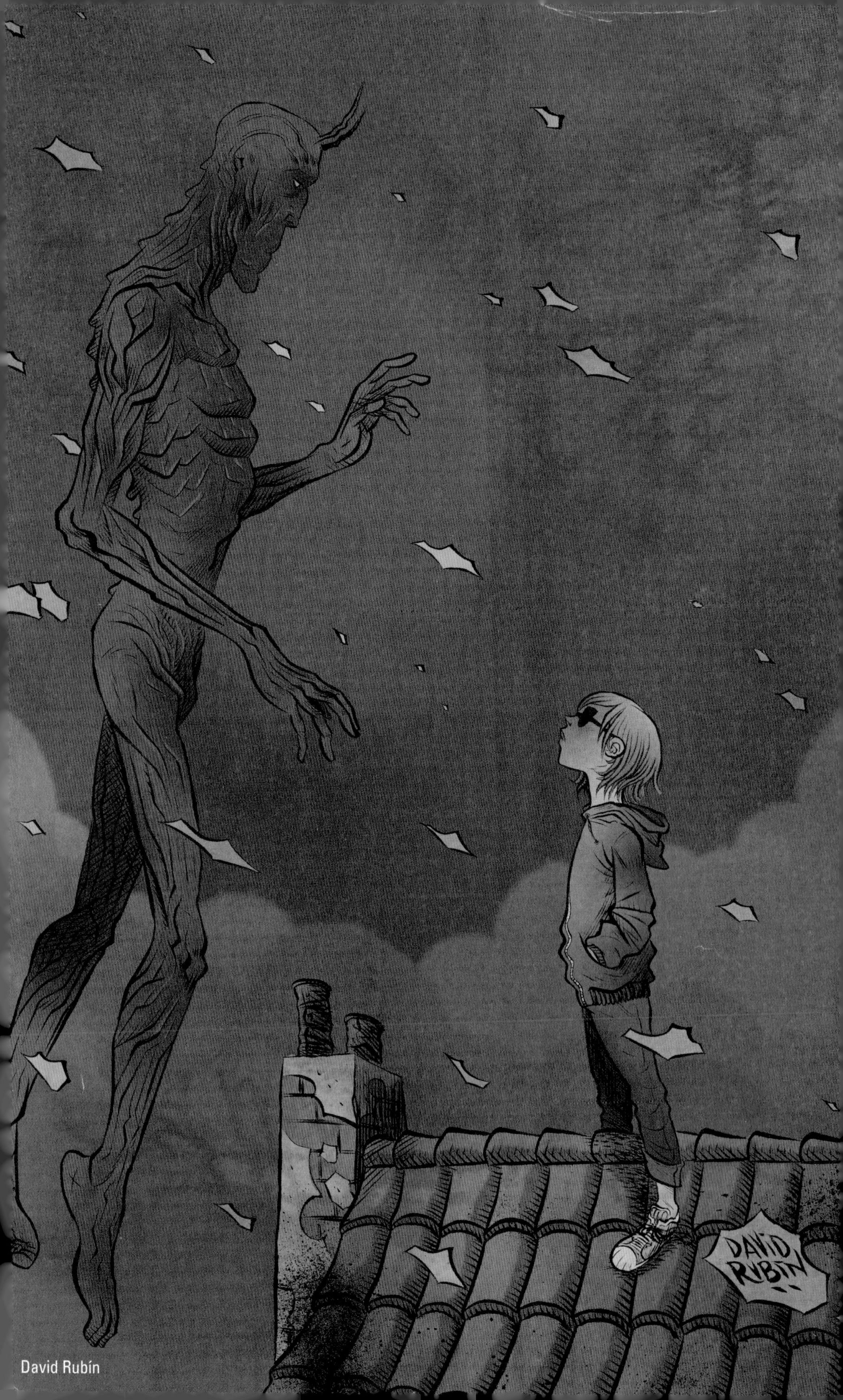
DAVID RUBÍN
David Rubín

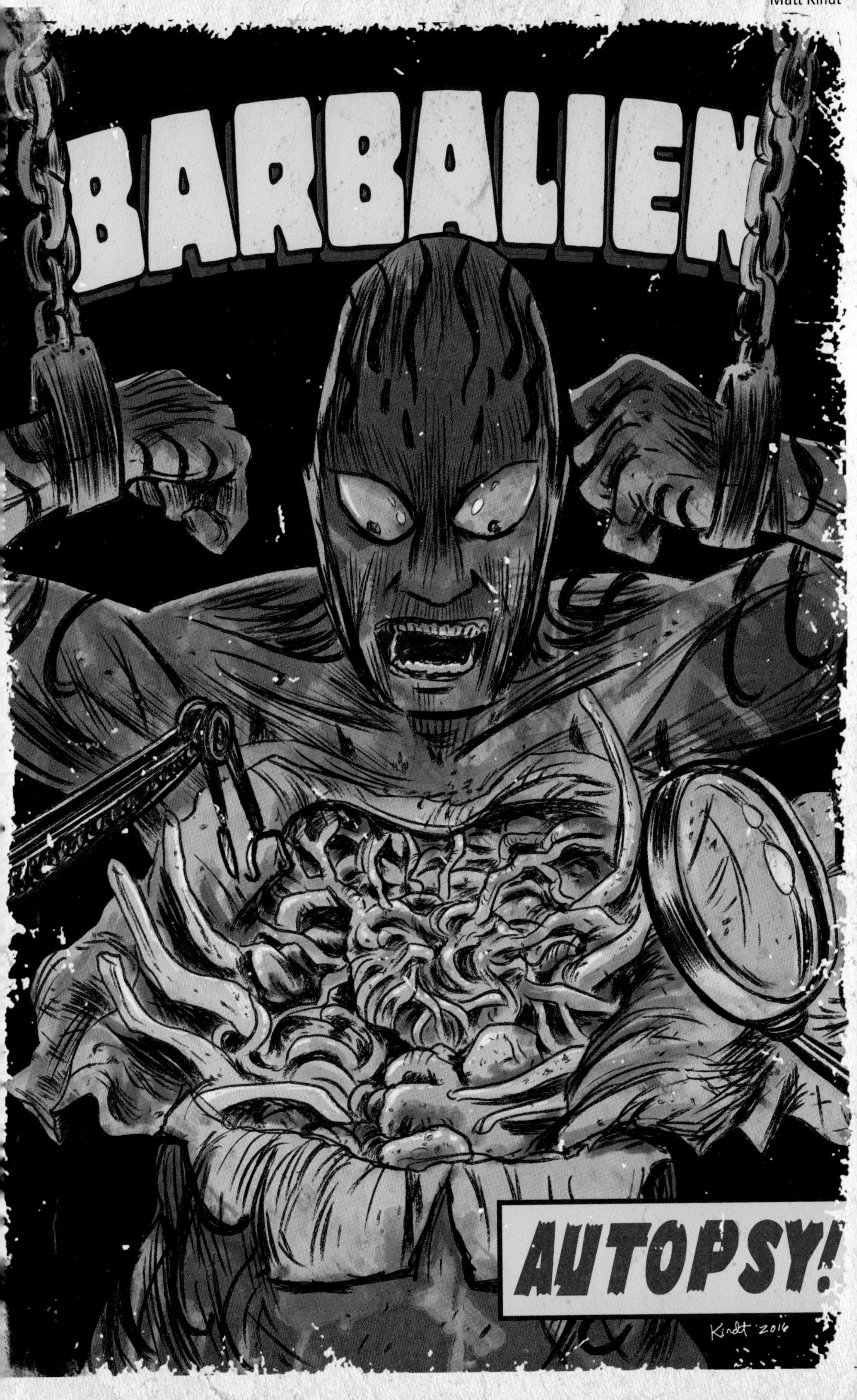
BARBALIEN
AUTOPSY!
Kindt 2016